D1452514

Spies and Provocateurs

Oh! what a tangled web we weave,
When first we practice to deceive!
—Sir Walter Scott, *Marmion*

Spies and Provocateurs

A Worldwide Encyclopedia
of Persons Conducting Espionage
and Covert Action, 1946–1991

Wendell L. Minnick

McFarland & Company, Inc., Publishers
Jefferson, North Carolina, and London

British Library Cataloguing-in-Publication data are available

Library of Congress Cataloguing-in-Publication Data

Minnick, Wendell L.
 Spies and provocateurs : a worldwide encyclopedia of persons
conducting espionage and covert action, 1946–1991 / [by] Wendell L.
Minnick.
  p. cm.
 Includes bibliographical references and index.
 ISBN 0-89950-746-8 (lib. bdg. : 50# alk. paper) ∞
  1. Intelligence officers — Biography.   2. Spies — Biography.
 3. Agents provocateurs — Biography.   I. Title.
 JF1525.I6M56   1992
 327.1'2'0922 — dc20
 [B]   92-50312
                                                             CIP

Manufactured in the United States of America

McFarland & Company, Inc., Publishers
 Box 611, Jefferson, North Carolina 28640

To Dr. John B. Stabler,
friend and mentor

Acknowledgments

I would like to acknowledge the libraries of Indiana State University and Old Dominion University. Within those walls I spent countless hours researching this book.

I would like to thank the following people for their support and encouragement: Scott Bell, Elizabeth Fauver, Rob Lancaster, Jeff Martin, Robert Puckett, Brent Rollings, and Yann-huei Song.

A special thanks goes to my family, particularly my mother and stepfather, for their unwavering support and encouragement.

Contents

Introduction

Spies and Provocateurs describes the activities of over seven hundred agents of espionage and covert action. The first group embodies the classical definition of espionage, which involves the gathering and transmission of intelligence to a foreign government. The second involves the clandestine activities of agents of covert action, which includes assassination, political coups, and sabotage. There are two types of agents that should be distinguished. The first are professional intelligence officers (CIA, KGB, MI6, etc.) who are motivated by conviction, duty, and tradition. The second are agents recruited by a foreign government who are motivated by blackmail, conviction, or money.

That this volume details far more Western intelligence personalities than their Eastern counterparts is due to the fact that Western-style democracies encourage freedom of the press and an open debate on sensitive national foreign policies. The lack of attention to Communist and Third World agents by other postwar works on intelligence and covert action has occasioned a need to collect the basic data in support of further study. I have endeavored to complement this work with as many non–Western individuals as possible.

The names that appear in this volume can be found in any public library. The activities of spies are well documented by the press, historians, and the participants themselves. The Bibliography lists books and articles written by former intelligence officers. The Glossary explains terms and acronyms and the Chronology sets forth milestones of espionage and covert action.

The reader may be confused by the fact that I have listed diplomats and reporters arrested for espionage. In the case of diplomats, many governments install intelligence officers in foreign embassies under the cover of "military attaché" or "cultural affairs attaché," and so on. Since there have been so many expulsions of diplomats on the basis of espionage activities, I have not been able to justify listing all of them. However, I have listed those expulsions that are explained in lengthy detail. With regard to reporters or journalists, this book lists only those where details of espionage, true or false, are extensive. Reporters are often considered spies in other countries that do not exercise freedom of speech rights (the former Soviet Union and other former Eastern Bloc nations, China, many parts of the Third World). Numerous intelligence organizations use and retain journalists as spies, and the CIA and KGB are no different. In fact, the Chinese government uses the China News Agency as a front for numerous espionage activities overseas.

Virtually every nation has an intelligence organization of some type. Prior to World War II, the United States lacked such an institution, and today many argue that if there had been a Central Intelligence Agency (CIA) during those early years, the Pearl Harbor attack would not have occurred. With World War II, the United States developed and implemented the Office of Strategic Services (OSS), an intelligence organization which focused on espionage and covert activities. After the conflict, the OSS was disbanded, and a new type of war ensued. The cold war brought to the surface old fears of a "nuclear Pearl Harbor," and with that came the creation of the CIA.

With the fall of Communism in the Soviet Union and Eastern Europe, one wonders how intelligence targets will be redefined in the next few years. The need for an intelligence service will not diminish, but the hysteria and paranoia that characterized the cold war has certainly become *passé*. Among its other functions, this book will give the reader an understanding of the motivations that defined espionage during this era.

Spies and Provocateurs

1 Abdoolcader, Sirioj Husein. When KGB agent Oleg Lyalin defected to the West in 1971, he named dozens of agents in Great Britain. One of those was Abdoolcader, of Malaysian origin, who worked as a civil servant in the Motor Licensing Department of the Greater London Council as a clerk. In March 1967, Abdoolcader was recruited by KGB agent Vladislav Savin and two years later was turned over to Lyalin, whom Abdoolcader knew only as "Alex." Though Abdoolcader's position seemed innocuous, it was a good source of information. Abdoolcader had access to a special list of cars used by MI5, the counterintelligence branch, which told the KGB the identity of the surveillance cars. He was arrested in September 1971 at his office, carrying a postcard addressed to Lyalin with a new list of registration numbers of MI5 vehicles. He pled guilty in February 1972 and was sentenced to three years. (Brook-Shepherd, *The Storm Birds*; West, *The Circus*)

2 Abel, Col. Rudolph Ivanovich (1903–71). Abel was born and raised in England under the name William Fisher to Russian émigré parents. Abel learned English while living in London, and in 1921 he returned with his father to the Soviet Union. When he returned to the Soviet Union, he joined the Young Communist League. Later he served in the radio corps of the Soviet Army (1922–26), then joined Soviet intelligence in 1927 as a spy in Germany during World War II, but in what capacity there seems to be some debate. Abel was described as a man of many talents: expert in radio technology; spoke perfect English and five other languages; knowledgeable of chemistry and nuclear physics; mathematician; cryptographer; accomplished musician, and painter. He was perfect for intelligence work, and in November 1948 Abel arrived on the SS *Scythia* in Quebec, Canada, under the alias Andrew Kayotis. The real Kayotis had been a naturalized U.S. citizen who in July 1947 returned to his birthplace, Lithuania, and died. Once Abel crossed the Canadian border into America, he shed the Kayotis identity and traveled around the

1

United States for the next sixteen months becoming acclimated with U.S. culture. In April 1950 he emerged as "Emil Robert Goldfus," posing as an artist and photographer in New York. Once there, he began establishing an extensive network of spies.

In October 1952, Abel, overburdened with work, was united with an assistant, Maj. Reino Hayhanen of the KGB. Hayhanen began drinking heavily, failing to complete assigned tasks. Abel was particularly angered by his misuse of intelligence funds for drinking and entertainment. Abel convinced him to return to the Soviet Union in April 1957, but Hayhanen changed his mind in Paris, defected, and turned Abel over to the U.S. government.

On June 21, 1957, the FBI arrested Abel at the Hotel Latham in Manhattan where he was registered under the alias Martin Collins. The FBI discovered a Hallicrafter shortwave radio with a schedule of message reception times, small electrical generator, a speedgraphic camera, hollowed-out secret containers, a codebook, coded messages, microfilm equipment, marked-up maps of major U.S. defense areas, and birth certificates for Emil Robert Goldfus (b. August 2, 1902) and Martin Collins (b. July 2, 1897). The FBI offered Abel his freedom and a $10,000 position in U.S. counterintelligence, but Abel refused. Abel was arraigned in federal court in August 1957 and convicted of espionage in May 1960. He was sentenced to 30 years but later traded for captured U-2 pilot Gary Powers in 1962. The exchange took place on February 10, 1962, on the Glienicker Bridge between East and West Berlin. After Abel returned to the Soviet Union, he was awarded the Order of Lenin.

What happened to Abel after his return to the Soviet Union seems confused. Soviet newspapers reported Abel all over the world — once in Saigon, once stationed in Leipzig as liaison officer between Soviet intelligence and the East German high command, other times living in Moscow teaching espionage trainees. All these reports are dubious except perhaps the latter. Moscow announced his death on November 15, 1971, at 68. His tombstone in a Moscow cemetery was marked: *Fisher, William Gnerykovich–Abel, Rudolf Ivanovich.* (Bernikow, *Abel;* Donovan, *Strangers on a Bridge;* Lamphere, *The FBI-KGB War;* Newman, *Famous Soviet Spies;* Rositzke, *The KGB*)

3   Abdullah, Fawzi, and Mahmoud el–Haihi.   Both convicted in January 1967 by a Jordanian court for spying for Israel. Sergeant Abdullah and el-Haihi were executed by hanging in Amman in February 1968. Both were arrested in 1966 and reportedly had spied for Israel since 1962, providing data on Jordanian Army troops. A third accomplice, Abdel-Karim Abdel-Nabi, managed to escape from prison. (*Facts on File,* 1968)

4   Abramov, Mikhail N. In April 1982, Abramov, Soviet trade representative, was expelled by Canadian authorities for espionage activities. Abramov was accused of attempting to steal high-technology equipment that had been banned for sale to the Soviet Union. The Royal Canadian Mounted Police (RCMP) had caught Abramov offering the president of the Canadian Northumberland Cable Company money for fiber-optics cable and other items. (Bittman, *The KGB and Soviet Disinformation; Facts on File*, 1982; *New York Times*, April 2, 3, 1982)

5   Adams, Samuel A. (d. 1988). Former CIA analyst; first served in the Congo in 1964, then transferred to the Southeast Asian Division. Adams discovered that military estimates of enemy troop strength were intentionally underestimated to give the illusion that the United States was winning the war in Vietnam.

For example, Adams discovered that enemy troop strength in 1966 in Binh Dinh Province was 50,000, not the 4,500 the Pentagon had announced. The U.S. military stated that in the entire country enemy troop strength was at 270,000. Adams discovered that its true numbers were closer to 500,000 to 600,000. Another report by Adams in November 1969 reported that 30,000 Viet Cong agents had infiltrated into the South Vietnamese Army.

He resigned in May 1973, claiming that the CIA had been lying about Vietnamese and Cambodian insurgency strength since 1967. In 1968 Adams became embroiled in a battle with DCI Richard Helms over his report that the U.S. military had been lying about troop strength of Vietnamese Communist forces. Adams went to the inspector general's office, filing a complaint which resulted in an investigation into Adams's assertion that Helms had attempted to hide the facts. Adams's action was surprising because he was a midlevel analyst in the CIA. During a meeting with Helms, Adams insisted that he would see him fired as DCI. The investigation resulted in no negative action against Helms and Nixon reappointed Helms as DCI. (Jeffreys-Jones, *The CIA and American Democracy;* Freemantle, *CIA;* McGehee, *Deadly Deceits;* Powers, *The Man Who Kept the Secrets;* Ranelagh, *The Agency*)

6   Afzali, Bahram. A former Iranian commander of the navy, Afzali was arrested along with several other members of the Tudeh Communist party for espionage and attempting to overthrow the government. Afzali had been the Iranian commander from 1980 till his arrest in February 1983. It is not known if Afzali was actually a spy for the Soviets or simply the target of a crackdown on the Communist party in Iran. According to Iranian authorities, Afzali had confessed to spying. (*Facts on File*, 1984)

7 Agee, Philip Burnett Franklin (b. 1935). One of the best-known ex–CIA employees to go public. Joined the CIA in 1957 after graduating from Notre Dame University, serving 1963–66 in Uruguay directing operations against Cubans and helping to build up the security forces. He was later assigned to the Mexico City station, where he finally resigned in 1969.

Agee then wrote *Inside the Company: CIA Diary* (1975), which created an intelligence crisis for the CIA when it listed the names of 250 agents working for the CIA, crippling CIA operations and assets in Latin America. He adopted a pro–Cuban Marxist-Leninist idealism, spending months in Cuba and France researching his book. His presence in Cuba raised some disturbing questions due to the fact that in a country that curbs freedom of information, the only obvious research source must have been the Cuban Intelligence Service (DGI). Therefore, should Agee be considered a spy or traitor? The book was published in over 20 languages and gave the CIA headaches for years to come.

In July 1978, Agee attended the International Tribunal of the 11th World Festival of Youth and Students in Cuba, where he announced the creation of the *Covert Action Information Bulletin.* The bulletin listed the names of CIA personnel and operations around the world. Agee's zeal also led to two books that listed hundreds of CIA agents actively engaged in operations: *Dirty Work* and *Dirty Work II.*

Many blame Agee for the assassination of Richard Welch, the CIA station chief in Athens, Greece. Agee had called for the "neutralization" of CIA personnel in an article in an anti–CIA magazine, *Counterspy*, in 1975. The same edition carried the name of Richard Welch as an employee. An Athens newspaper, *Athen News,* searched through the U.S. embassy personnel listing and discovered Welch's name under a diplomatic title. Welch was exposed in the paper, including the address of his residence. A month later, Welch was assassinated in front of his home by a leftist group called the Revolutionary Organization of November 17th. The U.S. government responded to the crisis by passing Public Law 97-200, allowing for the prosecution of those who reveal the identity of agents actively involved in U.S. intelligence operations. In 1979, Secretary of State Cyrus Vance ordered that Agee's passport be revoked due to his activities. In 1981, after a long legal battle, Agee lost his right to hold an American passport.

Agee has often been referred to as the "man without a country." In June 1977 Agee was forced to leave Great Britain and went to the Netherlands. In August 1977 the French government expelled Agee as an undesirable. In December 1977 the Netherlands government asked him to leave the country, and Agee attempted to enter Germany but was denied. In January 1978 the Netherlands announced that Agee had been denied permission to remain in Holland but did allow him to stay several more months.

In 1979 Agee was invited by the Iranian student militants to join in the tribunal that would examine the spy activities of the American hostages. Agee refused to participate unless the hostages were released but did send a proposal for the release of the hostages that included the release of all CIA files on their involvement in Iran since the 1950s. The Iranians rejected the idea.

In 1987 Agee returned to the United States after a 16 year absence by way of the Canadian border, using a Nicaraguan passport. Agee went to the United States to promote his new book, *On the Run*, which was his personal account of the CIA's attempts to stop him from writing *Inside the Company*. Agee feared arrest for espionage, but the Justice Department had no warrant against him (Agee, *Dirty Work*, *Inside the Company*, *On the Run*; Bittman, *The KGB and Soviet Disinformation*; Poelchau, *White Paper Whitewash*; Ray, *Dirty Work II*)

8 Ahern, Thomas Leo. Attended Notre Dame University, graduating in 1954. He joined the U.S. Army and served in the Counterintelligence Corps from 1954 to 1960. Later, during the 1960s, he served in Laos as a security officer. In December 1979, Iranian students holding American hostages at the U.S. embassy in Tehran accused Ahern of being a CIA agent. They produced a Belgian passport with Ahern's picture on it and instructions on how to portray himself as a Belgian businessman in Iran. Ahern was listed as the narcotics liaison officer for the State Department. In April 1980, Iranian TV showed a video taken of one of the American hostages, Army S.Sgt. Joseph Subic, discussing U.S. surveillance flights over Iran. One scene showed Subic showing Iranians a secret hiding place in the floor and ceiling in the embassy warehouse that held computer equipment. Subic also identified Ahern as a CIA agent. American TV networks refused to buy the tapes from the Iranians when they insisted that the tapes not be edited. (*Facts on File*, 1979–80; McFadden, Treaster, and Carroll, *No Hiding Place*; Moody, *444 Days*)

9 Aldridge, Philip Leslie. A young lance corporal in the British Army, Aldridge was sentenced in January 1983 to four years after pleading guilty to attempting to sell the Soviet Union classified documents from the Joint Intelligence Committee. Aldridge, part of the Intelligence Corps, was in charge of the burn bag of classified documents at the Defense Ministry and was able to remove documents without being caught. He was motivated to sell the data for money for a new car. He managed to make contact with Soviet officials by mail with instructions to run an ad in the *Daily Telegraph* which read, "I Love You Spider, Love Mum." Apparently MI5 had intercepted one of Aldridge's attempts to contact the Soviet embassy, and surveillance began. A search of his apartment revealed a diary with the phone numbers of the Soviet Embassy. (Pincher, *Too Secret Too Long*)

10   Allen, Michael H.   Arrested in 1986 for selling classified intelligence data to the Philippine military. Retired in 1972 as a senior chief radioman for the U.S. Navy. He worked as a civil service photocopy clerk at the naval air station in the Philippines when he was arrested. Since he was still a naval reservist, he was court-martialed by the military and sentenced to eight years. (Allen and Polmar, *Merchants of Treason; Facts on File*, 1987; *New York Times*, December 12, 1986)

11   Allen, Percy.   British army staff sergeant; worked in the Land–Air Warfare Directorate of the War Office where he had access to classified intelligence assessments of the Middle East. Desperate for money, he attempted to contact Egyptian and Iraqi embassies to sell classified documents, but the calls were being monitored by MI5. He was placed under surveillance and was arrested during a meeting with an Iraqi military attaché, Maj. Abdul Al-Abbasi, in March 1965 while passing classified documents. It was revealed during the trial that Allen had a previous criminal record in 1947 for vandalism and theft that had gone unnoticed during his original security background check. He was sentenced to ten years (Pincher, *Too Secret Too Long*; West, *The Circus*)

12   Althoff, William, and Bertram L. Parr.   In April 1966, Commander Althoff, U.S. naval attaché, and Lieutenant Colonel Parr, assistant military attaché, had been arrested in Poland outside Warsaw. The police discovered a variety of intelligence documents in the car. The Polish government described a briefcase found on the bank of the Vistula River which belonged to the two men, containing sensitive intelligence documents. (*Facts on File*, 1966; *New York Times*, May 24–25, 1966)

13   Ames, Robert Clayton (d. 1983).   Ames had a successful career in the CIA. Served as a case officer in Lebanon recruiting agents during Richard Helms's tenure as head of the CIA. Reportedly, he recruited Ali Hassan Salameh ("Red Prince"), head of security and intelligence for the PLO, who was later assassinated by Israeli agents in Beirut.

In April 1983 a massive car bomb destroyed the U.S. embassy building in Beirut, killing Ames and over 40 people, nearly wiping out the CIA's total staff in Lebanon. Ames had been sent as the CIA's top Middle East analyst to evaluate the hostage situation. (Raviv and Melman, *Every Spy a Prince*; Woodward, *Veil*)

14   Amin, Mustafa. In July 1965, Amin, founder and editor of *Al Akhbar*, was arrested by Egyptian authorities and accused of spying for the U.S. Amin pleaded not guilty to spying but did plead guilty to smuggling $46,000 in Egyptian pounds overseas. Reportedly, Egyptian security agents caught Amin in the process of transmitting sensitive security information to Taylor Odell, an officer stationed at the U.S. embassy in Cairo since 1964. Odell was arrested but was later released due to diplomatic privilege. According to Egyptian authorities, the CIA had recruited Amin several years before. Each week Odell would give Amin a list of questions to answer, and Amin would fill out the questionnaire and return it at the next meeting. He was caught giving Odell one of his weekly reports about the political and military situation in the country. Amin finally confessed to his activities and also implicated his twin brother, Ali Amin, a correspondent for the newspaper in London. Amin was giving Ali half his payments from the CIA as his share. The most recent amount sent to Ali was reportedly $56,000. State Department authorities denied that Odell belonged to the CIA or used Mustafa as an agent. He was released in January 1974. (Steven, *The Spymasters of Israel*)

15   Amit, Meir (b. 1921). Born in Tiberias, he grew up on an agricultural kibbutz in Palestine. He had joined the Haganah, the underground Jewish army, and later became deputy commander in the Golani Brigade in the 1948 War of Independence. He rose to serve as the head of military intelligence branch, the Aman, in 1961. In 1962 he became the head of Mossad and was responsible for revolutionizing and updating Mossad's techniques and equipment. He created a strong liaison relationship between the CIA and Mossad during the 1960s. (Black and Morris, *Israel's Secret Wars*; Eisenberg, Dan, and Landau, *The Mossad*; Raviv and Melman, *Every Spy a Prince*; Steven, *The Spymasters of Israel*)

16   Angleton, James Jesus (1917–87). After graduating from Yale, he attended Harvard Law School. In 1943 he joined the Office of Strategic Services (OSS) in the counterintelligence division and was sent to London. In 1944 he was put in charge of counterintelligence operations in Italy. When the war ended, the OSS was disbanded, but Angleton continued working in Italy in the Strategic Services Unit, which was later absorbed into the Central Intelligence Group (CIG), the forerunner of the CIA. In 1949 Angleton returned to the U.S. to find the creation of the CIA where he continued as chief of the Office of Special Operations. Angleton finally rose to become head of the CIA's counterintelligence division.

Angleton eventually began to let his paranoia effect his staff when he became obsessed in the search for an imaginary Soviet mole within the CIA. This finally forced the CIA director, William Colby, to ask Angleton to resign in 1974. After his resignation, his staff was cut from 300 to 80, and many of the techniques implemented by Angleton were phased out.

In the 1970s Angleton was accused of being a Soviet spy. A CIA investigation, concluded in 1979, rejected the accusation.

When Yuri Nosenko defected to the U.S., Angleton became obsessed that he was a disinformation agent. He had a special house built at Camp Peary surrounded by a fence and searchlights where he kept Nosenko captive over a three-year period of interrogations and druggings. Angleton was one of the first to become suspicious of Kim Philby, due to an Israeli source. (Colby and Forbath, *Honorable Men*; Halperin and Peake, "Did Angleton Jail Nosenko," *IJIC*; Mangold, *Cold Warrior*; Phillips, *The Night Watch*; Smith, *OSS*; Winks, *Cloak and Gown*)

17   Antipov, Mikhail Mikhailovich.   From as early as 1958, Antipov worked for the KGB's assassination and sabotage Department V. From July 1963 to September 1966, he worked under the cover of a UN diplomat for the Soviet mission, then returned to the KGB headquarters in Moscow. He returned to the UN in New York as first secretary from October 1969 to February 1972. (Barron, *KGB*)

18   Arguedas Mendietta, Antonio.   In July 1968, Arguedas, former Bolivian interior minister, escaped from Bolivia, smuggling Che Guevara's diary to Cuba. He stated that he had been forced to work for the CIA during his tenure as interior minister, claiming that the CIA approached him in January 1965 and that he provided a variety of services for the CIA for money. He returned to Bolivia in August 1968 to expose the CIA effort in his country. He named several people he claimed were CIA officers working in Bolivia: Air Force Col. Edward J. Fox, Lawrence (Larry) M. Sternfield, Nicholas Leondiris, Hugh (Hugo) E. Murray, and John S. Hilton. The Bolivian government argued that Arguedas should be tried for treason and for supporting the guerrilla movement of Guevara. (*Facts on File*, 1968; *New York Times*, July 1, 22, 24, 26; August 3, 1968)

19   Attardi, Joseph B.   In August 1969, Staff Sergeant Attardi provided to another soldier classified documents on the "Cosmic Top Secret" NATO defense plans, copying top-secret documents from the classified document section in Heidelberg, Germany. In 1969 he was sentenced to three years for espionage. (*Facts on File* 1969; *New York Times*, August 28, 1969; Rositzke, *The KGB*)

20   Attassi, Farhan.   In February 1965, Attassi, a naturalized U.S. citizen of Syrian birth was hanged for spying in Damascus, Syria.

Attassi came to the U.S. in 1951 and was naturalized in 1959. The U.S. protested the execution, claiming that Attassi was a U.S. citizen. According to Syrian authorities, Attassi had provided the second secretary of the U.S. embassy in Damascus, Walter S. Snowdon, who was later expelled, with Soviet-made equipment. They arranged to deliver Soviet-made machine-gun ammunition for $10,000. Attassi was arrested while offering an Iraqi military officer $2 million for information on a Soviet-made naval rocket. The officer contacted authorities about Attasi's offer and trapped him during the second meeting. Attasi was a nephew of the first president of the Syrian Republic, the late Hashem Attassi, and first cousin of Syrian Deputy Pres. Nureddin Attassi. The Syrian government also executed by firing squad Attassi's cousin, Maj. Abdel Moeen Hakimi, accusing him of being an accomplice. Both men were charged with spying for the U.S. (*Facts on File*, 1965; *New York Times*, February 18, 23–26, March 5, 1965)

21   Augustenborg, Lon David.   In September 1983, Augustenborg, a U.S. vice consul assigned to the U.S. consulate in Leningrad, and his wife, Denise, were expelled from the Soviet Union for espionage. The Soviet press reported that Augustenborg and his wife were caught in the act of picking up classified documents on the Soviet Navy at a drop. The State Department argued that the expulsion was in response to the U.S. expulsion of Soviet diplomats Yuri Leonov and Anatoly Skripko for espionage. (*Facts on File*, 1983; *New York Times*, September 13–14, 1983)

22   Azpillaga, Florentino Lombard.   Cuban intelligence major, defected to the West in 1987. While serving as the chief of Cuban intelligence in Czechoslovakia, he crossed the border into Austria and defected. Azpillaga provided the names of 350 Cuban agents around the world and a number of CIA double agents in Cuba who were feeding the CIA false information. Azpillaga claimed that Panamanian dictator Manuel Noriega had provided Cuba with high technology barred by U.S. law to the Cubans. Noriega was also described by Azpillaga as helping Cuba provide weapons to the rebels in Columbia, El Salvador, and Honduras. (*Facts on File*, 1987; *New York Times*, August 10, 1987)

23   Baba, Stephen A.   In September 1981, Baba, ensign in the U.S. Navy stationed on a frigate in San Diego, mailed classified data on electronic warfare to the South African embassy in Washington, D.C. The South African embassy officials returned the documents to the U.S. government, and Baba was immediately arrested. During the court-martial, it was reported that Baba was attempting to make enough money to bring his Filipino girlfriend to the U.S. to go to college. He was sentenced in January 1982 to eight years, but the sentence was later reduced to two years. (Allen and Polmar, *Merchants of Treason; Facts on File*, 1982; *New York Times*, January 20, 21, 1982)

24   Bagaya, Elizabeth.   In November 1974, Ugandan Pres. Idi Amin Dada fired Bagaya, often referred to as Toro Princess Bagaya, as foreign minister. He accused Bagaya of having contacts with British and U.S. intelligence agents, and of having engaged in sexual intercourse in a public toilet with an unnamed European in the Orly Airport in Paris. She was placed under house arrest but later released. United Nations and French government officials defended Bagaya against the charges. Bagaya had been a lawyer and former fashion model. She was appointed to replace Lt. Col. Michael Ondoga, who was dismissed in February 1974 and found dead floating in the Nile River. (*Facts on File*, 1974; *New York Times*, February 24; November 29, 30; December 1, 3, 6, 7, 1974)

25   Barmyantsev, Yevgeny N.   In April 1983 Lieutenant Colonel Barmyantsev, a Soviet GRU military intelligence officer, was expelled from the U.S. for espionage. On April 16, 1983, Barmyantsev was caught at a contact drop picking up film containing military secrets in rural Maryland. The FBI arranged a sting operation to help curb walk-ins. The FBI approached John Stine, chief of security of a local defense research company, to act as a false walk-in. Stine approached Soviet intelligence officials offering to sell classified data on ballistic missiles. It took the GRU intelligence officials five months to arrange a dead drop, at which the FBI was waiting. When FBI agents surprised Barmyantsev at the site, he wet his pants. Barmyantsev was well known by the FBI for his numerous attempts to recruit spies. (Allen and Polmar, *Merchants of Treason; Facts on File*, 1983; *New York Times*, April 22, 24, 1983)

26   Barnes, C. Tracy (1912–72).   Barnes attended Yale University, earning his B.A., then attended Harvard Law School; entered the U.S. Army Air Force, working in the Intelligence Division during World War II. He later transferred to the Office of Strategic Services (OSS) and became part of the famous Jedburgh special operations team making several covert parachute jumps into occupied France.

He joined the CIA in the early 1950s and was given overall responsibility for the CIA sponsored coup in Guatemala in 1954. The Guatemala operation, called Operation Success, involved the overthrow of the leftist president Jacobo Arbenz. When Arbenz nationalized the United Fruit Company and other industries in Guatemala, the CIA feared that Communism was in the making. The CIA was able to overthrow the government with a military junta headed by Colonel Carlos Armas in 1954. The CIA created a small army in the Nicaraguan jungle, complete with a small air force. The operation began in June 18 when the army crossed the border into Guatemala marching toward the capital, while CIA pilots flew missions against the capital and government facilities. By June 27, the government collapsed, Arbenz fled the country, and Armas was appointed president.

Barnes was awarded for his success and named chief of station in Frankfurt, West Germany, 1954–56, then chief of station in London from 1957 to 1959. From 1960 to 1961, he served as assistant to the deputy director of plans under Richard Bissell. During the Bay of Pigs invasion, Barnes served as CIA liaison with the State Department. After the failure of the operation, he served as chief of the Domestic Operations Division until his retirement in 1968. After his retirement, he served as special assistant to the president of Yale University. (Ambrose, *Ike's Spies*; Hunt, *Undercover*; Phillips, *The Night Watch*; Powers, *The Man Who Kept the Secrets*; Schlesinger, *Bitter Fruit*; Smith, *OSS*; Wyden, *Bay of Pigs*)

27   Barnett, David Henry.   Worked as a contract employee for the CIA in the Far East Division from 1958 to 1963, then became a career CIA intelligence officer. First assigned to Korea for two years, then assigned to Surabao, Indonesia, where he targeted Soviet delegation members for recruitment. Resigned in 1970, starting a seafood processing company, P. T. Trifoods, but it failed.

In October 1976, with his business in Indonesia failing and deeply in debt, he contacted the Soviet cultural attaché in Djakarta by passing a note stating that he had some CIA secrets to sell for $70,000. A week later, a KGB officer, Dmitri, met Barnett. At the time of the contact, he received an initial payment of $25,000. Barnett was instructed to fly to Europe in February 1977 to meet a KGB agent in Vienna for debriefing.

It was here that Barnett gave extensive details of CIA operations, including the names of 100 CIA agents and the names of KGB officers that the CIA targeted for recruitment. He was paid an additional $15,000 at this point. The KGB encouraged him to return to U.S. intelligence service as an agent for the KGB. He agreed to try and returned to Indonesia, where he received another $30,000.

He returned to Washington, D.C., and began actively looking for a job. While in the U.S. he was handled by KGB officer Vladimir Popov. He took a special interest in a staff position for the Senate Intelligence Committee but did not get the position. It was not until January 1979 that the CIA rehired him as a contract employee and assigned him to teach CIA agents how to resist interrogations. In March 1980 he went to meet with his students at a CIA safe house only to find two FBI agents waiting for him. After a brief discussion, the FBI was able to get him to confess.

Reportedly, the FBI had intercepted Popov's messages to Barnett after a Rumanian diplomat defected to the West. Nicholae I. Horodinca, third secretary of the Rumanian embassy, provided information that led to the arrest of Barnett.

In October 1980 he pled guilty to supplying the KGB with data on a variety of CIA intelligence operations and the names of CIA agents all over the world. One of the operations Barnett revealed was Operation H A Brink, which involved the collection of information about Soviet weapons supplied to Indonesia. This was one of the CIA's more important covert operations at the time. (Barron, *KGB Today;* Prados, *The Soviet Estimate;* Romerstein and Levchenko, *The KGB Against the "Main Enemy";* Turner, *Secrecy and Democracy*)

28   Batashev, Gennadi.   In February 1983, Batashev, a KGB officer, was arrested in West Germany while meeting a contact who provided classified data on decoding machines used by West Germany. Batashev was a member of a Soviet trade mission in Cologne and did not have diplomatic immunity. His contact had notified West German officials that a Soviet official had made contact with him. Reportedly, Batashev and the contact had met five times since 1981. Batashev had promised him 5,000 German marks ($2,000) for a decoding machine. (*Facts on File,* 1983; *New York Times,* February 19, 1983)

29   Bazoft, Farzad (d. 1990).   Convicted and executed by Iraq as a British spy, working as a freelance journalist for the British newspaper, the *Observer,* traveling to Iraq six times at the invitation of the Iraqi government. Bazoft, Iranian-born, was arrested September 1989 after making an unauthorized inspection of a military complex involved in a mysterious explosion. Bazoft had lived in Britain since 1975 but was not a British citizen. Though he had confessed to having spied for Israel and Britain, he later recanted his confession, claiming to have been forced into the confession during the interrogation. British authorities did acknowledge that Bazoft had contacted the British special branch police about providing data on Iraq. It was also revealed that Bazoft had been convicted of bank robbery in Britain in 1981 and sentenced to 18 months. Bazoft was hanged near Baghdad on March 15, 1990. (*Facts on File,* 1990; *New York Times,* July 17, 1990)

30   Beaufils, Georges.   In July 1978 a French court sentenced Beaufils to eight years for spying for the Soviet Union. He was a decorated hero of the French Resistance during World War II and a member of the French Communist party. Beaufils argued that he acted out of goodwill as a fellow Communist and did not suspect that his actions would be interpreted as espionage. The court rejected his argument. (*Facts on File,* 1978)

31   Bechtell, William (d. 1988).   Bechtell ("Big Bill") fought in the French Resistance during World War II and later served French intelligence services in a variety of areas. Bechtell served in French IndoChina in security and intelligence operations.

French intelligence's Action Branch, responsible for covert operations, recruited him to assassinate Felix Moumie, the leader of the Union of the Populations of Cameroon (UPC) who was leading a revolt against the French-backed government for a separate state. He traveled extensively around Africa and Europe, an easy target.

Posing as a Swiss journalist, he visited Moumie in the city of Accra in Ghana for an interview and managed to convince Moumie to travel to Geneva, suggesting several doctors who specialized in liver problems. Three months later in October 1960, Moumie appeared in Geneva for treatment and contacted Bechtell out of boredom. Bechtell invited him to dinner at the Plat d'Argent. While having dinner, Bechtell managed to pour thallium into Moumie's wine glass. Moumie ignored the glass for most of the dinner, frustrating Bechtell, but finally took a drink. He died the next evening in a Geneva hospital.

Swiss authorities issued an international warrant for Bechtell's arrest, and he was finally arrested in Belgium and extradited to Switzerland in 1975. Swiss authorities released Bechtell in 1980 due to pressure from France. Fortunately for Swiss authorities, an elaborate attack planned by Bechtell's friends using a helicopter and a small commando team on the prison where he was being held in an attempt to free him was stopped by his release. (*Facts on File,* 1975; Faligot and Krop, *La Piscine*)

32   Beck, Melvin (b. 1913).   Spent his first ten years in the National Security Agency as a Soviet communications analyst. In 1953 he joined the CIA as the chief of the Latin American desk in the Soviet Division of Clandestine Services where he analyzed counterintelligence operations using case studies and research on Soviet intelligence organizations.

In 1958 he became a case officer running operations against Soviet agents in Cuba and Mexico; while in Havana in 1960, Beck was able to observe the meeting between Castro and First Deputy Premier Anastas Mikoyan.

Beck was then assigned a deep-cover assignment in Mexico, where he conducted operations against Soviet agents and diplomats, which included bugging operations against Soviet diplomats. Beck describes a strange hypnotic experimental operation in Mexico, designed to test double agents, that failed miserably. After five years he returned to CIA headquarters and took a desk job till his retirement in 1971. (Beck, *Secret Contenders*)

33   Beer, Israel (1912–68).   Beer, born in Vienna, arrived in

Palestine in 1938. He served as chief of training operations of the Jewish underground army, the Haganah, till 1948 when he became the deputy chief of operations of the Israeli Army during the war for independence. Though retired in 1949, he continued to have access to classified data. Beer had been an active member of the Communist Mapai party till 1954 when he switched to Ben-Gurion's Mapai party. Beer became a close friend of Ben-Gurion and was asked to write the official history of Israel's birth. He was a committed Socialist while growing up in Vienna and reportedly fought in the Spanish Civil War with the Socialist against Franco. Beer had told his friends in Israel an elaborate story about his military academy training and fighting Nazis in Vienna during the invasion in 1938. Many believe the story to be untrue. It is possible that Beer was recruited in Spain by the Soviets as a "sleeper agent," one that would be activated at some future date — in this case, in Israel. In 1961 Shin Bet noticed his excessive spending, quite beyond his means, and started surveillance. They arrested him shortly after meeting a KGB officer. Lieutenant Colonel Beer was convicted in 1962 for spying for the Soviets and sentenced to 15 years. (Black and Morris, *Israel's Secret Wars*; Eisenberg, Dan, and Landau, *The Mossad*; Raviv and Melman, *Every Spy a Prince*)

34 Bell, William Holden (b. 1921).   Bell served in the U.S. Navy at Pearl Harbor during the Japanese bombing and was later wounded at Iwo Jima. After the war, he earned a physics degree from UCLA and went to work for Hughes Aircraft in California. Bell was an unlikely candidate to spy, but in the mid–1970s Bell would suffer a divorce, the tragic death of his son in a fire, bankruptcy, and an IRS investigation.

In 1977 Bell met a Polish neighbor, Marian Zacharski, who stated he was a manager for POLAMCO, an import-export machinery company owned by the Polish government. Zacharski was actually a Polish intelligence officer using the position with POLAMCO as a cover. When Zacharski discovered Bell's access to sensitive radar systems at Hughes, he quickly befriended him, becoming almost a surrogate son. Bell had been a project manager in the Radar Systems Group of Hughes Aircraft. Bell did not have top-secret clearance but did have secret clearance to many of the projects Hughes Aircraft was working on. Bell worked on the radar for the space shuttle and defense aircraft radar.

Zacharski showed an interest in Bell's career and strongly suggested that Bell could come to work for the Polish American Machinery Company (POLAMCO). Zacharski first paid Bell for suggestions and the names of contacts in the industry that would help POLAMCO establish business contacts, paying Bell $4,000 for the information, and asked Bell to sign a receipt, thereby setting the hook.

Bell would provide Zacharski a variety of information on Hughes radar systems. Bell provided secret project plans for the "Covert All-Weather Gun System" to impress him. Zacharski gave Bell a camera for taking pictures of documents at work. Bell was a projects engineer with Hughes Aircraft and photographed sensitive documents at Hughes, giving them to Polish agents in four trips to Austria and Switzerland between 1979 and 1980. Bell became Hughes specialist on military radar systems. Bell supplied classified information of the video correlator of the cruise missile, changes in the TOW antitank missile, radar systems data on the B-1 bomber and Stealth bomber and F-15 fighter, radar systems for the Phoenix air-to-air missile, Patriot missile, the towed array submarine sonar system, HAWK missile, and NATO air defense system. One of the items Bell gave the Polish agents was a document called "Dual Purpose Weapons System Study Effort Final Report." Reportedly, Bell had received $110,000 for photographing classified documents concerning weapons and radar projects.

In 1980 the FBI became aware that there was a spy in the aerospace industry due to information provided by a Polish defector from the UN. The leads led to Hughes Aircraft and Bell. The FBI began surveillance of Bell and asked the CIA to follow Bell during his trips to Europe. In June 1981 the FBI arrested Bell, and he agreed to meet with Polish intelligence agents under FBI supervision. In October 1981, Bell pled guilty in a U.S. court to espionage charges. In December 1981, Bell was sentenced to eight years. Zacharski was also arrested, and sentenced to life in prison. Bell claimed he was involved only in industrial espionage. Bell agreed to testify against Zacharski. Bell had been paid over $100,000 and $60,000 in gold coins for his services for Polish and Soviet intelligence. (Allen and Polmar, *Merchants of Treason*; Barron, *KGB Today*)

Bennett, Harvey C. see Kaminsky, Mark I.

35   Bennett, Meir (Max) (1917–54).   Born in Hungary to Orthodox Jewish parents from Germany. His family immigrated to Palestine in 1935. Bennett had a flair for languages and learned six fluently. This caught the attention of Israeli intelligence, and he was recruited into the Aman, rising to the rank of major.

In 1951 he was sent to Egypt under cover as a salesman of artificial limbs for a German company by the name of Emil Witbein as an ex–Nazi who hated Israel. Ironically, he established contracts with the Egyptian Army to supply artificial limbs to the victims of the Israeli wars. The Israeli government supplied the limbs to a German warehouse that shipped them to Egypt. He was able to make friends with numerous government and military officials.

While in Egypt, Bennett lost contact with his Israeli handlers and contacted another Israeli spy in Egypt, Marcello Ninio, to reestablish contact. Later, Ninio was captured by Egyptian counterintelligence agents. Under torture, she identified Bennett as an Israeli agent. Egyptian agents burst into Bennett's apartment and discovered a radio transmitter. On December 21, 1954, while waiting in prison for trial, Bennett removed a nail from his cell and cut open his wrists, killing himself. (Black and Melman, *Israel's Secret Wars*; Eisenberg, Dan, and Landau, *The Mossad*; Raviv and Melman, *Every Spy a Prince*; Steven, *The Spymasters of Israel*)

36   Berger, Helge.   In May 1976, Berger, a secretary at the West German Foreign Ministry, was arrested for spying for East Germany for ten years. Berger had worked in the West German trade mission in Warsaw from 1966 to 1970 and allegedly had blackmailed the head of the mission, Heinrich Boex, into supplying her with classified documents. In November 1977, Berger was sentenced by a West German court to five years for giving classified Foreign Ministry documents to East Germany. Berger had worked for the Foreign Ministry offices in Bonn, Warsaw, and Paris, spying for East Germany. (*Facts on File*, 1977; *New York Times*, November 3, 1977)

37   Bettaney, Michael John.   MI5 agent who was convicted of spying for the Soviet Union in 1984. Bettaney, a notorious drunk, was Oxford-educated and had bizarre beliefs, converting to Roman Catholicism at the age of 16, then switched to Nazism, then discovered Communism. He was recruited in 1975 for MI5, the British counterintelligence service. He was a midlevel officer in MI5 domestic counterintelligence service but eventually worked in a sensitive position within Section K, which was involved with the KGB and GRU operations in Britain.

He approached Arkady V. Guk on April 13, 1983, but received no response. He made another attempt on June 12, and another on July 12, giving them data on British MI5 operations against the Soviets. The Soviets remained unconvinced. Confused and desperate, he made plans to travel to Vienna to contact the Soviets, but on September 16 he was arrested. British intelligence was tipped off by KGB officer Oleg Gordievsky, a double agent for the British.

In April 1983 Bettaney was sentenced to 23 years for espionage. Bettaney had taken classified documents and dropped them into a mailbox of a GRU intelligence officer, Arkady Guk, who was under cover as the Soviet naval attaché. The Soviets believed Bettaney was attempting to bait them into a trap and refused the offer. Some believe that Bettaney's efforts were so clumsy and obvious that the Soviets believed Bettaney to be a double agent sent to fool them. When British officials asked Bettaney why he did it, he announced that the British system had become unjust and that the U.S.-British relationship was becoming dangerous, claiming he had converted to Communism. Guk was expelled from the country on May 14, 1983. (Andrew and Gordievsky, *KGB*; Costello, *Mask of Treachery*; Glees, *The Secrets of the Service*; Pincher, *Too Secret, Too Long*)

38 Biard, Henri. In March 1974, Biard, the head of the French counterintelligence agency DST, was forced to resign from the post after a political scandal erupted over the illegal wiretapping of the office of a publication called *Le Canard Enchaine*. Biard had refused to allow DST agents to testify during the investigation. The DST was reorganized after Biard's removal. (*Facts on File*, 1974; *New York Times*, March 28, 1974)

39 Bienstock, Natalie Anna. Between March 1962 and February 1963, Bienstock, a Czech graduate student and Russian language teacher at Cornell University, provided Soviet officials with the names of Russian artists touring the U.S. who might defect. A KGB officer, Viktor Petrovich Sorine, recruited her in March 1962 to spy on the students. She had worked for a company involved in the U.S.–Soviet cultural exchange program in New York. Her reports were forwarded to Leo Sorokine in New York. (*Facts on File*, 1964; *New York Times*, December 6, 1964)

40 Bingham, David James. Sublieutenant Bingham, a British torpedo specialist, was sentenced in March 1972 to 21 years for selling classified naval documents to the Soviet Union. The data included British naval movements and naval firepower. In 1970–72 he photographed classified documents from the British Navy. He was stationed on HMS *Rothesay* at the Portsmouth naval base. He was motivated by severe debt and family problems. Desperate, Bingham approached a GRU officer, Lori Kuzman, after Bingham's wife made contact with the Soviet embassy. In 1972, due to pressures at home, his job, and the demands of GRU, he turned himself in to authorities. The Soviets had paid him a total of $6,000 for his services. GRU officers had trained him in the use of photographing documents. According to his wife, Maureen, who was also charged with espionage, she had encouraged her husband into selling secrets to the Soviets to the point of nagging. She was sentenced to two years in November 1972. (Andrew and Gordievsky, *KGB*; West, *The Circus*)

41 Bittman, Ladislav. From 1954 to 1968 served in the First Directorate of the Ministry of Interior of the Czechoslovakian secret service. In 1964 he was appointed deputy chief of Department Eight (active measures), which was responsible for special operations. In 1966 he was posted in Vienna. With the Soviet invasion of Czechoslovakia in 1968, he decided to defect. He joined the Communist party in 1946, attended Charles University in 1950 in international law. In 1954, after his graduation, he was recruited into the Czechoslovakian intelligence service.

He was first appointed as a research officer in the Department of Research and Analysis. In 1958 he was appointed as a junior officer of the German-Austrian operational department, which was responsible for re-cruiting agents in West Germany. In 1961 he was sent to East Berlin, where he took over the control of a recruited agent. In 1963 he returned to Prague, appointed deputy chief of Department Eight in 1964. (Bittman, *The Decep-tion Game, The KGB and Soviet Disinformation*)

42   Blahut, Regis T.   In the summer of 1978 CIA officer Blahut was fired for the unauthorized entry into a locked safe containing the physical evidence and files relating to the 1963 assassination of Pres. John F. Kennedy. Blahut had been assigned to assist the House Assassinations Committee investigation into the assassination with CIA records. When committee members discovered that the files and evidence had been disturbed, they ordered an investigation. Blahut's fingerprints were found on the files. The safe contained autopsy photos, X-rays, and the "magic bullet" that hit both the president and Gov. John B. Connally. Reportedly, nothing had been taken from the safe.

Blahut stated that he had an innocent reason for entering the safe but refused to state it because of his oath of secrecy to the CIA. A polygraph indicated that he was lying when he was asked if anyone had ordered it. Blahut stated that he had passed the polygraph test without problems but reportedly failed three polygraph tests regarding the incident. (*Facts on File* 1979; *New York Times*, June 18, 1979)

43   Blake, George (1922–78).   When the Nazis invaded the Netherlands, Blake was interned in a prison camp but later escaped and joined the Dutch Resistance, helping to receive SOE officers parachuting into Holland. After arriving in London, he anglicized his name from Behar to Blake and was commissioned in the Royal Naval Volunteer Reserve as an intelligence officer and attached to the Dutch Section. Blake's knowledge of a variety of key languages — French, German, Dutch, and English — made him a valuable interpreter for the staff of the newly created Supreme Headquarters Allied Expeditionary Force and subsequently the Head-quarters Allied Naval Expeditionary Force, which was planning Operation Overlord (the invasion of Europe) where he translated and interpreted cap-tured German documents. After the war Blake was decorated with the Knights Cross of the Netherlands Order of Nassau and put in charge of his own naval intelligence unit, where Blake interrogated U-Boat commanders and technical experts in Hamburg.

He returned to London in 1947 and studied Russian at Cambridge. Afterward he joined the Foreign Office with the rank of vice-consul in the Far Eastern Department. This was a disappointment for Blake since he had hoped to return to Germany to work against Soviet spies. He was sent to Seoul, South Korea, as an assistant to Captain Vyvyan Holt in 1948. Blake managed to gather valuable information about political and military events in North Korea and China.

When North Korea invaded South Korea on June 25, 1950, Blake was captured. Blake later confessed that it was in Korea, before his capture, that he began to appreciate Communist society. Blake underwent brainwashing and, having personal doubts about his own society, was finally won over to the Communists. By the time of his release, Blake was a full-fledged Communist.

He returned to Great Britain and was given a sensitive assignment in Berlin in 1955, where he was attached to the MI6 outpost at the office of the British military commandant in West Berlin. Blake was joined by Horst Eitner, a West German intelligence officer who ran teams of agents in Eastern Europe. Ironically, Eitner and Blake were both double agents for the Soviets but did not realize it till 1958 when they then joined forces. The relationship with Eitner was a dangerous one for Blake, so in 1959 he asked to be reassigned.

In September 1960 they sent him to Beirut, where he became a student at the Middle East College of Arabic Studies with the intention of working as an MI6 agent in the Middle East. Back in Berlin, Eitner was arrested by the West German secret service, and in 1961 Eitner became bitter sitting in prison and decided to sell Blake out. But it was only when the Polish defector, Lt.Col. Michal Goleniewski, chief of Polish Military Intelligence, alerted them of Blake's activities that British began to act. Blake was asked to return to London where he was arrested April 3, 1961.

He confessed to being a Soviet spy for nine years and was sentenced to 42 years on May 3, 1961. Soon after his arrest, six British agents in Germany were captured by the Soviets, and a few weeks after his trial 40 British agents in Europe and the Middle East were also captured, including 12 German agents.

Among the possible connections between Blake and the Soviets was the kidnapping of General Bialek and the disappearance of the members of the National Alliance of Russian Solidarists, an anti–Communist Russian operation in the Eastern Bloc and the Soviet Union. Blake is also thought to be responsible for the arrest of an RAF officer, G.C. Cedric Masterman, in Czechoslovakia after a photoreconnaissance mission against the airfield installations in northern Bohemia. Blake exposed 40 Western agents to the Soviets and betrayed sensitive British and U.S. secrets. Blake also informed the Soviets of the Berlin tunnel (Operation Gold), which was built by the U.S. and British intelligence services into East Germany to tap Soviet intelligence communications. The Soviets used disinformation for a while but later captured it in 1956.

On October 22, 1966, Blake disappeared over the wall of Wormwood Scrubs Prison, escaping to the Soviet Union. In February 1970, the Soviet Union awarded Blake two medals for his service to the Soviet Union: the Order of Lenin and the Red Banner. (Blake, *No Other Choice;* Bourke, *The Springing of George Blake;* Cookridge, *The Many Sides of George Blake, Esq.;* Lucas, *The Great Spy Ring*)

44   Bloch, Felix Stephen.   Joining the State Department in 1958, Bloch, born in Austria, was a veteran diplomat serving several embassy posts throughout Europe for over 30 years. Though he was never charged with a crime, the FBI pursued him with a vengeance, and the State Department declared him the biggest spy in the department's history.

Counterintelligence agents trailed a Soviet agent, Reino Gikman, in Paris to a meeting with Bloch, who at the time was deputy chief of mission at the U.S. embassy in Vienna (1981–87). Bloch was filmed handing Gikman a briefcase, which Bloch later claimed was a stamp collection. Reportedly, Bloch was later tipped off that he was being followed by Soviet agents who had spotted the surveillance team.

The State Department withdrew his security credentials and transferred Bloch from his post to Washington, D.C. The FBI began overt surveillance of Bloch, which attracted a parade of reporters and cameramen. Bloch was described as a disgruntled employee of the State Department who may have been motivated by bitterness and revenge. The State Department finally dismissed Bloch in November 1990 on grounds of making false statements. Bloch was never charged or arrested for any crime. (Duffy, "Tinker, Tailor, Soldier, Deputy Chief of Mission," *U.S. News and World Report; Facts on File,* 1989–90; *New York Times,* July 22–31, August 1–7, 1989, January 3; February 8; March 8, 1990, April 26; May 13; July 20, 1990)

45   Blunt, Anthony Frederick (1907–83).   Former art adviser to Queen Elizabeth II from 1945 to 1979, knighted by the queen in 1956. In 1979 the British government announced that Blunt was a former Soviet spy, part of the Maclean-Burgess-Philby spy ring. Blunt had confessed to British intelligence officials in 1964 that he had recruited students to spy for the Soviets while he was a professor at Cambridge University in the 1930s. Blunt confessed only after being offered freedom from prosecution.

Blunt became disillusioned with the British social and economic system while a student at Cambridge during the Depression. Recruited by the Soviets in the early 1930s, he agreed to act as a recruiter while teaching at Trinity College, Cambridge, from 1932 to 1936. Blunt was a confirmed Marxist when he joined the Security Service in 1940, motivated by his political beliefs to help the Soviets. Blunt claimed that the intelligence he provided the Soviets during World War II was concerned with German activities.

In 1951 Blunt learned through his contacts in MI5 that Burgess and Maclean were about to be arrested and quickly notified them, allowing them to escape to the Soviet Union. Though he had been uncovered by MI5, he continued as the queen's adviser until he retired in 1972. He was stripped of his knighthood after the British announcement in 1979. Blunt was never formally charged with any crime. (Andrew, *Her Majesty's Secret Service*; Boyle, *The Climate of Treason* and *The Fourth Man*; Costello, *Mask of Treachery*; Penrose and Freeman, *Conspiracy of Silence*)

46   Boeckenhaupt, Herbert W.   U.S. Air Force Staff Sergeant Boeckenhaupt, a German-born U.S. citizen naturalized in 1948, was convicted of passing classified data on the Strategic Air Command (SAC) to Aleksey R. Malinin, a KGB agent, between June 1965 and October 1966. He worked at the Pentagon from April 1964 to August 1965 as a radio operator in the Air Force headquarters command post. He had access to SAC codes and cryptographic equipment and systems. He claimed that the KGB had threatened to harm his father living in West Germany if he did not cooperate. He was arrested in October 1966 by FBI agents at March Air Force Base in California, where he worked as a communications technician, and sentenced to 30 years in June 1967. (Allen and Polmar, *Merchants of Treason*; Romerstein and Levchenko, *The KGB Against the "Main Enemy"*; Rositzke, *The KGB*)

47   Bogdanov, Radomir Georgievich.   Served as KGB resident in New Delhi 1957–67, where he was engaged in recruiting agents and participated in propaganda operations. Responsible for recruiting Romesh Chandra to spy for the Soviets and is credited with building the foundations of KGB operations in India. Rose to the rank of colonel in Department Twelve in the First Chief Directorate. In 1989 he was named the deputy director of the Academy of Sciences Institute for the Study of the U.S. and Canada, which he used as a cover for covert operations. (Andrew and Gordievsky, *KGB*; Barron, *KGB Today*)

48   Bokhan, Sergei.   In 1985 Bokhan, deputy director of Soviet military intelligence in Greece, defected to the West. Bokhan gave the U.S. considerable data on Soviet intelligence operations in Greece. Due to this information, several Greeks were arrested for spying for the Soviets. These included Michael Megaloeconomou and Nikos Pipitsoulis, computer engineers, and Vasilis Serepisios, a Greek Navy lieutenant in the Records Office of the naval command. (*Facts on File*, 1985; *New York Times*, October 1, 1985)

49   Bordes, Pamella Chaudhury Singh.   She grew up in a middle-class family in Haryana, India. Her father, Maj. Mahendra Singh Chaudhury, was killed in 1962 during the IndoChina War. After she won the title of Miss India in 1982, she quickly gained the attention of the rich and powerful when she began traveling and socializing at high-class parties and restaurants in New York, Tokyo, Paris, and London.

Bordes later acquired a job as a parliamentary researcher for the British House of Commons, working for two conservative MPs of the Tory party, David Shaw and Henry Bellingham. Reportedly a high-class prostitute, she was spotted with a Libyan agent, a cousin of Muammar Qaddafi, Ahmed Gedda Feddem, who was stationed in Paris. Bordes would travel in his personal jet to Tripoli on several trips while working in the British Parliament. When MI5 learned of the relationship, an investigation was launched by both British and French counterintelligence services. The incident caused a major scandal in Britain and brought comparisons to the Profumo affair of the 1960s. Bordes was often referred to as a cross between Linda Lovelace and Mata Hari. Bordes was never convicted of any crime. (Bobb, "Indecent Exposures," *India Today; Facts on File,* 1989)

50   Borger, Harold N.   A former U.S. Air Force officer and businessman, he was sentenced to two years for espionage for East Germany. He had given classified military data on nuclear warfare to East German agents. (*Facts on File,* 1962; *New York Times,* April 29; May 8, 1962)

51   Borovinsky, P. F.   In January 1971, Borovinsky, first secretary at the Soviet embassy in Bonn, left West Germany after accusations of espionage activities. Reportedly, Borovinsky had made contact with two West Germans, Daniel Wlaczak and Hans Adolf Wlaczak (father and son), to provide military intelligence. Both were arrested. (*Facts on File,* 1971; *New York Times,* January 8, 1971)

52   Bossard, Frank Clifton (b. 1912).   Joined the Royal Air Force in 1940, lying about his education; he was able to get a commission as an officer. During World War II, he became a specialist in radar. In 1946, as a flight lieutenant, he left the RAF and joined the Ministry of Civil Aviation, then transferred to the Intelligence Division of the War Office. In 1956 he joined the Joint Intelligence Bureau at the British Embassy in Bonn, where he interviewed former Nazi scientists. He returned to Great Britain in 1958 and in 1961 met a Soviet GRU agent, Ivan Petrovich Glazkov, at a coin collector's meeting. During a subsequent meeting at a restaurant,

Bossard complained about his financial problems, and Glazkov quickly jumped on the opportunity, giving Bossard cash for information.

In July 1964 he joined the Naval Guided Weapons Branch of the Aviation Ministry as a project officer. He would photograph documents and deliver them to dead drops (actually an odd assortment of cubbyholes, gutter drains, notches in walls). Bossard would receive instructions from Radio Moscow, notifying him by the musical selections it played on certain evenings.

MI5 was tipped off by an FBI asset within GRU named Top Hat, who indicated there was a Soviet mole in the Aviation Ministry. In March 1965 MI5 officers surprised Bossard in the act of photographing sensitive documents. Bossard had provided guided missile secrets to the Soviets for $14,000. Bossard was sentenced to 21 years in May 1965. Upon his arrest, it was revealed that Bossard had been arrested for stealing watches in 1934 and sentenced to six months' hard labor for that crime. There was considerable criticism of the government for not conducting a background check. (Pincher, *Too Secret, Too Long*; West, *The Circus*; Wright, *Spy Catcher*)

53   Boyce, Christoper John (b. 1953), and Andrew Daulton Lee (b. 1952).   Boyce and Lee grew up in southern California as childhood friends. Both had been influenced by the antiestablishment forces of the late 1960s and early 1970s. Boyce, as an employee of TRW Systems in California from July 1974 to December 1976, was assigned to the "black vault," a secure communications room, as a security clerk. Here he worked with classified documents and encoded communications of the CIA. Boyce gave the data to Lee, who acted as a mediator with the Soviet KGB.

On January 16, 1977, the FBI arrested Boyce and Lee for selling classified documents to the Soviet Union. Lee had been arrested in Mexico City on January 6. Mexican authorities discovered three rolls of microfilm classified documents.

Boyce was convicted of selling classified data on two satellite systems, Rhyolite and Argus, which intercepted telemetry signals transmitted by Soviet missiles during test launchings. During his trial Boyce testified that he had seen data that the CIA had been involved in a covert operation to manipulate the political leadership of Australian labor unions. In April 1977 Boyce was found guilty of espionage and in September was sentenced to 40 years. He escaped in January 1980 and was caught a year later in August 1981. In April 1982 Boyce was given an additional 20 years for bank robbery after he had escaped from federal prison. He pled guilty to the bank robbery and was a suspect in 16 bank robberies.

Lee stated that he worked for the CIA in an effort to feed the Soviets false information. No one believed him. In May 1977 Lee was convicted of eight counts of espionage and sentenced to life. (Allen and Polmar, *Merchants of Treason;* Corson and Crowley, *The New KGB;* Lindsey, *The Falcon and the Snowman;* Turner, *Secrecy and Democracy)*

54   Brenneke, Richard.   Former CIA pilot and Oregon businessman, he announced in 1987 that he had been a liaison between an Iranian Air Force officer and the U.S. government. Brenneke had attempted to gain U.S. approval for a weapons sell to the Iranians in late 1984 for the exchange of information, which included a detailed map of Qaddafi's headquarters in Libya, details of the PLO headquarters in Tunisia, and positions of terrorist camps in Libya, Chad, Algeria, and Lebanon. (*Facts on File,* 1987)

55   Britten, Douglas Robert.   Britten, a chief technician in the Royal Air Force, sold classified data from RAF signal units in Cyprus and Lincolnshire. He was recruited in 1962 by a KGB officer, who first approached him in South Kensington Science Museum and addressed him by his ham radio call sign "Golf Three Kilo Foxtrot Lima." Britten was shocked by the announcement, and the two men began talking about amateur ham radio. Britten was offered money for an obsolete RAF transmitter which was widely available on the open market, called the 1154, but the KGB officer pretended that he thought it was a classified piece of equipment. Britten needed the cash and thinking the piece unimportant, provided it to them. The Soviets were aware that the device was nonclassified, but it was the hook needed to ensnare Britten into helping them. While stationed in Cyprus in 1962–66, the Soviets photographed Britten taking cash from a KGB agent in Cyprus for blackmail. The Soviets were able to coerce him into providing more data.

After 1966 he was assigned to the RAF signal unit in Lincolnshire. His new case officer was Aleksandr Ivanovich Bondarenko, working under cover of first secretary. He was caught by MI5, who photographed him delivering a package to the Soviet embassy after his case officer failed to show up at a scheduled meeting. In November 1968, Britten pled guilty to espionage for the Soviet Union and was sentenced to 21 years. (Andrew and Gordievsky, *KGB;* West, *The Circus)*

56   Brooke, Gerald.   Brooke, a professor of Russian at Molborn College, London, arrived in Moscow in April 1965 serving as a tour guide for a group of British students but was arrested several days later by Soviet authorities. According to Soviet authorities, Brooke was arrested at the apartment of Yuri Konstantinov, a Moscow physician, while handing over anti–Soviet propaganda. Konstantinov had apparently assisted security officials during the arrest. During the trial Brooke stated that an agent from the émigré organization People's Labor Alliance (NTS) had contacted him in 1964 in London, asking him to carry the materials to a contact in Moscow.

The NTS was formed in 1930 by Soviet émigré students in Europe and operated a radio station aimed at the Soviet Union. The Soviet government accused the NTS of trying to start an armed revolt in the country.

In July 1965, a Soviet court sentenced Brooke to one year in jail and four years in a labor camp for smuggling anti–Soviet propaganda into the Soviet Union for NTS. Brooke pled guilty to the charges. Soviet authorities also declared that Brooke was under orders to contact Second Secretary K. Anthony Bishop of the British embassy in Moscow if there were problems in distributing the materials, and expelled him from the country. The British government denied that Bishop or the government was connected with the NTS or Brooke. The British government retaliated by expelling Second Secretary Vitalij K. Boyarov, of the Soviet embassy in London. In 1969 Brooke was exchanged for the Krogers. (*Facts on File*, 1965; *New York Times*, April 29–30; May 6, 27; July 2, 23–25; August 18, 1965)

57   Broudre-Groeger, Joachim.   In September 1978, Broudre-Groeger, top aide to West German Social Democratic party manager Egon Bahr, was accused of being a spy for Rumania. The allegations were based on statements made by Ion Pacepa, who defected to the West, the vice minister of the Rumanian secret police. The charges were later dropped. (*Facts on File*, 1978; *New York Times*, September 3, 1978)

58   Bryen, Stephen D.   In April 1983 the National Association of Arab Americans (NAAA) sued the U.S. Justice Department for the right to review documents charging Bryen, a Senate aide, with passing sensitive data to Israel. Bryen, Jewish, had been a senior staff member of the Senate Foreign Relations Committee. An Arab-American leader, David Saad, with the NAAA had overheard Bryen in 1978 in the Madison Hotel coffee shop offering Israeli embassy diplomats data on a Saudi Arabian air base. Bryen was suspended due to the charges but was reinstated and promoted to deputy assistant secretary of defense, specializing in controlling high-technology exports to the Soviet Union in the Reagan administration. A memo from the Justice Department's internal chief strongly urged that Bryen's case be brought before a federal grand jury for prosecution. The NAAA was now suing to obtain a six-page report encouraging the Justice Department's recommendation for a grand jury. The group was also seeking 400 missing pages from the Justice Department's files concerning the investigation into Bryen's activities. The Defense Department officials defended

Bryen against the accusations, and no criminal charges were filed against him. (Blitzer, *Territory of Lies; Facts on File*, 1983)

59   Buckley, William (d. 1985).   CIA station chief in Beirut, Lebanon, he was kidnapped by Shiite terrorists in 1984 and tortured to death in the basement of the Iranian embassy in Beirut. The Islamic Jihad announced in September 1985 that Buckley had been executed and that Buckley had admitted being a CIA agent. Reportedly, Buckley was video-taped confessing to being a CIA officer and provided intelligence on the Middle East. The CIA made several desperate attempts to locate and rescue Buckley. A special FBI kidnapping team was sent to Beirut but failed to find him. (*Facts on File*, 1985, 1987; Woodward, *Veil*)

60   Buckley, William Frank, Jr. (b. 1925).   In 1950 Buckley joined the CIA's Office of Policy Coordination. E. Howard Hunt met the young Yale graduate and was impressed by Buckley's command of Spanish and French, inviting him to join Hunt's opening of the CIA's OPC station in Mexico City. Buckley was assigned to assist Communist ex-patriot Eudocio Ravines, a former Chilean Marxist intellectual, write *The Yenan Way*, a book reflecting Ravines's disaffection with communism. Once the work was published, it was circulated around Latin America. Buckley also translated the work into English.

Despite Buckley's exotic locale, he became bored with his assignments. During his tenure in Mexico, his publication *God and Man at Yale* had created a sensation back in the U.S. and in 1951, after nine months in the CIA, Buckley left Mexico and the CIA. He returned to the U.S. and became a well-known conservative spokesman who founded the *National Review* and the television interview program "Firing Line." Buckley has also written three spy novels featuring a fictional CIA agent, Blackford Oakes: *Saving the Queen, Stained Glass*, and *Who's on First*.

Hunt and Buckley maintained a close relationship over the years. Buckley became the godfather of Hunt's children and the executor of his estate. When Watergate exposed Hunt's involvement, Buckley solicited funds for Hunt's legal defense and had Hunt on as a guest on "Firing Line." Buckley's support for Hunt did not stop him from criticizing the Nixon administration for the Watergate affair in the *National Review*. (Judis, *William F. Buckley, Jr.*; Hunt, *Undercover*)

61   Bukreyev, Vladimir.   In June 1978, Bukreyev, a Soviet official for the International Labor Organization (ILO) in Geneva, Switzerland, was expelled after being accused by Swiss officials of being a KGB officer due to British intelligence reports. (*Facts on File*, 1978; *New York Times*, June 30, 1978)

62   Bunke, Haidee Tamara ("Tania") (d. 1967).   On April 31, 1967, Tania (Che Guevara's mistress and a leftist guerrilla) and a group of guerrillas were ambushed by the Bolivian Army. The CIA had trained a special Bolivian army to hunt down Guevara's guerrilla army. Tania, who reportedly was pregnant at the time of her death, is believed to have been spying on Guevara for the Soviets. Reportedly, she had helped the Bolivian Army find Guevara by leaving a guerrilla jeep with sensitive maps and information for them to find. These led the Bolivian forces to find his jungle headquarters. U.S. experts note that Cuba suddenly stopped promoting her as a revolutionary heroine in May, apparently after learning of her espionage for the Soviets. Many speculate she may have been ordered to betray Guevara, who was captured and executed. (*Facts on File*, 1968; *New York Times*, July 15, 1968)

63   Burchett, Wilfred (d. 1983).   Burchett, an Australian journalist, was accused of being a spy for the Soviet Union by U.S. officials. Former prisoners of war from the Korean conflict had also testified that Burchett had been a Communist agent and had participated in brainwashing of Americans in North Korea. Burchett later claimed the CIA offered him $100,000 to work for them while he was covering the war in North Korea and that he turned the offer down. He was a well-known Communist sympathizer. The KGB defector Yuri Krotkov stated that he had met Burchett in Berlin in 1947. Burchett revealed to Krotkov that he was a secret member of the Australian Communist party. Krotkov stated that he recruited him to work for the KGB. During the Vietnam War, he wrote a variety of anti-U.S. articles while living in luxury in Hanoi as a guest of the North Vietnamese government. (Bittman, *The KGB and Soviet Disinformation*; Burchett, *The Second Indochina War*; Toohey and Pinwill, *Oyster*)

64   Burger, Heinrich.   In June 1976, Burger, his ex-wife, Kathryn, and Kurt and Erna Nickel were arrested for espionage by West German agents. Burger, press spokesman for the Social Democratic party, was accused of spying for East Germany for five years. Reportedly, Burger's former wife, Kathryn, had told authorities of his activities. The Nickels served as couriers between East German agents and Burger. Burger supplied East Germany with information on the SDP and the West German government. In January 1978 East German authorities arrested Gunter Weinhold, a West Berlin city official, and accused him of espionage. In July 1979, Weinhold was exchanged for Heinrich Burger. (*Facts on File*, 1977–79; *New York Times*, June 15, 1976, July 20, 1979)

65   Burgess, Guy Francis de Moncy (1911–63).   British spy for the Soviet Union. Burgess attended Cambridge in 1930, studying history and becoming involved in Communist student activities. Burgess was an open and promiscuous homosexual in college. It was at Cambridge that Burgess met three of the most infamous Soviet spies: Kim Philby, Donald Maclean, and Anthony Blunt. It was Blunt who helped recruit him to spy for the Soviets. During his last year at Cambridge in 1934, he visited Russia. It was probably during this visit that the Soviets convinced Burgess to work for them. After his return from Russia, Burgess quit the Communist party and began befriending conservatives. By 1935, Burgess was submitting regular reports to Samuel Borisovich Cahan, the Soviet resident director of the Soviet secret service.

In 1936 he joined the BBC as a journalist and capitalized on the anti–Fascist fears to promote pro–Soviet causes. It was during this time that Burgess was arrested for making a homosexual advance in the men's bathroom. The charge was later dropped due to lack of evidence. In December 1938 he was offered a job in Section Nine of the secret service. Burgess helped prepare wartime propaganda against the Germans and organized an underground resistance to Hitler through the international trade union movement. For a time he acted as a liaison officer between the Ministry of Information and Section Nine. When the war actually did break out, Guy was sacked. By this time, Burgess was handled by Soviet agent Filipp Kislitsyn. Burgess returned to his old job at the BBC in 1941 and at the same time began working closely with MI5 uncovering Fascists in England. He stayed with the BBC for the next three years, then joined the Foreign Office News Department in 1946 where he became the personal assistant to the minister of state, Hector McNeil. It was here that Burgess supplied the Russians with data on foreign policy strategy. In 1944 Burgess invited Donald Maclean to a homosexual orgy where he was photographed and blackmailed into cooperation. In 1947 he was transferred to the Far Eastern Department as a political analyst of the Chinese Revolution.

He was sent to the British embassy in Washington, D.C., in 1950, charged with the special responsibility of explaining British policy on the Far East to the U.S. State Department. While in Washington, in November 1950 he was involved in a drunken brawl with another colleague in which he suffered a concussion after being tossed down a stairwell. After several other embarrassing incidents, he was recalled to London in 1951. That same year Burgess learned that he was about to be arrested by MI5. Fearing arrest for espionage, Burgess and Maclean defected to the Soviet Union. It was not until February 1956 that Burgess and Maclean summoned a news conference in Moscow and announced their defections. (Boyle, *The Climate of Treason, The Fourth Man*; Cookridge, *The Third Man*; Fisher, *Burgess and Maclean*; Newton, *The Cambridge Spies*)

66   Burke, Michael (1918–87).   Served in the Office of Strategic Services (OSS) in Algeria in 1942, then in Sicily and Italy in 1942. In July 1944 he parachuted into France as part of the Jedburgh team to organize resistance forces for the oncoming D-Day invasion.

In July 1949 Burke was recruited as the operational officer into the Eastern European Division of the CIA. His first assignment was to organize the Albanian refugees into a resistance force; called Operation Valuable, it was a joint CIA-MI6 operation. The idea was to send an Albanian resistance guerrilla force into Albania to stir up resistance to the Communist government.

Called Company 4000, 250 Albanian refugees were trained in guerrilla tactics in Germany and Great Britain; the force later grew to five hundred. The first team was parachuted into Albania by CIA-flown C-47s in April 1950, and the team disappeared. A second team went in by sea from submarines but also disappeared. At first Burke believed that the radio equipment of the teams was damaged, but additional teams were sent in with the same results. The operation was stopped in early 1952 with the belief that there was a leak in the Albanian group who was giving the Soviets the information about the drops and landing sites. In fact, it was an MI6 liaison officer with the CIA, Kim Philby, who was a Soviet double agent. Close to five hundred Albanians had been captured and executed.

After the operation Burke was transferred to Germany, where he coordinated agent drops into the Soviet Union as the Munich station chief. He quit the CIA in 1954 and became the manager of the Ringling Brothers Barnum and Bailey Circus. (Bethell, *Betrayed*; Hunt, *Undercover*; Knightley, *The Master Spy*; Page, Leitch, and Knightley, *The Philby Conspiracy*; Prados, *Presidents' Secret Wars*)

67   Burnett, Steve.   Burnett, former member of the British Special Air Service, admitted in a Botswana court to spying for South Africa on Ronald Watson, an ANC sympathizer, in 1987. Burnett accosted Watson in a hotel room in Botswana with a gun, but Watson was able to wrestle the weapon away from Burnett. Burnett later claimed to be working for MI6. Burnett was convicted of attempted murder. (*Facts on File*, 1987)

68   Bush, George Herbert Walker (b. 1924).   Director of the Central Intelligence Agency (DCI) from January 1976 to January 1977 under President Ford. He served in World War II as a naval pilot in the Pacific and was shot down by Japanese forces. Member of Congress, Seventh District, Texas, 1966–70. Ambassador to the United Nations 1971–72. Chairman of the Republican National Committee 1973–74. Chief of the U.S. Liaison Office to the People's Republic of China 1974–75. Vice President under President Reagan, elected president in 1988. Instituted reforms due to controversies of agency activities revealed by the commission on CIA activities headed by Nelson Rockefeller.

Bush flew the Avenger torpedo bomber for the U.S. Navy in the Pacific during World War II. In September 1943 Bush was shot down by Japanese antiaircraft guns over the island of Chichi Jima. Though hit by the fire and burning, he continued his bombing run, delivering the bombs to the target. He bailed out over the ocean and was rescued by the *Finback*, a U.S. submarine. While he was on the *Finback*, the Japanese attacked it with depth charges twice. Bush was awarded the Distinguished Flying Cross after returning to his carrier, the *San Jacinto*. Bush left the navy in 1945. He then attended Yale University, graduating in 1948.

From 1948 till 1964, he became a successful businessman in the oil industry. His first foray into politics came when he was elected to Congress from Texas. In 1971 he was appointed the U.S. ambassador to the United Nations till 1972. From 1974 to 1975, he served as the chief of the U.S. Liaison Office in Beijing, China. In January 1976 he was appointed director of the CIA by President Ford. He served in the position till January 1977 when President Carter replaced Bush with Stansfield Turner. While CIA director, Bush helped institute reforms brought on by the disclosures of congressional committees investigating CIA activities. (Hyams, *Flight of the Avenger*; Johnson, *America's Secret Power*; Ranelagh, *The Agency*)

69 Butenko, John William. Butenko, a U.S. electronics engineer and field administrator for the International Electric Corporation (IEC), had supplied the Soviets with information on IEC's work on an international data transmitting and processing system for the U.S. Strategic Air Command (SAC). A Soviet, Igor A. Ivanov, using the cover of a chauffeur for the Soviet Amtorg trade agency in New York City, was also arrested. The Soviet vehicle captured when Butenko was arrested had a special camera needed for document photography. Several Soviet diplomats were expelled from the U.S.: Gleb A. Pavlov, UN attaché; Yuri A. Romashin, third secretary of the UN mission; and Vladimir I. Olenev, UN employee. Ivanov did not have diplomatic immunity. In 1964 Butenko was ordered to undergo a mental examination. In December 1964, Butenko was convicted of spying for the Soviet Union. At Butenko's trial he stated that he had provided the information to the Soviets to get information about relatives living behind the Iron Curtain. Butenko was accused of providing information for the Soviets between April and October 1963. Butenko was sentenced to thirty years. Ivanov was also convicted of spying and sentenced to twenty years. (*Facts on File*, 1963–64, 1969; *New York Times*, October 30–31, November 16, 1963, January 18, 25, 31, November 26, December 19, 23–34, 1964; Romerstein and Levchenko, *The KGB against the "Main Enemy"*)

70 Bychkov, H. E., and Y. N. Poluchkin.   In May 1965 two Soviet diplomats were expelled from Canada for espionage activities in Ottawa — Bychkov, Soviet embassy commercial section, and Poluchkin, a chancery clerk. Canadian authorities accused both men of paying a Canadian government employee and a Canadian citizen thousands of dollars for sensitive technical data. Canadian authorities claimed that no information was transmitted to the Soviets. (*Facts on File*, 1965; *New York Times*, May 9, 1965)

71 Cabon, Christine.   French DGSE intelligence agent whose successes included the infiltration of the PLO. Her final assignment involved the *Rainbow Warrior* affair where she infiltrated the Greenpeace organization in Auckland, New Zealand. She successfully penetrated the organization and provided the DGSE with critical details allowing frogmen to place two bombs on the *Rainbow Warrior,* sinking it and killing one member of Greenpeace. (Faligot and Krop, *La Piscine*; Richelson, *Foreign Intelligence Organizations*)

72 Cairncross, John C. (b. 1913).   In 1930 attended Glasgow University for two years, studying a variety of languages, political science, and economic studies. He then spent 1933–34 in Paris studying at the Sorbonne. By the time he returned to England and attended Trinity College, Cambridge, in October 1934, he was a confirmed Communist and dedicated anti–Fascist.

His French literature teacher was the Soviet agent Anthony Blunt, who recognized Cairncross's potential. In 1935 Guy Burgess recruited Cairncross as an agent, putting him in touch with Arnold Deutsch (alias "Otto"). Cairncross was instructed to break off all contacts with the Communist party.

In 1936 he graduated with top honors and passed the Foreign Office examination with high marks. Served first in the Foreign Office in several different departments: American, Western, Central, and League of Nations. In October 1938 he transferred to the Treasury Department, then transferred to the Government Code and Cipher School where he supplied Enigma SIGINT information to the Soviets. He transferred to MI6 in 1944, first serving in the German counterintelligence division, then in the Balkan division. After the end of the war, he moved back to the Treasury Department and worked in the Defence Division (Material and Personnel).

In May 1951 a MI5 search of Guy Burgess's apartment revealed reports written at Treasury by Cairncross from 1940. Cairncross was put under surveillance, and MI5 agents followed him to a park where he was to meet with his Soviet controller, but the agent never showed up. MI5 then interrogated him, but he denied any espionage, admitting only that he had given

Burgess some papers from Treasury during the war. He resigned from Treasury and eventually worked for the Food and Agriculture Organization of the United Nations in Rome, where in 1964 he admitted to MI5 agents his activities during and after the war. It wasn't till Anthony Blunt admitted being a Soviet spy and named Cairncross and Leo Long that MI5 resumed its investigation into Cairncross's activities, and his final admission in 1964. He was never charged with a crime. (Andrew and Gordievsky, *KGB*; Costello, *Mask of Treachery*; West, *The Circus*; Wright, *Spy Catcher*)

73   Carey, George F., Jr.   Colonel Carey, while serving as the senior air attaché for the U.S. embassy in Warsaw, Poland, was expelled from the country in January 1965 for spying. According to Polish authorities, Carey had photographed a Polish military air base at Bydgoszcz. Carey denied the charges but did state that he had inspected and walked around the base without entering it. The U.S. retaliated by expelling Kazimierz Mizior in January 1965, a clerk in the office of Poland's military attaché. The State Department hinted that Mizior was involved in espionage. (*Facts on File*, 1965; *New York Times*, 14, 19, 1965)

74   Carr, Sam.   Born Schmil Kogan to Jewish parents in the Ukraine, he anglicized his name to Carr when he entered Canada. Part of GRU Colonel Nikolai Zabotin's spy network in Ottawa, serving as a talent spotter and agent handler for the GRU, Carr was the organizing secretary of the Canadian Communist party. He was elected to the Canadian Parliament in 1943 and reelected in June 1945. When Igor Gouzenko, Soviet cipher clerk, defected from the Soviet embassy in Ottawa in September 1947, Carr was named and fled to Mexico. Carr had been jailed in 1942 for being a security risk and well known to authorities for his Communist activities but was still able to maintain an extensive network of spies. (Andrew and Gordievsky, *KGB*; Brook-Shepherd, *The Storm Birds*; Gouzenko, *The Iron Curtain*; Rositzke, *The KGB*)

75   Carranza, Nicolas.   Colonel Carranza, then head of El Salvador's Treasury police, was reported in 1984 by various sources to have been on the CIA payroll as an informant. Reportedly, Carranza received more than $90,000 a year for his services over a period of five to six years. Carranza was linked to the death squads but denied any connection to the squads and to the CIA. U.S. congressional sources stated that Carranza had provided the CIA with data on Salvadorean rebel groups, political activities in El Salvador, and inside gossip from security and military circles. (*Facts on File*, 1984; *New York Times*, February 19, March 22–23, May 25, 1984)

76 Carrillo Colon, Humberto. In September 1969, the Cuban government accused Carrillo, a Mexican diplomat, counselor, and press aide, of being a CIA agent. Reportedly, Carrillo maintained radio equipment that he used to send reports to the CIA. The Cuban government stated that it had positive proof of Carrillo's activities. The evidence included a forty-eight-page document with 110 photographs and eighty-seven messages between the CIA and Carrillo. Carrillo was recalled to Mexico in September 8, 1969. (*Facts on File*, 1969; *New York Times*, September 6, 13, 1969)

77 Cascio, Giuseppe. U.S. Air Force staff sergeant stationed in South Korea, was arrested and convicted of espionage in 1952 for attempting to sell the North Koreans classified data on the F-86E Sabre fighter. He was working as a photo technician for the 49th Air Base Group in Korea and had accepted payments from a Korean civilian who was believed to be an enemy agent. Cascio was diagnosed as paranoid but capable of standing trial. His wife did not help his case when she referred to him as behaving "goofy" during testimony at his trial. A confederate, U.S. Air Force S.Sgt. John P. Jones was also arrested but was discharged from the Air Force after it was determined that he was insane and unable to stand trial. Cascio was sentenced to twenty years and dishonorably discharged. (*Facts on File*, 1952; *New York Times*, November 25–27, 1952)

78 Casey, William Joseph (1913–87). Director of Central Intelligence Agency (DCI) from January 1981 to January 1987 under President Reagan. Graduated from Fordham University in 1934, then attended Law School at St. John's University, graduating in 1937. Joined the U.S. Navy in 1943 during World War II and transferred to the Office of Strategic Services in 1944 as chief of the Special Intelligence branch in European theater of operations. He coordinated the effort to send Polish, Belgian, and French agents to the major crossroad cities of Germany. Deep penetration agents were parachuted far behind the lines.

After the war Casey became a successful businessman and lawyer. Served as chairman of the Securities and Exchange Commission 1971–73, then under secretary of state for economic affairs 1973–74; president and chairman of the U.S. Export-Import Bank 1974–76; member of the president's Foreign Intelligence Advisory Board 1976–77.

Casey managed the Reagan presidential campaign in 1980, and after the election was appointed director of the CIA. Casey's tenure included the largest peacetime hiring programs in the history of the CIA. His directorship came under scandal when the Iran-Contra program became public. During Casey's tenure as DCI, the CIA was involved in a variety of embarrassing scandals, including the mining of Nicaraguan harbors, the illicit sale of weapons to the Contras and the Iranian government, and lying to Congress. Casey became ill in January 1987 and resigned his position as DCI; he soon died from a brain tumor. (Byrne, *The Chronology*; Persico, *Casey*; Smith, *OSS*; U.S. Govt., *Tower Commission Report*; Woodward, *Veil*)

79   Cavanagh, Thomas Patrick.   Severely in debt, Cavanagh, a Northrop engineer, sold Stealth bomber secrets to FBI agents posing as KGB officers. Cavanagh had been an engineer at the Advanced Systems Division at the Northrop Corporation, where he stole blueprints and other documents detailing the Stealth bomber. Cavanagh contacted a Soviet diplomat by telephone, but the FBI intercepted the phone call and met Cavanagh instead of the Soviets. He offered to provide his services for ten years for a salary of $25,000 a month. The meeting was arranged for December 10, 1984, at the Cockatoo Motel near Los Angeles, where he introduced himself as Mr. Peters to FBI agents.

Cavanagh joined the Navy where he learned electronics and became an interior communications specialist. After leaving the Navy, he worked for Northrop, rising to senior engineer on the Stealth bomber project. He told the FBI agents at the motel that he was afraid of being caught and detailed the security problems he faced at Northrop. He displayed some classified documents as an example. He agreed to another meeting, and after a third meeting he was paid for the documents and arrested. On March 14, 1985, he pled guilty to two counts of espionage and was sentenced to life. (Allen and Polmar, *Merchants of Treason*; *Facts on File*, 1984–85; *New York Times*, December 19–20, 22, 1984, February 26, May 25, 1985)

80   Chebotarev, Anatoly Kuzmich.   In October 1971, Belgian authorities announced that Chebotarev, a member of the Soviet trade delegation in Brussels, had been missing since October 3, 1973. Chebotarev had defected to the U.S. and was granted political asylum.

Chebotarev, a GRU major in the Technical Directorate, was working in Brussels under the cover of a member of the Soviet trade delegation. On October 2, 1971, he went to the British embassy in Brussels and asked for asylum, only to be told that he would have to come back after the weekend. Chebotarev, no doubt baffled by the explanation, went to the U.S. embassy and was immediately given asylum.

He identified thirty-three Soviet KGB officers in Belgium, many working under the cover of Skaldia-Volga and Aeroflot. Many were involved in electronic-listening operations on NATO telephone communications at the NATO headquarters in Belgium and at the Supreme Headquarters, Allied Powers.

The Soviets demanded to meet with Chebotarev, and the CIA finally granted the request on December 21, 1971. No one is sure what was discussed, but three days later Chebotarev announced that he wanted to return to the Soviet Union. Two days later he was delivered to the Soviet embassy. What happened to him upon his return is uncertain, but many believe he was probably forced to return by threats against his family, and probably executed. (Barron, *KGB*; Brook-Shepherd, *The Storm Birds*; Corson and Crowley, *The New KGB*)

81   Chebrikov, Viktor Mikhailovich.   Appointed head of the KGB in December 1983, replacing Vitaly Fedorchuk. First joined the KGB in 1967 when he was appointed to head the KGB personnel department, then was transferred to head the KGB electronic surveillance operations division. In 1987 Chebrikov alienated Gorbachev by reintroducing an old KGB conspiracy theory involving an attempt by Western intelligence services to disrupt the Soviet ideological system. An angry Gorbachev replaced him with Vladimir Kryuchkov in October 1988. (Andrew and Gordievsky, *KGB*; Corson and Crowley, *The New KGB*; Knight, *The KGB*)

82   Chelpanov, Yuri, and Gennady Mikhailov.   In April 1973, Colonel Chelpanov, Soviet military attaché, and Captain Mikhailov, Soviet assistant naval attaché for the London Embassy, were ordered to leave Great Britain for espionage activities. Both men were accused of recruiting Cuban diplomats to spy in England. One Cuban diplomat, Aristides Diaz Rovirosa, was expelled from Great Britain for spying for the Soviets. Reportedly, the Soviets began recruiting Cubans when one hundred Soviet officials were expelled from Great Britain in September 1971. (*Facts on File*, 1973)

83   Chernov, Vladimir Alexandrovich.   In January 1983, Chernov, translator for the International Wheat Council, was ordered expelled from Britain for espionage activities. Oleg Gordievsky, KGB officer turned double agent for British intelligence, confirmed that Chernov was an agent for the KGB Department Twelve, which recruited Soviet civil servants and journalists as spies. (Andrew and Gordievsky, *KGB*; *Facts on File*, 1983; *New York Times*, January 13, 1983)

84   Chernyayev, Rudolph, Valdik Alexandrovich Enger, and Vladimir Petrovich Zinyakin.   Chernyayev, UN personnel official; Enger, an assistant to the under secretary-general of the United Nations; and Zinyakin, an attaché at the Soviet UN mission, were arrested in a joint FBI-NIS (Naval Investigative Service) sting operation called Operation Lemonade.

In the summer of 1977, under the guidance of the FBI and NIS, Arthur F. Lindberg, a naval lieutenant commander, took a Soviet cruise ship, *Kazakhstan*, for a cruise between New York and Bermuda. Before he left the ship, he handed a Soviet officer a note stating an interest in making extra money selling data on naval underwater warfare projects.

He met with the KGB agent seven times between October 22, 1977, till their arrest in May 20, 1978. They paid him $16,000 for unclassified or forged documents. In May 1978 the KGB agents were retrieving a roll of film hidden in an orange crate when they were arrested by FBI and NIS agents.

They were convicted in 1978 for espionage and sentenced to 50 years but later ordered confined to their Soviet-owned residences in New York. Zinyakin, was released due to his diplomatic status. Enger with Chernyayev was later traded for Soviet dissidents. (Allen and Polmar, *Merchants of Treason*; Rositzke, *The KGB*; Turner, *Secrecy and Democracy*)

85 Chin, Larry Wu-Tai (d. 1986).   Chin, a naturalized U.S. citizen, had supplied China with a variety of CIA classified documents, including the CIA's assessment of China's military, economic, scientific, strategic, and technical capabilities.

He began working in the U.S. Army liaison mission in China in 1943 as an interpreter during the Chinese civil war, as a translator in Foochow, Shanghai, and Hong Kong. While a translator at the U.S. Army liaison office in Foochow, he was approached by a Chinese intelligence officer, Dr. Wang of the Communist party. In 1948 he was an interpreter in the U.S. consulate in Shanghai till the fall of the Nationalists, then was sent to Hong Kong in 1950 as the secretary-interpreter at the U.S. embassy in Hong Kong. It was in Hong Kong that he began his espionage for the Communists. During the Korean War he was sent to South Korea to interrogate Chinese POWs. In 1952 he joined the CIA's Foreign Broadcast Information Service (FBIS) as a translator at the monitoring station in Okinawa, then in 1961 moved to the CIA monitoring stations in California till 1970. In 1970 Chin came across sensitive documents pointing to the possibility that Nixon was preparing to open relations with China. Chin copied the document and sent it to his handlers, then went to Washington, D.C., for the CIA's FBIS.

He retired in 1981 as an analyst in the FBIS office in Virginia but continued till 1985 in the CIA division of the U.S. Joint Publications Research Service as a translator. Chin received the title of Deputy Bureau Chief in China's Ministry of Public Security in 1982 while on a visit to Beijing and received $50,000 for his years of service.

Convicted of spying for China in 1986, Chin stated in court that he had sold China documents during the 1970s to better relations between the two countries. The discovery of Chin was a major blow for the CIA. Chin committed suicide in his cell after his conviction, awaiting sentencing.

He received a CIA medal for distinguished service upon his retirement. In 1985 one of Chin's Hong Kong handlers defected, revealing Chin's activities. Chin's Hong Kong bank accounts had grown to $564,000 by the time he was arrested. (Allen and Polmar, *Merchants of Treason;* Richelson, *Foreign Intelligence Organizations*)

Chisholm, Janet Ann see Chisholm, Roderick

86   Chisholm, Roderick, and wife, Janet Ann.   In early 1962 a KGB surveillance team followed Janet Chisholm to the Arbat area of Moscow where she was scheduled to meet with Oleg Penkovsky, a Soviet spy for the West. They made a brief exchange, and the KGB team split up to follow them as they departed. They followed Janet back to the British embassy, but lost Penkovsky. Roderick Chisholm was the MI6 officer assigned to serve as Penkovsky's handler in Moscow, operating under diplomatic cover of second secretary, but the KGB had a file on him from his stations in Singapore and Germany. Since the KGB was aware of his MI6 relationship, he used his wife for the meetings.

One meeting occurred at a park where Janet's children were playing. Penkovsky would stop to greet her and offer one of her children a box of candy filled with film. In January 1962 both Janet and Penkovsky noticed a KGB surveillance team and decided not to meet personally again but to use dead drops. But Penkovsky did pass film to her at the British embassy reception in March 1962 and the July 4 celebration at the U.S. embassy in 1962. When Penkovsky was arrested, Chisholm transferred to the Foreign Office as a diplomat. (Andrew and Gordievsky, *KGB;* Penkovskiy, *The Penkovskiy Papers;* Richelson, *American Espionage and the Soviet Target;* West, *The Circus;* Wynne, *The Man from Moscow*)

87   Chitov, Vasily I.   In 1982, Major General Chitov of the Soviet Union, assigned to the Soviet embassy in Washington, D.C., was expelled after a high-speed chase by the FBI. When the FBI was able to stop Chitov they found classified documents in the car. Since Chitov had diplomatic status, he was not charged with a crime. (*Facts on File,* 1982; *New York Times,* February 5–6, 1982)

88   Chow Tse-Ming (alias "Chou Chou").   In April 1955 an Air India Constellation airliner carrying the Chinese delegation to the African-Asian Bandung Conference in Indonesia was destroyed by two time bombs over the South China Sea. Chow was an employee of the Hong Kong Aircraft Engineering Corporation and reportedly admitted placing the bombs aboard the plane when it landed in Hong Kong for refueling. Hong Kong police discovered that Chow had been recruited by a Kuomingtang

(Nationalist party) intelligence organization to carry out the act. Chow escaped to Taiwan where he was given sanctuary. A clockwork device was later recovered from the crash.

An individual claiming to be an ex–CIA officer stationed in India in the 1950s, John Smith, claimed that he had delivered two time bombs to Chinese Nationalist agents. The main target was the Chinese premier Chou En-lai, but Chou departed the plane unexpectedly in Rangoon, Burma, for a brief visit with Egyptian President Nasser before continuing to Indonesia on a different flight. (Blum, *The CIA; Facts on File*, 1955–56; *New York Times*, March 12, 30; April 2, 3; August 1955)

89 Chung Ki Ryong. Chung was arrested by South Korean agents for heading a North Korean spy ring. While in South Korea, Chung had been a professor of political science in Seoul. All together, twelve Communist agents were arrested with ten collaborators. Reportedly, Chung had been sent to South Korea in 1955, developing an extensive espionage ring in Pusan, Taegu, and Seoul. On December 5, 1968, Chung was sentenced to death for his involvement. Reportedly, Chung had received spy training and money from North Korean agents in 1958–67. (*Facts on File*, 1968, 1972; *New York Times*, December 6, 1968)

90 Chuyen Thai Khac. Chuyen had been in charge of a team of Vietnamese units observing the movement of Communist troops on both sides of the Cambodian border. They had been trained by U.S. Special Forces, who used the data to coordinate ambushes. Reportedly, he notified the North Vietnamese agents of his activities in May or June 1969. The Communists ambushed the team, killing several members. When Chuyen met with his North Vietnamese contacts in Cambodia, he was secretly photographed. After being interrogated, he confessed his activities, and the CIA subsequently ordered his execution. Reportedly, the CIA had withdrew the order without the knowledge that Special Forces members had already killed him. Several Special Forces members involved in the case confirmed that the CIA had ordered the murder (Middleton and Marasco).

After ten days of interrogation, he was drugged with morphine and on June 20, 1969, taken by motorboat out into Nha Trang Bay. He was then shot twice in the head, weighted down with chains, and dumped into the water. Robert F. Marasco, Special Forces captain in Vietnam, was accused of assassinating Chuyen. CIA Director Richard Helms refused to allow CIA officers to testify in the case. Chuyen was killed, according to Marasco, on orders from the CIA with "extreme prejudice." Marasco had shot Chuyen in the head with a pistol, and it was Capt. Leland J. Brumley and CWO Edward M. Boyle who kidnapped Chuyen from the Special Forces base in Nhatrang and injected Chuyen with morphine before he was shot. In

August 1969, the commander of the U.S. Special Forces and seven others were arrested on suspicion of the murder.

Several others were accused from the Special Forces base in Nhatrang: Col. Robert B. Rheault, commander of the Fifth Special Forces Group (Airborne); Maj. David E. Crew; Maj. Thomas C. Middleton, Jr.; Capt. Robert F. Marasco; Capt. Budge E. Williams; and Sgt. First Class Alvin L. Smith, Jr. A U.S. Navy frog team searched for but did not find the body. In September 1969 murder charges were dropped against all the Green Berets connected with the case.

It became known as the "Green Beret Murder," and the movie *Apocalypse Now* made several references to the killing. The CIA denied any involvement and proposed an elaborate story of trying to convince Special Forces not to kill Chuyen. Considering the times, it is difficult to believe. (*Facts on File*, 1969, 1971; Stanton, *Green Berets at War*)

91   Cichy, Gerard.   In January 1970, Cichy, a courier for a French travel firm in Warsaw, was accused by Polish authorities of working for U.S. intelligence officers. Reportedly, Cichy conducted spying operations in Poland for French intelligence. (*Facts on File*, 1970)

92   Clark, Carlton W.   In December 1972, Clark, a British citizen, was sentenced to nine years in prison by a Zambian court for spying for Rhodesia and South Africa. He was also reportedly caught with weapons and committing sodomy. Clark denied the charges. (*Facts on File*, 1972)

93   Clines, Thomas G. (b. 1928).   Joined the CIA in 1949; CIA posts involved Laos, Congo, Vietnam, and Cuba. Clines was deputy chief of the Miami station during Operation Mongoose. As a private businessman in 1986, Clines helped arrange clandestine arms deliveries to the Contras out of Portugal, recruiting ex–CIA pilots for the supply operation. A veteran CIA clandestine services officer, Clines had numerous contacts with Ed Wilson, the CIA rogue agent who helped Clines set up CIA proprietary companies while still in the CIA. Clines retired in 1978 and formed several businesses with the help of Wilson. Wilson was arrested for gun smuggling for Libya. Wilson was angry at Wilson, who he believed owed him $200,000 for past business relationships. Wilson later claimed he would have Clines killed, offering $100,000 for his death. Convicted of four counts of income tax evasion stemming from the Contra supply network, Clines was sentenced to sixteen months. (Byrne, *The Chronology*; Goulden, *The Death Merchant*; Maas, *Manhunt*; Marshall, Scott, and Hunter, *The Iran Contra Connection*; McCoy, *The Politics of Heroin*; U.S. Govt., *The Tower Commission Report*)

94 Cloude, Robin Douglas. In November 1968, a British court sentenced Cloude, who served on an antisubmarine frigate, HMS *Duncan*, to five years for violating the Official Secrets Act. Cloude had visited the Soviet embassy in London shortly after the British Navy rejected his request for a loan to build a house. He then decided to sell some secrets for the money, confessed to visiting the Soviet naval attaché twice. He was arrested on August 21, 1968. (Allen and Polmar, *Merchants of Treason*; *Facts on File*, 1968; *New York Times*, November 5, 1968)

95 Cohen, Aharon. In 1962 Cohen was convicted in a secret trial in Israel of spying for the Soviet Union. Cohen supplied them with scientific and research data from 1956 to 1958. He had been an active member of Israel's Communist party, the Mapai party, serving as their Middle East specialist. Shin Bet agents, Israel's counterintelligence and internal security agency, caught Cohen meeting a KGB officer in Tel Aviv in October 1958. Though the Mapai party leader protested his arrest, denying that he spied, he did admit to meeting with the Soviets. He met with Vitaly Pavlovski, a member of the Soviet scientific delegation in Jerusalem, who fled the country when Cohen was arrested. He was freed in July 1963 after serving half of his five-year sentence. (Black and Morris, *Israel's Secret Wars*; Raviv and Melman, *Every Spy a Prince*)

96 Cohen, Baruch. Cohen spoke fluent Arabic while growing up in Palestine in an old Jewish family. He joined Shin Bet in 1959 after being rejected by the police for his height. He worked mostly in Arab villages in northern Israel and joined the investigations branch in 1966. After the 1967 war, he served with the security service in the city of Nablus in the Gaza Strip. In July 1970 he was recruited by Mossad and sent to the Israeli embassy in Brussels under diplomatic cover under the name Moshe Hanan Yishai. Here he ran Arab agents in Europe and kept tabs on Palestinian groups in Europe. He traveled extensively throughout Europe meeting contacts. One of his agents contacted him for a meeting in a café, a Palestinian medical student studying in Madrid. While waiting to meet the student on January 26, 1973, he was gunned down by Black September terrorists in an apparent ambush. (Black and Morris, *Israel's Secret Wars*; Ostrovsky and Hoy, *By Way of Deception*; Raviv and Melman, *Every Spy a Prince*; Steven, *The Spymasters of Israel*)

97 Cohen, Eliahu ben Shaul (1924–65). Born in Alexandria, Egypt, to Jewish parents, Cohen became a political instructor in Hachalutz and began teaching Zionist thought. Despite this, he was also committed to Egyptian nationalism. He attended a French high school in Alexandria, then attended Faruk University for two years, studying electrical engineering. While a student, he joined the Committee Guards, a vigilante group that responded to anti–Jewish attacks by Moslems in Egypt. In 1952 Eli was arrested on suspicion of engaging in Zionist activities, despite the fact that Cohen considered himself a loyal Egyptian.

He began to get involved with a clandestine operation called Goshen, which helped Jews emigrate from Egypt to Israel. Cohen helped bribe Egyptian passport and customs officials, and made friends with French, German, Italian, and British vice-consuls, who helped provide transit visa for bribes.

Later he joined an Israeli network based in Egypt in 1953, operating a transmitter between the Egyptian network and Israel. After a series of bomb attacks in 1954 were carried out by the network, Cohen and the group were picked up. After four months of questioning Cohen convinced them that he had nothing to do with the network and was released. He continued his work in illegal immigrations, was arrested again in November 1956, and after several torture sessions was ordered expelled from Egypt.

Arriving in Israel on February 12, 1957, he joined Shin Bet where he started work in a research department translating and analyzing Arab newspapers. He left Shin Bet after a reorganization and worked odd jobs for a while. In 1959 he was approached by a Mossad official, who asked him to join. He turned down the offer but finally accepted after he was laid off from his job, rather conveniently for the Mossad.

He began a six-month training program where he learned basic espionage tradecraft, part of his training specifically aimed at the Syrians. He studied every aspect of Syrian society, politics, customs, and economics. He was sent to a Moslem *kadi*, who instructed him on the Koran and Islamic practices. The Mossad gave Cohen the cover of Kamal Amin Taabet, a deceased Lebanese Moslem of Syrian descent who had been raised in Egypt and emigrated to Argentina.

To strengthen his cover, he was sent to Argentina in 1960. When he arrived, he was given Argentine identity papers and a passport. While there, he established a strong knowledge of the area. His Spanish improved, and he made some Argentine friends. Here he met influential Syrians, opened an account at a Syrian-Lebanese Bank, and subscribed to the Syrian-based *Arab World* newspaper. He joined the Islamic Club and met a variety of businessmen from Syria. He espoused anti–Zionist views and a progressive Arab nationalism. He joined the Argentine Arab Youth Movement, the Syrian Cultural Movement, and the Arab League Society. He became so well respected that he received invitations to Arab diplomatic missions. It was here that he voiced an interest in returning to his homeland, Syria.

After nine months in Argentina he returned to Israel in May 1961 and reported to the Mossad operations department for advanced training in microfilm and radio communications, drilled further on the Syrian military, weaponry, organization, and Soviet military equipment, nearly memorizing the Syrian *Who's Who.* He was assigned a mission to infiltrate the upper echelons of the Syrian government and gather intelligence on every level. He would represent himself as a militant Syrian nationalist.

Once in Syria in 1961, he started an import-export business. Portraying himself as a convert to the Baathist cause and an anti–Zionist, he constantly talked to senior military officials, insisting on stronger defenses against Israel, actually making them feel guilty. They made him an honorary major in the Syrian Army and took him on tours of secret military areas to assure him that there were proper defenses against Israel. He joined the Baath party and became an executive member of the National Revolutionary Council. He became so trusted that he performed unofficial tasks for the Syrian prime minister, Salah Bitar. He told the Israelis about the border fortifications and the strength and position of the forces. He was able to give Mossad an accurate analysis of Syrian Army strengths and an accurate forecast of the strength of the Baathist party. He became so well trusted and revered that they nominated him for the position of minister of information, with the possibility of being appointed deputy minister of defense.

Syrian counterintelligence service placed him under surveillance when Cohen was identified by Egyptian intelligence agents, who spotted him in Syria in 1964. It came to an end when a picture of Cohen in Egypt was found. Syrian agents raided his apartment on January 24, 1965, while he was waiting for a message from Mossad. They discovered a miniature Phillips radio transmitter, two codebooks, a bathroom dark room, a second transmitter, two bars of soap filled with explosives, a movie camera with infrared film, and a tape recorder built into the wall of the guest room. Cohen attempted to swallow a cyanide pill, but the guards stopped him. After two hours of interrogation, he revealed his identity as an Israeli operative employed by Mossad. The next day Cohen agreed to send a false message by radio to the Israelis if the Syrians spared his life. Cohen had actually warned the Israelis of his capture. During the past three years, Cohen's last line of every message sent to the Israeli's had been intentionally garbled. A coherent message was the prearranged signal that he had been arrested.

Cohen was physically and psychologically tortured. On February 28, 1965, he was put on trial, and on May 8, 1965, he was sentenced to death. On May 18, 1965, he was hung in Marjeh Square in front of spectators and a television crew. (Aldouby, *The Shattered Silence;* Black and Morris, *Israel's Secret Wars;* Eisenberg, Dan, and Landau, *The Mossad;* Raviv and Melman, *Every Spy a Prince;* Steven, *The Spymasters of Israel*)

98   Colby, William Egan (b. 1920).   Director of Central Intelligence (DCI) from September 1973 to January 1976 under Presidents Nixon and Ford. Graduated from Princeton in 1940 and entered the U.S. Army in 1941. In 1943 he was transferred to the Office of Strategic Services (OSS), special operation branch. As commander of the operational group, he parachuted into occupied Norway where his team carried out sabotage operations. He was awarded the Silver Star and Bronze Star for his efforts.

After the war he joined the CIA, served as CIA station chief in South Vietnam from 1959 to 1962, then served as chief of the Far East Division 1962–67; in 1968–71 served in South Vietnam with the rank of ambassador as director of the Civil Operations and Rural Development Program, which was responsible for the infamous CIA Phoenix program, responsible for the deaths of twenty to forty thousand members of the Vietcong. The Phoenix program was designed to identify members of the Vietcong, then "neutralize" them. This meant arrest, convert, or kill them. For the most part, it meant the death and torture of thousands of innocent Vietnamese suspected of being Vietcong.

In 1972–73 he served as executive director-comptroller, and deputy director for operations. In 1973 he was appointed director of the CIA. While director, he was forced to fire James Angleton as head of the counterintelligence division after Angleton began displaying a paranoid obsession that there was a Soviet mole in the CIA hierarchy.

Colby earned the Distinguished Intelligence Medal, the Intelligence Medal of Merit, and the Career Intelligence Medal from the CIA. Colby was often referred to by colleagues as the "soldier-priest," due to his strong Roman Catholic standards and his career choice. (Andrade, *Ashes to Ashes*; Brown, *Wild Bill Donovan*; Colby, *Honorable Men* and *Lost Victory*; Smith, *OSS*; Valentine, *The Phoenix Program*)

99 Conein, Lucien.   Born in France, he joined the French Foreign Legion as a captain. With the fall of France Conein joined the U.S. Army and transferred to the Office of Strategic Services (OSS). He parachuted into France and helped to organize resistance, later participated in French commando raids into northern Vietnam in 1945. Conein would find himself a fixed figure in Vietnamese affairs for the next two decades. Using the cover of a lieutenant colonel, he was assigned to the Vietnamese Interior Ministry. His mission was to cultivate contacts with Vietnamese generals. He was a CIA contact man with Saigon during the military coup against President Ngo Dinh Diem. (Cline, *Secrets, Spies and Scholars*; Colby, *Honorable Men*; Hunt, *Undercover*; Prados, *Presidents' Secret Wars*; Smith, *OSS*)

100 Conrad, Clyde Lee.   Retired U.S. Army sergeant; charged by West German authorities of spying for Hungary and Czechoslovakia and sentenced to life in 1990. He passed NATO secrets to Czechoslovakian and Hungarian agents for more than ten years. Conrad was the custodian of a storage vault for classified documents at the U.S. Army Eighth Infantry Division headquarters in Bad Kreuznach, West Germany. Conrad received millions of dollars for his spying. Roderick Ramsay, former Army sergeant, was also arrested for his participation. Ramsay had served with Conrad in 1983–85. The data sold to the Soviets was described as extremely sensitive. (*Facts on File*, 1989–90; *New York Times*, June 7–9; March 10; September 2, 1989)

101 Conway, Rosemary Ann. In June 1975 Laotian authorities arrested Conway, accusing her of being involved in espionage activities. Conway, an American, was accused by Pathet Lao radio of being a CIA agent, stating that she had offered money to Laotian Air Force officers to defect to a CIA air base in Thailand with their T-28 fighter-bombers.

She was released in August 1975 and left for Thailand. Laotian officials said she had confessed to being involved in espionage. U.S. officials said Conway taught English in Vientiane and was not a spy. (*Facts on File*, 1975; *New York Times*, June 10, 14, 1975)

102 Cooke, Christopher M. In February 1982 Air Force Lieutenant Cooke was released from jail by order of a military appeals court. Cooke was accused of passing classified data to Soviet agents. When Cooke was arrested in May 1981, he was given a promise of immunity from prosecution if he cooperated. The court ruled that the agreement had been violated, and he was released.

Cooke, a deputy commander of a Titan missile silo, visited the Soviet embassy in Washington, D.C., three times between December 1980 and May 1981. While there, he made a telephone call to inquire about his car, and the FBI monitored the conversation. Reportedly, Cooke admitted giving the Soviets sensitive data about Titan missiles. At his arrest he was questioned without being advised of his right to counsel. The contents of the data given to the Soviets had not been revealed, but the Air Force was forced to change its codes and targets of the 54 intercontinental Titan missiles. He was not court-martialed but released from the Air Force. (Allen and Polmar, *Merchants of Treason*; *Facts on File*, 1981–82; *New York Times*, June 1, 2, 16, 21; September 2, 6, 9–11, 15–18; October 26, 1981)

103 Cooper, Roger. Arrested in December 1985 by Iran security officials accusing him of being a British spy. In February 1987 Cooper appeared on Iranian TV confessing to spying for British intelligence while attempting to set up a spy network within Iran. The British government denied any involvement with Cooper and argued that he had been coerced into a confession. In May 1991 the Iranian government released Cooper in exchange for an Iranian student, Mehrdad Kokabi, who bombed a British bookstore selling Salman Rushdie's novel *The Satanic Verses*. Upon his release, he denied any involvement in espionage. (*Facts on File*, 1987, 1988, 1991).

104   Coplon, Judith (b. 1922), and Valentin A. Gubitchev.   FBI agents arrested Coplon, a Justice Department employee, and Gubitchev, a Soviet UN employee, on March 4, 1949. In her purse were FBI reports of counterintelligence operations against the Soviets. The FBI also discovered the address of Robert Soblen, another spy for the KGB.

Coplon was convicted of espionage for the Soviet Union in 1950. Her Soviet handler and lover, Gubitchev, was deported. She had been convicted both in 1949 and 1950 for espionage; one conviction was reversed in 1950 because the FBI had obtained evidence illegally; the other was upheld in 1951 but later reversed because telephone conversations between her and her lawyer were tapped. Seventeen years later, Justice dropped espionage charges against her in 1967. (*Facts on File*, 1949–50, 1952, 1967; Romerstein and Levchenko, *The KGB Against the "Main Enemy"*)

105   Cordrey, Robert E.   Cordrey, a private in the Marine Corps, was court-martialed in 1984 for attempting to sell classified data on nuclear, biological, and chemical warfare (NBC) to the Soviet Union. In April 1984 Cordrey contacted Soviet and Czech officials with an offer to sell NBC information. Cordrey was an instructor at the NBC Defense School in survival techniques at Camp Lejeune, North Carolina. He was convicted in August 1984 on eighteen counts of attempting to contact foreign representatives for the purpose of selling secrets. The case was not revealed to the public till January 1985. He was sentenced to twelve years hard labor, later reduced to two years. (Allen and Polmar, *Merchants of Treason*; *Facts on File*, 1985; *New York Times*, January 10, 1985)

106   Cotter, William J.   Cotter joined the CIA in 1951 and served from 1952 to 1955 as deputy head of the CIA field office in charge of the East Coast mail intercept. The CIA had had a mail cover project since 1953 which was aimed at mail going between the Soviet Union and the U.S., later expanded to include a variety of other targets. The project involved externally photographing the envelopes. They were generally never opened till 1955 when the contents of a few were photographed.

In April 1969 Cotter became the chief postal inspector of the U.S. Post Office Department. In January 1971 Cotter received a letter of inquiry from a group of American scientists concerned that the Post Office was involved in the illegal opening of first-class mail. Cotter became concerned that the project might be revealed if he was forced to testify before a government committee under oath. Cotter also became concerned about the legality of the project and expressed considerable doubt about the continuation of the project, informing the CIA that he would discontinue the operation on February 15, 1973, unless the CIA received approval for the project from a higher level (presidential). The CIA failed to get approval, and the operation was canceled.

The last year of the New York operation handled 4,350,000 pieces of mail which were externally photographed and not opened and 8,700 pieces opened for examination, many of those based upon a watch list which contained the names of six hundred people (varied each month, depending on intelligence assessments). The CIA argued that the project was successful and led to numerous counterintelligence leads. (Freemantle, *CIA*; U.S. Govt., *Rockefeller Commission on CIA Activities*, 1975)

107   Crawford, Iain.   Worked as a parachute rigger, or "kicker," with the CIA in its first air drops of weapons to the Nicaraguan Contras in April 1986 from the Ilopango air base. Crawford claimed that a Southern Air transport plane had been used for the drops and that he had personally briefed Oliver North during a flight from El Salvador to Washington, D.C. (Byrne, *The Chronology; Facts on File*, 1987)

108   Crews, Alvin.   In April 1979 the South African government expelled three U.S. Air Force personnel for espionage activities. All three were assigned to the U.S. embassy in South Africa and were in charge of flying and maintaining the U.S. ambassador's airplane. Colonel Crews, the defense attaché; Maj. Bernd McConnell, assistant air attaché; and Master Sergeant Horace Wyatt, airplane crew chief, were accused of using the ambassador's airplane to photograph sensitive areas of South Africa, including military installations. A special camera was discovered under the copilot's seat containing undeveloped film. The South African government stated that it was shocked by the discovery and compared the espionage to something it would have expected from the Soviets, not the U.S. government. Reportedly, the main targets of the photography was the nuclear research facility near Valindaba and the uranium enrichment plant at Pelindaba. The U.S. government retaliated by expelling two South African diplomats, Commodore Willem Du Plessis, defense attaché, and Colonel Gert Coetzee, air attaché. (*Facts on File*, 1979; *New York Times*, April 13, 14, 20, 21, 1979)

109   Cross, Ralph Bernard.   Cross, a private in the Canadian Army, defected to East Germany in 1955. He stated that he had fallen in love with an East German woman. The affair ended within a year, but Cross remained in East Germany till 1982 when he was arrested near an East German missile base. He was charged with espionage and spent thirteen months in prison. In November 1983 he was taken to the border and returned to West Germany. He surrendered to Canadian authorities and pled guilty in January 1984 to desertion, was sentenced to 60 days in jail. Cross's charges of espionage in East Germany were not explained. (*Facts on File*, 1984)

110   Cubela Secadas, Rolando.   In October 1956 Cubela assassinated Blanco Rico, Cuba's military intelligence chief under Batista. Cubela had been a well-respected guerrilla leader in the central Escambray Mountains during the 1959 revolution, and reached the rank of major in the Cuban revolutionary army. Cubela, a close friend of Castro, contacted the CIA in 1961 after becoming disenchanted with Castro's pro–Soviet leanings, providing the CIA with a variety of data. Cubela who wanted to replace Castro with himself, met with CIA officials in Paris on November 22, 1963, to discuss the possibility of assassinating Castro. Ironically, the same day in Dallas, Texas, President Kennedy was assassinated by Lee Harvey Oswald. It was not until 1965 that the CIA teamed Cubela with Manuel Artime, the former Bay of Pigs commander, to plot the attempt. The operation became known in the CIA as AM/LASH. In 1966 he went to the U.S. to meet with CIA contacts. He returned to Cuba with a high-powered rifle and plans to kill Castro. A Cuban double agent in Miami informed Cuban authorities of the plot, and he was arrested upon his arrival. He was sentenced to 25 years in 1966. In August 1979 Cuban authorities released Cubela. (Freemantle, *CIA*; Powers, *The Man Who Kept the Secrets*)

111   Cunningham, Alden, and Barbara Sims.   In 1986 Colonel Cunningham and Captain Sims were charged with spying in Nicaragua for the U.S. Both were U.S. military officers attached to the U.S. embassy in Managua. The charge stated that they had been caught by the Sandinista military in the war zone of northeastern Nicaragua. (*Facts on File*, 1986)

112   Da-Chuan Zheng, and Kuang-Shin Lin.   In February 1984, Da-Chuan and Kuang-Shin were arrested for attempting to smuggle classified high-technology military equipment to China. Da-Chuan, a Chinese citizen with strong ties to China's military community, had provided undercover agents a list of $1 billion worth of equipment that he wanted to smuggle to China. Da-Chuan and Kuang-Shin had already smuggled integrated circuit equipment to China, were arrested after offering to purchase equipment needed for missile guidance systems and radar jamming technology used on military aircraft. Kuang-Shin was employed with AT&T Information Systems when he was arrested. (*Facts on File*, 1984; *New York Times*, February 14, 1984)

113   Daniloff, Nicholas S.   In August 1986 Daniloff, a reporter for *U.S. News and World Report*, was arrested in the Moscow woods in Lenin Hills. Daniloff had just met a Soviet friend by the name of Misha, later identified as Mikhail A. Luzin, with whom he was exchanging departing gifts. Luzin had given Daniloff a package that he stated contained news clippings from the city of Frunze. When Daniloff left the woods, he was arrested by the KGB. When the package was opened, the Soviets claimed it contained secret photos of military bases and equipment related to the Soviet war in Afghanistan.

Many argued that Daniloff's arrest was in retaliation for the arrest of Gennadi Zakharov, a KGB agent working under the cover of a UN delegate. In September 1986 Zakharov was exchanged for Daniloff. *Izvestia* reported that Daniloff was linked to the expelled CIA agent Paul Stombaugh, who was exposed by Edward Lee Howard to the Soviets. Another Soviet article announced that "Misha" had stated that Daniloff had asked for secret data on the Soviet war in Afghanistan. (Daniloff, *Two Lives, One Russia*; Kessler, *Moscow Station*; Wise, *The Spy Who Got Away*)

114   Darakhshani, Ali Akbar.   After World War II, Darakhshani was sentenced to life in prison for his support for the pro–Soviet separatist movement in northwestern Iran. He was later pardoned and rose through the ranks of the Iranian military. In March 1978 Brigadier General Darakhshani was arrested as part of a Soviet spy ring. Darakhshani had met with three Soviet agents just before his arrest, but the Soviets escaped. Darakhshani confessed to spying and died of a heart attack shortly after being sentenced. (Dzhirkvelov, *Secret Servant*; *Facts on File*, 1978; *New York Times*, April 7, 1978)

115   Daubbertin, Rolf.   In January 1979 French authorities announced that Daubbertin, a nuclear scientist, and his wife had been arrested for spying for the East Germans. Daubbertin worked for 15 years at the National Center for Scientific Research (NCSR) and was accused of providing the East Germans with information about research at the NCSR. (*Facts on File*, 1979; *New York Times*, January 29, 1979)

116   Daugherty, William.   In December 1979, Iranian student militants holding American hostages in Tehran accused Daugherty of being a CIA agent. The allegations were based on a State Department cable that stated that Daugherty and Malcolm Kalp needed State Department covers of second and third secretaries, respectively. The Iranian students also claimed that Daugherty had admitted being a CIA officer.

In April 1980, Iranian TV showed a video taken of one of the American hostages, Army S.Sgt. Joseph Subic, who was shown being interviewed discussing U.S. surveillance flights over Iran. One scene showed Subic showing Iranians a secret hiding place in the floor and ceiling in the embassy warehouse that held computer equipment. Subic also identified Daugherty as a CIA agent. U.S. TV networks refused to buy the tapes from the Iranians with their condition that the tapes not be edited. (Bittman, *The KGB and Soviet Disinformation;* McFadden, Treaster, and Carroll, *No Hiding Place;* Moody, *444 Days*)

117 Davies, Allen John. In 1986 Davies, a naturalized U.S. citizen from England, was arrested for attempting to pass classified military data to the Soviets. Davies, a former U.S. Air Force staff sergeant, attempted to sell data on the Air Force's reconnaissance program. Davies left the Air Force in 1984 after a poor service record forced him out. His duty stations included Japan, West Germany, and Korea. He was working as a laboratory technician for an aerospace company at the time of his arrest. Davies met an undercover FBI agent he believed to be a Soviet agent. His motivations were based on revenge for being kicked out of the service. (Allen and Polmar, *Merchants of Treason; Facts on File*, 1986; *New York Times*, October 29; November 4, 9, 15, 1986)

118 Davis, Charles. In November 1973, Davis, a black U.S. journalist, was arrested in West Germany on suspicion of spying for East Germany. Davis had moved to West Berlin in 1970 under the alias Calvin Williams, claiming that he was working for a black newspaper, but the newspaper denied employing Davis. He was released for lack of evidence and expelled in January 1974. (*Facts on File*, 1974)

119 Debret, Jacques (alias "Debreton"). Debret, a French citizen, was charged with espionage and linked to the attempted coup in the Congo in May 1968. The military tribunal began in May 1969 in Brazzaville where authorities argued that Debret had been recruited by a Frankfurt-based international intelligence organization. Debret stated that he had been recruited in Geneva to make contacts in Brazzaville in preparation for the coup attempt. While in the Congo, he contacted Lieutenant Pierre Kinganga, who helped him make contact with other military officers. Debret was sentenced in May 1969 to life. Kinganga was sentenced to death in absentia. Four other officers received from one to 20 years for their involvement. (*Facts on File*, 1969; *New York Times*, June 1, 1969)

120   De Bruyeker, R. E.   While working for the Soviets in 1976, he successfully broke into the NATO naval base at Agnano, Italy, and removed a box of classified documents. However, he forgot his bag, which contained an odd collection of items: a hammer, a Bible, a copy of *Playboy*, and details about himself and his residence. He was immediately traced and arrested.

121   De Champlain, Raymond G.   In July 1971, De Champlain, a U.S. Air Force master sergeant stationed in Thailand, was arrested for attempted espionage for the Soviet Union. De Champlain was flown to the Philippines for further charges. He had been part of the Military Assistance Command in Bangkok and was charged with attempting to pass classified documents to Vassily I. Khlopianov and Victor V. Mizin, second and third secretaries at the Soviet embassy in Bangkok. Both left Thailand after De Champlain's arrest. In November 1971 he was convicted of espionage and sentenced to 15 years at hard labor by a military court-martial in Guam. (*Facts on File*, 1971; *New York Times*, July 26; September 21; November 13, 1971)

122   DeForest, Orrin.   Served in the U.S. Air Force Office of Special Investigations as a liaison with the Japanese National Police KGB-GRU section and the Public Safety Investigative Board (Japan's FBI) 1955–1964. From 1964 to 1967 served in the U.S. Army's Criminal Investigations Division (CID), and from 1966 to 1967 completed one tour in Vietnam as a CID investigator in Vung Tao, then CID chief in Binh Dinh where he gained considerable experience working with the Vietnamese National Police.

Joined the CIA in 1968 as the chief interrogator for Military Region Three (Hau Nghia Province) in Bien Hoa till the fall of Vietnam. Working under the cover of an OSA officer (Office of Special Assistance to the ambassador), Deforest's duties included the inspection of the Provincial Interrogation Centers (PIC), training Vietnamese field officers in interrogation techniques, monitoring intelligence production, and special attention to spotting operational leads with the possibility of turning prisoners into agents.

DeForest discovered that the PICs were poorly run, the Phoenix program was slipshod, and the CIA had been unable to generate a single agent. DeForest's actions created numerous agents and helped to revolutionize the system. Using methods learned while working with the Japanese National Police in identifying Communist agents, disregarding CIA methods, DeForest's efforts produced 80 percent of the CIA's hard intelligence in Vietnam.

During the fall of Saigon, DeForest managed to get some of his agents out of Vietnam but in the end was forced to leave many of the CIA's best agents to be captured by the North Vietnamese. DeForest severely criticized the CIA's handling of the evacuation, pointing out that the station chief (Thomas Polgar) depended too much on a Hungarian source who was working in the interest of the Communists and ignored dependable intelligence on the intentions of the North Vietnamese and the deteriorating conditions of the South Vietnamese Army.

DeForest was awarded the Intelligence Medal of Merit by the CIA for his activities in Vietnam. (DeForest and Chanoff, *Slow Burn*)

123 DeGeyter, Marc Andre. In August 1980, DeGeyter, a Belgian businessman, was sentenced to four months for involvement in industrial espionage activities for the Soviet Union. U.S. authorities accused DeGeyter of offering $500,000 for the secret internal source code for their Data Base Management System (called ADABAS) developed by Software AG of North America, Inc., for Techmashimport, a Soviet foreign trade company. DeGeyter was arrested after giving a $500,000 check to an undercover FBI agent posing as a representative of Data Base at Kennedy Airport in New York. DeGeyter denied being a spy and referred to allegations as a mistake. Eight felony charges were dropped after DeGeyter pled guilty to two misdemeanor charges. The Soviets were so desperate for the code that a second KGB agent, Georgi Veremey, posing as a Soviet embassy official, approached the executives of the company offering cash for the code but was refused. (Barron, *KGB Today; Facts on File*, 1980; *New York Times*, July 23, 27; August 2, 1980)

124 Dejean, Maurice. During his eight-year term as French ambassador in Moscow in 1956–64, both he and his air attaché, Col. Louis Guibaud, were seduced by KGB "swallows." The operation was set up by the head of the Counterintelligence Directorate, Lt.Gen. Oleg Mikhailovich Gribanov. Once, while Dejean was being entertained, the KGB introduced an "angry husband" who ran into the apartment and beat up Dejean.

When the KGB produced the photos to Guibaud, he committed suicide. One of the KGB officers in the operation defected, revealing the blackmail of Dejean and Guibaud. French intelligence was able to stop it before serious harm could be done, and Dejean returned to France in ruins. (Andrew and Gordievsky, *KGB*; Barron, *KGB*; Faligot and Krop, *La Piscine*; Rositzke, *The KGB*)

125 Delince, Francois. In March 1972, Delince, a Belgian, was charged in Belgium with stealing classified documents on the French Mirage V-B fighter-bomber. Delince had worked as a representative for the Soviet truck firm Skaldia-Volga till February. (*Facts on File*, 1972)

126   De Mohrenschildt, George (d. 1977).   In March 1977
De Mohrenschildt was found dead at the home of his daughter in Florida.
A police report cited suicide as the likely cause of death. De Mohrenschildt,
Russian-born, a professor of international commerce and engineering, had
testified to the Warren Commission concerning his relationship with Lee
Harvey Oswald. Reportedly, De Mohrenschildt had worked for the CIA
at the time of the Kennedy assassination. The Select Committee on
Assassinations sought his testimony on his relationship with Oswald due
to reports that De Mohrenschildt had been more acquainted with Oswald
than he originally reported during his testimony to the Warren Commission. De Mohrenschildt's sudden death, new reports of his relationship with
Oswald, along with the revelations of his involvement with the CIA, stirred
new debate about the role of the CIA in the assassination of President Kennedy. (*Facts on File*, 1977; *New York Times*, March 30, 31; April 1–4, 1977)

127   Deriabin, Peter Sergeyevich (b. 1921).   A KGB major
and chief of the Sovetskaia Koloniia (SK) intelligence section in Vienna at
the time he defected, he was put in charge of security surveillance of all
Soviet citizens in Austria. Ironically, one of his main responsibilities was
to stop defections. He escaped with the help of the CIA, which hid him in
a wooden crate, placing it on a train headed toward the West.

He joined the army in 1941 as a Komsomol secretary of an engineers'
battalion. As political officer he observed his fellow soldiers for disloyalty.
He was wounded in the leg in the fall of 1941 and a year later appointed
as a junior political commissar in the 284th Reconnaissance Detachment in
Stalingrad. In April 1944 he was shot in the back during a battle near Odessa.
Badly wounded, he was transferred to the Higher Military Counterintelligence School in Moscow, where he graduated in April 1945, then posted as
a state security captain to Barnaul, Siberia. A year later he was appointed
to the Kremlin Guard Directorate in Moscow, responsible for the surveillance
of the bodyguards of Stalin.

In 1952 he transferred to the Austro-German section of the Second
Directorate. It was here that he helped plan the kidnapping of Dr. Walter
Linse in West Berlin on July 8, 1952. Linse had been the head of an anti-
Communist group called the Association of Free German Jurists. When
Deriabin was offered the opportunity of being stationed in Vienna, he
jumped at the chance and was put in charge of the SK counterintelligence
unit at the Soviet Mission. Four months later, he defected.

In the KGB, he watched in horror his fellow members being arrested
and executed. It was this fear and the paranoid nature of the KGB that led
to his defection to the West in February 1953. (Andrew and Gordievsky,
KGB; Brook-Shepherd, *The Storm Birds*; Corson and Crowley, *The New
KGB*; Deriabin, *The KGB, The Secret World, Watchdogs of Terror*)

128   Derlig, Anna-Marie.   In August 1967, Hungarian officials announced that Derlig, a West German, had been extradited to East Germany for espionage. She had escaped from East Germany in 1960 after being charged with espionage. Reportedly, East German agents arrested her in Hungary. (*Facts on File,* 1967; *New York Times,* August 17, 1967)

129   Desai, Morarji R.   Reportedly, Desai served as a paid informer in 1967 for the CIA. Shortly after Desai's break with Prime Minister Indira Gandhi, he was recruited by the CIA. One former U.S. intelligence official stated that Desai, well known for his anti–Communist and pro–West sympathies, had been paid $20,000 a year for his services during the Johnson and Nixon administrations. During the Indian-Pakistani 1971 war, Desai supplied the CIA with India's planned invasion of East Pakistan, now known as Bangladesh. Desai, who later served as prime minister of India from 1977–79, called the charges false and outrageous. (Bobb, "The Hersh Heresy," *India Today;* Hersh, *The Price of Power*)

130   de Silva, Peer (b. 1917).   Joined the U.S. Army in 1936, assigned to the counterintelligence branch in 1942. During the development of the atom bomb at Los Alamos, de Silva served as chief of security. After World War II, de Silva joined the Strategic Services Unit (SSU), the remnant of the Office of Strategic Services, and began a Soviet studies program at Columbia University in 1946–47, where he learned Russian. In 1947 de Silva joined the CIA as a deputy to the CIA station chief in Pullach, West Germany.

In 1956 he was assigned to the East European division in Vienna as chief of station. In 1959 he was sent to Seoul Korea as chief of station. In 1962 he was assigned as station chief of Hong Kong. While station chief in Hong Kong, his mission was to gather intelligence on mainland China, particularly details concerning the construction of the uranium gaseous-diffusion plant in Lanchow and the plutonium plant at Pao Tou. He was unable to discover anything significant about either plant. It was not until the late 1960s with satellite reconnaissance that they were able to find out anything about the facilities.

In 1963 de Silva was assigned as station chief to Saigon, but in 1965 de Silva was injured during a car-bomb attack near the embassy and was forced to return to the U.S. After 1966 de Silva served in a variety of roles for the CIA. As special assistant for Vietnam affairs, he served under Graham Martin, ambassador to Thailand in 1966, as an advisor in counter-insurgency, in 1971 station chief to Australia, retired in 1973. (de Silva, *Sub Rosa;* McGehee, *Deadly Deceits;* Prados, *Presidents' Secret Wars;* Ranelagh, *The Agency*)

131   Devlin, Lawrence Raymond (b. 1922).   Served in the U.S. Army during World War II, then served as a civilian political affairs analyst for the U.S. Army from 1953 to 1957. Joined the CIA in 1957 as a political officer at the U.S. embassy in Brussels. In 1960 Devlin was appointed station chief to the Congo. As station chief, he organized the CIA attempt to assassinate Patrice Lumumba, a pro–Soviet Congolese leader of the secessionist movement. In September 1960 the CIA's Sidney Gottlieb delivered to the station a poison to be used on Lumumba. Though there was much discussion about how to slip Lumumba the poison, it was never used. The plan involved the hiring of two assassins, one code-named WI/ROGUE, a European mercenary wanted in a variety of European countries for bank robbery, and QJ/WIN, also a European, recruited by William Harvey. Each would be given the poison to be used on Lumumba, and it was assumed that at least one would manage to kill him. But before an operation could be launched, the UN placed Lumumba under protective custody. In November Lumumba left the protection of the UN and was captured by Mobutu's troops in early December 1960 and executed in February 1961. During the time that Lumumba left the UN custody and was captured, the CIA was trying desperately to find him. At the same time, the two assassins, WI/ROGUE and QJ/WIN, had discovered each other's presence after WI/ROGUE attempted to recruit QJ/WIN into the operation. Ironically, both were unaware that the other had been hired for the job. QJ/WIN reported to his CIA handlers that he had discovered the presence of the other, and a sharp argument erupted, forestalling any organized attempt to find and kill Lumumba. Though the CIA was unable to assassinate Lumumba, many argue that the CIA encouraged his demise. The Soviet Union named a terrorist training base in Moscow in Lumumba's honor, calling it the Patrice Lumumba Friendship University. In 1963 Devlin was sent to Laos as the head of the CIA's paramilitary program. In 1970 he was appointed chief of the Africa Division, retiring in 1974. (Freemantle, *CIA*; Heinz, *Lumumba*; Kalb, *The Congo Cables*; Prados, *Presidents' Secret Wars*; Stockwell, *In Search of Enemies*)

132   Dimski, Henryk.   In September 1980, West German authorities arrested Dimski, a Pole who worked in the budget office of the U.S. embassy in Bonn, for spying for Poland. According to West German authorities, Dimski supplied Polish agents with details of the U.S. embassy's financial, personnel, and security arrangements. Dimski originally worked in the U.S. embassy in Warsaw and resigned in August from his position in Bonn. No reason was given why a U.S. embassy would hire a Polish national for such a position. (*Facts on File*, 1980)

133   Dnyeprovsky, Geli A.   In August 1978 U.S. and British officials accused Dnyeprovsky of being a colonel in the KGB. He had served as the Soviet official in the UN secretariat in New York, but he was reassigned to a higher position as head of personnel at the UN headquarters in Geneva after the allegations, despite the complaints of the U.S. and other countries. As supervisor of UN civil servants in New York, he filled positions with people based on their loyalty to the Soviet Union and KGB. While in this position, he had access to the personnel files of all the employees, details that allowed the KGB to target possible recruits and remove those who appeared to be troublesome.

The allegations were based on the defection in June to Great Britain of a Soviet staff member of the Soviet mission to the UN in Geneva, Vladimir Rezun. Dnyeprovsky has also been identified by a variety of KGB defectors as a KGB agent. (Barron, *KGB Today;* Dzhirkvelov, *Secret Servant;* Shevchenko, *Breaking with Moscow*)

134   Dobson, Sue.   Escaping to Britain in October 1989, she claimed to have spied on the African National Congress in Namibia for nine years as a South African agent for the Bureau of Information. Her duties included propaganda projects aimed at influencing the elections in favor of the DTA and discrediting SWAPO and the UNTAG. The South African government denied her story. (*Facts on File*, 1989)

135   Dolce, Thomas J.   Former civilian weapons analyst for the U.S. army at the U.S. Army's Aberdeen Proving Ground in Maryland he was well known as an anti–Communist. Dolce pled guilty and was sentenced to ten years for espionage for South Africa from 1979 to 1983. This was the first espionage case in the U.S. involving South Africa. (*Facts on File*, 1989; *New York Times*, October 12, 1988)

136   Doole, George Arntzen, Jr. (1909–85).   Chief of CIA air proprietaries in Asia: Air America, Air Asia, and Civil Air Transport. Doole was a former airline executive who earned a B.S. in business administration from the University of Illinois in 1931. Joined the military and trained as a pilot, then joined Pan American Airways in 1934, flying in DC-2s in Mexico. Later joined Avianca as chief pilot in Colombia. In 1946 he became Pan America's regional director for the Middle East and Asia.

It was in 1951 that Doole, still an Air Force reservist, was called to active duty and began working with the CIA in the Middle East. Doole was offered a permanent job to head the CIA's air proprietary Civil Air Transport in 1953 and put in charge of all the air proprietaries in Asia. He finally retired in 1971.

Doole's reign of CAT and Air America saw missions in China to drop agents and supplies during the early 1950s, supporting French forces defending Dien Bien Phu in 1954, flying bombing missions in support of Indonesian rebels in 1958, parachuting agents and supplies into Tibet in 1958–61 in support of guerrillas fighting the Chinese, and heavy involvement in the Vietnam War. The Air America logo was very apparent on the blue and white helicopters landing on the roof of the Saigon embassy evacuating personnel during the dramatic fall of South Vietnam in 1975. Doole's Air America operations in Laos came under severe criticism for participating in the transport of opium. (Robbins, *Air America*; Leary, *Perilous Missions*; Marks and Marchetti, *The CIA and the Cult of Intelligence*; McCoy, *The Politics of Heroin*)

137   Dooley, Dr. Tom A. (1927–61).   Dooley, an American Navy doctor in Vietnam in the 1950s was also a CIA operative. It was his mission to encourage the Catholics in the northern part of Vietnam to flee to South Vietnam. His efforts were successful not only in encouraging fear among those living in the north of Communist aggression of Catholics but helping to stimulate U.S. public support for the South Vietnamese government. In 1955 he returned to the U.S. on a propaganda campaign of speeches and interviews describing the need to support Prime Minister Ngo Dinh Diem and told numerous stories about Communist atrocities to the people of Vietnam.

He wrote several books describing, inaccurately, Communist aggression against Christians. The stories included a description of Vietminh forces disemboweling one thousand pregnant women, beating a naked Catholic priest with bamboo sticks, and sticking chopsticks in the ears of children, preventing them from hearing the missionaries preaching the Bible. The stories were outrageous but were successful in stirring paranoia among Christians in the North and U.S. public support for the South Vietnamese government. Thousands of Catholics streamed south into South Vietnam, helping to offset the Buddhist majority in the South.

At one point he helped to organize a rally of 35,000 Catholics in North Vietnam demanding evacuation to the South. It was not until 1979, during a Roman Catholic sainthood investigation, that Dooley's propaganda work for the CIA was fully revealed. (Blum, *The CIA*; Dooley, *Dr. Tom Dooley's Three Great Books*; McGehee, *Deadly Deceits*; Monahan, *Before I Sleep*)

138   Dorey, Robert W.   U.S. Army private court-martialed in Berlin, West Germany, for crossing the border into East Germany and returning with two Soviet agents with whom he escorted around U.S. military facilities, sentenced to fifteen years in prison. He pled guilty to entering East Germany and returning twice with Soviet agents. (*Facts on File*, 1953; *New York Times*, October 31; November 1, 7, 1953)

139 Downey, John Thomas (b. 1930), and Richard George Fecteau (b. 1927). During the 1950s, the CIA was actively engaged in supplying Nationalist Chinese agents with weapons to fight the Communist Chinese in mainland China. A CIA program known as Operation Tropic, using CAT C-47's flown out of Japan, dropped supplies, Nationalist Commandos, and agents into Kirin Province to stir up resistance to the Communist government.

CIA officers Fecteau and Downey boarded a C-47 B-813 on November 29, 1952, to pick up Li Chun-ying, a special agent who had been sent in previously by parachute to help the CIA-supported Team Wen that operated against the Communist government. Upon the approach to make an air-to-ground pickup, known as an in-flight pickup, using a wire and two poles, the plane was shot down in an apparent ambush.

Team Wen, along with Li, had been captured and forced to cooperate, forcing Li to radio that he was ready to be picked up. Upon interrogation, Downey admitted his involvement and details of the operation. He had been in the CIA for less than a year and originally was an instructor in espionage tradecraft in Taiwan. The seven Taiwanese agents who were also aboard the downed craft and survived the crash were executed. Fecteau was sentenced to 20 years, and Downey was sentenced to life.

The State Department denied that they were with the CIA, stating that they were employed as civilian employees of the Army Department and were declared missing after a routine flight from Korea to Japan disappeared. Downey was released in March 1973, Fecteau in December 1971. Downey stated upon his release that his 20 years in prison were a waste and that the CIA had originally misjudged the support the Chinese people had for the Communist government. (Deacon, *The Chinese Secret Service;* Leary, *Perilous Missions;* Prados, *President's Secret Wars;* Wise and Ross, *The Invisible Government*)

140 Driberg, Tom (d. 1976). An aggressive homosexual and Communist, he was a left-wing Labour MP and a double agent, serving both the British and the Soviets. Driberg traveled to Moscow in 1956 to meet with Guy Burgess to write a book about his activities as a spy. When MI5 learned that Driberg was traveling to Moscow, they arranged for Driberg to provide copies of the work to MI5 before publication. MI5 was already aware of Driberg's Communist party affiliation and his work for the KGB in London. (Costello, *Mask of Treachery;* Driberg, *Guy Burgess;* Penrose and Freeman, *Conspiracy of Silence;* Pincher, *Their Trade Is Treachery;* West, *The Circus;* Wright, *Spy Catcher*)

141 Droller, Gerry (alias "Frank Bender"). Of German birth, he worked for the Office of Strategic Services during World War II in

France behind the lines. Joined the CIA and first served as the Swiss desk officer. In 1960 he was appointed as political action chief of the Bay of Pigs project, working closely with E. Howard Hunt at the Miami station. While planning the operation, they quickly became enemies. Droller's chain-smoking cigars and calling everyone "Popsy" irritated Hunt. Droller's liberal views and lack of Spanish were in conflict with Hunt's conservative views and knowledge of Spanish. Hunt was later able to ban him from the Miami field station. After the Bay of Pigs fiasco, he became chief of the Covert Action staff of the Western Hemisphere Division. (Agee, *Inside the Company*; Hunt, *Undercover*; Johnson, *The Bay of Pigs*; Phillips, *The Night Watch*; Wyden, *Bay of Pigs*)

142 Drummond, Nelson Cornelius.   As a clerk at the U.S. naval headquarters in London, he had access to COSMIC (NATO) classi-fied data. Drummond, a chronic gambler who suffered from debt, decided to make contact with Soviet intelligence. While in a London bar in 1957, Drummond met a Soviet who gave him some money for a favor (a Navy ID card for shopping at the Navy exchange). Later, the Soviets asked for classified data and supplied Drummond with equipment needed for es-pionage. In 1958 he was posted to a duty station in the U.S. and for the next four years continued passing data to the Soviets. His contacts in the U.S. were KGB agents working out of the UN mission in New York. FBI surveillance of the KGB in New York eventually led them to Drummond, arrested in 1962 selling classfied Navy documents on electronics to two Soviet agents, Second Secretary Yevgeny M. Prokhorov and Third Secre-tary Ivan Y. Vyrodov. Drummond, yeoman first class in the U.S. Navy, had been under FBI surveillance since 1958. Documents were discovered in his car, along with a miniature camera. In 1963 he was placed on trial for conspiracy to commit espionage.

Reportedly, the Soviets paid him $20,000 for classified documents. Drummond was sentenced to life in prison. Four Soviets were named as coconspirators: Second Secretary Yevgeny M. Prokhorov, Third Secretary Ivan Y. Vyrodov, First Secretary Mikhail S. Savelev, and Third Secretary Vadim Sorokin. (Allen and Polmar, *Merchants of Treason*; Rositzke, *The KGB*; Tully, *The FBI's Most Famous Cases*)

143 Dubberstein, Waldo H. ("Doobie").   Studying to be a Lutheran minister at the Concordia Seminary in St. Louis, he became in-terested in ancient Assyria. This led him to the University of Chicago's Oriental Institute, where he earned a doctorate in 1934. In 1942 he became an analyst for the Office of Strategic Services (OSS) in the Middle East branch. When the CIA was formed, he joined as a Middle East specialist. He retired from the CIA in 1970 and taught at the National War College but became bored and took a job as an analyst for the Defense Intelligence Agency's Directorate for Foreign Intelligence in 1975. He was back in the intelligence game as a Middle East specialist and had access to a wide variety of intelligence, from satellite data to agent networks.

In 1977 Edwin Wilson, the ex–CIA agent turned gunrunner for Libya, approached Dubberstein for data on the Middle East. Dubberstein had just suffered a divorce and was having financial problems. He sold him data on military dispositions in the Middle East, which was given to the Libyans. In 1978, under the alias John Heath, Dubberstein flew to Tripoli to meet with Libyan intelligence officers. For a week he revealed a variety of intelligence information in the Middle East.

After being indicted for selling military secrets to Libya, Dubberstein was found dead in April 1983, killing himself with a shotgun. Reportedly, Dubberstein had provided the Libyans with data between 1977 and 1980 and was paid over $32,000 for his services. (Freemantle, *CIA*; Goulden, *The Death Merchant*; Maas, *Manhunt*)

144   Dulles, Allen Welsh (1893–1969).

Director of the Central Intelligence Agency (DCI) from February 1953 to November 1961 under Presidents Eisenhower and Kennedy; served in the State Department 1916–26; head of the Office of Strategic Services (OSS) office in Berne, Switzerland, 1942–45; served as CIA deputy director of plans December 1950–August 1951; deputy director of Central Intelligence August 1951–February 1953; served on President's Commission on the Assassination of President Kennedy 1963–64; first CIA and OSS veteran to become DCI, helped define the role of clandestine operations in the CIA. In Dulles's tenure as DCI, the CIA participated in coups in Iran and Guatemala, and the Bay of Pigs invasion. The Bay of Pigs disaster forced Dulles out of the position. Relative of three secretaries of state (his brother, John Foster Dulles; his grandfather, John W. Foster; and his uncle, Robert Lansing). (Darling, *The Central Intelligence Agency*; Dulles, *The Craft of Intelligence* and *The Secret Surrender*; Ranelagh, *The Agency*)

145   Dunlap, Jack Edward (1928–63).

It was revealed by Pentagon officials that Sergeant First Class Dunlap had sold the Soviets classified data from the National Security Agency (NSA) over a period of several years. Reportedly, Dunlap had received $30,000 to $40,000 in his first year spying. He had joined the Army in 1952 after serving eight years as a merchant mariner. He saw combat in the Korean War with the 36th Infantry, earning the Bronze Star and Purple Heart.

First assigned to the NSA in April 1958 as a chauffeur, by 1960 he became a courier for the NSA and began selling the classified documents to the Soviets after going to the Soviet embassy and offering to sell classified

NSA documents. A GRU case officer was assigned to handle him. He had access to a broad array of classified documents. Dunlap suddenly became a playboy, supporting a mistress, two Cadillacs and a Jaguar, a 30-foot cabin cruiser on a salary of $100 a week with a wife and five kids.

In 1963 he took two polygraph tests, which revealed deceit and led to an investigation into his high living, and he was transferred to a nonsensitive position in the NSA. He foresaw a growing investigation and killed himself in July 1963. But it was not until his wife discovered a treasure trove of classified NSA documents a few months later that the NSA discovered the horrible truth. (Allen and Polmar, *Merchants of Treason*; Andrew and Gordievsky, *KGB*; Bamford, *The Puzzle Palace*)

146 Dzhirkvelov, Ilya Grigorevich (b. 1927). Born in Soviet Georgia, he volunteered in 1942 for a reconnaissance unit attached to a calvary division near his home, Tbilisi. In 1943 he joined the state security service, and in February 1944, at the age of 17, he was made a member of the cryptographic section. In April 1944 he joined a commando unit and for the first time saw combat against the German Army. He was one of eight Georgians selected to go to the KGB school in Moscow in 1945. In 1947 he was sent to Rumania for the KGB, searching for Nazi collaborators and agents. After a month he was ordered back to Moscow and placed in the Middle East Department of the KGB's First Directorate.

He was in the Iranian section at a time when the Iranian government was waging a civil war with the pro–Soviet northern provinces and the Iranian Communist party, Tudeh. When Tudeh leaders went into hiding to avoid being arrested in 1948, Dzhirkvelov helped in their rescue to the Soviet Union. Later he participated in the kidnapping of the double agent Sarkisyan in Iran.

In 1949 the KGB discovered that Dzhirkvelov's father had been arrested in the 1930s for anti–Soviet activity. This slowed Dzhirkvelov's rise in the KGB, and he was transferred to a menial job in the Archives Section and began studies at the Higher Party School in Lenin and Marx to complete his political education. In 1952 he was transferred to the American Department of the KGB, where he helped plan strategies against U.S. counterintelligence operations.

In 1955 he was transferred to the Tenth Department of the First Chief Directorate where he was in charge of operations against Turkey. He supervised the Georgian and Armenian KGB units near the border areas of Turkey. In 1957, he was dismissed from the KGB when he was involved in a fight with a drunk. While on the beach, a drunken Adzharian threatened him with a knife. Dzhirkvelov drew his gun and as a form of punishment forced the drunk to walk into the water up to his chin. It turned out to be the Adzharian minister of education.

Shortly after his dismissal he was rehired as a secret employee in the KGB to work in the Soviet media, first with the Central TV and the Union of Journalists, 1958–65, and then as a Tass correspondent. From 1967 to 1970, he was stationed as a Tass correspondent in Zanzibar, and in 1970 was transferred to Dar-es-Salaam. In 1970 he was sent to Khartum, then, 1972–74, put in charge of the Tass foreign news desk in Moscow.

Posted as press officer in 1974 to the World Health Organization in Geneva, in 1980 he was involved in a car accident. His KGB superiors saw the reports of the accident and believed he was involved in an embarrassing drunk-driving spree. He was recalled to Moscow to explain the incident and discovered that he was about to be fired from his position. Able to convince them that he needed to return to Geneva and help his wife pack for the return trip to the Soviet Union, he returned to his apartment in Geneva and defected with his family. (Dzhirkvelov, *Secret Servant*)

147   Edwards, Sheffield (d. 1975).   Director of the CIA Office of Security in the 1950s and 1960s. Edwards introduced the polygraph into personnel security examinations and advanced the idea of using the Mafia to assassinate Fidel Castro. Edwards approached former FBI agent Robert Maheu, whose private investigation agency occasionally did contract work for the CIA.

Maheu acted as a mediator between the CIA and Mafia crime figure Salvatore Giancana, the man selected to orchestrate the plan. Edwards instructed Maheu to offer $150,000 to Giancana to hire someone from the underworld to kill Castro. The Technical Services Division began developing poisons for the operation; several plans were formulated, and money was passed around, but no one came close to assassinating him.

Maheu and Edwards had worked together once before in an attempt to discredit Indonesian President Sukarno. They produced a bizarre pornographic film, purportedly showing Sukarno having sex with a blond Russian woman. (Freemantle, *CIA*; Johnson, *A Season of Inquiry*; Powers, *The Man Who Kept the Secrets*; Martin, *Wilderness of Mirrors*; Ranelagh, *The Agency*; Smith, *Portrait of a Cold Warrior*)

148   Efimov, Yuri A.   In 1987 Japanese authorities arrested Efimov, first secretary of the Soviet embassy, for conducting espionage in Japan. Four Japanese suspects were also arrested and confessed to providing the Soviets with classified information. The spy ring had operated since 1979. The principal spy was a Japanese national working as a technical librarian at the U.S. Yokota Air Base. Data given to the Soviets included technical manuals for the F-16 and Boeing E3C Hawkeye. Efimov was expelled from Japan. (*Facts on File*, 1987; *New York Times*, August 21, 22, 1987)

Egorov, Aleksandra see Egorov, Ivan Dmitrievich

149   Egorov, Ivan Dmitrievich, and his wife, Aleksandra. Egorov, UN secretariat personnel officer, and his wife were arrested in 1963 for espionage in New York. They were indicted for conspiring to deliver classified data on U.S. nuclear weapons, missile sites, and a variety of military secrets. They argued that they were entitled to diplomatic privilege, but it was denied due to their low positions at the UN. They pleaded not guilty to the charges.

In addition, two other Soviets using the real names of Robert Keistutis Baltch, a Roman Catholic priest, and Joy Ann Garber, a housewife, were arrested in Washington, D.C. It is unknown how the Soviets came to choose these names. The Egorovs were traded in 1963 for Soviet-held Marvin Makinen and the Jesuit priest Walter Ciszek. Robert Baltch was later identified as Aleksander Sokolov. The woman was not identified but was using Jane Doe and later Bertha Rosalie Jackson.

Two Soviet diplomats who had already left the U.S. were named as coconspirators: Aleksei Ivanovich Galkin, first secretary of the Byelorussian mission to the UN; Petr Egorovich Malsennikov, first secretary of the Soviet mission. They were accused of financing and organizing the espionage activities of the four arrested. (*Facts on File*, 1963; *New York Times*, July 3, 17, 1963; Wise, *The Invisible Government*)

150   Eitan, Rafi (b. 1926). Eitan, nicknamed the "Stinker," was born in Palestine in a Jewish kibbutz. He joined army intelligence in May 1948 and after the war for independence, he joined Shin Bet, becoming the head of the operations branch. He headed the team that kidnapped Nazi criminal Adolf Eichmann in 1960 from Argentina. In the mid–1960s he joined the Mossad operations in the European Division. In 1968 his name was linked to the disappearance of 200 pounds of uranium from the NUMEC nuclear processing plant in Pennsylvania in 1960. He rose to the rank of deputy head of Mossad's operations branch. He resigned from Mossad in 1976, becoming adviser to Prime Minister Rabin, and in 1978 Begin appointed him as his adviser on terrorism.

In 1981 Eitan was put in charge of the Israeli Defense Ministry's Liaison Bureau for Scientific Affairs (LAKAM). When the Jonathan Pollard scandal erupted, Eitan was blamed for conducting the operation despite U.S.-Israeli agreements that they not spy on each other. When Eitan returned to Israel, he was nominated to the post of chairman of the board of Israel Chemicals.

Eitan also headed the Israeli assassination squad that hunted down the members of the Palestine Liberation Organization's Black September, responsible for the terrorist attack on Israeli athletes at the 1972 Munich

Olympics. He got the nickname "Stinker" from the fact that during a sabotage operation against the British for the Palmach in the late 1940s, he was forced to crawl through sewage to reach the target. (Black and Morris, *Israel's Secret Wars;* Ostrovsky and Hoy, *By Way of Deception;* Wolf, *Territory of Lies*)

151   Eitzenberger, Dr. Josef.   In March 1968, West German authorities arrested Eitzenberger, a scientist, for spying for the Soviet Union. Eitzenberger had worked for the U.S.-owned Battelle Institute, where he worked as a researcher on Defense Ministry projects. Eitzenberger had also worked for the Pentagon. (*Facts on File,* 1968)

el–Haihi, Mahamoud see Abdullah, Fawzi

152   Elad, Avri (b. 1926).   Born in Austria with the name Avraham Seidenwerg, he was forced to escape to Britain during the Nazi anti–Jewish campaigns. When he arrived in Palestine in 1937, he changed his name to Elad. He participated in Palmach's battle for Jerusalem, serving as a major, but was caught stealing a refrigerator from an Arab and demoted to the rank of private and resigned in 1952.

In 1953 Israeli Aman (military intelligence) recruited him for a mission in Egypt. He was given the alias Paul Frank with an established history in Germany. To complete his new identity as a German businessman and ex–Nazi SS officer, he underwent a painful surgical operation that reversed his circumcision. He was sent to Germany for six months to help establish his history for his cover. He finally went to Cairo in December 1953 as a German businessman in the import-export of electrical equipment. He managed to secure information about Egypt's rocket plans and plans involving the building of an underground oil pipeline.

In May 1954 he was ordered to Paris where he was assigned as the case officer of Operation Suzanna. This operation involved the use of Arab Jews as sleeper agents already in place in Egypt to sabotage British and U.S. installations in the hope of drawing the blame on Egyptian anti–British groups and gaining the support of London and Washington for Israel. On June 29 he returned to Egypt to discover the agents unprepared and unprofessional. On July 2, 1954, bombs began exploding all over Alexandria. On July 14 another bomb detonated in the U.S. Cultural Centers in Cairo and Alexandria. On July 23 an agent carrying a bomb to its target prematurely ignited it in the pocket of Philip Natanson in front of the Rio movie theater in Alexandria. The bomb set Natanson on fire, but he was rescued by an Egyptian security officer, who promptly put the fire out and arrested him.

Under questioning, Natanson told the Egyptians details about the operation. Egyptian security agents immediately began arresting the rest of the agents: Moshe Marzuk, Shmuel Azzar, Marcelle Ninio (later committed suicide in his cell), Victor Levi, Robert Dassa, Meir Zaafran, Meir Meyuhas, Eli Yaakov, and Azzar Cohen. Another agent, Max Bennett, unrelated to the operation, who had revealed his identity to the group was arrested. Elad managed to escape Egypt and return to Israel.

Upon his return to Israel, there was speculation that he might be a double agent for the Egyptians, but Aman continued trusting him and sent him to Germany for operations against German targets. While there, he made an unauthorized contact with the Egyptian military attaché. Shin Bet notified Aman that Elad was a double agent, and Aman ordered him to return to Israel. He was put on trial for betraying the operation and sentenced to ten years. Upon his release, he moved to the United States. (Black and Morris, *Israel's Secret Wars*; Raviv and Melman, *Every Spy a Prince*; Steven, *The Spymasters of Israel*)

153 Ellis, Robert W.   Contacted the Soviet consulate in San Francisco in 1983 while stationed at the Moffett Field Naval Air Station in California, offering to sell classified documents for $2,000. He was arrested while selling documents to an undercover FBI agent posing as a Soviet agent. He was sentenced to five years' hard labor. (Allen and Polmar, *Merchants of Treason*)

154 Emmick, Frank Carl.   In April 1964, a Cuban court sentenced Emmick, former president of Havana's American Club, to 30 years in prison for spying for the CIA. Reportedly, Emmick headed CIA operations in Cuba.

Six other Cubans were convicted of supplying Emmick with data: Manuel Sanjuro Diaz, Guillermo Diaz Alvarez, and Juan Antonio Fernandez were given 30 years; Rafael Alvarez Fernandez 20 years; German Ruiz Martinez, 12 years; and David Feito Fernandez 6 years.

In 1977 Emmick was released from Cuba. Emmick denied being a CIA agent but did admit to smuggling a letter to the director of the CIA, Richard Helms, in 1973. (*Facts on File*, 1964, 1977; *New York Times*, April 10, 16, 1964)

Enger, Valdik Alexandrovich see Chernyayev, Rudolph

155 Entezam, Abbas Amir.   In June 1981, an Iranian Islamic revolutionary court sentenced Entezam to life for working for the CIA. Entezam had served in the first government formed after the Iranian revolution in 1979 as deputy prime minister. When Iranian students overran the U.S. embassy, authorities discovered classified CIA files implicating Entezam as a spy for the CIA. Though embassy employees were able to shred many of the files, Iranian students carefully pasted them back together over a period of a year after the takeover. (*Facts on File*, 1981; *New York Times*, March 12, 18, 29, April 5, 28, June 11, 1981)

156 Erb, Walter, and Eberhard Lippold. In November 1980, West German authorities arrested Erb, an engineer and union official, and Lippold, a musicologist, for spying for East Germany. Jurgen Kreisser was suspected of providing the East German government with information about the Working Group for Human Rights, which monitored East German human rights abuses. (*Facts on File*, 1980; *New York Times*, November 11, 1980)

157 Escartin, Ricardo. In February 1981, Escartin, first secretary of the Cuban interest section in Washington, D.C., was expelled for espionage activities. Reportedly, Escartin was accused of engaging in illegal trade and intelligence gathering of high technology. Escartin had established a wide variety of business contacts and encouraged them to violate the laws forbidding commerce with Cuba. No details of the espionage activities were given. Escartin was the first Cuban diplomat to be expelled since 1970. (*Facts on File*, 1981; *New York Times*, February 12, 1981)

158 Fabiew, Serge. In March 1977 Fabiew, a Yugoslavian-born French citizen, and three others were arrested by French agents on charges of passing French and NATO defense secrets to the Soviet Union. The spy ring had provided the Soviets with classified data on military equipment and data on the early-warning defense systems for eleven years, 1963–74. The data covered French aircraft production, aircraft test centers, civilian and military airports, and NATO committee reports. French counterintelligence (DST) agents also discovered advanced radio units used to contact the Soviet Union. Fabiew, the ringleader, had used a company that made fire protection systems as a front for the ring's espionage activities. In February 1978 a French court sentenced Fabiew to 20 years. (*Facts on File*, 1977–78; *New York Times*, March 23, 1977, February 2, 1978)

159 Falk, Elke. A West German government secretary who passed classified secrets to the East Germans, Falk had been entrapped in a sexual relationship with an East German spy, a common tactic used by East German intelligence. (*Facts on File*, 1988)

160 Farcetti, Paolo, and Gabriela Trevisin. Both were put on trial in Bulgaria in December 1982 for espionage. They were arrested in August 1982 for photographing Bulgarian military sites. Italy warned Bulgaria not to use the trial as a way of retaliating to the Italian investigation into the pope's shooting. (*Facts on File*, 1982)

161   Fedorchuk, Vitali Vasilievich (b. 1918).   Joined the Soviet security police (NKVD) in 1939. During World War II he served in the secret police units in the military called SMERSH. At the end of the war he joined military counterintelligence, serving in East Germany in the early 1960s. In the late 1960s he became chief of the KGB Third Directorate, which was responsible for internal security in the Defense Ministry. In 1970 he was made the KGB chief responbile for Ukraine. In May 1982 Andropov left the position of head of the KGB to become party general secretary, and Fedorchuk replaced him. In December 1982 Andropov made him minister of internal affairs (MVD) to fight corruption and waste, and Chebrikov succeeded him as head of the KGB. In 1986 Gorbachev transferred Fedorchuk to a position of military inspector and advisor to the Group of General Inspectors under the Ministry of Defense, obviously an attempt to remove Fedorchuk from power. (Corson and Crowley, *The New KGB*; Knight, *The KGB*)

162   Felfe, Heinz Paul Johan (b. 1918).   Joined the Nazi party in 1936 and during World War II served on the staff of Heinrich Himmler, head of the Gestapo. After World War II Felfe was sent to a Canadian prison due to his work in the Nazi SS, but in 1946 he returned to Germany and began working as a counterintelligence inspector for the Ministry of All-German Affairs and became an informer for British intelligence. In November 1951 Felfe was hired by BND. In 1961 East German intelligence officer Gunter Mannel defected to West Germany. Upon his interrogation by intelligence officials, he revealed that the head of the BND Soviet Counterintelligence Department, Felfe, was a double agent, and he was tried and convicted of espionage for the Soviet Union in a West German court in 1963. Felfe was sentenced to 14 years of hard labor. Felfe had received a total of $40,000 over a 10-year period. Reportedly, he gave the Soviets over 15,000 classified documents dealing with the agency's personnel, West German security, and reports dealing with suspected East German spies. Authorities stated that the Soviets were able to identify 95 operatives working for the agency. He was exchanged in 1969 for Walter Naumann, Peter Sonntag, and Volker Schaffhausen. (Cookridge, *Gehlen*; Corson and Crowley, *The New KGB*; Gehlen, *The Service*; Hagen, *The Secret War in Europe*; Rositzke, *The KGB*)

163   Fell, Barbara Janet Hunter.   Fell, an assistant overseas controller of the British Central Information Office and the acting controller of the Central Office of Information, was convicted of supplying classified Foreign Office documents to a Yugoslav embassy official, press counselor Smiljan Pecjak, who was her lover. The documents included economic and political assessments of Yugoslavia and East-West relations. Fell, a civil servant for 23 years, pled guilty in 1962 to espionage and was sentenced to two years. She had provided Pecjak documents from 1959 to 1961. British MI5 agents monitored her phone conversations with Pecjak after receiving a tip from a defector that there was a spy in Central Office. (Pincher, *Too Secret Too Long*; West, *The Circus*).

164   Felten, Peter.   East German authorities announced in August 1979 that Felten, a West German journalist, had been arrested for espionage. East German officials said Felten had a long association with West German intelligence. Felten's arrest followed new censorship rules regarding Western newsmen and journalists. Felten was sentenced to 12 years for espionage in an East German court in 1979. (*Facts on File*, 1979; *New York Times*, August 22, 1979)

165   Fernandez, Joseph F.   Former CIA station chief of Costa Rica, 1984–86, charged on several criminal counts for his involvement in the Iran-Contra affair. All charges were eventually dropped when the CIA refused to release evidence in Fernandez's defense that had been classified secret. Fernandez was charged for obstructing the 1987 Tower Commission inquiry into the scandal and lying to federal investigators. (*Facts on File*, 1989; U.S. Govt., *The Tower Commission Report*)

166   Field, Noel Havilland (d. 1970).   Graduated from Harvard in 1926, joining the U.S. State Department where he befriended Alger Hiss. In 1935 Field was recruited by Heide and Paul Massing, German Communists involved in the Communist underground network in the U.S., who convinced him to provide classified State Department documents. He was recruited on the basis of his disdain for Nazi fascism and pro–Communist sympathies. Under orders of Soviet intelligence, Field resigned from the State Department and joined the International Labor Organization in Geneva. In 1936 he went to work for the ILO in Geneva and began working directly for the Soviets. In 1941 he began to work as resident director of the Unitarian Services Committee in Marseilles, France. After the Nazis invaded France, Field escaped to Switzerland in November 1941. While in Switzerland in 1943, the OSS recruited Fields as a spy. Working under cover as a Unitarian representative, he helped to develop spy networks throughout Europe for the OSS but at the same time continued his work as a double agent for the Soviets.

When Field was notified that his name would be mentioned in the upcoming Hiss spy investigation in 1954, he decided to flee France for Hungary. When he escaped to Hungary in 1954, he was arrested and imprisoned on a variety of false charges by Communist authorities, who believed that he was an American secret agent. Apparently, Stalin's postwar attempts to eliminate the members of the Communist underground networks in Eastern Europe included Field. Stalin was afraid that if the networks remained intact, they would oppose Soviet domination of Eastern Europe. Obviously, the Soviets encouraged the arrest due to fears that the OSS had managed to turn him. He remained in Hungary till his death in 1970 in Budapest. (Lewis, *Red Pawn*; Romerstein and Levchenko, *The KGB against the "Main Enemy"*; Williams, *Klaus Fuchs, Atom Spy*)

167 Filatov, Anatoly N. In September 1980 it was revealed that Filatov, a Soviet who spied for the U.S., had not been executed as commonly believed in 1978.

Tass had reported in 1978 that Filatov had been sentenced to death for espionage. It was reported in 1980 that his sentence had been commuted to fifteen years. When Filatov was arrested in 1977, the U.S. intelligence authorities announced that an important CIA operative in Moscow, code-named Trigon, had disappeared. Reportedly, Trigon, later identified as Filatov, had supplied the CIA with important Soviet military, economic, and political information. The Soviet press reported that he had been recruited by the CIA in February 1974. There was considerable debate and speculation about the relationship of Filatov to the CIA and his identity as Trigon. (*Facts on File*, 1980; *New York Times*, September 23, 24, 1980; Prados, *The Soviet Estimate*)

168 FitzGerald, Desmond (1910–67). Graduated from Harvard Law School in 1935; with the outbreak of World War II, joined the U.S. Army. He was transferred to the Office of Strategic Services (OSS), serving as liaison officer to the Chinese forces in Burma and China fighting the Japanese, earning the Bronze Star for his service. After the war he joined the CIA in 1951, rising to deputy chief of the Far East Division of Clandestine services, then deputy chief of the Far East Division in 1958.

In 1966 he served as deputy director of the CIA's clandestine service. During his tenure in the CIA, he helped formulate the CIA Tibet covert operations during the late 1950s and early 1960s, was instrumental in CIA operations in China to help the nationalist Chinese attempt to overthrow the Communist in China, and served as head of the Cuban Task Force in 1963 where he helped plot CIA assassination and sabotage operations. (Agee, *Inside the Company*; Cline, *Secrets, Spies and Scholars*; Phillips, *The Night Watch*; Powers, *The Man Who Kept the Secrets*; Prados, *Presidents' Secret Wars*)

169   Flavell, Anthony Harold.   In June 1969, a Zambian tribunal found Flavell, a British-born Rhodesian resident, guilty of attempting to form a spy ring. Flavell confessed to having been trained in Rhodesia and assigned on a mission to Zambia to form a spy network. (*Facts on File*, 1969)

170   Fleener, Terry.   In October 1977, Fleener, an American, was arrested at Israel's Ben-Gurion Airport while attempting to escape the country. She photographed Israeli military installations. She confessed at her trial to charges of spying for the Palestinian Liberation Organization (PLO). She received a five-year sentence, but in June 1979 Fleener was released from an Israeli prison and deported after 20 months in jail due to U.S. government pressure. (*Facts on File*, 1978–79; *New York Times*, May 31; June 30, 1977)

171   Fletcher, Anthony A., and Richard W. Harcos.   In April 1973 Fletcher and Harcos, American citizens, were sentenced by a court in India for espionage and narcotics smuggling in Calcutta. Both pled guilty. They were released in September 1975. (*Facts on File*, 1975; *New York Times*, September 22, 1975)

172   Forbrich, Ernst L.   In August 1984, in a Florida courtroom, Forbrich, a West German citizen, was sentenced to fifteen years for attempting to purchase classified data for East Germany. Forbrich, a West German auto mechanic at the time of his arrest, was arrested after paying $550 for classified data from a U.S. Army intelligence officer working undercover. (Allen and Polmar, *Merchants of Treason*; *Facts on File*, 1984)

173   Forsyth, Olivia.   Forsyth, dual South African and British citizen, sought protection in the British embassy in Angola in August 1988 after agents in the African National Congress discovered that she was a South African spy. Forsyth admitted that she had been an agent of the security branch of the South African police. Angola expelled her, and she returned to South Africa. (*Facts on File*, 1989)

174   Frauenknecht, Alfred.   In April 1971, a Swiss court sentenced Frauenknecht, a Swiss engineer, to four years for spying for Israel. Reportedly, he supplied the Israel's Liaison Bureau for Scientific Relations (LAKAM) with blueprints and details for the jet engine of the French Mirage 3/C fighter. He was found guilty of both industrial and military espionage, but the military espionage conviction was later dropped. Frauenknecht was the director of the jet engine department of the Sulzer engineering works. Frauenknecht confessed that he had sold over 200,000 documents (two tons of paper) for $200,000 in 1968–69. He claimed he did it out of sympathy for Israel, despite the fact that he was not Jewish. Frauenknecht's responsibility was to make sure that classified blueprints were eventually incinerated. Frauenknecht's cousin was employed to deliver over 100 pounds of documents to the incinerator once a week. However, he would first stop at Frauenknecht's garage and switch the classified blueprints for blueprints bought by Frauenknecht from local companies. He was arrested in September 1969 and sentenced to four and a half years. The Israelis were able to use the technology provided by him in the development of the Kfir fighter. (Black and Morris, *Israel's Secret Wars*; Eisenberg, Dan, and Landau, *The Mossad*; Raviv and Melman, *Every Spy a Prince*; Steven, *The Spymasters of Israel*)

175 French, George H. U.S. Air Force captain arrested in 1957 after throwing a letter into the Soviet embassy compound declaring his wish to sell atom bomb secrets. He was sentenced to life. (Allen and Polmar, *Merchants of Treason*; *New York Times*, September 22, 1957)

176 Frenzel, Alfred (b. 1899). Born in Czechoslovakia in the Sudetenland, he joined the Communist party in 1920. In 1926 he was forced to resign due to charges of theft. In 1934 he joined the Social Democratic party (SDP), becoming a high official. In 1938 Germany invaded the Sudentenland, and Frenzel fled to England. He joined the RAF 311th Bomber Squadron, serving as a cook till 1945. After the war Frenzel moved to Germany in 1946 and rejoined the SDP, becoming a high official. He became a member of the Parliament in Bonn in 1953. In 1956 Czech intelligence officers approached Frenzel while he was serving on the Defense Committee and the Chairman of the Restitution Committee. The Czech agents suggested to Frenzel that he could play a role in helping to establish better ties between Germany and Czechoslovakia. They paid Frenzel 3,000 marks for his services. During the second meeting in Switzerland, they asked Frenzel to gather data on the German Navy, which he did. Frenzel was now an active agent for Czech intelligence, providing antimissile defense plans, military installations, military operations, and a variety of other data. West German counterintelligence, BfV, became aware that the Czechs had considerable detailed information during negotiations. It pointed toward Frenzel. BfV began surveillance of Frenzel and gathered enough information for an arrest. He was arrested in 1960 for espionage for Czechoslovakia. On April 28, 1961, Frenzel was sentenced to 15 years, hard labor. (Bittman, *The Deception Game*; Cookridge, *Gehlen*; Gehlen, *The Service*; Hagen, *The Secret War in Europe*)

177 Frolik, Joseph. A major in Czech intelligence service (StB), he defected in July 1969 to the CIA. Frolik served on the British desk of Czech intelligence in Prague 1960–64. When Frolik defected, he accused British Labour MP Will Owen of spying for Czechoslovakia since 1957. He served in the Czech embassy in London under the cover of "labour attaché." While in London, he recruited Labor and trade officials. It was the Soviet invasion of Czechoslovakia in 1969 that convinced him to defect. Frolik's defection caused the reorganization of Czech intelligence services. He revealed that the Czech intelligence had 200 contacts in British industry, government, and the military. He defected to the CIA and met personally with the director of the CIA, Richard Helms. (Andrew and Gordievsky, *KGB*; Frolik, *The Frolik Defection*; West, *The Circus*)

178 Fuchs, Klaus Emil Julius (1911–1988).   While a student at the University of Leipzig, 1930–31, he joined the Socialist party (SPD). In 1932 he attended the University of Keil where he studied physics, along with Marxist philosophy and left-wing political views. While attending college, he broke from the SPD and joined the anti–Nazi German Communist Party (KPD). When the Reichstag mysteriously burned, Hitler blamed the Communists, and Fuchs went into hiding. In July 1933 he escaped to Paris, and on September 21 he finally arrived in England where he made contact with the KPD organization in England. He continued his studies in physics at the University of Bristol, where he finished his doctorate in December 1936. In 1937 he joined Max Born's laboratory in Edinburgh. His work was becoming well known in the academic community in a variety of articles 1939–41 on quantized field equations, electromagnetic radiation, and wave functions.

Unfortunately for Fuchs, panic swept England when Germany invaded France, and Fuchs was interned as an enemy alien and sent to a Canadian internment camp near Quebec in 1940. But a few months later he was released and sent back to England where he was hired to work on the atomic bomb for Britain. Fuchs first worked on unclassified mathematical problems but later moved into developments related to gaseous diffusion theory, mainly the mathematics of hydrodynamics. Fuchs also helped resolve the problems concerning the equation for the sphere of uranium needed for a bomb and on isotope separation.

When Germany invaded Russia on June 22, 1941, Fuchs felt compelled to assist the Soviets in any way possible. He approached KPD leader Jurgen Kuczynski to see how he could be of help. Within months, Fuchs was delivering atomic secrets to Simon Davidovich Kremer (alias "Alexander"), a Soviet GRU agent. In 1942 he was handed over to another GRU agent, "Sonia," who was really Jurgen Kuczynski's sister Ursula. He gave her the reports, and she transmitted them to Moscow by radio.

In 1941–42 Fuchs conducted research on German scientific periodicals to determine German progress on the atomic bomb. Fuchs also gained classified American reports of early work on the atomic bomb. All of this was given to the Soviets. In 1943 Fuchs was sent to the U.S. as a member of the British mission to the top secret Manhattan Project. Before he left, Sonia gave him instructions for contacting another agent in New York, "Raymond," who was actually Harry Gold.

By 1944 he was passing data on the Oak Ridge, Tennessee, gaseous diffusion plant for producing fissionable uranium. He also passed data on the process of isotope separation, electromagnetic separation of uranium, and the security techniques of the Manhattan Project. But by August 1944, Fuchs was transferred to Los Alamos, New Mexico, where the atomic bomb was designed and assembled. He was assigned to the T-1 group (implosion dynamics).

In February 1945 Fuchs delivered considerable data about the bomb to Gold. This included the process of assembling the bomb, noting the problems with predetonation of plutonium through spontaneous fission; the advantages of the implosion method of detonation over the gun method; and the critical mass of plutonium.

In June 1945 Fuchs met Gold in Sante Fe where he delivered details of the bomb that was about to be tested at Alamogordo and the one that was to be dropped on Nagasaki. Fuchs was present at the first atomic blast, the Trinity Test, in the New Mexico desert on Juy 16, 1945. Fuchs gave the data on the results of the testing and other new data to Gold.

When Fuchs returned to England in June 1946, he joined the British project to build an atomic bomb. Fuchs became the deputy chief scientific officer at the Atomic Energy Research Establishment at Harwell on August 1, 1946, making him the leading scientist on the project. Fuchs was assigned to do the theoretical work on the plutonium bomb, based on Fuchs's experience with plutonium reactions and implosion techniques at Los Alamos. While here, he gave the Soviets data on the plutonium bomb.

By 1949, Fuchs began to have doubts about his participation with the Soviets and began to miss meetings. About the same time the Signal Corps, stationed at Fort Meade, Maryland, had accumulated a large number of intercepted messages between the Soviet embassy and Moscow during World War II but had no way of decoding them till 1949. When they discovered Fuchs's name mentioned in one of the telegrams, the FBI notified British MI5, who placed Fuchs under surveillance. Not wanting to alert the Soviets to the fact that their codes had been broken, the British successfully managed to coax a confession out of Fuchs.

On January 27, 1950, Fuchs signed a confession at Scotland Yard that in 1942–49 Fuchs had been working for the Soviets. On February 2, 1950, Fuchs was placed under arrest, and during his trial on March 1, 1950, he pled guilty and was sentenced to 14 years.

Evidence supplied at the confession led the FBI to Harry Gold, Fuchs's American handler. Gold's confession in turn led to David Greenglass and Julius and Ethel Rosenberg. After his release from Wakefield Prison on June 23, 1959, he went to East Germany, where he accepted a job as deputy director of the Institute for Nuclear Research at Rossendorf. Fuchs also lectured at the Akademie der Wissenschaften, an academic institute in Dresden. He was accepted into the German Communist party. He was elected to the German Democratic Republic's Academy of Sciences, and also to the Communist party Central Committee. He was awarded the Order of Merit of the Fatherland and the Order of Karl Marx. He retired in 1979, and died January 28, 1988, at the age of 76. Debate surrounds the true value of the data he supplied the Soviets.

Many argue that Fuchs left the H-bomb program too early to have gleaned sufficient and accurate data to have helped the Soviets. (Hyde, *The Atom Bomb Spies*; Moorehead, *The Traitors*; Moss, *Klaus Fuchs*; Williams, *Klaus Fuchs, Atom Spy*)

179   Fuelle, Rainer, and Johannes Koppe.   In January 1979, West German authorities attempted to arrest Fuelle, an accountant at the Karlsruhe nuclear facility, and Koppe, who worked in the public relations division of a nuclear construction company, for espionage. Police were able to arrest Fuelle, but he jumped from the police car and escaped. Koppe was able to escape his Hamburg home along with his wife before they were able to arrest him. Though both were sought for espionage charges, neither was believed part of a ring. An East German defector who was a member of East Germany's State Security Ministry had identified Fuelle and Koppe, along with several other spies, involved in industrial espionage for East Germany. (*Facts on File*, 1979)

180   Furnival-Jones, Martin.   Director-general of MI5 after Roger Hollis retired in 1965. His job was difficult due to revelations of a major Soviet spy ring in Great Britain that had operated since the 1930s and had gone undetected by MI5 (Blunt, Burgess, Carincross, Maclean, and Philby). He joined MI5 in 1940 and served in the security detail at Eisenhower headquarters. He was awarded the Bronze Star for his service during the war. Despite his deep respect for his former MI5 boss, Roger Hollis, he was forced to investigate him due to charges that he was a spy for the KGB. (Andrew, *Her Majesty's Secret Service*; West, *The Circus, MI5*; Wright, *Spy Catcher*)

Gallaher, Alfred Trevor see **Nicholson, John Roger**

181   Garbe, Ingrid.   In December 1980 Garbe was sentenced to four years in a West Germany court for spying for East Germany but was released on $49,000 bail. Garbe had worked as a secretary in the Foreign Ministry and for the West German delegation to the NATO office in Brussels. Reportedly, two East German intelligence operatives had started a love affair with Garbe and convinced her to give them classified data. (*Facts on File*, 1980)

Garcia, Nestor see Hernandez, Gladys Garcia

182 Gates, Robert Michael (b. 1943). Deputy director of the CIA in April 1986, acting director of the CIA when William Casey fell ill in December 1986. Gates was nominated for the position of DCI when Casey resigned in February 1987, but his ties to the Iran-Contra scandal forced Gates to withdraw his name for consideration in March 1987. Gates, a career intelligence analyst, joined the CIA in 1966 after graduating from Indiana University with a master's degree in history. He earned a doctorate in Soviet history from Georgetown University in 1974. Gates served as the CIA's chief Soviet analyst. In 1974–79 he was a staff member of the National Security Council. From 1982 to 1986 he was deputy director of intelligence. In May 1991 he was appointed to replace William Webster as DCI under President Bush despite continued criticism of his possible role in the Iran-Contra scandal and his lack of clandestine operations experience. Gates has been awarded the Intelligence Medal of Merit. (Byrne, *The Chronology*; Jeffreys-Jones, *The CIA and American Democracy*; Johnson, *America's Secret Power*; *New York Times*, February 3, 1987)

183 Gehlen, Reinhard (1902–79). Joined the provisional Reichswehr in 1921; attended Staff College in 1933–35. In November 1938 he was battery commander in the 18th Artillery Regiment of the German Army. In September 1939 he was assigned as operations officer to the 213th Infantry Division. In October 1940 he became chief of the Eastern Group of General Staff's operation branch. In April 1942 he was appointed chief of Branch 12 of the German Army's General Staff, concerned with intelligence operations on the Soviet Union. In December 1944 he was promoted to brigadier general.

His intelligence networks in the Soviet Union were extensive, and he was able to collect an exhaustive file on Soviet military and political leaders. When the war was drawing to an end, he hid these files in the Bavarian mountains and in May 1945 surrendered to US forces. His intelligence on the Soviet Union was quickly recognized by Allied intelligence, and he was quickly appointed to head his own intelligence organization in July 1946, the "Gehlen Organization."

In April 1956 the organization was transferred to the West German government and renamed the Federal Intelligence Service (BND), with Gehlen as the chief till his retirement in April 1968. Gehlen created the biggest intelligence organization in Europe. (Cookridge, *Gehlen*; Gehlen, *The Service*; Reese, *General Reinhard Gehlen*)

184   Gengenbach, Werner.   In October 1974, Gengenbach, a West German journalist, was sentenced by a Czech court to ten years for economic espionage. Reportedly, Gengenbach confessed that he had collected economic data for the West German intelligence service. (*Facts on File*, 1974)

185   George, Clair Elroy (b. 1930).   In September 1991 George was indicted on ten counts of lying and obstructing justice and accused of participating in the cover-up of the Iran-Contra operation. He joined the CIA in 1955 after a two-year stint in the Army in South Korea. He learned Chinese, and in 1957 the CIA sent him to Hong Kong. In 1962 he was sent to Mali in West Africa, where in 1968 the CIA sponsored a coup against the socialist regime. After the coup he was sent to India to serve as a clandestine services officer.

In 1975 he was sent to Beirut just as the civil was broke out in Lebanon. When Richard Welch was assassinated by terrorists in Athens, George was sent to take over the post of station chief in January 1976. In 1977 he took over the Africa desk at CIA headquarters. In 1981 he was appointed assistant deputy of operations. In 1983 he was appointed CIA liaison to congressional intelligence committees. After fourteen months, he was appointed director of operations. At the time of his appointment, several major crisis had occurred. The CIA station chief in Beirut, William Buckley, had been kidnapped, and George worked frantically to get him back. Buckley was later tortured to death in the basement of the Iranian embassy in Beirut.

George also participated in the sale of weapons to the Iranian government for the release of US hostages in Lebanon. In the fall of 1986, George was called before Congress to explain the incident and lied to the committees. George is considered one of the best covert-action specialists in the history of the CIA. (Byrne, *The Chronology; Facts on File*, 1991; Persico, *Casey*; US Govt., *The Tower Commission Report*)

186   Georgiev, Ivan-Assen Khristov.   Former counselor of the Bulgarian mission to the United Nations, 1956–61, he was convicted and sentenced to death for spying for the CIA. Reportedly, Georgiev was accused of spying from 1956 till his arrest. Authorities in the Bulgarian government announced that Georgiev had supplied the U.S. with classified data on political, economic, and military situation in the country. Georgiev pled guilty to the charges, stating that he made contact with the CIA immediately upon his arrival at the UN. Georgiev received $200,000 for his services and used the money on several mistresses in New York City. According to Georgiev, the first agent he met was at the American College in Sofia, Bulgaria, a professor of Slavic studies, Cyril Black, head of Princeton's Slavic department. But Black denied any connection to the CIA and called the charges false. The Soviets announced in January 1964 that Georgiev had been executed by firing squad. He was convicted of spying in a Soviet court. (*Facts on File*, 1963–64; *New York Times*, November 10, 16, December 22, 28, 1963, January 1, 5, 1964)

187   Gerhardt, Dieter Felix.   Nicknamed "Jumbo," in 1983, Commodore Gerhardt and his wife, Ruth, were arrested for spying for the Soviet Union for twenty-three years. Gerhardt was the commander of South Africa's largest naval shipyard in Simonstown. Gerhardt had access to a variety of classified military data. He had offered his services while serving in the British Navy as a South African naval officer during World War II. He had approached the Soviet embassy in London and was quickly recruited by the GRU. His motivation was based on revenge on the South African government, who had imprisoned his German father for his right-wing extremism. He returned to South Africa after the war and rose in the ranks of the South African military. Over the years he provided the Soviets with an astonishing amount of data.

While attending Syracuse University in New York in 1983, he was arrested and interrogated by CIA and British counterintelligence agents. He was then shipped back to South Africa to stand trial. He was sentenced to life in a Cape Town court for high treason and espionage. The South African intelligence service had been tipped to Gerhardt by the capture of Yuri Loginov, a KGB agent captured in 1967, though they did not know his actual identity till 1983 when Gerhardt was finally identified. (Bittman, *The KGB and Soviet Disinformation*; Pincher, *Too Secret, Too Long*)

188   Gerlach, Manfred.   Arrested by East German authorities in 1960 for spying for West Germany. Gerlach had been a research director of the East German aircraft industry. Code-named "Ferdiand," he was the technical manager of the aircraft factory at Pirna, East Germany, where parts for MIGs were built. He brought out 600 microfilms of technical drawings and photographs. Sentenced to life. (Cookridge, *Gehlen*; *Facts on File*, 1960; *New York Times*, August 26, 1960)

189   Gessner, George John.   Gessner had just served a sentence for desertion from the U.S. Army when he was arrested leaving the Leavenworth federal penitentiary. He was indicted in 1962 for espionage for the Soviet Union. Gessner provided classified documents on the U.S.

nuclear weapons program to Soviet agents. Gessner, a U.S. Army private at the time, was working at the U.S. missile program at Fort Bliss, Texas, until he deserted in 1960 as a nuclear weapons technician. Gessner had delivered the data to the Soviets in Mexico City between December 1960 and January 1961. In June 1964 he was convicted of spying for the Soviet Union. He was sentenced to life in prison. Gessner was the first to be tried under the 1946 Atomic Energy Act. Gessner's attorney argued that Gessner was insane at the time of the espionage. In March 1966 a U.S. court dismissed atomic espionage charges against Gessner. (*Facts on File*, 1962, 1964, 1966; Rositzke, *The KGB*)

190   Ghouse, Mohammad.   Ghouse, an aide to Mahathir bin Mohammad, who took office as the prime minister of Malaysia in July 16, was arrested for spying for the Soviets on July 13, 1981. Three Soviet diplomats accused of being KGB agents were expelled for recruiting Ghouse. (*Facts on File*, 1981; *New York Times*, July 14, 1981)

191   Glover, Paul John Gerald.   In January 1973 an Israeli court sentenced Glover to 12 years for spying for Jordan. Reportedly, Glover had given the Jordanians details of airports in Israel, information on military equipment and training installations. According to Israeli officials, Glover had made contact with Jordanian officials in London in 1968. While working for a British electrical engineering company, Glover was able to travel between Israel and Jordan regularly. (*Facts on File*, 1973)

192   Gold, Harry (alias Raymond) (b. 1910).   Gold, a biochemist, was arrested by the FBI on espionage charges in 1950. Fuchs turned over atomic bomb secrets to Gold, who gave them to the Soviets. Gold was originally recruited by Soviet spy Jacob Golos. He was released from prison in May 1966. He had been sentenced to 15 years in December 1950.

When Klaus Fuchs began working at the Tube Alloys project in Canada, it was Gold who served as his contact for the Soviets. Gold was born in Switzerland to Russian parents under the name of Golodnitsky. When his family emigrated to the U.S., they changed their name to Gold. From 1936 he worked for Soviet intelligence in the U.S. as an industrial spy and courier. Gold was also a courier for David Greenglass at Los Almos, New Mexico. When Fuchs was arrested, Gold identified Greenglass, who turned on the Rosenbergs, thus unraveling the Soviet atomic spy ring in North America. The Soviets awarded him the Order of the Red Star, though he never had the honor of accepting it. (Hyde, *The Atom Bomb Spies*; Moorehead, *The Traitors*; Moss, *Klaus Fuchs*; Williams, *Klaus Fuchs, Atom Spy*)

193 Goleniewski, Michal. A member of the First Department of the Polish intelligence service who worked in collaboration with the KGB, when he defected in 1960, he revealed Harry Houghton to MI5 and provided clues that led to George Blake. He provided hundreds of rolls of film on classified documents. When he was debriefed by American intelligence services, he told a wild story about how he was really Russian Grand Duke Aleksei Nicholaevich Romanoff, who escaped from Russia to Poland in 1917 when the Communists took over. In 1963 Goleniewski stated that he was aware of a KGB spy ring involving an agent code-named "Bor," who was Henry Kissinger, a Harvard professor and foreign affairs advisor. (Andrew and Gordievsky, *KGB*; Bittman, *The KGB and Soviet Disinformation*; Pincher, *Too Secret, Too Long*; Rositzke, *The KGB*)

194 Goliath, Inge. In March 1979 the West German government announced that an East German spy ring had infiltrated the Christian Democratic Union. Goliath, the secretary of Werner Max, CDU's specialist on East European affairs, escaped to East Germany. Other CDU officials were accused of espionage for East Germany: Christel Broszey and Ursula Hoefs. (*Facts on File*, 1979)

195 Golitsyn, Anatoly Mikhailovich. In 1962 Golitsyn, a Soviet intelligence officer, defected to the West. Golitsyn was stationed in an unnamed East European country when he contacted the U.S. embassy and requested asylum. Golitsyn provided the Western intelligence services with a great deal of data on Soviet espionage operations. Golitsyn later settled in Great Britain. When he was interviewed by the British MI5, he gave them information connecting Kim Philby to the disappearance of Burgess and Maclean. A lieutenant colonel in KGB counterintelligence, operating against NATO countries stationed in Helsinki, Finland, he was flown to West Germany and then the U.S. He defected due to the corruption of the Communist system and had become frustrated by his career stagnation. In 1944, while in the Soviet Army, he attended the counterintelligence school. After graduation, he joined the KGB. In 1951 he became a case officer in the First Chief Directorate's Anglo-American Department. In 1953–55 he served in Vienna, assigned to spy on Soviet émigrés. In 1960 he was assigned to Finland where he quickly began to fight over control of the KGB station with the KGB resident in charge. He lead British MI5 to Hugh Hambleton and helped identify Kim Philby as a Soviet mole. (Andrew and Gordievsky, *KGB*; Brook-Shepherd, *The Storm Birds*; Golitsyn, *New Lies for Old*; West, *The Circus*; Wright, *Spy Catcher*).

196 Golovanov, Vladimir. In June 1980, Iranian officials announced that Golovanov, first secretary of the Soviet mission in Tehran, was engaged in espionage and expelled him from the country. Golovanov was the first Soviet diplomat to be expelled since the 1979 revolution. The Iranian government also announced that the number of Soviet personnel at the mission would be scaled down. The Iranian government was angry with Soviet support of the Iranian Communist Tudeh party. (*Facts on File*, 1980; *New York Times*, July 1, 1980)

197   Gordievsky, Oleg (b. 1938).   Since 1974, a spy for MI6. In 1956 he attended the Moscow Institute of International Relations. He joined the KGB in 1962 and was first assigned to KGB headquarters in Department S of the First Directorate that analyzed illegal agents working in the West. In January 1966 he was sent to Copenhagen, running agent networks in Denmark. It was at this post during the 1968 Soviet invasion of Czechoslovakia that he lost his faith in the Communist system. In 1973–78 he served as political intelligence officer in Copenhagen, then KGB headquarters from 1978–82, then head of station 1982–85 in London. He provided MI6 with KGB personnel lists, intelligence targets and operations. Gordievsky also exposed several Soviet spies in the West. (Andrew and Gordievsky, *KGB*; Brook-Shepherd, *The Storm Birds*)

198   Gottlieb, Sidney.   Head o the CIA's Technical Services staff, he helped direct numerous projects: MKUltra, Artichoke, and Bluebird. The projects involved biological and chemical experiments involving truth drugs, and poisons. Gottlieb, biochemist and head of the CIA LSD experimental program, was accused of giving LSD to numerous unknowing test subjects.

Gottlieb was sent to the Congo in September 1960 to deliver a bacterial poison to kill Patrice Lumumba, but before it could be used, Lumumba was captured and killed by his opponents. He helped develop poisons to be used against Castro. A CIA plan to assassinate Egypt's President Nasser also involved Gottlieb, who produced a botulism poison to be injected into some Kent cigarettes to be given to Nasser. The plan was later dropped.

In 1953, Dr. Olson, a U.S. Army civilian scientist, had with several other scientists working on the CIA's MKUltra project been given LSD by Gottlieb on November 18, 1953. Dr. Olson, who conducted research for the CIA in biological warfare at Fort Detrick, Maryland, began to suffer from depression and personality changes a week later, and the CIA decided to send him to a New York psychiatrist for evaluation. He was escorted to New York with another CIA employee, Robert V. Lashbrook, to see a psychologist, who recommended that he be committed to a sanatorium for observation. But Olson dived through the glass window of the tenth-story of the Statler Hotel in Manhattan, plunging to his death (November 28). His family did not discover the nature of the death till the release of the

Rockefeller Report on CIA activities in 1975. His wife stated that Olson had behaved strangely after a meeting at which, it was later revealed, he had been given LSD. The Olson family stated that they believed that Lashbrook and another CIA employee, Sidney Gottlieb, had given Dr. Olson LSD. President Ford apologized to the Olson family. Lashbrook stated that Olson had agreed to take the LSD but was unaware when the experiment would actually begin. Unfortunately, there was no medical background check of the participants. If there had been, they might have discovered that Olson suffered from mental depression and had suicidal tendencies. Lashbrook had stated that he himself had been a subject of drug experiments by the CIA and did not like being a test subject. Lashbrook stated that he had contacted Sidney Gottlieb to inform him of Olson's death.

Reportedly, Gottlieb destroyed 150 files on the drug-testing program in 1973. Gottlieb admitted during testimony that 20 to 50 people had been unwitting subjects of mind-control drug experiments between 1952 and 1965. (Blum, *The CIA*; Freemantle, *CIA*; Marks, *The Search for the "Manchurian Candidate"*; Powers, *The Man Who Kept the Secrets*)

199   Gougleman, Tucker (d. 1976).   A former Marine colonel who was wounded during the Korean War, he joined the CIA and served as the national director of provincial reconnaissance units in South Vietnam. He retired in 1973 and lived in Saigon with his Vietnamese wife. He lived in Vietnam so long that he considered himself half Vietnamese and refused to leave when the fall of Saigon came. He was captured by North Vietnamese forces and tortured to death six months later. (Colby, *Lost Victory*; De Silva, *Sub Rosa*; DeForest, *Slow Burn*; Snepp, *Decent Interval*)

200   Gouzenko, Igor (d. 1982).   Soviet defector; served as the cipher clerk in the Soviet embassy in Canada in 1946 and disclosed a major Soviet spy ring in Canada involving Fred Rose, Samm Carr, Kathleen Mary Willsher, Raymond Boyer, and Emma Woikin. Gouzenko provided Canadian authorities with one hundred documents from the embassy with details about the spy ring. The ring was attempting to steal U.S. and British nuclear weapons secrets. (Gouzenko, *The Iron Curtain*; West, *The SIGINT Secrets*)

201   Greenglass, David (b. 1922).   Arrested in 1950 for espionage for the Soviet Union, Greenglass, brother of Ethel Rosenberg, was a physicist who gave Soviet agents data on atom bomb construction. He grew up in New York with his sister, Ethel Rosenberg, joined the U.S. Army in 1943. He was posted to Los Alamos, New Mexico, where they were building the atomic bomb. He had been heavily influenced by his sister's Communist activities during the 1930s and 1940s and had dedicated himself to the movement. Julius Rosenberg, upon discovering his brother-in-law's sensitive post, quickly recruited him to spy for the Soviets. A courier, Harry Gold, was sent to New Mexico to act as liaison. When Gold was arrested, he revealed Greenglass, who quickly implicated the Rosenbergs. At their trial, Greenglass testified against the Rosenbergs. At Los Alamos he made drawings of the atomic bomb and components. Greenglass was sentenced to 15 years. (Hyde, *The Atom Bomb Spies;* Philipson, *Ethel Rosenberg;* Radosh and Milton, *The Rosenberg File;* Williams, *Klaus Fuchs*)

202 Grey, Anthony. Released from Chinese prison in October 1969 after two years, reason not given. When he was released, he was named an "Officer of the Order of the British Empire" for his courage under duress. He described in a serious tone during an interview being tortured, explaining he had been painted and was forced to watch a crowd of angry Chinese shouting "Hang Grey, Hang Grey" as they hung his pet cat with a rope. (*Facts on File*, 1969; *New York Times*, May 10, July 15, 1969)

203 Grohman, Josef. In January 1977 Czech authorities announced the arrest of Grohman, former deputy minister of Education and Culture, for espionage. Reportedly, Grohman was arrested in October 1976 after he returned to Prague from Paris. In December 1977 he was sentenced to thirteen years for espionage. Two defectors had identified Grohman as an agent of the West, a former employee of Radio Free Europe and a former U.S. Army intelligence sergeant, Glen Roy Rohrer. (*Facts on File*, 1977; *New York Times*, January 7, 1977)

204 Grunert, Rolf. In May 1977, West German agents arrested Grunert, a senior detective on the Hamburg police force, for spying for East Germany. Grunert served as chairman of the Federation of German Detectives Officers, which gave him access to a variety of classified data. (*Facts on File*, 1977; *New York Times*, May 23, 1977)

Gubitchev, Valentin A. see **Coplon, Judith**

205 Guerrier, Patrick. Arrested by French officials for giving the Soviets industrial secrets, she had been a librarian for a French company. France expelled close to forty Soviet diplomats for their involvement. Two specifically targeted for expulsion were Nikolai Chetverikov, the third-ranking member of the Soviet embassy, and Oleg Chirikov, Paris bureau chief for Tass. (*Facts on File*, 1983; *New York Times*, April 2, 1983)

206 Guillaume, Guenther. Guillaume, a personal assistant to

West German Chancellor Willy Brandt, was arrested in April 1974 for espionage. Under questioning, Guillaume admitted being an officer in the East German Army and working for East German intelligence. Guillaume came to West Germany in 1956 and joined the Social Democratic party (SPD) in 1957. He began working in the chancellor's office in 1970 and became Brandt's personal assistant in 1973. Guillaume was described as a moderate Socialist by friends. In 1975 he was sentenced to 13 years for treason. Guillaume's wife, Christel, who was also convicted, was traded in March 1981. In 1981, Guillaume was released to the East Germans in a spy exchange with West Germany. The scandal caused Brandt's resignation.

Guillaume was considered East Germany's best penetration agent into the West German political system. During World War II his father, Dr. Guillaume, gave shelter and medical treatment to Willy Brandt when he was being hunted down by the Gestapo. In 1955 his father contacted Brandt, then mayor of West Berlin, to help his son escape East Germany. Brandt was able to get him accepted into the West German Emergency Refugee Relief program in 1956 as a "political" refugee. What Brandt did not know was that he was actually an East German spy. He was able to get a job in the Socialist party of West Germany (SPD) and rose to become Brandt's secretary in 1970. (Andrew and Gordievksy, *KGB*; Bittman, *The KGB and Soviet Disinformation*; Corson and Crowley, *The New KGB*; Rositzke, *The KGB*)

207   Haarlem, Erwin Van.   A Czechoslovakian spy using the name of Haarlem, his real name is unknown. He infiltrated Jewish groups in London, seeking data on the Strategic Defense Initiative ("Star Wars"). He was caught while receiving a secret message from Prague. The name Haarlem was taken from an individual who had disappeared as a child. A Dutch woman claimed that he was her long-lost son, but genetic tests proved that was not possible. The name was probably taken from a birth certificate with the knowledge that the individual was either dead or missing, a common practice with spies. In 1989 a British court sentenced him to ten years for espionage. (*Facts on File*, 1989)

208   Haase, Werner.   Served in a German engineers' regiment during World War II until his capture by Allied forces. After he was released from a British POW camp, he attended a technical college, becoming a telecommunications specialist. Reinhard Gehlen, West German intelligence chief, personally chose him for a special mission. Haase had served in the Wehrmacht since 1936, attended military college in Munich and the signals school in Doberitz. He saw combat in France and the Soviet Union. He was perfect for the job of installing permanent eavesdropping taps on

East German telephone cables. It would be a dangerous mission due to the fact that the East German border guards would be guarding the area. In November 1953 the operation began. In order to get the wire across to the eastern side of the canal between East and West Berlin, he had to use a model boat that would ferry the line across to the other side. While he was operating the controls of the toy boat, a car stopped nearby, and a group of East German agents captured him. The man on the east side of the canal waiting for the wire was also seized. When East German security forces captured Haase, they discovered a fake identity card with the name Wilhelm Heisler. A show trial followed, and he was sentenced to life but was exchanged in 1958. (Cookridge, *Gehlen*; Gehlen, *The Service*)

209 Haavik, Gunvor Galtung.   Haavik served as the confidential secretary to the Norwegian ambassador to Moscow from 1947 to 1956. It was here that she renewed a love affair with a Soviet, Vladimir Zolov, whom she fell in love with while she nursed him to health in a POW hospital during World War II while Norway was under Nazi occupation. She later helped him escape to Sweden. She was blackmailed in a "honey trap" (sexual trap) with Zolov in 1950 and agreed to work for Soviet intelligence. While working in Moscow, her code name was Vika, but when she returned to Norway, she was assigned the code name Greta. After her return to Norway, she worked in the department dealing with trade and political matters. She had over 250 meetings with her Soviet contacts, passing a variety of information, going through eight case officers before her arrest.

In the mid-1970s a British double agent in the KGB, Oleg Gordievsky, working in Copenhagen, became aware of her operations and reported her to British intelligence. She was arrested in January 27, 1977, while meeting with her case officer, Aleksandr Kirillovich Printsipalov. The Norwegian government expelled six Soviet KGB officers in January 1977, and the Soviet Union retaliated by expelling three Norwegian diplomats. Reportedly, she was involved in both industrial and military espionage. She died six months later in prison. (Andrew and Gordievsky, *KGB*; Brook-Shepherd, *The Storm Birds*; Martin, *Wilderness of Mirrors*)

210 Hadden, John.   CIA station chief in Tel Aviv, Israel, during the mid-1960s. His main job was to act as liaison between the U.S. and Israeli intelligence services and to monitor Israeli secret operations. He was particularly concerned with the development of nuclear weapons in Israel and made an extensive effort to discover what was happening at the nuclear research facility at Dimona in the Negev Desert.

During his tenure as chief, he investigated the attack by Israeli Air Force jets and torpedo gunboats on the USS *Liberty*, a signal intelligence ship off the coast of Sinai monitoring the Six Day War in June 1967, the attack effectively blinding U.S. intelligence in covering the war in the Sinai desert. The Israelis claimed it was an accident, explaining that the ship had been confused with an Egyptian naval vessel. (Ennes, *Assault on the "Liberty"* Raviv and Melman, *Every Spy a Prince*)

211   Hagen, Mary Frances.   U.S. journalist at the United Nations headquarters in New York with pro–Arab sympathies, she was recruited to spy on Israel by her fiancé, Syrian diplomat Galab al-Khieli. She went to Israel in 1956 as a journalist and began to send intelligence reports back to her Syrian handlers. Her interest in Israel's sensitive border areas sparked the surveillance of Shin Bet, Israel's internal security service. Convicted of espionage in a closed court in Israel and sentenced to one year in 1956, she was released in April 1957 after serving eight months. When she returned to New York, she discovered that her Syrian boyfriend was no longer interested and refused to see her. (*Facts on File*, 1957; Raviv and Melman, *Every Spy a Prince*)

212   Haguewood, Robert Dean.   He was convicted in 1986 and sentenced to two years. A U.S. Navy petty officer third class while stationed at Point Mugu Naval Air Station, California, he was arrested after selling classified documents to undercover agents of the Naval Investigative Service (NIS). The case was described as low level, and no foreign nationals were involved. (Allen and Polmar, *Merchants of Treason*; *Facts on File*, 1986; *New York Times*, March 11; May 10; June 20, 1986)

213   Haiducu, Matei.   In April 1982, Haiducu, former senior officer in the Rumanian secret service, appeared at a news conference in Paris with Rumanian dissident writer Virgil Tanase to discuss Haiducu's espionage activities in France for the last eight years. Haiducu had been cooperating with French counterintelligence officials for the past three months. Reportedly, Haiducu had worked in France for eight years involved in economic and scientific intelligence gathering. But in February Haiducu was ordered to kill Tanase and Paul Goma, dissident Rumanian writers. Haiducu refused to carry out the order and went to French intelligence (DST). While working with French agents, he faked an assassination attempt with Goma in a Paris lounge. Haiducu, with other Rumanian agents looking on, used a special pen to squirt a poison into Goma's drink. Before Goma could take a drink, a French agent, in what appeared to be an accident, knocked the glass from his hand. Haiducu then reported to Rumanian agents that he had hired French gangsters to kidnap and kill Tanase. Using French agents posing as gangsters they kidnapped Tanase in front of Rumanian agents and drove off. Tanase's disappearance for the next three months convinced Rumanian officials that he was dead. Both Tanase and Goma cooperated in the fake attempts. Haiducu then returned to Rumania where he was decorated for his successful mission and arranged a vacation for himself and his family abroad. When they left Rumania, the French government granted him asylum. (*Facts on File*, 1982)

214   Hall, James W.   A U.S. Army warrant officer, Hall accepted $100,000 for giving Soviets and East Germans classified military data from 1983 to to 1988. Hall was arrested in December 1988, and a confederate, Huseyin Yildirim, was also arrested. Hall pled guilty and was sentenced on March 9, 1989, to 40 years for espionage. (*Facts on File*, 1989; *New York Times*, February 28; March 7; July 17–21, 1989)

215   Hall, Sam Nesley.   Hall was arrested by Nicaraguan security agents in December 1986 near the Punta Huete air base while photographing the base. He claimed he was on a reconnaissance mission on Cuban activity at the base. He claimed he had met with Robert Owen, a consultant with the State Department who served as Oliver North's liaison with the Contras. The Nicaraguans discovered maps of the air base, the Tipitapa prison where Eugene Hasenfus was held, and two nearby towns in his car. Hall claimed at a news conference that in 1984 CIA and Defense Department officials had asked him to create a secret antiterrorist group called the Phoenix Battalion, to be based in the Middle East, similar to the French Foreign Legion. He was asked to head the organization and paid $12,500. However the project was dropped due to lack of funding. Hall named two retired U.S. naval officers who encouraged him in the project: Capt. William Hamilton and Cmdr. Francis Fane; both acknowledged knowing Hall. Hall also claimed that an independent private organization approached him to renew the Phoenix Battalion program and that he was its only member. Reportedly, Hall would meet with three different agents with code names "Tinker" in Washington, D.C., "Evers" in Great Britain, and "Chance" in Miami.

Reportedly, a confederate of Hall's stated that Hall provided intelligence on the Nicaraguan government to Adolfo Calero, a Contra leader, and to a private U.S. Nicaraguan Contra aid organization, Civilian Material Assistance, in 1985. Hall stated he had worked as a mercenary in Angola and Rhodesia. Hall's brother, Representative Tony P. Hall (D, Ohio), claimed his brother was mentally unstable and should be released. The Nicaraguan government agreed, and he was released in January 1987.

Hall had an impressive life. He had won a silver medal in diving in the 1960 Olympics in Rome and had been a Democratic representative in the Ohio House of Representatives in 1964–65. Hall worked for the Civilian Military Assistance (CMA) where he taught guerrilla warfare skills to

Nicaraguan Miskito Indians. The CMA claimed that Hall had been expelled from the organization due to recklessness. Hall's name came up during an investigation of Jesus Garcia in Miami, under investigation for illegal possession of weapons. Garcia had stated that he had attended a meeting in February 1985 with Hall, who was planning the assassination of the U.S. ambassador to Costa Rica, Lewis Tambs, placing the blame on the Sandinistas. After his release he was flown to Miami Veterans Hospital to undergo psychological testing. (Byrne, *The Chronology*; Cockburn, *Out of Control*)

216 Halm, Hilde (b. 1923). During World War II she served as a secretary in the Wehrmacht quartermaster general's office. She was awarded the Iron Cross for saving critical files during the shelling of Berlin by the Soviets in 1945. After the war she became a staunch Communist, and by 1946 she was working in the Soviet-German security and intelligence headquarters in Karlshorst. In 1950, while visiting an old teacher in West Berlin, she was approached by West German intelligence agents, who convinced her to work as an agent in East Germany. She returned to East Germany on a mission to infiltrate the Ministry of State Security. She proved to be a critical source during the Berlin uprising in June 1953. In 1954 she managed to get a job in the ministry, but in April 1956 she was arrested by East German security officers and sentenced to life. (Cookridge, *Gehlen*)

217 Halperin, Israel. Halperin, a mathematics professor at Queen's University, Kingston, Ontario, was one of the 13 Canadians arrested in February 1946 as a result of Igor Gouzenko's defection. Although acquitted of conspiracy charges, his notebook contained the name of Klaus Fuchs, but nothing was done about it. In 1942 Halperin joined the Canadian Army with the rank of major and in 1945 was recruited by GRU intelligence and given the code name Bacon. (Costello, *Mask of Treachery*; Pincher, *Too Secret, Too Long*; Williams, *Klaus Fuchs, Atom Spy*)

218 Halperin, Maurice H. Attended Harvard University and the University of Paris, where he earned his doctorate in 1931. He joined the Office of Strategic Services (OSS), serving as the head of the Latin American Division during World War II, and in 1942 urged a major OSS effort in Mexico against German operations. After Halperin's dismissal in 1953 from Boston University for refusing to state whether he was a Communist, he traveled to Mexico to live. FBI Director J. Edgar Hoover told a congressional committee that Halperin had been a Communist agent while in the OSS. He helped Alfred and Martha Dodd escape Mexico to Czechoslovakia in 1957 when U.S. authorities attempted to extradite them from Mexico for trial on espionage. Halperin left Mexico in 1958 for

Moscow to help in their analysis of Latin America. Halperin denied being a Soviet spy. In 1960 Halperin was discovered living in Moscow, working on research for the Soviet Academy of Sciences. He denied a State Department allegation that he had defected and was a Soviet spy. (*Facts on File*, 1960; Smith, *OSS*; Smith, *The Shadow Warriors*)

219   Hambleton, Hugh George (b. 1922).   Hambleton's parents had numerous friends in Soviet diplomatic circles during the 1930s in Canada, and he grew up with an interest in the Soviet Union. Graduating in 1940, he joined the Free French forces led by Charles de Gaulle. Since he spoke French, German, and Spanish as well as English, he quickly began to get special assignments. He was assigned to the General Directorate of Intelligence in Algiers as a translator of agent reports from Spain. When Paris was liberated, he was assigned to French intelligence headquarters in Paris and became the liaison officer to the U.S. Army's 103d Division. In 1944 he transferred to the Canadian Army where he interrogated POWs and translated and analyzed intelligence reports till he left the military in 1946. After the war he attended the University of Ottawa, received his master's in economics, and then began working for the Canadian National Film Board (NFB).

His parents had continued their close association with Soviet diplomats despite the cold war atmosphere during the 1950s. In 1951 Hambleton met First Counsel Vladimir Borodin of the Soviet embassy at a party, and in 1953 Borodin casually asked for information from the NFB. There was nothing of a classified nature at the NFB, but it was an exercise in conditioning that helped to cultivate Hambleton for future projects. Hambleton had missed the excitement and intrigue of espionage from the war.

When Hambleton finished his course work for his Ph.D in economics at the University of Paris (1954–1956), the Soviets suggested that he apply for a position at NATO headquarters in Paris. He was accepted and began working in NATO's Economic Directorate as an analyst. In 1958 his case officer, KGB Major Aleksei Fedorovich Trichin, gave him a special short-wave radio to transmit messages. In 1964 he took a position as a professor at Laval University in Quebec, continuing his relationship with the KGB. While at Laval, he visited Israel on a mission for the KGB to gather economic and military data and data on the South African and Israeli nuclear relationship.

In 1971 Hambleton received an invitation by the Canadian International Development Agency as an economic adviser for the Peruvian government and provided data to the KGB. In 1973–1975 he taught in Haiti for the Canadian government and the Organization of American States, and continued to spy for the Soviets. On a second trip to Israel in 1975, he completed an extensive demographic study.

Hambleton had met Yuri Andropov, the head of the KGB, in 1975 during a visit to Moscow. During the meeting Andropov strongly encouraged Hambleton to enter into Canadian politics and offered financial support to run for office. KGB officers urged him to get a job at the Hudson Institute, but he had become tired of the espionage game. When he left Moscow, he went to Belgrade, met a beautiful young Yugoslav girl, and fell in love. She later died a slow death by cancer, and the event was a major blow for Hambleton.

In 1979 Royal Canadian Police searched his apartment, found a short-wave radio in his basement with codebooks, and arrested him. In May 1980 Canadian officials announced that no charges were to be filed, and he was released. Since the espionage occurred overseas, no Canadian court could convict him. But in July 1982 he went on a trip to Great Britain where British officials had him arrested. Since he held dual Canadian-British citizenship, he could be tried there. In December 1982, he was sentenced to ten years by a British court for spying for the Soviet Union. He confessed to providing classified data to the Soviets while he was employed for the NATO in Paris from 1956–1961.

When Hambleton was first arrested, he confessed that he passed information to the Soviets but claimed it was as an agent working with French and Canadian intelligence services; Canadian and French intelligence officials denied the story. (Barron, *KGB Today*; Brook-Shepherd, *The Storm Birds*; Raviv and Melman, *Every Spy a Prince*; Romerstein and Levchenko, *The KGB Against the "Main Enemy"*)

220   Hamilton, Carl Edwin, and Richard Hammond.   In March 1977, Ethiopian authorities expelled two U.S. nationals, Hamilton and Hammond, for espionage. Reportedly, both had admitted spying for the Ethiopian Democratic Union, which opposed the military government. Authorities at the U.S. embassy in Ethiopia denied any U.S. relationship with the two. (*Facts on File*, 1977)

221   Hamilton, Victor Norris.   Hamilton was a naturalized U.S. citizen who had emigrated from Libya in the 1950s, changing his name from Hindali to Hamilton. He was a cryptoanalyst working in the NSA's code-breaking Production Organization (ALLO or All Other Countries) Division, which focused on the Middle East starting in June 1957. In 1959 Hamilton began exhibiting psychological problems and was dismissed. In 1963, Hamilton defected to the Soviet Union. A letter published in the Soviet newspaper *Izvestia* in July 1963 stated that Hamilton had notified the Soviets that the NSA was intercepting and decoding messages between Arab countries and their missions to the UN. The NSA responded by stating that Hamilton had been dismissed for psychiatric reasons in 1959 and that he had no knowledge of NSA codes and activities regarding the surveillance of communication channels of Arab states. The NSA claimed Hamilton had been released from his position due to paranoid-schizophrenic behavior. (Allen and Polmar, *Merchants of Treason;* Bamford, *The Puzzle Palace;* Wise and Ross, *The Invisible Government*)

Hammond, Richard see Hamilton, Carl Edwin

222 Hanselmann, Hans. In January 1969, Hanselmann, a West German official in the Foreign Ministry, threw himself in front of a train. He was a possible spy suspect and possibly killed himself in the belief that he had been discovered. (*Facts on File,* 1969)

Harcos, Richard W. see Fletcher, Anthony A.

223 Harel, Isser (b. 1912). The first head of the Israel intelligence branch of Mossad, Harel was famous for going into the field himself. He personally directed the capture of Adolf Eichmann in Argentina in 1960. He is noted for forming Mossad into one of the world's best intelligence services.

Born in Viebsk, Russia, he emigrated to Palestine in 1931, joined the underground Jewish army, the Haganah, in 1942. He changed his name from Halperin to the Hebrew Harel. During World War II he served in a British Army unit in Palestine but at the same time spied on the British for Haganah. In 1944 he became chief of intelligence for Haganah, and in 1951 he was made head of Mossad. He resigned in 1963.

In 1962 Harel authorized a terrorist operation against former Nazi scientists working on the Egyptian missile program. Mossad agents in Egypt began sending threatening letters, which escalated into letter bombs. The agents were arrested and put on trial. The operation turned into an international scandal, and Harel was forced to resign. He was replaced by Meir Amit. (Black and Morris, *Israel's Secret Wars;* Eisenberg, Dan, and Landau, *The Mossad;* Harel, *The House on Garibaldi Street;* Raviv and Melman, *Every Spy a Prince;* Steven, *The Spymasters of Israel*)

224 Harmen, Paul Lance. Corporal Harmen, an undercover British intelligence agent, was assassinated by members of the Irish Republican Army in Belfast, Northern Ireland, in December 1977. British intelligence agents had to be withdrawn from Northern Ireland because papers taken from Harmen after he was killed identified many of them. (*Facts on File,* 1978; *New York Times,* January 9, 1978)

225 Harper, James Durward, Jr. Harper, during a two-year hitch in the Marines, received training in electronics. After he was honorably discharged in 1955, he worked in a series of jobs in electronics firms.

In 1975 he struck out on his own, and that year William Hugle introduced Harper to two men identified as members of a Polish trade delegation shopping for U.S. electronics technology. The two men showed Harper what they said was a "shopping list" of high-tech data and equipment Poland needed. One of the items on the list was a tank-launched rocket.

In November of 1975 he delivered technological data on a trip to Geneva for $5,000. For the next four years, Harper made no further exchanges with the Poles. But in 1979, broke, divorced, and unemployed, he contacted the Poles. Harper's girlfriend, Ruby Louise Schuler, who died in June 1983, served as executive secretary to Dr. Robert E. Larson, the cofounder and president of Systems Control, Inc., a defense contractor that conducted research for the U.S. Army Ballistic Missile Defense Advanced Technology Center in Huntsville, Alabama. He received over $250,000 for his services. The classified documents concerned research on the intercontinental Minuteman missile.

U.S. officials learned about Harper's activities from a Polish agent working for the West. In 1981 Harper, identifying himself as "Jay," went to William Dougherty, the lawyer who represented the spy Christopher Boyce, to see if he would represent him to the CIA in hopes of turning into a double agent and gaining immunity from prosecution. The CIA rejected the offer and alerted the FBI that someone was spying for Poland.

In October 1983, Harper was arrested by the FBI for spying for Poland. Harper identified several other members of the ring: his wife, Ruby Louise Schuler Harper; business partners William Bell Hugle and John Philip Stouffer; and Hugle's wife, Bevalyn Iverson Hugle. Authorities maintained that William Hugle was the key member of the ring. Hugle denied any involvement, but government officials reported that Hugle had acted as a mediator between Harper and the Polish intelligence agents. In 1984, Harper was sentenced to life for spying for Poland. (Allen and Polmar, *Merchants of Treason; Facts on File*, 1983–84; *New York Times*, October 18–20, 23; November 10; December 10, 13, 1983, January 13; April 17, 18; May 15, 1984)

226 Harvey, William King (1915–76). Graduating from Indiana University in 1937 with a law degree, he joined the FBI in 1940 where he worked in the counterintelligence division. In 1947 Harvey resigned from the FBI and joined the CIA's counterintelligence division. Reportedly, FBI director J. Edgar Hoover took the defection personally.

In 1952 he was made chief of Project Gold, which involved digging a tunnel from West Berlin to East Germany to tap Soviet communication cables. The CIA-British built what was termed an experimental radar station, the construction of which was actually a cover for the digging of a tunnel. The digging began in the summer of 1954 and reached the cables in early 1955, costing between $4 to $6 million. They tapped the lines for about a year until April 1956 when the double agent George Blake warned the Soviets about the tunnel.

In 1961 the CIA began Operation Mongoose, covert political and economic operations against Cuba, organized by Task Force W. Harvey was put in charge and supervised the operations from CIA headquarters in Langley, Virginia, leaving the Miami station under the direction of Ted Shackley. Task Force W base in Miami consisted of 400 CIA officers and 2000 Cuban agents, at a budget of $50 million. Missions of Cuban commandos would enter Cuba on small raids and sabotage operations. Task Force W was finally closed down after the Cuban missile crisis because they had sent in ten commando teams of six men each into Cuba without authorization during the crisis. Trying to stop a potential nuclear war, the White House was horrified to discover that the task force had sent in commandos without authorization. Harvey was replaced by Desmond Fitz-zGerald in charge of Task Force W till it was closed down.

Harvey's final assignment was chief of station in Rome, Italy, in 1963, and when he returned, he resigned in 1969. He earned the Distinguished Intelligence Medal for his service. (Freemantle, *CIA*; Martin, *Wilderness of Mirrors*; Powers, *The Man Who Kept the Secrets*; Prados, *Presidents' Secret Wars* and *The Soviet Estimate*; Ranelagh, *The Agency*)

227 Hasenfus, Eugene.   Hasenfus served in the U.S. Marine Corps 1960–65, then quit the Marines to work for CIA's Air America in Laos, supplying the CIA-backed Hmong army with arms and supplies in 1965–73. Hasenfus was working a construction job in Wisconsin in June 1986 when he received an offer to join the secret war in Central America. He received a salary of $3,000 a month and a $750 bonus for every trip into Nicaragua. Between July and October, he flew ten missions. Hasenfus was in charge of dropping the parachute cargo out the door, called a kicker.

The two pilots, Wallace Blaine "Buz" Sawyer and William J. Cooper, had teased Hasenfus for bringing a personal parachute. All three men had flown missions in Southeast Asia for CIA's Air America. On October 5, 1986, a Southern Air Transport C-123K carrying 70 Soviet-made automatic rifles, 100,000 rounds of ammunition, and 7 RPGs was shot down over southern Nicaragua. The plane had taken off from Ilopango military base in El Salvador. When the plane came near a drop zone, a Sandinista army post, Light Hunter Battalion Third Company fired a rocket launcher and downed the aircraft.

Hasenfus was captured by the Sandinistas and paraded in front of journalists. At first the U.S. government denied knowledge of or responsibility for Hasenfus, but the barrage of evidence was overwhelming. Despite orders to the contrary, the team carried identification and paperwork detailing other missions. Hasenfus declared at a press conference that he was working for the CIA, explaining that the CIA air operation was run by two Cuban-Americans, Felix Rodriguez (aliases Gustavo Villoldo and Max Gomez) and Ramon Medina (later identified as the Cuban terrorist Luis Posada Carriles, who escaped a Venezuelan prison in August 1985 for the bombing of a Cuban airliner).

Hasenfus had worked for Corporate Air Services, which was reportedly part of Southern Air Transport. Southern Air Transport had been owned by the CIA till 1975 when it was sold. Hasenfus had participated in ten supply flights from the base in Ilopango, El Salvador, and four out of the base in Aguacate, Honduras.

Documents found on the plane included business cards of Robert W. Owen and P. J. Buechler. Buechler worked for the State Department's Nicaraguan Humanitarian Affairs Office, which oversaw nonlethal aid to the Contras. Owen was a close associate of Oliver North and was later identified as one of the individuals responsible for the air supply network.

In November 1986 Hasenfus was found guilty in a Popular Anti-Somocista Tribunal for terrorism, association to commit illicit acts, and violation of the public security laws. Sentenced to 30 years, he was released in December 1987 due to his cooperation with the Sandinistas. Hasenfus later filed a $35-million lawsuit against Major General Richard Secord and Albert Hakim. The lawsuit also named three companies that were reportedly engaged in the covert war in Central America: Corporate Air Services, Southern Air Transport, and Stanford Technology Trading Group, Inc. The case was lost. (Byrne, *The Chronology;* Cockburn, *Out of Control;* Marshall, Scott, and Hunter, *The Iran Contra Connection;* Sklar, *Washington's War on Nicaragua;* U.S. Govt., *The Tower Commission Report*)

228   Haury, Jean-Michel.   French authorities claimed that Haury, who worked at the Ariane rocket plant, had passed secrets about the Ariane rocket, including data on the rocket propulsion system, called cryogenic propulsion. He was arrested in 1987 for spying for the Soviet Union. (*Facts on File,* 1987)

229   Hayhanen, Reino (1920–61).   Born in Leningrad, he joined the NKVD in 1939 as an interrogator during the Soviet-Finland war (1939–40). During World War II he continued in intelligence till 1948 when he was sent to study English and espionage tradecraft for four years. In 1952 he was sent to New York to assist Rudolf Abel. But while there, he began to drink heavily and failed to carry out missions. Abel ordered him home in 1957, and during the trip he decided to defect in Paris. The CIA returned him to the U.S. where he testified against Abel. He was killed in a car accident on the Pennsylvania turnpike in 1961, but others dispute the story, saying he died of liver problems. He also identified Master Sergeant Roy Rhodes as a spy for the Soviets. (Bernikow, *Abel*; Donovan, *Strangers on a Bridge*)

230   Heiser, Carl John, and Carl Lutz Weischenberg.   In July 1977 FBI agents arrested Heiser, an American, and Weischenberg, a West German, in Florida for conspiring to sell cruise missile secrets and components to Soviet-bloc countries. Weischenberg, who lived in the Bahamas, had previously been charged by West German authorities for treason. Heiser reportedly had a recent unexplained infusion of cash. He had made numerous trips to Europe, leased a $400 apartment, and bought a 35 foot power cruiser that authorities believed he was planning to use to make secret trips to Cuba to ferry documents. Neither was charged with espionage; they were charged with failing to register as agents of a foreign country. Reportedly, neither was able to gain access to classified data, but they were actively seeking cruise missile data and nuclear bomb materials, such as uranium oxide and thorium. (*Facts on File*, 1977; *New York Times*, November 8, 12, 1977)

231   Helbig, Erich.   In April 1965 a West German court convicted Helbig of spying, accepting bribes, and committing acts of treason with the Communists. Helbig had been a senior counselor to Chancellor Konrad Adenauer for eight years. The court sentenced him to two years' hard labor. (*Facts on File*, 1965; *New York Times*, March 30, 1965)

232   Helin, Eila.   In March 1980, a court in Helsinki, Finland, sentenced Helin to four years for spying for the Soviet Union. Helin, formerly the head of the data library for Kemina Oy, a chemical firm owned by the government, gave Soviet agents classified data from 1974 to 1979 and was paid $8,600 for her services. (*Facts on File*, 1980)

233   Helmcke, Hans.   In January 1965, Helmcke was arrested in West Germany for spying for East Germany. Helmcke was the operator of a well-known and high-style brothel that catered to high political and military officials. Helmcke was accused of informing East German agents of the identities of his patrons. (*Facts on File*, 1965)

234   Helmich, Joseph George, Jr.   In September 1981, U.S. Army Warrant Officer Helmich pled guilty in a U.S. court to conspiring to sell military secrets to the Soviet Union and was sentenced to life. As a code specialist at SACEUR headquarters in Paris, Helmich was accused of selling maintenance and operating instructions, coding lists, and technical details of the KL-7 coding machine between 1963 and 1964, receiving $131,000 for his services. U.S. authorities believe that the Soviets may have been able to decode intelligence messages during the Vietnam War and may have severely damaged U.S. efforts in the war thanks to Helmich's help, but many argued that the use of the KL-7 coding machine had minimal use during the war.

After several checks bounced at military clubs in early 1962, he was threatened by a court-martial to pay the $500 he owed. Helmich attempted to get a bank loan but failed. He walked into the Soviet embassy in Paris and offered American and NATO communications secrets.

Helmich also had extensive access to U.S.-NATO diplomatic and military communications. In 1964 authorities questioned him about his high living, but the investigation was later dropped. He was transferred to Fort Bragg, North Carolina, where he continued as a spy for the KGB while working as cryptographic custodian. He traveled to France and Mexico City to meet with his Soviet case officers. In early 1981, Helmich was spotted in Canada with known Soviet agents during a surveillance operation. He was questioned and confessed. He was charged with espionage and sentenced to life. Reportedly, Helmich was given the rank of colonel by the Soviet government and awarded a hero's medal. (Allen and Polmar, *Merchants of Treason; Facts on File*, 1981; *New York Times*, July 16–18; September 22, 24, 25, 27, 29; October 10, 17, 1981)

235   Helms, Richard McGarrah (b. 1913).   Served as director of the Central Intelligence Agency (DCI) from June 1966 to February 1973 under Presidents Johnson and Nixon. He was one of the most diversely skilled individuals to serve as DCI.

He worked as a journalist until 1942 when he joined the U.S. Naval Reserve; served in the Office of Strategic Services (OSS) 1943–46 in the Strategic Services unit, then joined the CIA's Office of Special Operations; served 1962–65 as CIA deputy director of plans, then deputy director of the CIA from April 1965 to June 1966. Fired by President Nixon when he refused to allow the use of the CIA in the cover-up of Watergate, Helms pled no contest in 1977 to misdemeanor charges that he failed to testify fully and accurately before the Senate Foreign Relations Committee in 1973, which was investigating CIA involvement in covert activities in Chile. Helms was given a two-year suspended sentence. He served as ambassador to Iran from March 1973 to January 1977. In October 1983 he was awarded the National Security Medal by President Reagan. He served as a member of the President's Commission on Strategic Forces in 1983. (Johnson, *A Season of*

Inquiry; Leary, *The Central Intelligence Agency;* Powers, *The Man Who Kept the Secrets;* Ranelagh, *The Agency)*

236 Herczynski, Ryszard.   In June 1982, Herczynski, a professor at the Polish Academy of Sciences, was sentenced by a Polish military court to two years for passing sensitive information to two U.S. diplomats. The U.S. diplomats, John Zerolis, scientific attaché, and Daniel Howard, first secretary for cultural affairs, were expelled in May. Herczynski and the two diplomats were arrested after Polish security agents raided his apartment in Warsaw. The U.S. retaliated by expelling Andrzej Koroscik, Polish scientific attaché, and Mariusz Wozniak, a Polish political officer. The U.S. also suspended travel for important scientists and engineers to Poland involved in joint research projects. (*Facts on File,* 1982; *New York Times,* May 11; June 25, 1982)

237 Hernandez, Gladys Garcia, and brother Nestor Garcia.   Gladys, a Cuban exile visiting her brother in Cuba, and Nestor, who worked in the Cuban ministry of construction, were arrested by Cuban authorities in May 1987 for spying for the U.S. Accused of providing the U.S. with economic, sociopolitical, and military data, they were sentenced in 1988 to eight years for spying for the CIA. (*Facts on File,* 1987–88)

238 Herrmann, Rudolph Albert.   FBI officials revealed at a news conference that a Soviet spy had been turned into a double agent. Herrmann, real name unknown, was presented at the conference behind a special screen to hide his identity. Herrmann was described as a Soviet KGB colonel who studied in East Germany under KGB tutelage and was given the alias Herrmann (the name of a real German who had died in the Soviet Union during World War II). Herrmann stated that he had been engaged in espionage activities while posing as a freelance photographer in New York City. His main duties were running special errands for the KGB. He claimed that he never handed over classified data to the KGB or was engaged in military espionage.

Herrmann described writing a letter to NASA threatening the Apollo 8 space mission. Herrmann specialized in the reactivation of sleeper agents and was responsible for activating Hugh Hambleton in 1967. His duties also included gathering intelligence on presidential candidates, and he met one of the candidates in an airport in San Francisco, but unfortunately the candidate failed to win the election (the candidate's name was not disclosed). When Herrmann was turned, he began providing information about KGB communications, cipher systems, secret meeting places, and secret writing.

In 1968 he obtained a U.S. visa and moved to a suburb of New York

City where he freelanced as a photographer and filmmaker. He taught his older son, Peter, espionage tradecraft and recruited him into the KGB. It was hoped that Peter would be able to gain a sensitive government position, but in 1977, when he was a junior at Georgetown, the FBI was able to turn him and his parents into double agents. After two years it was feared that the KGB was suspicious, and they were given new identities. (Allen and Polmar, *Merchants of Treason*; Pincher, *Too Secret, Too Long*)

239 Hillenkoetter, Roscoe Henry (1897–1982). Third director of Central Intelligence Agency (DCI), serving from May 1947 to October 1950 under President Truman. Oversaw the transformation of the Central Intelligence Group into the Central Intelligence Agency in September 1947, making him the first director of the CIA. He was a graduate of the U.S. Naval Academy, 1920. In November 1946 he was promoted to Rear Admiral; November 1950–September 1951, commander of the Naval Task Force during the Korean War; April 1956, promoted to Vice Admiral; in August 1956, inspector general of the Navy; retired from the U.S. Navy in May 1957. He commanded a destroyer in the Pacific in World War II and a Navy task force in the Korean War. Resigning in 1950 after criticism that the CIA was unable to predict the revolution in Colombia, he was replaced by Walter Bedell Smith. (Darling, *The Central Intelligence Agency*; Leary, *The Central Intelligence Agency*; Ranelagh, *The Agency*)

240 Hinchcliffe, Leonard Michael. In October 1971, British officials charged Hinchcliffe, the British Foreign Service administrative officer in Algiers, with passing classified documents to an unidentified person while he served at the British embassy in the Sudan between July 1968 and April 1971. Reportedly, Hinchcliffe had not provided classified data to either the Sudanese or Algerian governments. (*Facts on File*, 1971; *New York Times*, October 12, 1971; West, *The Circus*)

241 Hirsch, John Vladimir. U.S. Air Force Captain Hirsch failed a polygraph test in July 1989. A search of Hirsch's house in West Berlin revealed classified documents and photographs of sensitive military installations. Hirsch, born in Czechoslovakia, became a U.S. naturalized citizen in 1971, was stationed at Tempelhof, West Berlin, where he had been in a high position that involved classified communications. (*Facts on File*, 1989; *New York Times*, August 5, 6, 1989).

242 Hiss, Alger (b. 1904). Hiss attended Johns Hopkins University, was an officer in the ROTC, and can be described as the "all-American boy." He graduated in 1926, then went to Harvard Law School and was named editor of the *Harvard Law Review*. He joined the State

Department in 1936 and was the assistant to Assistant Secretary of State Francis B. Sayre. When World War II broke out, Hiss was the assistant to political adviser Stanley Hornbeck, which involved the complex job of getting military aid to Chinese Nationalists who were battling the Japanese. Hiss then took part as an adviser to the U.S. delegation in 1944 to the Dumbarton Oaks and San Francisco conferences on the formation of the United Nations. Hiss left the State Department in 1946 and became president of the Carnegie Endowment for International Peace in February 1947.

In August 1948 Whittaker Chambers went before the House Committee on Un-American Activities and accused Hiss of being a Communist spy. Chambers charged that Hiss had been a member of a Communist spy ring while a federal employee in the mid-1930s.

Hiss was called before the committee and underwent extensive questioning, particularly from Richard Nixon, a junior member of the committee. Chambers admitted to being a member of the Communist underground but claimed to have left the party in 1939 with the signing of the Nazi-Soviet pact. After Chambers left the party, he became a senior editor at *Time* magazine. Chambers stated that he joined the Communist party in 1925 and was recruited into the underground movement by Max Bedacht, a member of the secretariat of the Communist National Committee, but Bedacht denied ever knowing Chambers. Chambers stated that in 1934 in Washington, D.C., he had been introduced to Hiss by the heads of the Communist underground section in the U.S. Chambers's primary task was to act as a courier between Washington, D.C., and New York.

According to Chambers, Hiss provided State Department confidential documents. Chambers claimed that he was known only as "Carl" to Hiss and that he delivered the Hiss data to two Russians who used the aliases "Herbert" and "Ulrich." Chambers described Hiss as a romantic but dedicated Communist. In 1931–32 Hiss did attend some Socialist party meetings with his wife to hear about proposals to feed and clothe the poor. His wife, Priscilla, even worked in a Socialist-sponsored food line preparing sandwiches and identified herself as a Socialist when she registered to vote in 1932. They stopped in 1933 when Hiss joined the International Juridical Association.

No one besides Chambers accused Hiss of being a spy. Psychologists described Chambers as a "psychopathic" liar, and his friends described him as having a brilliant imagination and extraordinary fantasies. Hiss claimed he did not know him as Chambers, but as George Crosley. Hiss claimed that Crosley had approached him in 1934 at the Nye Committee office in the Senate Office Building as a freelance writer. He told Hiss that he was writing for the *American Magazine* on the aircraft sales to Nazi Germany. They met several times, but Hiss claims that there was not much of a relationship except for the fact that he lent Chambers his apartment when he moved to another apartment. Though this was all rather innocent, it hurt Hiss later in the committee questioning.

Chambers claimed no relationship with *American Magazine* and that the use of the apartment was a gift from one Communist to another. Chambers had joined the Communist party in 1925 while a student at Columbia University; he had become disillusioned after World War I with the way things were run and began reading Marx and Lenin. He left Columbia University without graduating to work for the *Daily Worker*, became editor of *New Masses*, which had a strong Communist readership. He claimed that he was recruited to the Communist underground movement by Max Bedacht, a member of the secretariat of the Communist National Committee, but Bedacht claimed it was a lie.

Chambers did produce two microfilm strips that had 58 pages comprising five memoranda dealing with trade-agreement negotiations with Germany and three mimeographed copies of cables stamped in 1938 and initialed by Hiss. The pages were unimportant. They were called the "Pumpkin Papers" because Chambers claimed he had hidden them inside a hollowed-out pumpkin. (Andrews, *A Tragedy of History*; Chambers, *Witness*; Cook, *A Generation on Trial*; de Toledano and Lasky, *Seeds of Treason*; Hiss, *In the Court of Public Opinion*; Smith, *Alger Hiss*; Weinstein, *Perjury*)

243 Hodic, Josef.

In 1981, Hodic, posing as a Czechoslovakian dissident who supported the Charter 77 human rights document, was accused of being a Czech intelligence agent by the Austrian government. Hodic received Austrian citizenship and in 1979 began working for the Austrian Institute for International Politics. Hodic disappeared from Austria in July 1981, and shortly after, Czechoslovakian radio reported that an important undercover agent had returned home. (*Facts on File*, 1981)

244 Hoefs, Ursula.

In March 1979 the West German government announced that an East German spy ring that had infiltrated the Christian Democratic Union (CDU) had been broken. Hoefs, who was a secretary at the CDU headquarters, was arrested for spying for East Germany. Two other CDU members were accused: Christel Broszey and Inge Goliath. (*Facts on File*, 1979)

245 Hoeke, Margret.

Hoeke worked as a secretary for West German presidents since 1959 and senior secretary in the office of President Richard von Weizsaecker. As a secretary, she had passed confidential information to a Soviet agent, Franz Becker, who had become her lover. Hoeke admitted spying for 12 years and providing the Soviets with over 1,700 secrets. She had worked for the Soviets since 1968. She was connected to an East German couple who were arrested in London in August, Reinhardt and Sonja Schulze. She was uncovered when Oleg Gordievsky, a senior KGB agent, defected in London. Becker (real name unknown) escaped the country. She was arrested in August 1985 and sentenced to eight years for espionage for the Soviet Union in 1987. (*Facts on File*, 1987)

246 Hoffman, Mary. In March 1969, Hoffman, former clerk for the Japanese embassy in Sidney, Australia, stated that she had spied since 1958. She stated that she had passed classified documents to the Australian Security Intelligence Organization (ASIO). She considered it counterespionage since the Japanese had approached her husband, who worked in the Department of Customs and Excise, for classified data on Australian trade and tariff policy. (*Facts on File*, 1969; *New York Times*, March 9, 1969)

247 Hoistad, Ole Martin. In April 1973, Hoistad, a student, was sentenced in Oslo, Norway, for spying for the Soviet Union for seven years. His motivation seems to have been an attempt to gain an exit visa for his Russian fiancée. Hoistad had served as a guard at the Norwegian embassy in Moscow in 1972 and had given classified data to Soviet agents. (*Facts on File*, 1973)

248 Hollis, Roger (1905–73). British MI5 director general from 1956 to 1965. In 1984, Peter Wright, a former MI5 investigator, charged that Hollis had been a Soviet spy and had helped the KGB infiltrate British and Australian intelligence services. This was not the first time that Hollis had been accused of being a spy for the Soviets. But a KGB defector, Oleg Gordievsky, disputed Hollis's involvement with Soviets, pointing to several conversations with Soviet KGB officials who found the British paranoia about Hollis amusing and ironic.

He attended Oxford in 1924 but quit before completing his degree. He traveled to Asia where he landed a job with an American tobacco company in Shanghai for nine years. He became ill and was forced to return to Great Britain. In 1938 he joined MI5. During his career he helped in the creation of the Australian Security Intelligence Service (ASIS) in 1949. He was sent by MI5 in 1945 to debrief the Soviet defector Igor Gouzenko in Canada. (Andrew and Gordievsky, *KGB*; Pincher, *Their Trade Is Treachery*; West, *The Truth about Hollis*; Wright, *Spy Catcher*)

249 Holt, Harold. According to Anthony Grey, who wrote *The Prime Minister Was a Spy*, Harold Holt, former Australian prime minister, had been a spy for 36 years for China. According to Grey's theory, Holt did not die in a drowning in 1967 while swimming in the ocean but was secretly taken by Chinese frogmen to a submarine just off shore. Grey also argued that Holt planned his escape for fear of being caught by the Australian intelligence service. According to the book, Grey had started his espionage work for the Nationalist Chinese but began working for the Communists when they took power in 1949. Australians, the British, and Holt's family called the theory outrageous and without merit. (*Facts on File*, 1983; Grey, *The Prime Minister Was a Spy*; *New York Times*, November 21, 1983)

250 Holtz, Uwe.   In September 1978, Holtz, Social Democratic Party (SPD) deputy to the West German parliament and chairman of its Committee for Economic Development, was accused of spying for Rumania. The allegations stemmed from a statement made by Ion Pacepa, vice minister in the Rumanian secret police, who defected to the West. Holtz denied the allegations, and the charges were later dropped. (*Facts on File*, 1978)

251 Horton, Brian P.   In January 1983 U.S. Navy intelligence specialist Horton was sentenced to six years' hard labor for conspiring to sell classified documents to the Soviet Union. Horton, a second-class petty officer, pled guilty. He had contacted Soviet officials to offer selling U.S. military plans and war strategies. In June 1982, while stationed at the Fleet Intelligence Center in Norfolk, Virginia, he contacted the Soviet Military Office in Washington. Horton made four phone calls and wrote one letter offering data on U.S. war plans. Horton was convicted at a general court-martial on five counts of failure to report contact with a hostile country and one count of solicitation to commit espionage. His six-year sentence was later reduced to three. (Allen and Polmar, *Merchants of Treason*; *Facts on File*, 1983; *New York Times*, January 14, 1983)

252 Houghton, Harry Frederick.   Houghton was arrested in 1961, along with Gordon Lonsdale, the Krogers, and his fianceé, Ethel Gee, for espionage for the Soviet Union. Houghton had served as a naval attaché in Poland and may have been recruited there to work for the Soviets. Both he and Ethel Gee worked as civilian employees at the Portland naval base and had access to classified documents, supplying Lonsdale with classified data. Police searches of their homes discovered $15,000, some of it buried in a tin box in Houghton's backyard. Houghton and Gee were convicted in 1961 and sentenced to 15 years each. (Bernikow, *Abel*; Houghton, *Operation Portland*; West, *The Circus*; Wright, *Spy Catcher*)

253 Howard, Edward Lee (b. 1951).   Aliases: Patrick Brian, Edward L. Houston, Roger H. Shannon. His father served in the Air Force, and Howard and his family moved frequently around the country. In 1969 at the University of Texas (Austin) he joined the Army ROTC in the Engineer's branch to avoid the draft. He graduated in 1972 with a bachelor's degree in international business and economics, joined the Peace Corps in 1973, and was stationed in rural Colombia. While in Colombia he experimented with a variety of drugs, including cocaine.

He completed his tour in August 1974, and in 1975 he enrolled as a graduate student at American University, earning a master's in business administration in 1977. He then joined the trainee program in the Agency for International Development and was sent to Peru. He resigned in March 1979 and worked in the private sector.

He joined the CIA in 1981 and was considered perfect by the CIA upon his recruitment. In January 1982 he was assigned to the Soviet/East European Division for training as a case officer in Moscow. He had been given all the data needed to work in Moscow — names of agents, surveillance operations, and the identities of other CIA officers in the division. At the end of training, just before his assignment to Moscow in 1983, he was given a final polygraph and failed it. Another was given, but Howard had difficulty passing the polygraph when it came to questions concerning theft. He was asked to resign, and in bewilderment and anger Howard left the CIA with feelings of revenge.

Howard began drinking heavily and hanging around the Soviet consulate. Apparently he managed to contact Soviet officials in the consulate in Washington, D.C., and arranged a meeting in Vienna. Howard approached the Soviets, making three trips to Vienna with meetings with KGB officers from 1984 to 1985. Howard moved to New Mexico and began working for the New Mexico legislature as a budget analyst.

Vitaly Yurchenko, KGB defector, identified Howard as the spy from the CIA who identified agents and assets in the Soviet Union. Yurchenko had described Howard under the code name "Robert." Howard was placed under FBI surveillance in New Mexico but managed to escape the country. He was granted political asylum by the Soviet Union in 1986. Howard was the first CIA officer to defect to the Soviet Union. (Allen and Polmar, *Merchants of Treason*; Kessler, *Escape from the CIA*; Wise, *The Spy Who Got Away*; Woodward, *Veil*)

254 Huang, Hanson.   China arrested Huang, born in Hong Kong, for spying for the U.S. in 1983. Reportedly, Huang had provided the U.S. with data on Chinese energy resources. He was sentenced to 15 years but was released in 1985. Huang, trained in the U.S. as a lawyer, graduated from Harvard Law School, served for a short period as a partner in a New York law firm. (*Facts on File*, 1984–85; *New York Times*, January 20, 1984; May 16, 1985)

255 Hull, John. Linked to the CIA arms-supply network for the Nicaraguan Contras, he was arrested in Costa Rica January 12, 1989, on suspicion of drug and weapons trafficking and spying for the Contras. He was also charged with violating Costa Rica's neutrality. Hull held dual United States-Costa Rican citizenship and lived in Costa Rica for 20 years. A Colombian drug trafficker who flew cocaine to the United States from Hull's ranch in Costa Rica had accused Hull of complicity, but drug charges were later dropped. Costa Rican authorities were seeking the extradition of Hull from the United States in February 1990, claiming that he had participated in the 1984 bombing at La Penca, Nicaragua, aimed at assassinating Contra leader Eden Pastora Gomez, who survived the attack. As reporters gathered to cover the press conference in which Pastora was to reveal CIA involvement and support, a bomb detonated, killing five journalists. Costa Rican authorities announced that Hull and a Cuban exile, Felipe Vidal, had arranged the bombing. Pastora later claimed that Hull was a CIA asset who was controlled by Philip Holtz at the U.S. embassy in San Jose. (Byrne, *The Chronology*; Cockburn, *Out of Control*; U.S. Govt., *The Tower Commission Report*; Walker, *Reagan Versus the Sandinistas*)

256 Humphrey, Ronald L., and Truong Dinh Hung. Humphrey, a U.S. Information Agency (USIA) official who had served in South Vietnam during the war, and Truong Dinh Hung (David Truong), a Vietnamese graduate student, were arrested for espionage by the FBI on January 31, 1978. Humphrey handed over classified cables from U.S. embassies overseas to Truong to give to the government of Vietnam.

Humphrey had hoped that the document transfer would win the release of a Vietnamese woman, Nguyen Thi Chieu ("Kim"), he had fallen in love with while he was stationed in Vietnam (Nguyen was released in 1977). Truong acted as liaison for Humphrey and the Vietnamese government.

At one point Truong handed over the documents to a Vietnamese woman, Dung Krall, who offered to hand-deliver the documents to Vietnamese agents in Paris. Krall, however, turned out to be an FBI agent. The one hundred documents included a report by a United States embassy on anti–Communist activity in Laos; United States political, military, and diplomatic relations, and intelligence assessments in Thailand, Singapore, Vietnam, China, and Ethiopia; a report on the attempted coup in Thailand; and an assessment of Sino-Vietnamese relations.

Truong entered the U.S. in 1964 as a student. His father, Truong Dinh Dzu, was the "peace candidate" in the South Vietnamese elections in 1967. Truong's motivation appears to have been a belief that the documents would help improve relations between Vietnam and the U.S. The U.S.

government also indicted Dinh Ba Thi, Vietnamese ambassador to the UN, but he left the United States in February 1978. Humphrey and Truong were found guilty of espionage by a federal jury on May 19, 1978, and sentenced to 15 years each. (Allen and Polmar, *Merchants of Treason;* Turner, *Secrecy and Democracy*)

257   Hunt, Everett Howard (b. 1918).   One of the most infamous characters in the history of the CIA. He graduated from Brown University in 1940, then entered the Naval Academy at Annapolis in 1941. In 1943 he joined the Army Air Force and was sent to the Air Force Intelligence School at Orlando, Florida. After finishing the program, he was transferred to the Office of Strategic Services (OSS) and was assigned to Detachment 202 in China, where he helped organize resistance to the Japanese. When the OSS disbanded, Hunt joined the Economic Cooperation Administration (ECA) in 1948 as a staff member of the European administrator in Paris, serving as a press aide to Ambassador Averell Harriman. He then returned to Washington and joined the CIA.

1950 Hunt opened the CIA station in Mexico City under the cover of a Foreign Service reserve officer. While Hunt was station chief in Mexico City, he learned that a Communist organization was planning a banquet in honor of some Soviet visitors. Hunt acquired a copy of the invitation and had three thousand extra invitations printed and distributed. Hundreds of extra guests appeared, packing the halls inside. Hundreds of angry guests were stuck outside waiting to get in when the doors closed on them. Both the legitimate Mexican guests and the Soviets were angry at the sponsors. The technique became popular in CIA tactics and was coined "The Monster Rally."

He left Mexico and returned to CIA headquarters to become chief of the Balkans covert operations. CIA's Southeast Europe (Balkan) Division was responsible for Albania, Yugoslavia, Greece, Bulgaria, and Romania. All agent operations in Albania were carried out jointly by the CIA and MI6. From Greece's northern borders, CIA agents crossed into Bulgaria, and air operations were run from an airfield near Athens into all Balkan countries except Yugoslavia and Albania. Hunt helped to manage the Albanian airdrops of men and supplies. Almost all were captured and killed, no doubt with the help of Kim Philby, the MI6 liaison officer with the CIA who later turned out to be a Soviet spy.

After two years he transferred back to the Western Hemisphere Division where he was assigned as chief of the propaganda and political action staff in the project to overthrow Guatemala's Communist government. The Guatemala project was set up as a semiautonomous unit within the Western Hemisphere Division. The project was created as the result of the massive lobbying efforts of American companies with business in Guatemala, particularly the United Fruit Company. The operation managed to overthrow the Arbenz government by a CIA–sponsored rebel army made up of former Guatemalan officers led by Armas. Arbenz was captured along with his followers, one of them a young Argentine medical student by the name of Ernesto Che Guevara. The CIA managed to convince the new government not to execute Arbenz and his followers, and they were sent into exile. Arbenz went to Czechoslovakia, and Guevara went to Cuba and joined Castro's partisans. But before the actual invasion could take place, Hunt was reassigned to Tokyo as chief of covert operations for the North Asia Command under the cover of an Army civilian adviser to General Matthew Ridgway's Far East Command. During this period, Hunt worked on propaganda projects against North Korea and China.

In 1956 he became chief of station in Montevideo, Uruguay, under the cover of a State Department first secretary. At the time, the CIA had a small pool of assets and agents in Uruguay. Hunt managed to build an extensive agent network in all branches of the government. When Robert Woodward, the new U.S. ambassador, arrived in Uruguay, Hunt and Woodward became enemies. Due to the conflict, Hunt was summoned back to D.C. and reassigned as the chief of political action for the Cuban project, what later became known as the Bay of Pigs.

During this period, Hunt was sent to Miami under the cover name "Eduardo" to assist Cuban exiles in overthrowing Castro. The failure of the operation and the problems in Uruguay with Ambassador Woodward cast a dark shadow on Hunt's career. In 1965, unable to advance further, he was given a minor political assignment in Madrid, Spain. But in 1966 he returned to Washington, where he stayed in the Western Europeans Division working as the chief of covert action for Western Europe. Hunt was granted an early retirement from the CIA on May 1, 1970.

In July 1971, Hunt was hired at the White House as a "dirty-tricks" expert by Charles Colson. Hunt and G. Gordon Liddy formulated the Gemstone Project, actually several operations under the same name. One was the break-in of Daniel Ellsberg's psychiatrist's office. Ellsberg, a State Department employee, had given the *New York Times* the *Pentagon Papers*, a detailed history of U.S. involvement in Vietnam. Hunt was attempting to gather data to formulate a psychological profile of Ellsberg.

Hunt was finally caught in the break-in of the Democratic party's campaign headquarters at the Watergate Hotel. Hunt knew he was in trouble when Bob Woodward of the *Washington Post* telephoned him to ask about the notebook found on one of the burglars with his name and telephone number. Hunt received a prison sentence for his activities involving the Watergate affair. Despite the fact that the CIA denies Hunt was an employee at the time of the Watergate break-in, Hunt was also an employee of the Robert R. Mullen public relations firm, which had a strong relationship with the CIA, providing covers for agents in several other countries.

In the CIA and after, Hunt wrote a variety of spy yarns under several pen names: Robert Dietrich, John Baxter, Gordon Davis, and David St. John. Hunt was a well-known conservative in the CIA, one of the best psychological warfare and propaganda specialists in the history of the CIA. (Hougan, *Secret Agenda*; Hunt, *Give Us This Day* and *Undercover*; Prados, *Presidents' Secret Wars*; Schlesinger, *Bitter Fruit*; Szulc, *Compulsive Spy*; Wyden, *Bay of Pigs*)

258   Hussein, Talal, King of Jordan (b. 1935).   From 1957 to 1977, the CIA made payments to King Hussein for a variety of services. When President Carter learned of the payments in February 1977, he ordered the CIA to stop the operation. The CIA paid Hussein from $500,000 to $1 million each year and provided Hussein with female companions. In return, Hussein allowed CIA personnel to operate freely within the country. Hussein reportedly also provided the CIA with important intelligence. (*Facts on File*, 1977; Woodward, *Veil*)

259   Huttenmeister, Frowald.   In November 1964 Huttenmeister was released from a Egyptian prison after six months, after West German government appeals for his release. He had been serving a ten-year sentence for espionage for Israel. Huttenmeister had been a West German archeology student when he was arrested in Egypt. (*Facts on File*, 1964)

260   Imre, Nahit.   Imre, a Turkish citizen married to a Hungarian, became financial comptroller in December 1967 after working for several years as a financial specialist in NATO's finance department. While serving in this position, he had access to a variety of classified documents detailing NATO's financial expenditures. Imre was arrested in 1968 carrying twenty NATO classified documents. In June 1972, after admitting spying since the late 1950s, he was sentenced by a Turkish court to death for spying for Rumania and Yugoslav agents while in Brussels. (*Facts on File*, 1972; Rositzke, *The KGB*)

261   Infante, Cesar Diaz.   In June 1964 Cuba announced that Infante, director of the Internal Commerce Ministry of Oriente Province, was executed for spying for the CIA, one of the highest-ranking members of Castro's government to be executed for espionage. (*Facts on File*, 1964)

262   Ionov, Vassily Vladimirovich.   In September 1983, Ionov, Soviet attaché to the trade mission, was ordered expelled for espionage activities in Great Britain. The Soviets denied any espionage activity by Ionov. (*Facts on File*, 1983; *New York Times*, September 30, 1983)

263 Isacsson, Haakan. In 1973, Isacsson, a Swedish intelligence agent, provided details of a secret Swedish intelligence agency, the Information Bureau (IB), to two editors of the left-wing magazine *Fib Kulturfront*, Peter Bratt and Jan Guillou, who published the report in January 1974. Bratt and Guillou were convicted of espionage and sentenced to one year. Isacsson was also sentenced to one year for providing classified data to the editors. The article in the magazine detailed the liaison relationship of the IB with Western intelligence organizations, espionage operations against Arab embassies, a break-in by Swedish intelligence agents at the Egyptian embassy in Stockholm, and the infiltrations of IB agents into Swedish unions and political organizations. (*Facts on File*, 1974; *New York Times*, January 5, 1974)

264 Ismailov, Vladimir Makarovich. Colonel Ismailov, Soviet Air Force military attaché attached to the Soviet embassy in Washington, was actually a GRU intelligence officer. He attempted to steal classified data on the cruise missile and Stealth bomber. He was arrested at a drop site in Maryland in 1986. Ismailov had approached a U.S. Air Force officer in a local tavern near Washington, D.C., but the officer went to the FBI, and a sting operation was planned and operated, supplying him with fake documents until his arrest in June 1986. After the approach at the tavern, he approached the officer in stalled traffic while he was on his way to work at the Pentagon a couple of months later. It was obviously to the FBI that Ismailov had done his homework on the officer's movements. He was expelled shortly after his arrest. (Allen and Polmar, *Merchants of Treason*; *Facts on File*, 1986)

265 Jama, Abu. In February 1973, Israeli authorities arrested Jama and his family for participating in a Syrian spy ring. Reportedly, Jama had been linked to Syrian intelligence before the 1967 war that gave the Golan Heights, which is where Jama lived, to Israel. His mission was to gain intelligence on Israeli Army operations and fortifications in the Golan Heights area. The ring was also responsible for mailing letter bombs to a variety of political leaders. (*Facts on File*, 1973; *New York Times*, February 2, 1973)

266 James, Francis. In January 1973, James, an Australian journalist, was released from China after being arrested in 1969 on espionage charges. His release coincided with the establishment of diplomatic relations between China and Australia. James had been arrested after writing articles about his visits to the Chinese nuclear testing ground at Lop Nor in Sinkiang Province. The Chinese denied that he had been in the area. (*Facts on File*, 1973; *New York Times*, January 15, 1973)

267   Jeanmaire, Jean-Louis.   In August 1976 Brigadier General Jeanmaire, a well-known anti–Communist, was arrested by Swiss agents for spying for the Soviet Union. In June 1977, General Jeanmaire was sentenced to 18 years by a Swiss military court. Jeanmaire had been commander of the Swiss civil defense forces and chief of the Swiss air defense troops before his retirement in 1975 but remained an adviser to the air defense system till his arrest. Information given to the Soviets included the capacity of Switzerland's reserve militia of 680,000 men. Jeanmaire confessed to the charges and stated that he had met with a Soviet military attaché in 1959 who he claimed had entrapped him into spying. Jeanmaire claimed that he never received money for his services and felt compelled to assist them in fear of being exposed. (Bittman, *The KGB and Soviet Disinformation; Facts on File*, 1976–77; *New York Times*, November 11, 25, 1976; June 15, 18, 21; October 28, 1977)

268   Jeffries, Randy Miles.   Jeffries was a messenger handling confidential transcripts of closed committee hearings of the House of Representatives, including the Armed Services Committee. Jeffries approached the office of the Soviet military attaché with some samples. Jeffries had taken the documents from the Acme Reporting Company, a transcription company, where he was a messenger. A few days later he met what he thought to be a Soviet contact, actually an undercover FBI agent, and offered to sell documents. He was sentenced in 1986 to three years for espionage. Jeffries was motivated by his heroin habit. (Allen and Polmar, *Merchants of Treason; Facts on File*, 1986; *New York Times*, January 15, 24; March 14, 1986)

269   John, Otto.   First director of the Federal Internal Security Office, West Germany's version of the FBI. During World War II John participated in the conspiracy against Hitler and escaped to Spain when it failed, then to England where he participated in British radio propaganda effort against Nazi Germany. After the war, he helped interrogate Nazis for the trial at Nuremberg. He returned to Germany to head the Federal Internal Security Office in 1950, which was responsible for Soviet counterintelligence.

In 1954 he attended the ten-year memorial service for those who died during the coup attempt against Hitler. After the service witnesses saw John leave in the car of Dr. Wolfgang Wohlgemuth, unknown to John an East German agent. They drove through an East German checkpoint, no doubt to the surprise of John. Evidence indicating John's defection and betrayal was fabricated in East Berlin. He was encouraged to write propaganda tracts and fulfill the role of a defector, no doubt with apprehension. In 1955 he managed to escape back across the border where he was arrested by West

German officials for treason. During the interrogation, he maintained that he had been drugged and kidnapped. The star witness against him was Dr. Carl Wittig, supposedly a West German agent but later revealed to be a double agent for East Germany. He was found guilty and sentenced to four years.

Ironically, Wittig was later arrested by East German officials and accused of being a double agent for West Germany. The East Germans interrogated Wittig, who disclosed his prewar relationship with Nazi and Czechoslovak intelligence. (Bittman, *The KGB and Soviet Disinformation;* Frischauer, *The Man Who Came Back;* John, *Twice Through the Lines*)

270   Johnson, Robert Lee, and James Allen Mintkenbaugh.   Johnson in 1953 approached the Soviets to defect, but they convinced him that if he wanted to get revenge on the army, he could work as a spy for them. As a military clerk in Berlin in the fall of 1952, he became angry at not receiving a promotion. In February 1953 he went to East Germany and met with two KGB officers. He had met his wife while stationed in Vienna in 1948. She had been a prostitute, and he agreed to marry her only if she would help him contact the Soviets, which she finally did. On what was supposed to be his honeymoon, Johnson took leave from the army and went to East Germany to be trained in espionage techniques. His Austrian wife was taught some courier and espionage responsibilities. He was assigned a case officer by the name of Paula, real name Vladimir Vasilevich Krivoshey, who encouraged him to get a position in G-2 (intelligence) in Berlin Command where he was able to get a clerk position and pass unimportant documents to the Soviets.

It was at Berlin Command that Johnson met an old friend from three years before at Fort Hood, Texas — Sergeant James Allen Mintkenbaugh. Johnson admitted to him that he was making extra money spying for the Soviets and convinced him to do the same. He introduced him to his KGB contact, and Paula reasoned correctly that he was a homosexual. He asked Mintkenbaugh to identify other homosexuals in the military, particularly those in security positions, and the KGB later ordered Mintkenbaugh to disassociate himself from Johnson.

Johnson was sent as a finance clerk to France; the KGB lost interest in him at the new position and began concentrating on developing Mintkenbaugh, later discharged from the Army in July 1956. In January 1957 Mintkenbaugh contacted Johnson in the United States and said he had left the army in 1956 and was working with the KGB on different projects. He suggested that Johnson could go back to work for the KGB if he reenlisted, which he did.

His first position was at the Nike-Hercules missile site in Palos Verdes Peninsula, California, where he had access to a variety of documents on the missile site in 1957–58. Mintkenbaugh served as his KGB contact and courier. He would take the data to his KGB contact at the embassy in Washington, D.C., Petr Nikolaevich Yeliseev, who called himself Charles. In 1958 he went to Fort Bliss near El Paso, Texas, and gathered more missile data. At one point Mintkenbaugh flew to Moscow and met with KGB officers. When Johnson was reassigned at the Armed Forces Courier Station at Orly Airport outside Paris, Mintkenbaugh continued to act as liaison with the KGB. Here he had access to the top secret vault which contained communications between U.S. commands in Europe and Washington, D.C., and the rest of the world. From December 1961 to April 1963, he gave the KGB a treasure trove of classified documents. Some of them were top secret contingency plans for a war in Europe.

His KGB case officer in Paris, Feliks Ivanov, brought in a special KGB technical team to help Johnson get past the sophisticated locks and security systems. They provided him with a portable X-ray machine to photograph the mechanics of the lock on a safe to learn the combination. At midnight Johnson would give the documents to the KGB, who would take them to the embassy and photograph them and return them to Johnson at 3:00 A.M. Johnson entered the vault seven times between December 1962 and April 1963. One night Johnson fell asleep and missed the KGB courier, who had placed the bags in his car out of desperation. Johnson was able to find them in time.

In December 1962 Khrushchev sent congratulations to Johnson and ordered that he be awarded the rank of major in the Soviet Army. In May 1964 he was transferred to a position in the Pentagon, and his wife was in psychiatric counseling. His wife nagged him and threatened to turn him in as a spy. Johnson had suffered a court-martial demotion when he was absent without leave from his courier responsibilities for the Pentagon in December 1964 (from staff sergeant to sergeant). Six months later he deserted his post and went to Nevada.

The FBI investigated his disappearance and discovered his wife in a psychiatric ward telling a story about her husband's spying for the Soviets. Despite her condition, her details were convincing.

In November 1964 FBI agents arrested Johnson and Mintkenbaugh for spying for the Soviet Union. The FBI officials stated that the espionage had taken place in numerous locations around the world: Berlin, Paris, California, Texas, and the Soviet Union. They provided classified data on missile sites, military facilities, and intelligence operations.

After being discharged as a sergeant in 1956, Mintkenbaugh is believed to have taken a special espionage course in Moscow. The FBI named Vitaly Ourjoumov, a former attaché at the Soviet embassy in Paris, as a coconspirator, along with 11 other Soviets as contacts. Both were sentenced to 25 years.

In May 1972 Johnson's son, Robert, fresh from a tour in Vietnam and bitter about his father's treason, stabbed him to death during a family visit at the federal prison in Lewisburg, Pennsylvania. His son explained to the FBI that he killed him for personal reasons. (Andrew and Gordievsky, *KGB*; Barron, *KGB*; Rositzke, *The KGB*; West, *The Circus*)

271 Jordan-Rozwadowska, Lucia. She was a Polish native but was a British citizen at the time of her arrest. She was arrested in 1961 while engaged in espionage against Polish military units, convicted in 1962 for espionage in Poland for an unidentified Western country, and sentenced to six years. (*Facts on File*, 1962; *New York Times*, January 19; March 8, 1962)

272 Kahlig-Scheffler, Dagmar. In October 1978, Kahlig-Scheffler, former secretary in the office of Chancellor Helmut Schmidt, was convicted of spying for East Germany and sentenced to three years. She had a love affair with an East German agent, Herbert Schroter, who encouraged her to get a job in the chancellor's office so that she could pass information to him. This was a common tactic by East German intelligence agents. (*Facts on File*, 1978)

273 Kahr, Alouis. In July 1969, a Vienna court sentenced Kahr, former Austrian Foreign Ministry code specialist, to two years for passing classified data to the Soviet Union. (*Facts on File*, 1969; *New York Times*, July 5, 1969)

274 Kalinin, V. G. In January 1975 *Izvestia* announced that Kalinin had been found guilty of spying for an unidentified country. Reportedly, he was executed. (*Facts on File*, 1975; *New York Times*, February 21, 1975)

275 Kalmanovitz, Shabtai. Prominent Israeli businessman arrested for espionage for the Soviet Union in December 1987. Had extensive business links with the Soviet Union and Africa, with high-level contacts within the Israeli government. He arrived in Israel in 1971 from the Soviet Union as a spy for the KGB; with their financial help, he became a successful businessman and a member of the Labour party. He made a variety of high-level contacts in Israeli political and military leadership. South African intelligence officials warned Israeli intelligence that Kalmanovitz was building a Soviet spy network in South Africa. Shin Bet, Israel's security service, trailed him to Europe where he made a drop for his KGB controllers. Upon his return to Israel, he was arrested and sentenced to nine years in 1989. (Black and Morris, *Israel's Secret Wars*; Raviv and Melman, *Every Spy a Prince*)

276   Kalp, Malcolm.   One of the 52 Americans held hostage in Tehran during the hostage crisis. Kalp was singled out by the Iranians as a CIA agent. He was severely beaten for attempting to escape on three occasions and spent a total of 374 days in solitary confinement. In December 1979, Iranian students announced that a State Department cable confirmed that Kalp had been a CIA agent. The cable stated that Kalp needed State Department cover as third secretary. In April 1980, Iranian TV showed a video of one of the American hostages, Army S.Sgt. Joseph Subic, being interviewed, discussing U.S. surveillance flights over Iran. One scene showed Subic showing Iranians a secret hiding place in the floor and ceiling in the embassy warehouse that held computer equipment. Subic also identified Kalp as a CIA agent. United States TV networks refused to buy the video from the Iranians under the condition that the tape not be edited. (*Facts on File*, 1979–81; McFadden, Treaster, and Carroll, *No Hiding Place*; Moody, *444 Days*)

277   Kaminsky, Mark I., and Harvey C. Bennett.   Arrested in the Soviet Union in August 1960 for espionage, they were accused of gathering data on the Soviet military. They had entered the Soviet Union from Finland on an auto tour. Kaminsky was tried and convicted of espionage, receiving a sentence of seven years, but was released the same year along with Bennett. Both were U.S. Air Force veterans, and both spoke fluent Russian. Reportedly, Kaminsky confessed in a Kiev court to espionage but denied it when he was released in October. They were recruited by the CIA to gather data on the Soviet military, using fake travel grants given out by the Northcraft Educational Fund of Philadelphia, which was not publicly listed, later traced to the CIA. (*Facts on File*, 1960; *New York Times*, October 7, 17, 1960; Wise and Ross, *The Invisible Government*)

278   Kampiles, William Peter.   Kampiles joined the CIA in March 1977 after graduating from Indiana University, on the basis of his knowledge of modern Greek. He had an overrated image of himself as a master spy, but instead of being involved in James Bond–style operations, he was assigned to the Watch Center. The Watch Center received reports 24 hours a day from CIA stations around the world. Kampiles worked as a watch officer for the CIA from March to November 1977. Despite the access to inside information to some of the most exciting CIA operations around the world, Kampiles became bitter about not being part of the action.

He attempted to transfer to Clandestine Services (CS), but at the time DCI Stanfield Turner was cutting back the division in what has been called the "October Massacre." He claimed that he quit the CIA because he could not advance above a clerk position to a covert operations position.

He resigned within a year of joining the CIA, in November 1977, stealing copy 155 of a KH-11 photoreconnaissance satellite manual. The KH-11 ("Big Bird") satellite was state of the art, able to provide "real time" pictures of events on the surface. Launched in December 1976, the KH-11 was equipped with an infrared and multispectral photographic device. The CIA reportedly did not notice the manual missing for over a year.

In March 1978 he traveled to Athens, Greece, and visited the Soviet embassy where he sold the manual for $3,000. The Soviets encouraged him to rejoin the CIA as spy for the Soviets. Kampiles liked the idea of being a double agent, returned to Washington, and contacted the CIA about rejoining. He hoped to be rehired and admitted during an interview that he had met with Soviet agents in Greece in an exercise of disinformation to prove his abilities as a first-rate agent. The CIA was disturbed by the revelation and contacted the FBI, who questioned Kampiles till he confessed about the theft of the manual and its sale to the Soviets.

In August 1978, the FBI arrested Kampiles for selling a classified U.S. document to a Soviet agent in Greece in March 1978. The CIA discovered that thirteen other satellite manuals were missing but could not prove that Kampiles was involved. The Kampiles case was a security embarrassment for the CIA and raised questions of a Soviet mole in the higher echelons of the CIA. (Barron, *KGB Today;* Ranelagh, *The Agency;* Turner, *Secrecy and Democracy;* West, *The SIGINT Secrets*)

279   K'ang Sheng (b. 1903).   Director of the Chinese Social Affairs Department, responsible for internal security–foreign intelligence till the 1960s. One of the earliest members of the Chinese Communist party (CCP), K'ang attended Shanghai University where he joined the Communist Youth League. In 1924 he became a full member of the CCP and he began working as a labor organizer in Shanghai, a cover for espionage.

In 1925–27 he was director of the Organization Department of the CCP in Shanghai. In 1933 he was sent to Moscow to study Soviet intelligence and security methods. In 1937 he returned to China to take charge of intelligence operations in the new Communist capital of Yenan in North Shensi, replacing the director of the Political Security Bureau. In November 1938, the Political Security Bureau was abolished, and intelligence and security functions were consolidated within the newly formed Social Affairs Department (SAD).

In 1939 K'ang became the director of the SAD, which was responsible for internal and external security and intelligence tasks and also responsible for the CCP's security policies and plans, intelligence gathering, and counterintelligence functions. (Deacon, *The Chinese Secret Service;* Rice, *Mao's Way;* Richelson, *Foreign Intelligence Organizations;* Wise and Ross, *The Espionage Establishment*)

280   Kao Liang (b. 1930).   In 1971 Kao was sent as part of the first Chinese delegation to the UN in New York City. The CIA was well aware that Kao was an intelligence officer from his operations in Africa under cover of a journalist for the China News Agency.

A specialist in African, Middle Eastern, and Far Eastern Affairs, Kao was chief African correspondent of the CNA. Before joining the CNA, he was secretary of the Chinese Communist party committee in Hungchao, a suburb of Shanghai.

Over the years Kao managed to get expelled from both India and the Mauritas for espionage activities. In 1961 he was sent to Africa where he made contacts with Tanzanian politicians and political opponents. He instigated the Chinese-inspired coup in Zanzibar in 1964, providing arms and cash for Sheik Babu. (Deacon, *The Chinese Secret Service*; Wise and Ross, *The Espionage Establishment*)

281   Kapustin, Y. A.   In 1981, Kapustin was arrested by Soviet authorities and accused of being a spy for the CIA. Reportedly, Kapustin was discovered with sensitive documents. No other information was disclosed. (*Facts on File*, 1981)

282   Katkov, Mikhail.   In December 1987, Katkov, second secretary at the Soviet UN mission, was arrested for espionage and expelled. The FBI arrested Katkov after he attempted to gain U.S. military secrets. (*Facts on File*, 1987; *New York Times*, December 18, 19, 1987)

283   Kauffman, Joseph P.   A U.S. Air Force captain convicted of espionage for the East Germans while stationed in West Germany in 1962. He claimed that he had been entrapped into spying while visiting East Germany. He provided data from duty stations in Japan and Greenland where he provided information about personality traits of his fellow Air Force officers. This provided them with a list of individuals, with personality and personal traits to target for recruitment in the future. He also provided data on U.S. Air Force installations in Japan and Greenland. It was the East German defector Guenther Maennel, a former intelligence agent, who identified Kauffman. Kauffman was court-martialed in 1962 and sentenced to twenty years' hard labor. (Allen and Polmar, *Merchants of Treason*; Rositzke, *The KGB*)

284   Kazan-Komarek, Vladimir.   In February 1967, the Czech government expelled Kazan-Komarek, a Czech-born U.S. travel agent, after a Prague court found him guilty of spying for French intelligence from September 1948 to December 1950. He was sentenced to eight years but was expelled at the end of the trial. He had been arrested in October 1966 when his flight to Paris was forced to make an unscheduled landing in Prague. The U.S. government reacted by stopping all visas for Czech students and businessmen. The Czech authorities accused Kazan-Komarek of attempting to form an opposition group in Czechoslovakia against the Communist government from 1948 to 1950.

Reportedly, Kazan-Komarek had participated in the killing of three border guards when he was attempting to smuggle three Czechs into West Germany in 1950. Kazan-Komarek left Czechoslovakia in 1948, living first in West Germany, then France, and later moved to the U.S. in 1955, becoming a citizen in 1960. He admitted after his release that many of the charges were true. (*Facts on File*, 1967; *New York Times*, January 17, 31; February 2, 16, 1967)

285   Kearn, Bruce L.   Officer aboard the tank landing ship *Tuscaloosa* who stole classified documents, including cryptographic information, on an unauthorized leave from his ship in March 1984. A search of his room revealed 147 microfiche in his briefcase. The microfiche contained seven classified cryptographic publications. Authorities also found a large cache of child pornography. He was arrested in 1984 and sentenced to four years. (Allen and Polmar, *Merchants of Treason*)

286   Kedar, Mordecai ("Motke").   Kedar was born in Poland in the early 1930s as Mordecai Kravitzki. He was abandoned by his mother and brought by his grandfather to Palestine where he lived in the agricultural town of Hedera. In the 1948 war, he served in the Israeli Navy but went AWOL. In the early 1950s he became a gang leader of a small violent group in Hadera. They stole cars and were linked to armed robbery and murder cases. Kedar was finally arrested, but residents of Hadera feared retaliation by the gang, and they refused to testify against him.

He moved to Tel Aviv and started to go to a psychiatrist, Dr. David Rudi. What Kedar did not know was that Rudi was on the payroll of the intelligence community. Dr. Rudi introduced Kedar to General Yehoshafat Harkabi, head of Aman, who recruited Kedar for Unit 131 in the summer of 1956 for a mission to Egypt.

In March 1957 he was sent to Argentina to develop a cover story as an Argentine-Egyptian before being sent to Egypt. He lived in the home of a prosperous Argentine Jew who was helping to construct a cover story before his mission to Egypt. While there, he had an affair with his host's daughter, and after an argument he stabbed his host 80 times, stealing $80,000, which he said he needed to set up a secret meeting between Israeli and Egyptian officials.

Kedar went to Paris but returned to Israel in 1962 where he was arrested and sentenced by a secret military court to life. While in the Ramle prison, he was held in complete secrecy, known as "prisoner X." He was released in 1974 after 17 years. (Black and Morris, *Israel's Secret Wars;* Raviv and Melman, *Every Spy a Prince*)

287   Keenan, Helen.   Keenan, a shorthand typist at the British cabinet office, one of the famous "garden girls" of Downing Street, was recruited as an agent for the Rhodesian Special Branch. In May 1967 she resigned, complaining that her job was dull and boring. The supervisor became suspicious and notified the Special Branch, who discovered her real reason for leaving.

Keenan had visited the Zambesi Club, a well-known bar frequented by South Africans and Rhodesians. She had met a young surveyor, actually a South African intelligence service agent, Norman Blackburn. He asked for any documents on Rhodesia that she could find. On July 25, 1967, both were convicted; Keenan was sentenced to six months, Blackburn to five years. (West, *The Circus*)

288   Kerenyi, Maria.   In July 1970, Kerenyi, German-language specialist employed by Hungarian radio, was arrested in Budapest on charges of spying for West Germany. Reportedly, she had given classified documents to West German agents since 1968. (*Facts on File,* 1970)

Kerst, Kenneth A. see **Stolz, Richard F.**

289   Khokhlov, Nikolai Evgenevich (b. 1922).   During World War II he learned German and infiltrated a German POW camp in Russia, posing as German Army officer. In 1943 he parachuted behind German lines on an assassination mission against Wilhelm Kube at the German headquarters in Minsk. After careful planning, Kube was killed while lying on his bed, a bomb underneath.

In February 1954 he was ordered to assassinate Georgi Sergeevich Okolovich in Frankfurt, West Germany (called Operation Rhein). Fed up with the bureau's activities, he decided to defect. He went to Okolovich and introduced himself as a member of the KGB Special Bureau, not to kill him but to warn him. Okolovich was a leader of the Russian anti–Communist émigré organization, the National Alliance of Russian Solidarists (NTS), headquartered in Frankfurt, West Germany. Khokhlov identified East German agents who were to perform the killing, Feliks Kukovich and Franz Weber. Khokhlov identified them and their location to Western intelligence, who arrested them. Khokhlov then led the CIA to a hidden battery in the woods near Munich. The battery contained a gold cigarette case that transformed into an electric pistol that fired poison bullets.

Khokhlov continued to identify other agents and operations in Europe.

He went on speaking tours, warning of the Soviet threat. The KGB was not amused and placed his name on a death list. In September 15, 1957, he collapsed at a Frankfurt convention after being poisoned. After an exhaustive battle between life and death, he managed to survive, with the help of American doctors. Medical doctors discovered that he had been poisoned with radioactive thallium. (Andrew and Gordievsky, *KGB*; Barron, *KGB*; Brook-Shepherd, *The Storm Birds*; Khokhlov, *In the Name of Conscience*; Romerstein and Levchenko, *The KGB Against the "Main Enemy"*)

290   Khvostantsev, Lev G.   In February 1977, Khvostantsev, a Soviet scientist, was expelled from Canada for espionage activities. Khvostantsev had been in Canada on an exchange program but was caught attempting to buy classified data from a researcher at the National Research Council. The research notified the Royal Canadian Mounted Police (RCMP) about the approach, and the RCMP arranged for two unclassified documents to be sold to Khvostantsev during a sting operation. (*Facts on File*, 1977; *New York Times*, February 25, 1977)

291   Kianuri, Nureddin.   The leader of the Communist Tudeh party in Iran, he was arrested in 1983 for spying for the Soviet Union. This was part of a large crackdown on Tudeh party officials. Scholars viewed this as an attempt to eliminate the Tudeh party and charged that the charges were false. The Iranians were angry at the Soviet Union for backing Iraq in the war and blamed the Tudeh party; according to former KGB agent Ilya Dzhirkvelov, who worked in Iran, the Tudeh was a popular target of recruitment by the KGB. (Dzhirkvelov, *Secret Servant*; *Facts on File*, 1983)

292   Kim Hyung Wook.   In June 1977, the former director of the Korean Central Intelligence Agency (KCIA) from 1963 to 1969, stated that Park Tong Sun (also known as Tongsun Park) had served as a KCIA agent in the United States Kim had assumed the post after taking part in the 1961 coup which brought President Park Chung Hee into power. Kim asserted that Park had been involved in a KCIA lobbying operation to influence the United Sstates Congress, using cash for military aid. Park and the South Korean government denied any involvement in the scheme. Kim stated that Park continued to work for the KCIA after 1969 and from 1971 to 1975 was paid between $500,000 to $1 million annually for his efforts. According to Kim, the KCIA in 1975 began to suspect that U.S. authorities suspected Park's activities. Kim claimed another Korean, Kim Han Cho (known also as Hancho C. Kim)) received payments for lobbying efforts in the U.S. for the KCIA (a trustee of the American University in Washington, D.C., and a well-known businessman). Kim Han Cho allegedly gave U.S. public officials $200,000 in cash in 1975–76. Kim also alleged that Moon

Sun Myung, head of the Unification Church (commonly referred to as "Moonies"), and an aide, Pak Bo Hi, had worked for the KCIA in propaganda purposes. Moon denied any involvement with the KCIA.

Kim reported that Han Byung Ki, former South Korean ambassador to Canada and former member of South Korea's UN observer mission, had worked for the KCIA to strangle political opposition by Korean nationals to the Park government in the United States.

Kim also named several minor agents of the KCIA: Alexander Kim, New York lawyer, and his brother Charles Kim, former chairman of the Diplomat National Bank in Washington, D.C.; Jhoon Rhee, head of a karate business in Washington, D.C.; and Sue Park Thomson, former congressional aide to Speaker of the House Carl Albert (D, Okla.).

On one occasion Kim stated (and then withdrew the statement) that the KCIA had given money to the presidential campaigns of President Johnson in 1964 and Sen. Hubert Humphrey (D, Minn) in 1968. (Boettcher, *Gifts of Deceit; Facts on File*, 1967, 1977)

293   Kim Kyoo Nam.   In July 1972, Kim, former South Korean National Assembly deputy, was executed by hanging for spying for North Korea. Kim, reportedly the head of the ring, had been arrested in February 1968 as part of an extensive spy network based in Japan and Europe. Twenty-two men and ten women were also arrested. (*Facts on File*, 1968–69, 1972)

294   Kim Yong Kyu.   The Korean Central Intelligence Agency (KCIA) announced the defection of a North Korean spy, Kim, in October 1976. Reportedly, Kim, along with two bodyguards, landed on an isolated island 250 miles south of Seoul but changed his mind about the operation and decided to defect. When his bodyguards refused to join him, he killed them. Kim identified 12 communist agents working in South Korea. (*Facts on File*, 1976; *New York Times*, October 31, 1976)

295   King, Jerry M.   In 1983 it was revealed that a top secret U.S. Army intelligence unit, called the Intelligence Support Activity, which was formed in 1980 to deal with the Iranian hostage crisis, was still in operation. Reportedly, Colonel King was in charge of the unit, which comprised a variety of Army specialists around the world. Originally designed to gather intelligence for the disastrous rescue mission of the hostages in Iran, the unit stayed together after the crisis. The size and budget of the unit was classified, and the army would acknowledge only that it was not operating in Central America.

In 1983, former Army Lieutenant Colonel James G. Gritz had been approached by the group during a mercenary trip into Laos looking for POWs in 1982 and 1983. The unit, calling itself "the activity," originally offered to help by sending commandos into Laos to find the location of POWs but withdrew its support when jurisdictional disputes erupted with the CIA. It is not known whether the unit survived after 1983. (*Facts on File*, 1983)

296 Kinsman, N. Richard. In July 1980 three men attacked the Jamaica home of Kinsman, a U.S. embassy diplomat, spraying it with machine guns and throwing a grenade into his yard. The attack came as the result of allegations made by the *Covert Action Information Bulletin* (CAIB) that Kinsman was a CIA agent. The bulletin was dedicated to exposing CIA agents and operations around the world. Louis Wolf, the coeditor of the bulletin, had stated at a news conference that the CIA station in Jamaica was one of Latin America's largest. Wolf identified Kinsman and several other members of the embassy as CIA agents bent on undermining the Socialist government of Michael Manley. Philip Agee later claimed that the shooting was a hoax. (Agee, *On the Run; Facts on File*, 1980; *New York Times*, July 5, 10, 1980)

297 Kirkpatrick, Lyman Bickford, Jr. (b. 1916). Kirkpatrick had been a leading candidate to succeed Allen Dulles as Director of the CIA, but when he contracted polio in 1952, he was confined to a wheelchair. He attended Princeton, then in 1942 joined the Office of Strategic Services (OSS), serving as a major in the war. In 1947 he joined the CIA as division chief from 1947 to 1950, then assistant director for special operations from 1950 to 1953, then inspector general from 1953 to 1961, and till 1965 he served as executive director. While in Bangkok, Thailand, in July 1952 he contracted polio, returning to the CIA in March 1953 physically devastated. After retirement he served as a political science professor at Brown University.

It was Kirkpatrick who interviewed three hundred CIA officers on the Cuban Bay of Pigs operation and came out with a devastating negative report on the planning and implantation of the invasion, claiming that the secrecy of the invasion had been blown by the Miami Cuban community. Kirkpatrick earned the Distinguished Intelligence Medal for his service. (Freemantle, *CIA*; Kirkpatrick, *The Real CIA, The U.S. Intelligence Community*; Powers, *The Man Who Kept the Secrets*; Smith, *OSS*; Wyden, *The Bay of Pigs*)

298 Kiryczenko, Wiktor. In January 1977, Kiryczenko, first secretary and consul for the Polish embassy in Denmark, was expelled for espionage activities. Kiryczenko was the first Polish diplomat to be expelled by the Danish government. (*Facts on File*, 1977)

299 Kisilev, Lev. Kisilev, second secretary at the Soviet embassy in Reykjavik, was arrested in February 1963 for espionage. According to reports, he had approached members of the Icelandic Communist party (ICP) to spy on the U.S. military base at Keflavik. He was later expelled from the country. Apparently, members of the ICP had informed authorities of the approach. One member, Ragnar Gunnarsson, acted as a double agent and trapped the Soviet in a meeting outside Reykjavik. (*Facts on File*, 1963)

300   Kislitsyn, Filipp Vasilyevich.   Worked as a KGB cipher clerk in the London embassy 1945-48. While in London, he handled the files and documents that Guy Burgess would deliver to his Soviet handlers. In 1949 Kislitsyn was appointed to the top secret English archives at the Moscow KGB headquarters, primarily material from Donald Maclean and Guy Burgess. Ten years later he was with the Soviet legation in Canberra, Australia, as first director of information. (Andrew and Gordievsky, *KGB*; Boyle, *The Fourth Man*; Brook-Shepherd, *The Storm Birds*; Costello, *Mask of Treachery*)

301   Kisseleff, Andrei.   In August 1975, the Soviet Union withdrew Kisseleff, a military attaché at the Soviet embassy in The Hague, after the Dutch government accused him of espionage activities. According to government officials, Kisseleff had attempted to gain classified documents from a senior Dutch official in NATO. (*Facts on File*, 1975)

302   Klingberg, Marcus.   Arriving in Israel in 1948 from Eastern Europe, Russian-born, he had served in the Soviet Army as an epidemiologist. He studied natural sciences and in the late 1960s was appointed deputy director of the government's high-security Biological and Chemical Warfare Institute in the town of Nes Ziona. While in this position, he would frequently travel to Switzerland for health reasons. Shin Bet became curious and began a surveillance operation. While he was in Switzerland, Shin Bet agents rushed to his office and searched his apartment and office. The surveillance and growing evidence led to his arrest in 1983 for espionage, and he was sentenced to life. He was going to Switzerland not to see a doctor but to meet his Soviet contacts. (Black and Morris, *Israel's Secret Wars*; Raviv and Melman, *Every Spy a Prince*)

303   Klopfleisch, Erich, and Hubert Obieglo.   In February 1978 a West German court sentenced Klopfleisch and Hubert and Johanna Obieglo, to three years for spying for East Germany while Klopfleisch was employed by the Zeiss optical firm. Klopfleisch was accused of giving Hubert Obieglo photographs of the Orion 80 targeting optical device, made by Zeiss for West German tanks, in 1976. (*Facts on File*, 1978)

304 Knoppe, Wolf Diethard, and Josef Linowsky. In
October 1968, West German authorities arrested a West German Air Force
pilot, Warrant Officer Knoppe, and a mechanic, Linowsky, for stealing a
Sidewinder air-to-air missile and shipping it to the Soviet Union. Both men
stole a ten-foot Sidewinder missile from the NATO Zell Air Base in Bavaria
in October 1967. They placed the missile in their car and were forced to
break out the back window to fit it in wrapped in a carpet. They drove over
one hundred miles while it hung out of the rear window. They disassembled
the missile and shipped it to the Soviet Union. Both men were also accused
of stealing air navigation equipment and shipping it to the Soviet Union.
(*Facts on File*, 1968; *New York Times*, October 27, 30, 1968)

305 Knufelmann, Manfred, and Valerian Kuzniak. Knu-
felmann, West German citizen, and Kuzniak, a Belgian, were arrested by
West German agents for attempting to sell NATO aircraft plans to Eastbloc
agents. Kuzniak was arrested in July 1976 in Munich while attempting to
pass plans for NATO's Tornado fighter. Knufelmann was described as an
accomplice. The Tornado documents were stolen from a computer center
of Messerschmitt-Boelkow-Blohm, an aircraft construction company. (*Facts
on File*, 1976)

306 Knuth, Maria. Part of the Kolberg spy ring. Kolberg was
the code name of a Polish spy ring in West Germany headed by Col. Gregor
Kowalski, who recruited Heinko Kunze, who posed as an art historian. His
mistress, Maria Knuth, an aspiring actress, was recruited as a "swallow" for
seducing British and American targets. Kunze became depressed at having
his mistress used as a spy-whore and committed suicide. Knuth continued
her activities unabated.

The main target was to recruit people involved in the German rearmament program. She was able to seduce and blackmail Theodore Blank, a
cabinet minister, who was involved in the program. The German counterintelligence agency (BfV) sensed an operation and an agent, Ernst Boldt,
went undercover as "Dr. Petersen," an official of the rearmament project.
Knuth was sent to seduce him, and they met. Boldt described to her his
disillusionment with the rearmament process and discussed the possibility
of getting her a job in his office. For a while, Boldt would pass false data
to her, but in May 1952 she was arrested retrieving a letter from a dead drop
in Cologne. (Cookridge, *Gehlen*; Gehlen, *The Service*; Hagen, *The Secret
War for Europe*)

307 Kobayashi, Kazuo. In August 1971, Japanese authorities
arrested Kobayashi on charges of buying classified data from U.S. ser-
vicemen and selling them to an assistant military attaché at the Soviet

embassy, Lieutenant Colonel D. Kononov, actually a GRU intelligence officer. Kobayashi, a Japanese dealer in radio equipment, was caught with diagrams of the U.S. F-4 Phantom fighter. Kononov left Tokyo after Kobayashi's arrest. (*Facts on File, 1971*)

Koecher, Hana see Koecher, Karl F.

308 Koecher, Karl F., and wife, Hana. Czech-born couple arrested by the United States in 1984 for spying for Czechoslovakia. Koecher had been a contract employee for the CIA in Washington, D.C., 1973–75 as a translator and in New York City from 1975 to 1977. The FBI reported that Koecher had been recruited by Czechoslovakian intelligence in 1963. Koecher's duties in the CIA allowed him extensive access to classified data on Czechoslovakia. Koecher admitted his activities and implicated his wife. Koecher's lawyer insisted that they had been double agents for the CIA, feeding their Czech handlers false information, but the FBI and CIA discounted their version. They had been arrested a few hours before they were to leave the United States for Switzerland. The couple had emigrated from Czechoslovakia in 1965. They were later exchanged in 1986 for Soviet Jewish dissident Anatoly Shcharansky. (Allen and Polmar, *Merchants of Treason;* Corson and Crowley, *The New KGB;* Ranelagh, *The Agency*)

309 Kolasch, Helmut Stefan. Arrested by West German authorities in March 1988 for selling classified data on the Euro-fighter and NATO's Tornado fighter. Kolasch was an engineer who had worked on both projects and had spied for the Soviets since 1971. (*Facts on File, 1988*)

310 Koleshnikov, Yuri. In January 1985, Koleshnikov, cultural attaché at the Soviet embassy in Spain, was expelled for attempting to buy secret data on Spanish technology and scientific policy. (*Facts on File, 1985*)

311 Konstantinov, Oleg V. In April 1983, several Soviet diplomats were expelled from the U.S. Konstantinov, a member of the Soviet mission to the UN, had been caught after approaching a double agent for the FBI, seeking military information. (*Facts on File, 1983; New York Times, April 21, 22, 1983*)

Koppe, Johannes see Fuelle, Rainer

312 Korisko, Frantisek. In April 1972, Korisko, third secretary in the Czechoslovakian embassy in Paris, was arrested for receiving classified documents and expelled. The Czech government retaliated by expelling Georges Vaugier, third secretary for the French embassy in Prague, on the charge of espionage. (*Facts on File*, 1972)

313 Korolyuk, Viktor N. In late 1980, Korolyuk, the ranking Soviet interpreter at the Mutual and Balanced Force Reduction negotiations in Vienna, defected to West Germany. Reportedly, Korolyuk was believed to be a KGB major who delivered a variety of sensitive negotiation papers. Korolyuk had used a diplomatic passport to escape to West Germany; it was considered unusual for a mere translator to possess a diplomatic passport. (*Facts on File*, 1981; *New York Times*, January 9, 1981)

314 Korotkov, Alexander Mikhailovich ("Sasha"). In the late 1940s and 1950s, head of KGB Illegals Directorate. He was in charge of recruiting Jews to spy on Israel. Jews leaving the Soviet Union to emmigrate to Israel were a popular target for recruitment. Many shared both a Socialist belief and Jewish tradition. (Andrew and Gordievsky, *KGB*; Black and Morris, *Israel's Secret Wars*; Dzhirkvelov, *Secret Servant*; Romerstein and Levchenko, *The KGB Against the "Main Enemy"*)

315 Kostadinov, Penyu B. Bulgarian trade official indicted for spying in 1984, exchanged for East German–held spies in 1985. Kostadinov, assistant counselor at the Bulgarian Commercial Office in New York City, was arrested after obtaining classified documents on U.S. nuclear weapons. Reportedly, Kostadinov was identified as an agent for the Durzhavna Sigurnost, Bulgaria's secret police and security agency. Kostadinov had been trapped by an FBI sting operation, using a U.S. graduate student that Kostadinov had approached a few months before (the student had notified the FBI). While having dinner at a restaurant, the student gave Kostadinov the classified documents, and Kostadinov paid the student an unspecified amount and provided a new list of classified documents. Kostadinov was released briefly in the belief that he was eligible for diplomatic immunity, but after authorities discovered that his name was not listed, he was rearrested. (*Facts on File*, 1984–85; *New York Times*, January 18; May 11; October 10, 1984)

316 Kozlov, Alexei Mikhailovich. In 1981 KGB Major Kozlov was arrested by South African authorities. He was sent to South Africa to gauge the strength of the African National Congress in South Africa and the strength of the South-West Africa People's Organization. Kozlov had visited South Africa four times since 1976. In 1982 Kozlov was exchanged for a South African prisoner of war, Johan van der Mescht, an explosives specialist, who was captured by guerrillas of the South-West Africa People's Organization in Namibia and moved to a POW camp in Angola. The exchange took place in an unnamed European country. (*Facts on File,* 1981–82)

317   Krobock, Richard (1956–87).   Graduated in 1979 from West Point and became a second lieutenant in charge of a support troop servicing M-60 tanks at Fort Hood, Texas. In 1981, Krobock, now a first lieutenant, was accepted to the army's aviation branch, where he began helicopter training. After training he was sent to South Korea where he flew scout helicopters along the demilitarized zone between North and South Korea. While in South Korea, he began training in the AH-1 Cobra attack helicopter. In 1984, now a captain, he transferred to the Rapid Deployment Force in California and took command of a group of Cobra pilots.

Fearing a desk job as the next step in the promotion, Krobock applied for admission to army intelligence but was denied. Around the end of 1985, Krobock approached the CIA for employment and was accepted. In January 1987 Krobock was sent to El Salvador to keep tabs on U.S. financial aid to the Salvadorean government and as a military adviser. In March 1987 Krobock called home complaining of boredom and homesickness. On March 26 a UH-1 Huey helicopter carrying Krobock and four Salvadorean soldiers crashed outside the town of Chinameca, killing everyone on board. The CIA chiseled a two-inch star in his memory into the marble wall inside the entry foyer of the agency's headquarters. (Healy, "The Life and Death of an Intelligence Man," *U.S. News and World Report*)

Kroger, Helen see **Kroger, Peter John**

318   Kroger, Peter John (b. 1910), and Helen (b. 1913). Both immigrants from Poland, their real names were Morris and Lola Teresa Petra Cohen, U.S. citizens who used the alias Kroger. The Krogers were arrested, along with Gordon Lonsdale, Harry Houghton, and Ethel Gee, in Great Britain in 1961. When MI5 agents searched their home in 1961, they found photographic equipment, tape recorders, a shortwave radio transmitter hidden in the floor of the kitchen, microfilm inside a hollowed-out Bible, codebooks, cipher pads, and seven fake passports. The Krogers home appeared to be the main communication center for the ring for Moscow.

British intelligence discovered the Krogers after placing surveillance on Gordon Lonsdale. After a careful examination of fingerprints with the FBI and British intelligence, it was determined that the Krogers were really the Cohens who escaped the United States the day the Rosenbergs had been arrested. The Krogers moved to England in 1955 where Peter ran a small but specialized antiquarian bookstore in London, books on torture and sadomasochism, used as a cover for their operations. The Krogers had spied for the Soviets since World War II when Peter was in the U.S. Army. They were convicted of espionage in 1961 and sentenced to 20 years. They were exchanged for Gerald Brooke, Michael Parsons, and Anthony Lorraine, all British citizens, in July 1969 and returned to their native Poland. (Bernikow, *Abel*; Rositzke, *The KGB*; Pincher, *Too Secret, Too Long*; West, *The Circus*; Wright, *Spy Catcher*)

319 Krotkov, Yuri Vasilevich. In 1963, Krotkov, a Soviet film writer, defected to MI5 while visiting London with a group of Soviet writers and artists. As a KGB informant and agent, he specialized in blackmail operations to entrap foreign diplomats. His information indicated that the Canadian ambassador for whom the RCMP was searching was John Watkins, who served in Moscow 1954–56. Watkins, upon hearing the charges from the RCMP, had a heart attack and died. Since World War II he had operated blackmail operations all over the world but was not a member of the KGB, simply a contract agent.

When he attended Moscow University to study literature, he made contacts with friends in the KGB. The KGB helped him get a job with Tass and later Radio Moscow. As he began to meet foreigners, the KGB would use him as a contact. He would bring in female KGB "sparrows" to seduce foreigners while they were unknowingly being photographed. He helped blackmail the French ambassador to Moscow, Maurice Dejean. (Barron, *KGB*; Dzhirkvelov, *Secret Servant*; Faligot and Krop, *La Piscine*; Pincher, *Too Secret, Too Long*)

320 Krybus, Marie Hildegarde. In May 1964, Krybus, a phone operator, was sentenced by a Polish military court to 15 years for espionage for the United States. Reportedly, she had given U.S. intelligence agents in West Germany classified data on Polish defense and economic information. Krybus's fiancé, Joachim Sobek, was sentenced to ten years for encouraging her to commit espionage. Both pled guilty to the charges. (*Facts on File*, 1964)

Kuang-Shin Lin see **Da-Chuan Zheng**

321 Kunkle, Craig D. Kunkle had attempted to sell classified data on antisubmarine warfare to FBI undercover agents posing as Soviet KGB agents. A former navy petty officer, he was arrested January 10, 1989, on espionage charges. Kunkle had been discharged from the navy in 1985 for indecent exposure. The FBI believed he was motivated by revenge. The FBI became aware of Kunkle's activities when he telephoned the Soviet embassy in Washington, monitored by counterintelligence agents, and revealed his plans to sell data to the Soviets. Kunkle pled guilty and was sentenced to 12 years. (*Facts on File*, 1989; *New York Times*, January 11, 19, 1989)

322 Kurochkin, Nikolai Ivanovich.   Third secretary of the Soviet embassy in Washington, deported in 1958 for attempting to buy U.S. Army manuals, including classified documents. Kurochkin approached Charles T. Beaumet, a writer, to gain access to documents. Beaumet notified the FBI, but Kurochkin could not be charged with espionage because he had registered himself as a foreign agent with the State Department. (*Facts on File*, 1958; *New York Times*, June 8, 1958; Newman, *Famous Soviet Spies*)

323 Kuzichkin, Vladimir Andreyevich (b. 1947).   In October 1982, Kuzichkin, under cover as vice consul of the Soviet embassy in Iran, defected to the British. Kuzichkin, a KGB officer, defected from Directorate S. He attended Moscow University, studied Farsi and Iranian issues, then joined the KGB in 1975. He was assigned to Directorate S, the department responsible for handling KGB agents who do not have diplomatic status, often referred to as "illegals" (deep cover agents). He was posted to Teheran in 1977 as an illegals support officer. By 1982, he was a major in the KGB, and that same year he defected to the British embassy in Teheran. (Andrew and Gordievsky, *KGB*; Barron, *KGB*)

Kuzniak, Valerian see **Knufelmann, Manfred**

324 Kyu Myung.   A research physicist at the University of Frankfurt, he was sentenced to death by a South Korean court for participating in a North Korean spy ring. Reportedly, Kyu had received spy training and money from North Korean agents between 1958 and 1967. (*Facts on File*, 1968)

325 Lansdale, Edward Geary (1908–87).   Served in the Office of Strategic Services (OSS) till the end of World War II when he became the chief of the intelligence division of the U.S. Army. In 1947 he transferred to the U.S. Air Force. He was assigned to the CIA in the Far East Division in 1950.

Sent to the Philippines in 1950, he created the Civil Affairs Office in the Philippines that studied the folk tales and superstitions of Filipino peasants. The result was a variety of bizarre psychological warfare operations that succeeded in wearing down the Huk insurgents. One operation involved using a mysterious voice from the sky who gave food and shelter to the Huk. The most famous and successful operation involved the *asuang*, the Filipinos' version of the vampire. A group of Filipino agents would infiltrate villages spreading rumors of a *asuang* living among the Huk. A special unit would then capture Huk soldiers as their patrols passed and kill them. They would be drained of their blood, and two holes would be punctured in their necks. The bodies would then be returned to the trail where they would be found the next day. It terrified the Huks, who quickly disbanded. Those who remained were unable to recruit from the frightened villagers. Another tactic was to use disguised Filipino soldiers dressed as Huks who would enter one village after another terrorizing the inhabitants. With the Huk rebellion falling apart, Lansdale created the Economic Development Corps that gave land to the Huks and helped provide agricultural assistance, helping gradually to settle the Huks back to peaceful coexistence. He received the National Security Medal for his work in the Philippines.

After the Philippines operation was wrapped up, he was sent to Vietnam in 1954 where he used propaganda tactics to encourage Christian Vietnamese in the North to the South, helping to destabilize the Buddhist majority in the South. One of Lansdale's key propaganda assets was Tom Dooley, who wrote outrageous stories of Communist atrocities on Christians in the North. Lansdale arrived in Vietnam shortly after the fall of French forces at Diem Bien Phu. His activities attracted the attention of Graham Greene, who based *The Quiet American* after him. Lansdale supported the Ngo Dinh Diem regime with a variety of projects. Lansdale helped set up the Saigon military mission in July 1954 as a cover for intelligence operations in South Vietnam. Lansdale helped convince Diem to claim nation status for South Vietnam and to become president, despite the Geneva agreement for nationwide elections by 1956. The assumption of the CIA and the U.S. military was that the North would oppose Diem with the use of conventional warfare. But the North abandoned the tactics used at Diem Bien Phu and switched to clandestine guerrilla warfare tactics, catching the U.S. military and CIA unprepared.

In 1961 Lansdale served as the Pentagon liaison for Operation Mongoose, helping to coordinate military support for the operation. Lansdale became chief of the Washington task force running the operation, with a CIA group under him called Task Force W headed by William Harvey, who supervised Shackley's Miami station. Lansdale coordinated CIA covert operations with the task force headquarters in Miami. (Ambrose, *Ike's Spies*; Colby, *Honorable Men, Lost Victory*; Hunt, *Undercover*; Lansdale, *In the Midst of Wars*; McCoy, *The Politics of Heroin*; Prados, *Presidents' Secret Wars*)

326   Larrimore, Don, and Joseph Shaw.   In 1963, Larrimore, a correspondent for the United Press International in Poland, and Shaw, a professor of Slavonic studies, were charged by *Izvestia* of attempting to recruit a Soviet youth for espionage purposes. Shortly after the article, the Polish government requested that Larrimore be replaced with another correspondent. (*Facts on File*, 1963; *New York Times*, August 2, 1963)

Lee, Andrew Daulton see Boyce, Christopher John

327 Lee, Robert. Soviet news agency Tass reported in 1980 that an American with links to the CIA had been arrested in Afghanistan during an anti–Soviet riot in February. The State Department had no record of Lee being in Afghanistan. Lee was released in May 1980 and left the country. Another American businessman, Charles Brockunier, was also arrested but later released after stating his regret for the incident. (*Facts on File*, 1980)

328 Leonov, Yuri Petrovich. In August 1983, Lieutenant Colonel Leonov, Soviet assistant air attaché, actually a GRU intelligence officer, was expelled after being caught with a briefcase full of classified documents. Serving as a GRU officer in September 1981, assistant military air attaché at the Soviet embassy in Washington he visited the office of Representative David F. Emery (R, Maine). He asked John Rabb, an aide, for a copy of a plan the congressman had developed for basing the MX missile. Rabb called the FBI as soon as the Soviet left the office. He was put under surveillance and expelled in August 1983. (*Facts on File*, 1983; Romerstein and Levchenko, *The KGB Against the "Main Enemy"*)

329 Levchenko, Stanislav Aleksandrovich. Levchenko attended Moscow University's Institute of Asian and African Studies in 1958. He studied the Japanese language in hopes of becoming a diplomat. He graduated in 1964, and in 1965 he was given a job as an interpreter in the International Department of the party's Central Committee, for the Soviet Peace Committee, which allowed him to visit Japan on several trips. In 1966 he began working in the Afro-Asian Solidarity Committee, helping in propaganda against the Vietnam War.

In 1966 he was drafted into the Soviet Army and underwent espionage training under GRU officers. In 1971 the KGB recruited him into the First Chief Directorate (foreign operations); after a year of training he was assigned as a lieutenant in the KGB and placed at the Japan desk. He worked under the cover of a journalist for the Moscow journal *New Times*, and in February 1975 he was sent to Tokyo as its Tokyo correspondent. Levchenko cultivated and maintained Japanese contacts in political, military, and economic circles.

In October 1979 Levchenko strolled into a party attended by U.S.

military and diplomatic personnel at the Sanno Hotel in Tokyo and requested to see a representative of U.S. intelligence. He was bitter about the harsh treatment and political infighting he had suffered in the KGB. He was the first KGB active measures agent to defect to the United States. In 1983 Levchenko named eight Japanese contacts from the 1970s, and stated that there were another 18 he named only by code name. The Japanese National Police Agency (NPA) was unable to prove any of the allegations made by Levchenko. Levchenko also described a code clerk who worked in the Foreign Ministry who provided thousands of classified documents to him, but the NPA was unable to identify the individual. Levchenko stated that there were at least two hundred Japanese on the KGB payroll and that he did not want to name all of them because he feared that many would commit suicide.

Levchenko did name three Socialists — Shigeru Ito, Seiichi Katsumata, and Tamotsu Sato — and a former Liberal Democratic labor minister, Hirohide Ishida; also named Takuji Yamane, who resigned as managing editor of the Tokyo daily *Sankei Shimbun.* The Soviet government condemned him to death in absentia, and when KGB agents recruited FBI agent Richard Miller, they requested information on the location of Levchenko in the United States, presumably in the hope of assassinating him. (Barron, *KGB Today;* Bittman, *The KGB and Soviet Disinformation;* Brook-Shepherd, *The Storm Birds;* Levchenko, *On the Wrong Side;* Romerstein and Levchenko, *The KGB Against the "Main Enemy")*

330   Li Ching-sun (alias Johnson Li).   In December 1970, Li, deputy director of the Broadcasting Corporation of China, was arrested by Taiwan authorities and charged with espionage for the Communists. Two conspirators, also arrested, committed suicide. Li was given a life sentence in December 1971 by a military court in Taipei. Li had served as a board chairman of the *Great China Evening News* and vice president of the Broadcasting Corporation of China. He was accused of having been engaged in Communist subversive activities.

Yu Chi, former deputy editor in chief of the *China Daily News* in Tainan, was sentenced to five years in jail for being a Communist party member. He had confessed to all his activities during the investigation, and his relatively brief sentence was said to be due the fact that his confessions had led to the arrest of Li. The military prosecutor read out a long statement charging that the defendants had been members of the Chinese Communist party since 1935 and had engaged in subversive activities against the government. Yu disclosed that he and Li belonged to the same cultural subcommittee of the Communist party in Fukien Province in 1938 when they were both working at the *Nanfang Daily News.* Yu went to Taiwan in 1946 and said that Li contacted him after his arrival in Taiwan in 1949.

Li, however, denied the entire contents of his alleged confession, charging that he had written it under threats by his interrogators and claiming that he had never been a member of the Communist party. The prosecution alleged that Li had followed directives to use newspapers as weapons to launch a bloodless revolution in Taiwan and that as far back as 1949, he had been ordered by his Communist boss, Pu Hsihsiu to use the newspapers in Taiwan to help weaken the people's support for the government and to strengthen Communist front organizations in Taiwan. (Deacon, *The Chinese Secret Service; Facts on File*, 1970)

331 Li Hung-shu. According to the Chinese, Li was recruited in 1967, sent to the Soviet Union for training, and returned to China in 1971 to spy. In January 1974 Chinese authorities expelled five KGB officers working out of the Soviet embassy in Beijing. The agents were accused of meeting Li under the Paho River bridge outside the outskirts of Beijing where they gave him a clandestine radio and fake border passes for espionage activities. During the meeting they were arrested by agents of Chinese Public Security. Li confessed to his activities, explaining that the Soviets had given him a password, "Allen." (Deacon, *The Chinese Secret Service*)

332 Liao Ho-Shu. In January 1969, Liao, China's chargé d'affaires in The Hague, Netherlands, defected to the United States. But in April 1972 he returned to China, claiming that he was unhappy in the West. Reportedly, when Liao defected, he spent 17 months in the custody of the CIA until July 1970 when he was given a job at Georgetown University in Washington, D.C. Reportedly, he said the Chinese center of espionage in Europe was in The Hague, Netherlands. Holland was used by the Chinese because there were a large number of Indonesians of Chinese descent living there. He used his diplomatic cover to organize agent networks in Holland. (Deacon, *The Chinese Secret Service; Facts on File*, 1969, 1973)

333 Lichtenecker, Karl. In September 1971, Lichtenecker, editor of the official Austrian Federal Press Service, was sentenced to ten months by an Austrian court for spying for Czechoslovakia. Lichtenecker was described as a civil servant in the chancellery press department. (*Facts on File*, 1971)

334 Liebetanz, Reinhard. In August 1985, Liebetanz, a West German intelligence officer in the Office for the Protection of the Constitution (BfV), was arrested on suspicion of espionage. Liebetanz was the chief of a department in charge of watching right-wing extremists. According to officials, Liebetanz was contacted by Eberhard Severin, an East German intelligence agent and close friend, who queried Liebetanz about defecting while he was vacationing in Austria. He was later released. (*Facts on File*, 1985)

335 Lieblang, James W. In August 1972, Italian authorities arrested Lieblang, former U.S. Army captain, on espionage charges, but later reduced the charges to sabotage and trespassing on a military base. Reportedly, he was arrested at Bressanone near a NATO installation. He was caught with maps, drawings, and photographs of missile facilities. He was charged originally with stealing classified documents from the NATO base, but he denied any espionage. (*Facts on File*, 1972; *New York Times*, August 2, 1972)

336 Lincoln, Alexandra. Lincoln, a U.S. citizen, was arrested by Swiss authorities in Bern for political espionage activities. Lincoln, while working as a barmaid, had collected information on Swiss officials and delivered it to a Libyan diplomat, Muhammad Abdul Malek, in Bern. Swiss authorities ordered Malek out of the country and gave Lincoln a two-and-one-half-month suspended sentence. (*Facts on File*, 1983; *New York Times*, March 18, 1983)

337 Lindsay, Franklin Anthony (b. 1916). Graduating in 1938 from Stanford University, he joined the U.S. Army in 1940 and later transferred to the OSS. He served deep behind German lines in Yugoslavia, working with Tito's partisans. After the war in 1945 he was appointed chief of the U.S. military mission to Yugoslavia. In 1949 he joined the CIA and was put in charge of the East European Division. He helped plan and operate the Albanian operation 1949–50. He was deputy chief of the Office of Policy Coordination 1949–51, then served as chief of East European Division till he quit the CIA in 1953. The Albanian operation involved the training of a small force of Albanian refugees into an army. They were parachuted in small groups inside Albania to carry out sabotage and attempt to overthrow the Communist government. Each time a group was sent into the country, it would lose radio contact. Unfortunately, the entire operation had been revealed to the Soviets by British double agent Kim Philby. (Bethell, *Betrayed*; Powers, *The Man Who Kept the Secrets*; Prados, *Presidents' Secret Wars*; Smith, *OSS*)

338 Linney, Brian Frederick. Working as an electronics engineer for the aerospace company Shoreham, he was sentenced for 14 years in a British court for selling secrets to a Czech military attaché in Britain, Colonel Oldrich Pribyl. Pribyl met Linney at a reception in London in 1955. Pribyl befriended him and two years later recruited him as an agent. Linney began working at Shoreham, which had access to RAF classified documents in 1957, mostly radar projects. After MI5 spotted him with Pribyl, they accused him of being a spy. After Linney confessed, he was sentenced to 14 years. (Pincher, *Too Secret, Too Long;* West, *The Circus;* Wright, *Spy Catcher*)

Linowsky, Josef see **Knoppe, Wolf Diethard**

Lippold, Eberhard see **Erb, Walter**

339   Lo Chengxun.   In 1982, Chengxun, editor in chief of the Communist newspaper in Hong Kong, was arrested in Beijing and jailed for 10 years for spying. He was charged with supplying U.S. intelligence with military, political, and diplomatic classified data over several years. He pled guilty. (*Facts on File,* 1983; *New York Times,* May 16, 1983)

340   Loginov, Yuri Nikolaevich (b. 1923).   In September 1967, South African authorities arrested Loginov, a Soviet spy. After questioning he revealed the names of Soviet agents in 23 Western countries. Loginov had entered South Africa with a Canadian passport in the name of Edmund Trinka in January 1967. In July 1969 he was exchanged for ten Soviet-held West German agents. The South Africans agreed to the exchange after receiving important military equipment. In September 1967, he was arrested by the South African Bureau of State Security (BOSS) while photographing a building that had previously been used by the South African police. Reportedly, Loginov had been briefed on Western customs by the famous Rudolf Abel. Loginov was under orders to study Rhodesia's relationship with South Africa and find out what Western country was helping South Africa in its atomic and missile research. (Barron, *KGB;* Carr, *Spy in the Sun;* Corson and Crowley, *The New KGB*)

341   Lonetree, Clayton J.   Lonetree, a Native-American, assigned to the Moscow embassy from 1984 to 1986, then as a Marine guard at the Vienna embassy from March to December 1986, was convicted in 1987 for spying for the Soviet Union and sentenced to 30 years. The prison term was reduced when Lonetree cooperated with intelligence debriefers. Reportedly, Lonetree's involvement in the espionage-security scandal was an act of revenge for the treatment of the American Indian by the U.S. government. He allowed the KGB into the communications center and the U.S. military attaché's office. Lonetree was also charged with providing the KGB with information on covert agents in the Soviet Union, classified documents, and blueprints of the Moscow embassy.

Lonetree, while at the U.S. embassy in Moscow, had been confined to quarters for 45 days for drinking and went out on the town after his confinement. By what he thought chance, he met, at a Moscow metro stop in

September 1985, Violetta Alexdrovna Seina, KGB agent. She worked as a translator at the embassy. Lonetree, lonely and desperate for female company, was seduced by Seina in January 1986. She introduced him to an "Uncle Sasha," actually Aleksiy Yefimov, a KGB intelligence officer. He was asked to help the Soviet Union, and he agreed to help him identify individuals at the embassy.

When Lonetree was transferred to Vienna, the KGB continued contact with him, paying him $1,000 for the identities of embassy personnel and floor plans of sensitive areas of the embassy. Lonetree provided a variety of data on the personalities, relationships, and work schedules of embassy personnel of both embassies. While in Vienna, he stole the contents of burn bags that contained classified documents to the Soviets. In December 1986, desperate to get out of his KGB relationship, he approached the CIA station chief in Vienna and confessed.

The CIA wanted to use him as a double agent, but the Naval Investigative Service arrested him. The entire marine guard force was replaced. Additional marines were also arrested for espionage. A second marine, Corporal Arnold Bracy, who served at the U.S. embassy in Moscow from July 1985 to September 1986, was also arrested. Bracy had also become involved sexually with an embassy cook. Though Bracy confessed to the charges, he later recanted his statement, and the charges were dropped in June 1987. A third marine was arrested — S.Sgt. Robert S. Stufflebeam, who had served as assistant commander of the guard detachment from May 1985 to May 1986. Stufflebeam was arrested for having contacts with Soviet women and not reporting it. No charges of espionage were filed against him, and he was discharged from the military on January 22, 1988. He had been demoted from staff sergeant to sergeant in September 1987 after he was convicted of two counts of dereliction of duty while serving as a guard at the U.S. embassy in Moscow.

Sergeant John J. Weirick was arrested on suspicion of espionage. Weirick had been a marine guard at the U.S. consulate in Leningrad from November 1981 to December 1982. Weirick was suspected of helping the KGB in Leningrad after a sexual liaison with a Russian woman. There was no direct connection between Weirick and the other three marines who served at the Moscow embassy. The charges were later dropped. (Allen and Polmar, *Merchants of Treason*; Headley, *The Court Martial of Clayton Lonetree*; Kessler, *Moscow Station*; Wise, *The Spy Who Got Away*)

342 Long, Leonard Henry ("Leo"). Long arrived at Trinity College, Cambridge, already a strong convert to communism, on a scholarship for modern languages. He grew up in a working-class family and was deeply aware of the class differences in British society. He met Anthony Blunt, who taught French literature and recruited him to spy for the

Soviets, personally handling Long during and after World War II. Long graduated in 1938 and taught 1938–39 in Frankfurt, Germany, where he got a taste of Nazi Germany.

When the war started, he joined the Intelligence Corps as a second lieutenant. In December 1940, he was assigned to MI14 in the War Office, which analyzed German troop movements from SIGINT intelligence, particularly from Ultra and later Enigma. He met Blunt during weekly meetings to pass information on German intelligence. Blunt would then pass information to his Soviet handlers. In 1943 MI14 was renamed the Military Intelligence Research Section. In 1945 Long moved from MI14 to the British Control Commission in Germany where he eventually became deputy director of intelligence. In 1946 Blunt tried to get Long transferred to a position at MI5, but Long was denied the post.

Long argued during his interrogation with MI5 in 1964 that he stopped spying at that point, but he contradicted himself by stating that it was the Burgess and Maclean defection in 1951 that convinced him to stop spying for the Soviets, and quit his post in Germany in 1952. In 1963 Blunt named Long and John Cairncross as spies, thus precipitating Long's interrogation by MI5. Long was not publicly exposed till November 1981, by Margaret Thatcher. Despite Long's admission, he was not prosecuted for his involvement. It was argued that since Long admitted to spying only during the war years, a time when the Soviet Union was considered an ally, there was no strong case for a conviction.

It is difficult to believe that the Soviets would have dropped an asset in Long's position in Germany so easily after Blunt stopped making contact with Long in 1946. (Andrew and Gordievsky, *KGB*; Costello, *Mask of Betrayal*; Pincher, *Too Secret Too Long*; West, *The Circus*; Wright, *Spy Catcher*)

343 Lonsdale, Gordon Arnold (1922–70).   Arrested in 1961 by British agents for espionage for the Soviets. He was revealed to MI5 when Harry Houghton was arrested. Born in Russia, his real name was Konan Trofimovich Molody. He was sent to Berkeley, California, in 1929 to live with relatives till 1938 when he returned to the Soviet Union. He joined the Soviet Army and fought in World War II.

He was recruited into the KGB and in 1954 was sent to Canada under the cover Lonsdale. The real Lonsdale was a Canadian citizen who had died in Finland during World War II. He spent a year in Canada, then moved to England. While in Great Britain, he operated Harry Houghton, who worked at the Portland Naval Base. He would take the data from Houghton and relay it to the Krogers, who transmitted it by radio to the Soviet Union. Though Russian, he passed himself off as a U.S. naval commander, traveling salesman, and Canadian student.

In 1961 MI5 spotted Houghton and Lonsdale at a meeting in a park and placed him under surveillance. A search of the Lonsdale home produced a Canadian passport and personal letters from the Soviet Union. They found undeveloped film of a classified naval document on the British naval building program, details of Britain's first nuclear submarine HMS *Dreadnought*, and documents about antisubmarine experiments.

He was convicted and sentenced to 25 years in 1961, but later exchanged for Greville Wynne in April 1964 at Heerstrasse on the border between East and West Germany. When he returned to the Soviet Union, he published a memoir of his spy adventures, calling it *Spy*. He earned the Red Star and Red Banner for his service. (Bernikow, *Abel*; Lonsdale, *Spy*; Maclean, *Take Nine Spies*; West, *The Circus*; Wright, *Spy Catcher*)

344   Loo, Roland Shensu.   In 1986 Loo was convicted of espionage in China for Taiwan. Loo, who emigrated to the United States in 1980, was sentenced to 12 years. He was arrested along with several others: Ning Nianci, an engineer; Yu Defu, director of the Beijing Science and Education Film Studio, Nianci's husband; and Zhu Junyi. The Chinese announced that Loo had traveled to China in 1984 and 1985, and received secret data on military, political, and economic conditions from Ning and Yu. Zhu began supplying information in 1985. Reportedly, Loo reported to an alleged spy for Taiwan, Yang Peng (Edward Yang), a professor at the University of California in Los Angeles. According to the Chinese, Professor Yang, Loo's connection, was connected to the Sino-American Cooperation Organization, which the Chinese described as an organization that had trained spies for Taiwan to infiltrate mainland China since 1941. (*Facts on File*, 1986; *New York Times*, August 24, 1986)

345   Lorenzen, Ursel.   In March 1979, Lorenzen, a secretary at NATO headquarters in Brussels, defected to East Germany. Reportedly, Lorenzen took classified documents along with her that detailed NATO war exercise plans and nuclear warfare plans with the Soviet bloc. Before her defection she was a secretary in the Office of Council Operations and Communication, responsible for NATO war exercises. According to East German authorities, Lorenzen defected when she discovered that NATO Secretary General Joseph Luns had been a member of the Dutch Nazi party (1933–36). She joined NATO headquarters in 1966 and was recalled to East Germany in 1979 when her identity was revealed by an East German defector. She gave a TV interview in East Berlin complaining that Luns was a former Nazi. (*Facts on File*, 1979; *New York Times*, March 7, 14, 1979; Rositzke, *The KGB*)

346   Lotz, Johann Wolfgang Sigmund (b. 1921).   Born in

Germany to a gentile father and Jewish mother who divorced his father and moved to Palestine in 1933. Wolfgang changed his name in Palestine to Ze'ev Gur-Aryeh. While at the Ben Shemen agricultural school, he learned horsemanship. He joined the underground in 1937, the Haganah, then the British Army at the outbreak of World War II. His work as an interrogator of POWs in the British Army in North Africa gave him insight in the German Army. He mastered Arabic, English, Hebrew, and his native German made him indispensable to the British Army and later to Israeli intelligence. In 1948–49 he served in the Israel defense forces and fought in the war of independence and the 1956 Suez campaign. After this, he was recruited by Aman, Israel's military intelligence.

He was sent to Egypt in December 1960 as a rich German who bred horses. Using the cover of an ex–Nazi officer he arrived in Cairo and bought a horse ranch near the experimental rocket base. He quickly became friends with upper-class Egyptians and with Youssef Ali Ghorab, the officer in charge of the Egyptian police force. On a trip to Europe to report to his handlers, he took a train trip from Paris on the Orient Express in June 1961 and met a beautiful German. Two weeks later he was married without notifying his Israeli handlers or his wife in Israel. During Operation Damocles, he helped terrify German rocket scientists helping Egypt build a rocket program. Lotz was accused of sending letter bombs to German scientists — one, in 1962, which blinded the secretary of Wolfgang Pliz, who headed the Egyptian rocket research team.

In 1963 Mossad took over control of the operation, and he provided them with a variety of intelligence on the project. The Mossad accounting department referred to him as the "champagne spy" due to his luxurious lifestyle. In February 1965, Egyptian agents stormed his Cairo apartment. Lotz's radio transmitter had been detected by Egyptian intelligence using direction-finding equipment provided by the Soviets.

Lotz finally pled guilty to spying for Israel but denied the charge of attempting to assassinate Germans involved in the rocket project for Egypt. He was sentenced to life. His wife was given three years, but they were released three years later in an Israel-Egyptian spy swap of Six Day War POWs in 1967. (Black and Morris, *Israel's Secret Wars;* Eisenberg, Dan, and Landau, *The Mossad;* Cookridge, *Gehlen;* Lotz, *A Handbook for Spies* and *The Champagne Spy;* Raviv and Melman, *Every Spy a Prince;* Steven, *The Spymasters of Israel*)

347 Lubman, Leonid.   In April 1978, Soviet authorities announced that Lubman, a Leningrad resident, had been sentenced to 15 years for spying for the United States. He was arrested after classified documents were found on a foreign exchange student attempting to leave the country. (*Facts on File*, 1978; *New York Times*, April 11, 1978)

348   Ludwig, Horst Heinz.   A former lieutenant commander in the West German military, he pled guilty in a West German court in 1960 for spying for the East Germans for three years. This included the period that Ludwig underwent naval pilot training in the United States, 1956–57.

Confederates Fritz Briesemeister and Werner Jaeger were on trial for espionage with Ludwig. Ludwig stated that he spied for the East Germans to prevent his family in East Germany from being imprisoned.

He began his military career in the Wehrmacht. He was captured and placed in an American POW camp. After the war, he returned to his home in Soviet-occupied East Germany. In 1950, after graduating from Jena University in engineering, he fled to West Germany. He joined the West German Air Force as a pilot. In 1958 he was sent to a British naval station in Scotland for training in NATO Vixen aircraft. He had been recruited in 1954 with threats to his family. He was sentenced to five years. (Cookridge, *Gehlen; Facts on File*, 1960)

349   Luedke, Hermann.   In October 1968, West German Rear Admiral Luedke committed suicide. He was a major spy suspect and possibly committed suicide due to the impending investigation. He had been deputy chief of logistics at NATO Supreme Headquarters in Belgium. An investigation was prompted when a West German photo-processing store reported that Luedke had processed a roll of film that showed classified NATO documents. His death prompted a reorganization of West German intelligence services. (Cookridge, *Gehlen;* Gehlen, *The Service*)

350   Lueneburg, Sonja.   In August 1985, Lueneburg, personal secretary of West German Economics Minister Martin Bangemann, disappeared. This brought about charges that she had been an East German spy. A search of her apartment revealed expensive camera equipment. Her failure to return from a three-day trip to Brussels sparked concern. There were several other disappearances at the same time: Ursula Richter, believed to be the control officer in charge of an East Germany spy network, a secretary in the accounts department of the League of Expellees; Lorenz Betzing, a close friend of Richter and a messenger with an army administrative office in Bonn; and Hans Tiedge, division head in the counterintelligence service (BfV), who later defected to East Germany. (*Facts on File*, 1985)

351   Lugovoy, Vladimir.   In February 1983, Lugovoy, assistant to a Soviet military attaché, was arrested by Swiss authorities while trying to meet a recruited spy. The Swiss government detained Lugovoy for questioning and then expelled him from the country. (*Facts on File*, 1983)

352   Luk, Mordecai (b. 1934).   In November 1964, Luk, an

Israeli, was discovered by Italian authorities drugged, gagged, and bound in a trunk labeled for air express in the Egyptian diplomatic mail addressed to the Foreign Ministry in Cairo. Luk first identified himself as a Moroccan linguist, Joseph Dahan, but later admitted to being Luk. Luk stated that he had been working as an interpreter for the Egyptian embassy in Italy when he was kidnapped by Egyptian officials. The Italian government expelled two Egyptian first secretaries of the embassy: Abdel Moneim el-Naklawy and Selim Osman el-Sayed. Reportedly, Luk had crossed over armistice lines to the Egyptians in 1961 and had participated in anti–Israeli radio propaganda broadcasts from Egypt. Italy deported Luk back to Israel, and he was arrested for providing Egypt with security information. In February 1965, Israel charged Luk with spying for the Egyptian government. Luk was convicted and sentenced to 13 years on six counts of espionage. (Black and Morris, *Israel's Secret Wars*; Eisenberg, Dan, and Landau, *The Mossad*)

353   Lumbwe, Webster Kayi.

In June 1981, Lumbwe, a high official in the Zambian Foreign Ministry, was arrested for spying for the CIA. Lumbwe worked in the political section of the ministry's Africa section. Several U.S. diplomats were expelled: John David Finney, political affairs officer; Michael Francis O'Brien, public affairs officer and director of the U.S. International Communications Agency office; and Frederick Boyce Lundahl, who was declared persona non grata and had recently been expelled from Mozambique for espionage activities in March. The Zambian government accused the diplomats of encouraging a coup. (*Facts on File*, 1981; *New York Times*, March 5, June 23, 24, 1981)

354   Lundahl, Frederick Boyce, and Louis Leon Olivier.

Mozambican authorities announced in March 1981 a major U.S. spy ring that had been operating in Mozambique since 1975 when the country gained its independence from Portugal. The government accused the U.S. embassy of providing information to formerly white-ruled Rhodesia on guerrilla movements and reporting to South Africa on black exiles living in Mozambique. The network was also reported to have provided aid to an anti–Mozambican guerrilla group.

Mozambique's Foreign Ministry expelled several U.S. diplomats for espionage and subversive activities. Lundahl and Olivier were both second secretaries at the U.S. embassy but were accused of being CIA agents. The Mozambican government identified 13 other American diplomats who had engaged in espionage activities in the past.

The U.S. State Department announced that the Mozambique government had retaliated for an unsuccessful attempt by a Cuban intelligence agent to recruit a U.S. diplomat Mozambique. The diplomat was threatened and offered money for his services. The expulsion order came a few hours after the attempt was made. The State Department also claimed editors of the *Covert Action Information Bulletin,* an anti–CIA organization that identified CIA officers overseas, had visited Mozambique just before the Cuban attempt and may have informed the Mozambique government of suspected CIA intelligence officers stationed in Mozambique. The editors denied giving any information to the government.

Subsequently to their expulsion, a Mozambique Air Force captain, Joao Carneiro Goncalves, claimed that he was a double agent working against the CIA. Goncalves claimed that his CIA contact had told him that the United States would try and initiate a coup in Mozambique through South Africa. The Mozambique government announced that the CIA had arranged South African raiders to attack anti–South African guerrillas in the capital of Mozambique, Maputo, in January of that year. In retaliation to expulsion and accusations, the State Department canceled the U.S. food-aid program to Mozambique. (*Facts on File,* 1981; *New York Times,* March 5; June 23, 24, 1981)

355 Lunt, Lawrence K. In May 1965, Cuban authorities arrested Lunt, an American, on espionage charges and sentenced him to 30 years. In 1957 he had bought a ranch in the Pinar del Rio Province of Cuba where he hid anti–Castro Cubans. Reportedly, Lunt had seen Soviet missiles hidden in a nearby cave. Lunt was released in September 1979. He claimed that he had worked for the CIA. (*Facts on File,* 1965, 1979)

356 Luther, William Joseph. In May 1984, Luther, an American citizen, was arrested in Nicaragua for counterrevolutionary activities and espionage. Luther admitted to supplying a U.S. diplomat in the embassy in Managua with data on the status of Sandinista troops. Luther was paid for his services. A Nicaraguan army lieutenant was also arrested for supplying Luther with the data. (*Facts on File,* 1984; *New York Times,* July 5, 1984)

357 Lutz, Lothar Erwin, and Jürgen Wiegel. In June 1976 members of a spy ring working for East Germany were arrested in West Germany. The ring reportedly gave the East Germans structural plans of the NATO army, NATO military contingency plans, arms information, and a variety of classified documents. In June 1979, Lutz and his wife, Renate, were convicted in a West German court for treason. Lutz was sentenced to 12 years, and Renate was given six years. Both had worked in the West German Defense Ministry.

Renate was former chief secretary to Herbert Laabs, head of the Defense Ministry's social department. Lutz was employed in the Defense

Ministry's weapons department. Wiegel was a civilian employee in the West German naval operations staff with access to NATO documents.

They had given East Germany hundreds of pages of classified data, including the alarm plan of the West German military, an account of the West German pipeline system of the NATO forces, and data on planned tank armament. In April 1987 West Germany reportedly swapped Lutze for Western spies held in East Germany. (*Facts on File*, 1976–77, 1979, 1987; Rositzke, *The KGB*)

358   Lyalin, Oleg Adolfovich.   Member of Department V (as in Victor), a sabotage and assassination department, the First Chief Directorate. Six months before he defected, he was recruited by the British counterintelligence service, MI5, who used him as an *agent in place*. He provided sabotage plans for London, Washington, Paris, Bonn, and Rome in the event of war. Also gave a list of assassination targets.

Lyalin's revelations stunned the British government, and over one hundred Soviet intelligence officers were expelled. Due to the defection of Lyalin, Department V personnel around the world were recalled to Moscow, and operations were ceased, though this was only temporary and Department Eight later emerged to take over the responsibilities of Department V.

Lyalin was the first Soviet intelligence officer to be recruited by MI5 since World War II. Some of the sabotage plans he revealed included a bizarre plan to drop nerve-gas pellets onto the floors of the Foreign Office where unsuspecting officials would step on them and be killed. Lyalin named several KGB assets in Britain, including Sirioj Husein Abdoolcader, Constantinos Martianon, and Kyriacos Costi. (Andrew and Gordievsky, *KGB*; Barron, *KGB*; Brook-Shepherd, *The Storm Birds*; West, *The Circus*)

359   McCone, John Alex (b. 1902).   Director of Central Intelligence Agency (DCI) from November 1961 to April 1965 under Presidents Kennedy and Johnson; member of President's Air Policy Commission, 1947–48; deputy to the secretary of defense, March–November 1948; under secretary of the Air Force, 1950–51; chairman of Atomic Energy Commission, 1958–60. After his DCI position, he became counselor to the President's Commission on Strategic Forces in 1983. He was considered an outsider in the CIA. Many considered McCone unqualified for the position. He helped repair the CIA's reputation after the Bay of Pigs. (Cline, *Secrets, Spies and Scholars*; Leary, *The Central Intelligence Agency*; Ranelagh, *The Agency*)

360   McCord, James Walter, Jr. (b. 1924).   He joined the FBI in 1942 but left the FBI for the U.S. Army Air Corps in 1943. In 1945 he attended the University of Texas, and in 1948 he returned to the FBI but quit in 1951 to join the CIA's Office of Security. Sent to Europe, 1962–64, as senior security officer, after his return, he was named chief of the Physical Security Division.

Retiring in 1970 he was hired in 1972 to serve as chief of security for the Committee to Re-Elect the President (CREEP). Arrested at 2:00 A.M. with four others while installing wiretaps in phones at the Democratic National Committee at the Watergate Hotel. Several other former CIA employees were involved in the break-in. Eugenio Martinez, a veteran of the CIA's Operation Mongoose, was still on the payroll of the CIA, reporting on the activities of Cuban exiles in Florida. Another former CIA intelligence officer, E. Howard Hunt, was responsible for the planning and implantation of the break-in.

The White House began pressuring McCord to implicate the CIA in the burglary to get the Nixon administration off the hook. But McCord refused and warned the director of the CIA, Richard Helms, about Nixon's intentions. He was sentenced in 1973 for his role in Watergate and was released in 1975. Nixon subsequently fired Helms for his refusal to participate in the cover-up. (Freemantle, *CIA*; Hougan, *Secret Agenda*; Hunt, *Undercover*; Powers, *The Man Who Kept the Secrets*; Ranelagh, The Agency)

361 McDonald, Irving T.   Assistant air attaché at the U.S. embassy in Moscow, he was expelled from the Soviet Union for espionage in 1960. The Soviets reportedly accused McDonald of posing as a tourist and entering a secure military facility in Kharkov in October 1960. The U.S. State Department declared that McDonald's expulsion was in retaliation for the arrest in the United States of Soviet UN employee Igor Y. Melekh. (*Facts on File*, 1960)

362 McGehee, Ralph W., Jr. (b. 1928).   After graduating from Notre Dame, McGehee joined the CIA in 1952. His first tour was in Japan in 1953, where he was assigned to the China Operations Group (COG). His first job was as a mundane file checker in the records office. In 1955 the COG was moved to the Philippines, where he continued in the same position till 1956 when he returned to the CIA headquarters and was assigned to the administrative office of the Far East Division.

In 1958, McGehee got his first big break and was sent to case officer training at Camp Peary. In 1959 he was sent to Taiwan where he worked as a liaison officer with the Nationalist intelligence service. He also participated in sending Chinese agents to the mainland to gather intelligence on Communist Chinese activities.

In 1961 he was sent back to CIA headquarters and reassigned to Thailand a year later. Sent to a rural northern outpost near the Laos border, he gathered intelligence concerning Communist subversion and at the same time taught the Thai counterinsurgency force how to develop its own intelligence capability. McGehee also helped run a nonmilitary training and support program for peasants.

In 1964 he returned to CIA headquarters and was assigned to the Thai desk, responsible for keeping track of the programs that he had worked with in Thailand. It was here that he first worked with the Far East Division chief William Colby. In 1965 he went back to Bangkok, Thailand, where he assisted in liaison with the Thai counterinsurgency force, which also collected data on the Thai Communist party. After a year he was assigned to establish an intelligence-collection program for the Thai national police. In 1967 he took a job in the China activities department at CIA headquarters. In 1968 he was sent to Vietnam, working in Military Region Five as officer in charge of Gia Dinh, supervising the various CIA programs in that province. He supervised other case officers working with specific elements of the special police in and around Saigon. McGehee became distraught about the CIA's role in the war. Complaining that the CIA was misrepresenting the facts of the conflict for political reasons and humiliated by the death and destruction to the Vietnamese people, he considered suicide. He finally left Vietnam in 1970, embittered and depressed by the experience.

McGehee went to Thailand as deputy chief of the anti–Communist party operations branch, supervising case officers. But in 1971 he left Thailand, increasingly depressed about the CIA's activities in the region. After writing a negative memo on Theodore Shackley's activities, he was assigned as the East Asia Division referent to the international communism branch of the Directorate for Operations for the next four years. It was a depressing and unproductive time for McGehee, and he retired in 1977. When he retired, he was awarded the Career Intelligence Medal, but ironically, at the ceremony the citation which was read aloud described his excellent work in Malaysia, a country he had never been in. He later wrote an extremely negative book about his experiences in the CIA and attacked the CIA for its poor performance. (McGehee, *Deadly Deceits*)

363 McGiven, Arthur. In January 1980, McGiven, a former agent with South Africa's Bureau of State Security (now called the Department of National Security, DONS), announced that the bureau had kept files on businessmen and politicians in South Africa. McGiven had escaped to Great Britain with 50 classified documents supporting his claim. McGiven's announcement caused a political scandal in South Africa and a reorganization of DONS. McGiven stated that surveillance included mail opening and telephone bugging. The documents included a surveillance file on Helen Suzman, member of the Progressive Federal party and a member of Parliament. Another file described the activities of Harry Oppenheimer, a mining operator and owner. (*Facts on File*, 1980)

364 Machekhin, Alexander. In May 1976, Japanese authorities arrested Machekhin, a Soviet GRU major, in Tokyo for military espionage. He was using the cover of a journalist for the Soviet press agency Novosti. Reportedly, Machekhin had attempted to steal U.S. military information. Machekhin was arrested in the company of a U.S. Navy chief petty officer assigned to the Seventh Fleet aircraft carrier *Midway*, who was not charged. Reportedly, the chief petty officer, unidentified, had been offered $1,000 for information on the Seventh Fleet communications network codes and details of radar and electronic installations at the naval base near Yokosuka. Machekhin was given a roll of film at the meeting but threw it away when he saw Japanese counterintelligence agents rushing toward him.

Since he was working under the cover of a journalist, he did not have diplomatic immunity, and the Soviets feared that he would be imprisoned. Though Japanese investigators argued there was enough evidence to place him on trial for espionage, he was later released after an intensive KGB disinformation campaign was launched to discredit the case against him. (Barron, *KGB Today; Facts on File,* 1976; *New York Times,* May 15, 23, 25, 1976)

365 Maclean, Donald Duart (b. 1913). British spy for the Soviets. While attending Trinity Hall, Cambridge, in 1931 on a modern languages scholarship, he explored Communist theory and his homosexual tendencies. He became active in left-wing causes and a student of Marxism. Maclean developed a strong anti–American and anticolonial attitude. During a political demonstration for the unemployed, he was arrested, but due to his father's status as a cabinet minister, no charges were filed.

Maclean was recruited to work for the Soviets by Theodore Maly, known as "Teddy"; he was told to cut off all political ties to the Left and enter into the Diplomatic Service. It was a long-term strategy. He entered the Foreign Office in 1935, working as a junior member in the League of Nations and Western Department, which dealt with the Netherlands, Spain, Portugal, and Switzerland, as well as the League of Nations. In 1938 he took a post as third secretary at the British embassy in Paris. As third secretary, Maclean had access to virtually everything, including telegraphs, dispatches, even personal letters from the ambassador.

It was in Paris that Maclean met his wife, Melinda Marling, and married. Despite his occasional homosexual behavior, Maclean no doubt loved his wife. After the fall of France to Nazi Germany, Maclean began meeting with Kim Philby, another spy for the Soviets, on a regular basis. Maclean was appointed second secretary in 1940 in the newly created General Department, which dealt mainly with the wartime ministries Shipping, Supply, and Economic Warfare.

Maclean received a new Soviet controller, Anatoli Gromov (code-named "Henry"), who was the attaché at the Soviet embassy in London. Gromov was different from his previous handlers. Gromov insisted on copies of documents and photographs rather than the common gossip and observations Maclean provided his previous handlers. To keep Maclean in line, Guy Burgess is reported to have taken pictures of Maclean in the arms of a male lover, nude, in 1941.

In 1944 Maclean traveled to the United States to become the first secretary of the British embassy. It was here that Maclean learned of the Manhattan Project to create an atomic bomb. While in Washington, Maclean gained information on the Berlin airlift and details of the North Atlantic Treaty being negotiated. The data given to the Soviets no doubt helped shape Soviet foreign policy.

In 1948 Maclean was sent to Egypt where he took the post of head of chancery at Cairo on promotion to counselor. It was here that Maclean became unhappy with his post and duties, despite the apparent promotion. The area was poor by Western standards, and Israeli and Arab conflicts were common. He became depressed and began drinking heavily, his morale deteriorating.

Back in the West, Anglo-American cryptologists had discovered a Soviet agent named "Homer" in Soviet embassy communications to Moscow, who had been stationed in Washington. The hunt was on for Maclean, and Kim Philby managed to warn him in Cairo. Maclean became even more despondent.

After a fit of violence, Maclean was sent back to London in 1950 where he began seeing a psychiatrist. At the urging of Burgess, he returned to the Foreign Office and resumed his career. He was made the head of the American Department, and the Soviets assigned him a new controller, Yuri Modin, code-named "Peter." But MI5 had Maclean as a suspect as "Homer." The vital evidence against Maclean was the fact that Homer and Maclean had visited New York City at roughly the same time. The fact that Maclean had been given an important post just before his disappearance became an embarrassment for the British. (Boyle, *The Climate of Treason* and *The Fourth Man*; Cecil, *A Divided Life*; Fisher, *Burgess and Maclean*; Hoare, *The Missing Macleans*; Newton, *The Cambridge Spies*)

366 McMahan, Dennis, and John Massey. In January 1985, they were arrested for taking pictures of the communications tower located at the residence of Premier Felipe Gonazalez. Both were expelled in February. McMahan was a political staff member of the U.S. embassy in Spain. Massey was an official at the U.S.-Spanish air base at Torrejón de Andoz, near Madrid. (*Facts on File*, 1985; *New York Times*, February 16, 1985)

367   Madsen, Lee Eugene.   In August 1979, Madsen, a yeoman third class in the U.S. Navy, was arrested for espionage. Madsen worked on the strategic warning staff in the Pentagon. He was accused of selling classified military and intelligence data, documents concerning international drug trade, and locations of administration agents to a private citizen. He was sentenced to eight years in October 1979. He pled guilty to a single count that he sold seven top secret intelligence and military documents to an informer of the FBI. None of the documents was given to a foreign government. Madsen claimed that he had attempted to sell the documents to capture a Soviet agent and become famous. This would prove, in Madsen's perspective, that he could be a man *and* gay. One of the documents he sold was satellite photographs of amphibious troop and tank movements of an unnamed Communist country. Madsen's roommate, Gary Miller, stated that Madsen had sold the documents to get enough money for a car. (Allen and Polmar, *Merchants of Treason;* Turner, *Secrecy and Democracy*)

368   Mafart, Alain, and Dominique Prieur.   Major Mafart and Prieur, French DGSE agents, posing under the aliases Alain-Jacques and Sophie-Claire Turenge, were involved in the sinking of the *Rainbow Warrior.* In 1985, Mafart and Prieur arrived in New Zealand with Swiss passports claiming to be the Turenges. Their role in the operation was to arrange an escape after the attack. Several members of the DGSE arrived in New Zealand on an operation called Operation Satanic. The *Rainbow Warrior,* part of the Greenpeace organization, was sunk by two bombs, killing one crew member. The Turenges were arrested when they tried to return a rental car that had been spotted near the port where the ship was docked. The police traced their passports, which were discovered to be fake. The scandal in France caused the resignation of the head of the DGSE, Admiral Lacoste. (Faligot and Krop, *La Piscine; Facts on File,* 1987)

369   Mahdavi, Ahmed Malek.   In August 1976, Swiss authorities expelled Mahdavi, first secretary for the Iranian mission to the UN in Geneva, for espionage activities. Mahdavi was believed to head a SAVAK (Iranian intelligence service) unit in Geneva. The Iranian government retaliated by expelling a Swiss diplomat in Tehran. (*Facts on File,* 1976)

370   Maheu, Robert A.   From 1954, the CIA paid Maheu a monthly retainer of $500 to do jobs the CIA felt it could not perform within the boundaries of the law. Maheu helped in the CIA bugging of Aristotle Onassis's hotel room in Rome while he was working on contract negotiations with Saudi Arabia to become the single shipper of oil from that country.

The CIA was able to disrupt the contract negotiations and prevent Onassis from getting the contract.

His connections extended to the underworld, and he was approached by the CIA to arrange to have the Mafia assassinate Castro, his brother Raul Castro, and Che Guevara. Maheu turned to John Rosselli, an underworld fixer in Las Vegas, to help recruit Mafia figures for a CIA assassination plot against Castro. When Maheu approached Rosselli, he first indicated he was representing Cuban businessmen who wanted Castro out for $150,000. When Rosselli later discovered the CIA was involved, he contacted Salvatore Giancana. At the time, Giancana, a boss in the Chicago Mafia, was sharing a mistress, Judith Campbell, with John F. Kennedy. Giancana was sent to Miami in 1960 to recruit Cuban exiles for the operation.

The FBI discovered that the CIA was using Mafia gangsters to kill Castro and began a surveillance operation of Giancana. Giancana's phone was tapped, and when Giancana was away, his mistress, Judith Campbell, called John F. Kennedy, recording the phone call. No doubt, when Kennedy attempted to oust FBI Director J. Edgar Hoover, he quickly changed his mind.

In February 1961, Dr. Sidney Gottlieb provided a botulinum poison to be injected into Castro's cigars. They established a base in Miami, but the operation was later dismantled. The assassin assigned to complete the job could not get into position in Cuba.

Giancana was forced to appear before the Church committee, investigating CIA assassinations plots in July 1975. His testimony apparently was not appreciated by his fellow Mafia members; that evening, after he spoke to the committee, he was shot to death in the basement of his home. He was shot seven times in the mouth, a Mafia way of killing someone who breaks the vow of silence (*omertà*).

Maheu also worked on a black propaganda pornographic film with Sheffield Edwards, *Happy Days,* purportedly featuring Indonesian President Sukarno. The idea was to shock the morals of the Muslim population in the country. The film was produced and funded by the CIA, using an unlikely looking Mexican as Sukarno. The film backfired in Indonesia. Indonesian Muslims were proud of their leader's sexual prowess. (Freemantle, *CIA;* Powers, *The Man Who Kept the Secrets;* Ranelagh, *The Agency;* Wyden, *The Bay of Pigs*)

371 Makinen, Marvin William. While on a tour of the Soviet Union in 1961, Makinen took some photographs of a Soviet military installation in Kiev, Ukraine. Makinen was a chemistry student from the University of Pennsylvania who became a Fulbright exchange student at West Berlin's Free University. The CIA regularly recruited students at the

Free University during the 1950s and 1960s for short spying missions into Eastern Europe and the Soviet Union. Makinen reportedly bragged about his relationship with the CIA to friends before his arrest. Makinen spoke fluent German and Finnish. Sentenced to eight years, he was imprisoned at the infamous Vladimir Prison where U-2 pilot Gary Powers had been held. Though Makinen confessed to the Soviets, the CIA and State Department denied his role as a spy. He was exchanged in October 1963 for U.S.-held Ivan and Aleksandra Egorov. (Ranelagh, *The Agency;* Wise and Ross, *The Invisible Government*)

372   Marchetti, Victor L.   He served in the U.S. Army in Germany in 1952, where he studied Russian at the European Command's school. After the military he earned a degree in Soviet Studies at Penn State, joining the CIA in 1955, first as a Soviet military specialist, then as an analyst of Soviet activities in the Third World, including activities in Cuba during the missile crisis in 1962. From 1966 to 1969 he served as a staff officer in the office of the director of the CIA in various positions, including chief of planning and special assistant to the deputy director.

During the late 1960s, he became disenchanted by CIA activities and resigned in 1969. In 1974 a book on the CIA, *The CIA and the Cult of Intelligence,* was published by Marchetti and a former State Department intelligence officer, John D. Marks. It caused a major crisis for the CIA, who successfully had the book edited of material it considered classified. While he was writing the book, the CIA hounded him with threats and proposals. One was to purchase every copy of the book to prevent its release to the public. The book became necessary reading for students of intelligence and the CIA. The CIA successfully edited the book, and over the years additional paragraphs of deleted portions were added to the book as italic or bold script, giving the book a puzzlelike quality. (Agee, *On the Run;* Marchetti and Marks, *The CIA and the Cult of Intelligence*)

373   Markelov, Valery Ivanovich.   In February 1972, Markelov, a Soviet employee at the UN, actually a KGB officer, was arrested for attempting to steal classified documents detailing the U.S. Navy's F-14A Tomcat fighter. He was arrested in February 1972 by FBI agents while meeting an engineer of the Grumman Aerospace Corporation who had worked with the FBI, staging 11 meetings since 1970. The espionage charges were dismissed, and he was released and returned to the Soviet Union. (Allen and Polmar, *Merchants of Treason;* Barron, *KGB;* Newman, *Famous Soviet Spies*)

374   Marshall, William Martin (b. 1924).   In April 1952, a member of the British MI5 Watcher Service accidently came across Pavel

Kuznetsov, Soviet third secretary, talking to an unidentified man on a London street. Kuznetsov, actually a GRU agent, and the individual were watched for a while, and when they split up, the watcher agent followed the unidentified person to his home. He was later identified as Marshall, who worked for the Diplomatic Wireless Service (DWS) as a Foreign Office radio operator, who had recently returned from a one-year tour at the British embassy in Moscow as a cipher clerk.

Marshall had served three years in the Royal Signals Corps till 1948, serving in Palestine and Egypt, when he joined the Diplomatic Wireless Service (DWS). During a one-year tour as cipher clerk in the embassy in Moscow, he was trapped in a homosexual blackmail operation.

In June 13, 1952, an MI5 surveillance team monitoring a meeting between Marshall and Kuznetsov in a London park were accosted by uniformed London police, giving away the team. Without anything else to do, they arrested Marshall and Kuznetsov. Kuznetsov claimed diplomatic immunity and was released and expelled from the country. A search of Marshall revealed classified data, and a search of his home revealed a diary detailing the numerous meetings and Kuznetsov's phone number.

In June 1952, Marshall was found guilty and sentenced to five years for espionage. Marshall was coined "the Hanslope Park spy" because he met Kuznetsov there on numerous occasions. (Lucas, *The Great Spy Ring*; Rositzke, *The KGB*; West, *The Circus* and *The SIGINT Secrets*)

375 Martelli, Giuseppe E.   Dr. Martelli, Italian nuclear physicist, was arrested in 1963 in London for espionage for the Soviet Union. Martelli had joined the European Atomic Energy Commission at the Culham Laboratories of the British Atomic Energy Authority in Oxfordshire, England, in September 1962. While Martelli was on vacation in Europe, MI5 searched his office and home, revealing a diary with the name Nikolai Karpekov, a Soviet KGB officer, a cipher pad, hollowed-out cigarettes used for hiding messages, hollowed-out shoe heels, and cigarette packs with coding devices hidden in them. The diary also contained information for special codes used by the KGB. When he returned, he was arrested at the airport.

He later identified Nicolai Karpekov, John Vassall's former case officer, as the man he was meeting. It was later revealed that several members of Martelli's family were Communists and that he had been part of an underground Communist group in Italy. A Soviet KGB double agent working in the Soviet delegation at the UN had informed the FBI that the KGB had a source in the British nuclear research community and that he had been in place between a year and two. Martelli fit the description despite the fact that he had no access to sensitive data.

He went on trial in July 1963 and was found not guilty. Martelli intentionally pled not guilty, arguing that he had no access to classified data and that though he had meetings with KGB agents, they had blackmailed him. Martelli argued that the KGB hinted that there would be visa problems in visiting his children, who were going to the Soviet Union with their mother, who had been educated in that country. His defense lawyers argued that he had contact with KGB agents but that that was not against the law, nor was the espionage paraphernalia that was discovered. Since no evidence could be produced that Martelli was providing classified data to the Soviets, he was acquitted of the charges. (Andrew and Gordievsky, *KGB*; West, *The Circus*; Wright, *Spy Catcher*)

Martin, William H. see **Mitchell, Bernon F.**

Massey, John see **McMahan, Dennis**

376 Mazurier, Jean-Paul. Mazurier, a Paris lawyer, worked for the French intelligence service (DGSE), while handling the Arab terrorist, Georges Ibrahim Abdallah of the Lebanese Armed Revolutionary Faction. Mazurier had met Abdallah in 1982 but did not approach DGSE until 1984 after becoming frustrated with the violent tactics used by Abdallah's group. While working for the DGSE, code-named "Simon," he reported on Abdallah's activities until 1986 when he became disenchanted by DGSE's failure to stop the Paris bombing campaign. Ironically, Mazurier represented Abdallah in his 1986 trial for weapons and fraudulent documents charges. Mazurier's activities were chronicled in a book by journalist Laurent Gally, *The Black Agent*. (*Facts on File*, 1987)

377 Medjeber, Smail (alias Claude-Pascal Rousseaux). Medjeber, an Algerian with a French passport, was accused of being the head of a French spy network in Algeria. In January 1976, Algerian authorities arrested Medjeber and two other members of the ring — Javier Lucumberri-Martinez, a Spaniard, and Gregorio Villagran Anderson, a Paraguayan who had entered Algeria in December 1975 with false Italian passports carrying bombs for targets in Algeria and Oman. All three were condemned to death in March 1976.

All three were accused of working for the French intelligence service (SDECE), which reportedly had recruited them as mercenaries for sabotage operations against the Algerian government for the benefit of the Soldiers of the Algerian Oppositon (OAS). The OAS was a terrorist organization aimed against the Algerian government. It was accused of bombing the office of the government-run newspaper *El Moudjahid* in January 1976.

Anderson was also accused of bombing the Algerian embassy in London in 1975, under orders from a SDECE agent, Jean Laurent. Medjeber stated that he had been recruited by Jacques Benet, an intelligence agent linked to the OAS, in 1973. Medjeber reportedly was suspected of bombings of Algerian embassies in Europe since 1973. Medjeber stated that he had participated in the assassination of Amilcar Cabral, the former leader of the African Party for the Independence of Portuguese Guinea and Cape Verde (PAIGC) in 1973. In March 1976, all three were sentenced to death by an Algerian state security court in Medea. (*Facts on File*, 1976)

378 Medrano, Alberto Cesareo Fernandez. In 1964 several members of Cuba's Lion's Club were arrested for spying for the CIA. Medrano, a counselor for the Lion's Club, was described as the ringleader of the spy network. Medrano was executed, along with two other confederates — president of the anti–Castro Rescate Group, Marcelino Martinez Tapia, and, accused as the chief CIA agent for Camaguey Province, Manuel Paradela Gomez. Two others were given undetermined prison sentences: former Camaguey governor under the Batista government Manuel Zayas Bazan and Jorge Bermudez Compar. All conspirators were members of the Lion's Club and were accused of participation in a CIA spy network in Camaguey Province. All five were identified as having associations with rural landowners upset about the loss of their land under Communist land reforms. (*Facts on File*, 1964)

379 Mehta, P. E. In 1986 Mehta was sentenced in India for spying for the United States. Mehta admitted to providing the United States with a variety of classified data, including political, military, and economic information. Reportedly, he received up to $420,000 in payments from 1962 to 1977. Mehta's trial lasted nine years. (*Facts on File*, 1986; *New York Times*, October 30, 1986).

380 Meissner, Herbert. Former deputy director of the East German Academy of Sciences, he was arrested in July 1986 for shoplifting a shower attachment in a West German store. Meissner demanded to be interviewed by West German intelligence officials, claiming that he was an East German spy. After convincing West German officials that he was an East German agent, he asked for political asylum, but after several days Meissner fled to the East German mission in Bonn, telling them he had been kidnapped and drugged by West German authorities. West Germany finally dropped all charges against Meissner and allowed him to return to East Germany. The incident brought comparisons by the media to the Yurchenko scandal in the United States (*Facts on File*, 1986; *New York Times*, July 16, 17, 19, 22, 1986)

381 Merrin, Jacques. French intelligence (DGSE) agent assassinated in East Beirut on February 2, 1988. Merrin was killed in his car when assassins in a passing car fired automatic weapons with silencers. Merrin, using the cover of a businessman, had just left a meeting with Lebanese internal security officers. (*Facts on File*, 1988)

382 Meyer, Paul Carl. In February 1965, Meyer pled guilty to fraudulently obtaining 15 U.S. passports in November 1962 and giving them to Soviet agents in East Berlin. While he was in East Berlin, the Soviets placed Meyer through some special espionage training. They gave him a camera disguised as a portable radio. He was given orders to befriend a female employee of the U.S. mission in Berlin to gain access to the grounds and photograph classified documents. He was unsuccessful. Reportedly, Meyer confessed to the FBI when he returned to the United States in June 1963 that he had worked for the Soviets for only ten weeks. He was sentenced in February 1965 to two years for providing 15 passports to the Soviet Union. No espionage charges were filed. He had obtained the passports after running an advertisement for 15 people to work overseas. He took their passports, explaining that he needed to get proper visas. (*Facts on File*, 1965; *New York Times*, February 3, 4, 27, 1965; Romerstein and Levchenko, *The KGB Against the "Main Enemy"*)

383 Miagkov, Gregory. In July 1978, the International Labor Organization in Geneva dismissed ILO official Miagkov of the Soviet Union for being a KGB agent. The Swiss cited intelligence reports that implicated Miagkov. Miagkov had been with the UN since 1968. (*Facts on File*, 1978)

384 Michelson, Alice. In October 1984, Michelson, an East German courier, was arrested by FBI agents at Kennedy Airport in New York as she was boarding a flight bound for Czechoslovakia. A search of her luggage uncovered classified cables stolen by a U.S. Army sergeant in army intelligence who was a double agent. She had been given classified material by a U.S. Army sergeant posing as a KGB-recruited spy. Before she was put on trial, she was exchanged in 1985. (Allen and Polmar, *Merchants of Treason*; Corson and Crowley, *The New KGB*)

385 Michiels, Eugene. In 1983 Michiels, a Belgian Foreign Ministry official, was arrested for espionage. Michiels, who was a senior official in the office that coordinated Belgian trade policies with the European Community and Comecon, was accused of providing classified economic data to Soviet and Rumanian intelligence agents. The Belgian government expelled several Soviet and Rumanian diplomats. Reportedly, an electronics company in Brussels acted as a front for Rumanian agents. (*Facts on File*, 1983; *New York Times*, August 21, 1983)

Mikhailov, Gennady see Chelpanov, Yuri

386   Mikheyev, Aleksandr N.   In April 1983, several Soviet diplomats were ordered expelled from the United States. Mikheyev, a member of the Soviet UN mission, was accused of trying to obtain classified data from an aide to Rep. Olympia Snowe (R, Maine). (*Facts on File*, 1983; *New York Times*, April 22, 24, 1983)

387   Miles, Jennifer.   In October 1970, Miles, a South African working as a receptionist in the South African embassy in Washington, was arrested after supplying two Cubans with information. The Cubans, Rogelio Rodriguez Lopez, counselor to the UN, and Orlando Prendes Cutierrez, first secretary at the mission, were expelled from the United States. Miles returned to South Africa in late October 1970. (*Facts on File*, 1970; *New York Times*, October 23, 30, 1970)

388   Miller, Richard W.   The only FBI agent ever convicted of spying for the Soviet Union. Miller, 20 veteran of the FBI, was arrested in 1984 after having an affair with a female Soviet agent, Svetlana Ogorodnikova, giving her an FBI manual on U.S. counterintelligence techniques. The FBI had had Ogorodnikova and her husband under occasional surveillance since 1980 but did not consider them a serious threat.

Svetlana had bragged about being a major in the KGB, but the FBI regarded her and her husband as amateurs who carried out small-time operations. Miller met her during an investigation, and she expressed sympathy for his financial and personal problems. Miller was overweight, suffered from severe financial burdens, trying to support eight children and several properties on a salary of $50,000. Miller's personal and financial problems made him an obvious target of Soviet recruitment.

Ludmila Kontratjeva, a Soviet immigrant to the United States who had testified at the trial, was found dead in the back of a car in the Pacific near Malibu, California. Her lover, Vladimir Ratchikhine, also a Soviet immigrant, was arrested for her murder.

In July 1985, Ogorodnikova was sentenced to 18 years for espionage. Ogorodnikova, and her husband, Nikolai (sentenced to eight years), had pled guilty to conspiracy to commit espionage. Both had come to the United States in 1973.

The FBI noted Svetlana's frequent trips to the Soviet consulate in San Francisco and restored their surveillance on her, which led to the discovery of Miller. In 1991, Miller was finally sentenced to 20 years for espionage. Miller claimed that he had attempted to infiltrate the KGB network in California. Miller was also charged with providing classified data to a private investigator for $1,185 and stealing $2,000 in FBI funds earmarked for informants. (Allen and Polmar, *Merchants of Treason;* Corson and Crowley, *The New KGB;* Romerstein and Levchenko, *The KGB Against the "Main Enemy")*

Mintkenbaugh, James Allen see Johnson, Robert Lee

389 Mishukov, Yuri A. Mishukov had paid Richard A. Flink, a Republican candidate for New York's state assembly, $3,000 for data on U.S. government agencies, information on individuals in the Republican party, and specific topics and policies favorable to the Soviet Union. He also offered to finance his campaign. Flink went to the FBI, and Mishukov and a confederate, Yuri V. Zaisev, were trapped in an FBI sting operation and forced to leave the United States. In 1962 Mishukov, a UN translator, was ordered out of the country for espionage. (Barron, *KGB; Facts on File,* 1962; *New York Times,* September 16–18, 1962)

390 Mitchell, Bernon F. (b. 1929), and William H. Martin (b. 1931). Both were code clerks and mathematicians for the Cryptology Department, National Security Agency (NSA) when they defected to the Soviet Union in 1960. Both stated that they had been disenchanted by U.S. intelligence activities aimed against the Soviet Union and had planned their defections for a year.

At the press conference, they cited several examples of classified clandestine operations that had been staged against Soviet targets, attempts to recruit agents from friendly governments, and Third World coup attempts. Reportedly, they delivered valuable cryptographic secrets to the Soviets when they defected. They stated that the NSA had given cryptographic machines to friendly countries and was then able to intercept the signals. They also reported that the NSA regularly intercepted thirty to forty countries' signal communications.

Reportedly, Martin and Mitchell were homosexual lovers. When it was disclosed that they were homosexuals, the NSA began firing 26 homosexual employees and fired the NSA personnel director for failing to detect their sexual behavior.

They had met when they were assigned to the National Security Group's listening post in Kamiseya, Japan, when they were in the U.S. Navy. Mitchell had spent two years at the California Institute of Technology, where he studied philosophy, languages, and statistics. To avoid the draft, he joined the navy. He was assigned to the Kamiseya station where he met Martin. They shared similar beliefs, agnostics, a love of math. They were introverted and shy with homosexual tendencies.

Martin (nicknamed "Ham") was a young math genius who graduated early from high school and joined the navy. He was assigned to cryptographic duties for the National Security Group, first at the intercept station in Alaska, then at Kamiseya, Japan. After their stint in the navy, Martin stayed on in Japan as a civilian cryptologist for the Army Security Agency.

Mitchell returned to college, enrolling at Stanford, where he completed his degree in mathematics. Martin also returned to college in the United States at the University of Washington. They maintained their friendship after the navy, and both were hired by the NSA in July 1957. They underwent a polygraph for their security clearance, and it was Mitchell who confessed during the interview of sexual experiments with chickens and dogs between the ages of 13 and 19. Despite the bizarre admission, he was hired.

Both attended the training schools for the NSA and were assigned to the NSA Office of Research and Development. Shocked by the revelation that there were electronic intelligence missions being flown into the Soviet Union, they approached Congressman Wayne Hays, but no action was taken. Frustrated by the fact that nothing was done, they began to focus their disenchantment not only on the NSA but American society. A few months later, they decided to defect and began to make plans.

Martin was awarded an NSA scholarship for his master's degree in mathematics at the University of Illinois, Urbana, where he studied math and Russian in September 1959. It was here that he began associating with the college's Communist party. In December 1959, he and Mitchell flew to Cuba and met with Soviet diplomats. They returned to the United States and began making additional plans, naively reading Soviet magazines published in English, which gave a romantic view of the Soviet Union.

They took leave at the same time from the NSA, between June and July 1960. First going to Mexico City, then Cuba, they took a Soviet freighter to the Soviet Union. It took the NSA a month to realize they were missing. After a press conference in Moscow in which they revealed a variety of NSA operations and their disillusionment with American society, they began their new lives in the Soviet Union.

Two years later, Martin had changed his name to Sokolovsky. Martin had married and was studying for his candidate's degree, essentially a Ph.D. He complained to a journalist of his disillusionment. In 1979, Mitchell made an inquiry to the State Department on whether he could return but was rejected and his citizenship revoked. (Andrew and Gordievsky, *KGB*; Bamford, *The Puzzle Palace*; West, *The SIGINT Secrets*; Wise and Ross, *The Invisible Government*)

391   Miyanaga, Yukihisa.   In January 1980, Japanese authorities arrested Miyanaga, retired army general, and two aides, Warrent Officer

Tsunetoshi Oshima and Lieutenant Eiichi Kashii, for spying for the Soviet Union. When KGB officer Stanislav Levitchenko defected to the United States, he described a Japanese spy ring, which led authorities to Miyanaga. According to Japanese authorities, Miyanaga had received over $20,000 for his services over a period of ten years. His aides confessed to their involvement and stated that when Miyanaga served in the intelligence branch of Japan's defense force, they provided the general with classified documents.

This was the first spy affair involving the military since World War II. Most of the classified data involved information about U.S. and Chinese military activities and Japanese counterintelligence operations. The scandal brought about the dismissal of Enji Kobota, the director-general of Japan's defense agency, and forced the resignation of Shigeto Nakana, army chief of staff. (Bittman, *The KGB and Soviet Disinformation*; Suvorov, *Inside Soviet Military Intelligence*)

392 Mizrahi, Baruch. In March 1974, Israel exchanged 65 Arab terrorists to Egypt in exchange for Mizrahi, an Egyptian-born Israeli who had been arrested in Yemen in 1972 and given to the Egyptians. Mizrahi was in Syria in 1965 as a principal of a foreign-language school in Aleppo, Syria, when Eli Cohen was arrested by Syrian counterintelligence.

In the early 1970s, he was sent to North Yemen to spy on the Egyptian Army, still involved in a civil war there, and to report on shipping traffic in and out of the Red Sea. In June 1971 a unit from the Popular Front for the Liberation of Palestine (PLFP) operating out of the Yemeni Red Sea port of Hodeida, shot rockets at an oil tanker heading northward to Eilat. Mizrahi, sent in 1972 under cover as a Moroccan businessman, was captured while taking photographs in Hodeida. He was handed over to Egyptian authorities till a POW exchange in March 1974 for two Israeli Arabs who had been spying for Egyptian intelligence. (Black and Raviv, *Israel's Secret Wars*; Raviv and Melman, *Every Spy a Prince*)

393 Modin, Yuri Ivanovich. Stationed in London from 1947 to 1953 and from 1955 to 1958, he was the last KGB agent to handle Anthony Blunt, Kim Philby, Donald Maclean, Guy Burgess, and John Cairncross (the "Magnificent Five"), who knew him only as "Peter." He helped in the escape of Burgess and Maclean in 1951 to the Soviet Union, and the escape of Philby in 1958 when Modin traveled to Beirut to warn Philby of his impending arrest. Modin also handled George Blake when he returned from a North Korean POW camp in 1953, and again in 1958.

In 1958 Modin became involved in a heated argument with the head of the KGB station in London, Nikolai Borisovich Rodin. As a result Modin, was recalled to Moscow.

In 1967 Modin emerged in New Delhi, India, under the name Yuri Lyudin, helping to prepare disinformation stories that were planted in Indian newspapers to influence the 1967 election. The main target was an anti–Communist candidate by the name of S. K. Patil.

In April 1967 after only nine months, Modin returned to Moscow. In the early 1980s he was teaching offensive intelligence techniques at Faculty Number One (political intelligence) in the FCD Andropov Institute. (Andrew and Gordievsky, *KGB*; Barron, *KGB*)

394 Moncada, Marlena. In the summer of 1983, Nicaragua announced that an attempt by the CIA to poison Defense Minister Miguel d'Escoto Brockman had been prevented with the help of Moncada, a double agent. At a news conference Nicaraguan security chief Lenin Cerna displayed a bottle of poison, two booklets for decoding radio messages, and note paper that dissolved in water. The CIA was accused of giving these items to Moncada.

Moncada stated that the CIA had recruited her in 1982 while she was assigned to the Nicaraguan embassy in Honduras. Moncada identified her recruiter as Ermila Rodriguez. The Nicaraguan government expelled three U.S. diplomats accusing them of being CIA agents: David Greig, reported to be the chief of CIA operations at the U.S. embassy in Managua; Linda Pfeifer, a case officer assigned to agents in the anti–Sandinista movement; and Ermila Rodriguez.

The U.S. government denied involvement and retaliated by closing all six of the Nicaraguan consulates in the U.S. and expelling twenty-one consular officials. The Nicaraguan security forces arrested Mario Castillo, member of the opposition Democratic Conservative party, accusing him of taking part in the assassination plot. Another, Carlos Icaza, was accused, but took refuge in the Venezuelan embassy. The Nicaraguan government accused Icaza of participation in the assassination plot and of being the CIA's main agent responsible for recruiting in Nicaragua. A third member of the plot, Enrique Sotelo Borge, a member of the Democratic Conservative party, was also arrested. (*Facts on File*, 1983; *New York Times*, June 7, 1983)

395 Moore, Edwin G. In December 1976, Moore, a former CIA officer, was arrested by FBI agents for attempting to sell CIA documents to the Soviets. Moore, retired in 1973 from the CIA, who worked in the map-making and logistics section, had thrown a package of classified documents, including a directory of CIA intelligence officers names and office telephone numbers, into the grounds of a Soviet residence in Washington with a note explaining that he had classified CIA documents for sale for $200,000. But the Soviets believed the package might be a bomb and turned it over to the Executive Protection Service. They notified the FBI and responded to Moore's offer.

The note asked for $200,000 to be left at a drop site in a residential suburban neighborhood. The FBI left a drop at the site, and agents watched nearby. A man raking leaves in his yard across the street from the drop walked over to the package and picked it up. It was Moore.

Moore had worked for the CIA from 1952 to 1953; he was fired after being arrested for arson of his home in North Carolina. Acquitted on that charge, he appealed for reinstatement and was rehired in 1967.

After his arrest, the FBI searched his home and discovered boxes of classified documents. In May 1977, Moore was found guilty of attempting to sell classified data to the Soviet Union and sentenced to life, but paroled in 1979. (Allen and Polmar, *Merchants of Treason;* Corson, *The Armies of Ignorance*)

396 Moore, Michael R. A lance corporal in the Marine Corps while working at the Naval Air Station in Cubi Point, Philippines, he was caught with photographs and classified data while attempting to give them to a Soviet contact in February 1984. Reportedly, Moore had expressed an interest in defecting. He was not prosecuted and was discharged from the service. (Allen and Polmar, *Merchants of Treason*)

397 Moqarrebi, Ahmed. In December 1977, Major General Moqarrebi was executed for attempting to pass classified Iranian Army documents to the Soviet embassy in Teheran. He confessed to spying for the Soviet Union for nine years. Some of the data he passed included Iran's purchase of military equipment, including aircraft, from the United States (*Facts on File,* 1977; *New York Times,* December 26, 1977)

398 Morrison, James. In 1983 the former Royal Canadian Mounted Police (RCMP) corporal was charged with espionage for the Soviet Union between 1955 and 1958. But in 1984 a Canadian court ruled that the government had waited too long to prosecute the case and therefore dismissed it. Morrison admitted being the individual on whom John Sawatsky based his spy novel *For Services Rendered.*

Morrison was charged with three charges of espionage for providing two Soviet agents with information. Morrison pled not guilty to the charges. Morrison's arrest did not come till after Sawatsky's book, which detailed Morrison's activities under the code name Long Knife. Morrison admitted in a TV interview that he was the Long Knife of the book. Ironically, Morrison had given the RCMP notification of his espionage activities when he left the RCMP in 1958 but was not charged with any crime. (*Facts on File,* 1983–84; *New York Times,* June 10, 1983)

399 Mueller, Gustav Adolph.
U.S. Army Corporal Mueller was court-martialed for espionage and sentenced to five years in West Germany for attempting to provide classified documents to the Soviet Union in 1950. Mueller was arrested after telegraphing an offer to sell secrets to the Soviet consulate in Berne, Switzerland. (*Facts on File*, 1950; *New York Times*, April 14, 16, 1950)

400 Mufti, Aminah (b. 1935).
Born to a Circassian Muslim family in Jordan, she was recruited by the Mossad in Vienna in 1972 after she fell in love with an Israeli pilot visiting Austria. The Circassian community in Jerusalem had been a valuable source of agents within the Muslim population. She was probably intentionally chosen by Mossad, who sent an attractive pilot for her seduction. She hated the PLO and blamed them for the wars in the Middle East.

She was sent to Beirut in 1973 to infiltrate the PLO. Her medical education made her valuable to the PLO, who let her set up a clinic. When the civil war broke out in Lebanon in 1975, she treated numerous PLO soldiers, making contact with top-level PLO leaders. Ironically, her clinic was being financed by the Mossad. She was able to gather a variety of intelligence. Her reports were left in dead drops in Beirut, and emergency data was sent by a small radio transmitter. The PLO discovered her activities and tortured her into revealing her mission. She was held in a cave near the Lebanese port of Sidon. She was finally traded for two PLO terrorists and given a job as a doctor in Israel. (Raviv and Melman, *Every Spy a Prince*)

401 Munsinger, Gerda (Olga) Hessler.
In 1966 a major scandal erupted in Canada when a former German citizen, Munsinger, was reported to have been a spy for East Germany while having romantic affairs with several members of Canada's Conservative cabinet under former P.M. John Diefenbarker during the late 1950s and early 1960s. Reportedly, she was commonly seen with former Associate Defense Minister Pierre Sevigny from 1958 to 1960. She was born in Koenigsburg, East Germany, and had escaped to West Germany in 1949. She married a U.S. soldier, Michael F. Munsinger, in the early 1950s, but when he applied to have her return to the United States with him, he was informed by the U.S. State Department that she had a history of espionage and was considered a security risk.

Mrs. Munsinger denied being a spy and claimed she left Canada because she had become bored. From 1960 until she left Canada, she was under surveillance. Soviet KGB agents would frequently visit her at her Canadian home. She was described as a known prostitute in West Germany and had been arrested in 1949 for prostitution and theft. (*Facts on File*, 1966; *New York Times*, March 12; April 26, 29, 1966)

402   Myagkov, Aleksei (b. 1945).   A counterintelligence KGB officer stationed in East Germany, he defected in February 1974. A captain at the time he defected, he had been stationed at the headquarters of the Motorized Rifle Regiment. While on a tour of West Berlin with several other KGB officers, he slipped away and contacted British authorities.

In 1962 he attended the officers' cadet airborne school at Ryazan for four years. After this he was posted to an intelligence subunit at Kaunas in an airborne division. Recruited by the KGB in December 1967, he went to KGB training school in Siberia. In 1968 he finished his studies and was appointed to the East Germany Directorate of Special Sections, KGB, Group of Soviet Forces in Germany. He became disillusioned with the Soviet system of violence and oppression. (Myagkov, *Inside the KGB*)

Myer, Barbara see **Myer, Frederick**

403   Myer, Frederick, and wife, Barbara.   In February 1985 U.S. Army Colonel Myer and his wife were arrested in Poland in a restricted military area. Reportedly, their car was stopped after being discovered in a restricted military zone. The police found several rolls of film, cameras, and military maps. The Polish government claimed that the couple had intentionally destroyed six rolls of film before the police could arrest them. Apparently, the Polish police mistreated the couple upon their arrest, strip-searching her. They were expelled from Poland a few days later. The United States retaliated by expelling Colonel Zygmunt Szymanski, Polish military attaché in Washington. (*Facts on File*, 1985; *New York Times*, February 26, 1985)

404   Narain, Coomar.   On the evening of January 16, 1985, special agents of India's Intelligence Bureau arrested Narain as the ringleader of a complex spy ring working for France, East Germany, the Soviet Union, and Poland. Coomar was the regional manager of Maneklal Group Industries when he was arrested. Narain confessed to being involved in espionage for 25 years obtaining military, economic, and political data. Narain reportedly had infiltrated the prime minister's office in 1982 during the reign of Indira Gandhi.

Several diplomats were named as conspirators: former French deputy defense attaché Col. Alain Bolley; former Polish commercial attaché Jan Haberka; and an East German, Otto Wicker. Altogether, nineteen Indian nationals were charged with espionage. Data transmitted by the spy ring included military and economic, intelligence and political data. (Bobb, "The Spy Sensation," *India Today; Facts on File*, 1985; *New York Times*, February 5, 6, 1985)

405 Nassar Haro, Miguel.   In 1982, Nassar Haro, former Mexican police chief, was identified as an important intelligence source for the CIA. Nassar Haro was indicted by a federal court in an international car theft case in California. The ring was believed responsible for stealing six hundred cars in southern California and moving them into Mexico. High officials in Mexico would resell them. The U.S. attorney in San Diego, William H. Kennedy, informed news reporters of Nassar Haro's relationship with the CIA and that he was forced to release him. Kennedy was dismissed by the Justice Department for revealing an agent of the CIA. The indictment was dropped in the $8-million case because of complaints from the CIA that Nassar Haro had been a valuable asset in Mexico and Central America. United States authorities reported that his intelligence gathering included the activity of guerrilla leaders in El Salvador and Guatemala. He was also a key intelligence source on foreign influence in El Salvador. Nassar Haro had been supplying the CIA with data since 1977 when he was head of Mexico's Directorate of Federal Security. (*Facts on File*, 1982; *New York Times*, March 28–30; April 2, 3, 5–7, 24, 1982)

406 Negrino, Azelio, and Victor Pronine.   In February 1983, Negrino, Italian businessman, and Pronine, the assistant commercial director of the Soviet Aeroflot's Rome office, were arrested by Italian authorities for espionage. Negrino was the owner of a microfilm company in Genoa and was planning to give Pronine, who did not have diplomatic immunity, sensitive microfilm data on classified weapons and military installations. The carabinieri, Italy's paramilitary police, made the arrests and confiscated classified documents in Negrino's possession. A third party was arrested a few days later — Viktor Konaiev, deputy commercial director of an Italian-Soviet company, Nafta-Italia, who did not have diplomatic immunity. Police confiscated classified documents from Konaiev's office. Konaiev was accused of complicity to commit espionage with Negrino and Pronine. (*Facts on File*, 1983; *New York Times*, February 15, 17, 18, 25, 1983)

407 Nelson, William.   The CIA operations deputy director (DDO), resigned April 1976. Nelson had served as chief of the East Asia Division and was then appointed deputy director of operations in 1973. As DDO, he participated in the creation of the Angola Task Force, with John Stockwell as chief, described as a covert operation directed to supply the National Front for the Liberation of Angola (NFLA) with weapons and material to fight the Cuban-backed government. Nelson was replaced by Bill Welles as DDO. (Phillips, *The Night Watch*; Prados, *Presidents' Secret Wars*; Stockwell, *In Search of Enemies*)

408 Nenninger, Ursula Maria. A former librarian for the European Atomic Energy Agency in Brussels, she was sentenced to two years for espionage in 1962 for East Germany. She provided East Germany with classified data on the European atomic bomb project from 1956 till her arrest in 1961. A confederate, Heinz Werner, a philosopher who had lectured in East Germany, was also sentenced to two years for cooperating. (*Facts on File*, 1962; *New York Times*, February 2, 1962)

409 Netrebsky, Boris, and Viktor S. Sharovatov. In May 1970 the Netherlands announced that two Soviet embassy diplomats were expelled for espionage activities: Netrebsky, second secretary, and Sharovatov, who had already left Holland in March. Reportedly, Dutch authorities found a military map in Netrebsky's car that detailed military installations. Netrebsky's car had been found in a canal after a car accident. (*Facts on File*, 1970; *New York Times*, May 7, 1970)

410 Nguyen Song Hai, and Tran Ngoc Duc. Nguyen, second secretary, and Tran, North Vietnamese press agency correspondent, along with four minor officials from the North Vietnamese embassy, were arrested when their car was rammed by Laotian military police jeep in Vientiane to prevent them from reaching the North Vietnamese embassy. A search of their car revealed maps of Sam Thong and Long Cheng, two secret military bases where U.S. Special Forces and CIA officers helped train and run the Laotian military against the Pathet Lao in northeastern Laos. Reportedly, Laotian authorities had received a tip that the North Vietnamese had made contact with a Laotian army officer who provided the maps. In August 26, 1969, Laotian officials expelled five North Vietnamese diplomats and a North Vietnamese correspondent for espionage activities. All six were arrested August 9 and were flown out of the country on an International Control Commission plane but returned for some unknown reason to the Laotian capital of Vientiane where they were rearrested. They were put on another ICC plane on August 17 but had to return again to Vientiane due to poor weather conditions for landing in Hanoi. (*Facts on File*, 1969; *New York Times*, August 11, 14, 1969)

411 Nicholson, Arthur D. United States Army Major Nicholson was shot by a Soviet sentry on March 24, 1985, in East Germany. The Soviets argued that Nicholson was in a restricted military zone and was taking pictures of Soviet military equipment. Nicholson had been part of the U.S. liaison unit that was authorized to observe Soviet and Warsaw Pact military forces.

The Soviet version stated that Nicholson, wearing camouflage fatigues, had been caught by a Soviet guard at a military facility taking photographs of Soviet military equipment. According to their version, the Soviet soldier ordered him to stop, firing warning shots before shooting Nicholson as he fled.

The U.S. version, according to a companion of Nicholson at the scene, Sergeant Jesse Schatz, admitted that Nicholson had taken pictures of Soviet military equipment inside a building in the facility, but Nicholson had left the facility and was outside the restricted military zone when shot. Nicholson was not wearing camouflage fatigues but a regular army uniform. Both were not running but standing next to their Jeep when three shots were fired. The United States complained that it was an hour before the Soviets gave Nicholson medical attention. (*Facts on File*, 1985; *New York Times*, March 26–31; April 4, 5, 11, 16–18; May 2, 10, 1985)

412   Nicholson, John Roger, and Alfred Trevor Gallaher.
In December 1969, these Rhodesian citizens were convicted by a Rhodesian court for spying for the United States. They were released in January 1970 and surrendered their Rhodesian citizenship before being expelled. Reportedly, Nicholson was recruited by the CIA in 1968 and made regular contact with the U.S. consul general's office in Salisbury. Gallaher worked independently of Nicholson as a spy for the U.S. State Department. Both men were released reportedly under an agreement between the United States and Rhodesia that if they were released, the United States would not close its diplomatic mission in Rhodesia. (*Facts on File*, 1970; *New York Times*, November 2; December 10, 11, 1969; January 4, 5, 1970)

413   Noriega, Manuel Antonio (b. 1934).
Recruited by the CIA in the mid–1950s at a military academy for $25 a month. After he graduated, the CIA lost interest till 1968 when the CIA took control of all intelligence activities in Panama; they inherited Noriega from U.S. Army Intelligence, then a major in the National Guard. By 1972, Noriega was the intelligence chief and the most important CIA asset in Panama, receiving $100,000 annually for his services. He provided critical intelligence on Central America and Cuba.

In 1972 the Nixon administration considered assassinating Noriega for his drug activities, but the Watergate affair forced Nixon to drop the plan. The CIA also suspected Noriega of providing intelligence on U.S. military operations to Cuba. Noriega also became a human rights problem for the United States when in 1971, after throwing the wounded priest Hector Gallegos from a helicopter, he complained to a CIA official that he had learned a valuable lesson from the incident: "Always kill a man before throwing him out of the helicopter."

Noriega depended on a Brazilian "healer" or "mentalist" by the name of Ivan Trilha, whom he met in the mid–1970s, to help him control the cosmic forces of the universe. While Noriega was head of the Panamanian intelligence, he met Trilha, who would cure Noriega's severe migraines, calling them "demon" headaches. Trilha told Noriega that he would become a great leader of Panama. Noriega's ego latched onto these words, and Trilha accompanied Noriega on his journey to power. Noriega also believed in Santeria, a Cuban black-magic religion involving animal sacrifice.

By the mid–1980s, U.S. intelligence had collected enough data on Noriega's connections to Colombia's drug cartel to warrant concern and the desire to unseat Noriega. Noriega latched onto power, using "dignity battalions" and the secret police to terrorize his opponents. Noriega's favorite style of murder was beheading. The most famous victim was Hugo Spadafora; in 1985 he was found beheaded in a U.S. mailbag in Costa Rica.

Noriega's childhood was difficult. His alcoholic father abandoned him, and his mother died at an early age. He grew up in poverty with a severe case of acne, for which he was coined "pineapple face." Reportedly, Noriega was raped by one of his older brothers while he was young.

Despite his poor beginnings, Noriega managed to attend the Instituto Nacional (high school) in 1947, which was famous for political activism. In 1958 Noriega attended the Chorrillos Military Academy in Peru. He was an unruly student and was arrested once for beating and raping an unwilling prostitute.

It was at the military academy that Noriega spied on his fellow students and instructors, looking for leftists for the CIA. When Noriega returned to Panama, there was no officer's billet, so the U.S. government gave him a road-surveying job in the Canal Zone. In 1964 the 470th Military Intelligence Brigade recruited Noriega when he was hired on by Torrijos. On December 20, 1989, U.S. troops invaded Panama, arresting Noriega and extraditing him to the U.S. Despite advanced warning of an invasion, Noriega was with a prostitute when he heard U.S. forces attacking the city. (Hersh, "The Creation of a Thug," *Life*; Johnson, *America's Secret Power*; Kempe, *Divorcing the Dictator*; Woodward, *Veil*)

414   North, Oliver ("Ollie") Lawrence (b. 1943).   National Security Council aide and covert action specialist for the U.S. military. North attended the state college in Brockport as an English major and joined the Marine ROTC. He entered Annapolis and graduated in 1968.

Officially North served in Vietnam as an infantry platoon commander from December 3, 1968, to August 21, 1969, and then in a G-3 operations billet at Headquarters Battalion, Third Division, until November 23, 1969. While in Vietnam, his unit was referred to as Blue's Bastards, derived from North's radio call sign "Blue." They were stationed just south of the demilitarized zone (DMZ) and on one occasion led a successful covert mission into North Vietnam to capture an NVA soldier for interrogation.

North was first assigned to Basic School, Quantico, Virginia, from November 29, 1969, to February 2, 1973. While in the United States, Randy Harrod, one of the soldiers in his unit back in Vietnam, was court-martialed for the murder of sixteen Vietnamese women and children at Son Thang. North returned to Vietnam to testify as a character witness on Harrod's behalf. While the trial dragged on, North became bored and began participating in search-and-destroy missions with a nearby Marine unit. The lawyers were terrified that North would be killed in action before he was called to testify. Reportedly, North was involved in the Special Operations Group headed by General John Singlaub, which conducted covert counterinsurgency missions into Laos. While testifying as a character witness at the New York securities fraud trial of NSC aide Thomas Reed, North stated that he was on active duty in Vietnam from 1968 through the early part of 1970, then again in 1971, claiming to have been the team commander in the Special Operations Force.

North then went to Okinawa to work with the Special Operations Detachment, where he ran the Northern Training Area, a jungle combat school. North was then assigned to the Naval War College, where he served as an instructor. North was voluntarily hospitalized for emotional problems between December 6, 1974, and January 7, 1975, at Bethesda Naval Hospital. One night North was discovered nude, carrying a .45 automatic pistol, wandering a suburb in Virginia mumbling about the Vietcong and suicide. Afterward, North returned to active service in the Marine Corps. When North applied for a staff position on the National Security Council, apparently no one was informed of his past emotional problems. Several pages from North's outpatient treatment record describing his hospitalization had mysteriously been removed. National Security Council Advisor Richard Allen was not informed of North's hospitalization and later admitted that if he had known, he might not have hired North for such a sensitive position.

In 1980, North was based at Camp Lejeune, North Carolina. He led a secret team of marines into eastern Turkey in April 1980 to back up the Iran hostage rescue mission. When the mission failed, North helped plan a second rescue plan with Richard Secord, but the plan was aborted. In August 1981, North joined the National Security Council under the Reagan administration.

In May 1986, North participated in the secret U.S. delegation to Iran to discuss hostage release. Along with North was Robert McFarlane, NSC staffer Howard Teicher, former CIA officer George Cave, and Israeli counterterrorist adviser Amiram Nir. The plane was carrying parts for Hawk missiles, and the delelgation brought odd gifts for the Iranian government: six Blackhawk .357 Magnums in presentation boxes and a chocolate cake shaped as a key. The Iranians were unaware that the delegation had arrived, and they were forced to wait in the plane. In the meantime, the Revolutionary Guards guarding the group ate the cake. Once Iranian officials showed up, they were taken to the Independence Hotel, and discussions began. The Iranians were upset that the Americans had brought only half the Hawk parts promised. Two days later, the U.S. delegation left Teheran, leaving an unpaid $4,000 hotel bill.

Money earned from the sale of arms to Iran was used to buy weapons and supplies for the Contras in clear violation of congressional ban on weapons sales to the contras. (Byrne, *The Chronology*; Cockburn, *Out of Control*; Lamar, "North's Other Secret," *Time*; Marshall, Scott, and Hunter, *The Iran-Contra Connection*; U.S. Govt, *The Tower Commission Report*; Walker, *Reagan versus the Sandinistas*)

415   Nosenko, Yuri Ivanovich (b. 1927).   In 1964, Nosenko, a staff member of the Soviet secret police, defected in Geneva to the United States. Nosenko had been attached to the Soviet delegation to the disarmament conference in Geneva as the KGB security officer in 1962. He contacted the CIA in 1963 and suggested that he could spy for them in the KGB. But at a second meeting in January 1964, he requested asylum. Nosenko stated that he was a lieutenant colonel in the KGB, but it was later discovered that he was a captain.

Nosenko attended the Naval Preparatory School in 1942, then attended the State Institute of International Relations in Moscow in 1945, excelling in English. After he graduated, he was recruited by GRU Naval Intelligence and assigned to the Seventh (Far Eastern) Fleet in the Vladivostok region for three years, working in the signal intelligence analysis branch monitoring U.S. military communications in Asia and the Pacific. In 1953 he joined the KGB and returned to Moscow. He worked for the Second Chief Directorate (foreign intelligence operations) as a security officer and for the Seventh Department that recruited American tourists visiting the Soviet Union. In 1957 he visited the West for the first time as a KGB security officer, under cover as an official of the Ministry of Culture under the alias Nikolaev, traveling with a Soviet athletic team. He was stunned by the high standard of living in Great Britain.

By 1959, he was working with the Seventh Department again, assigned as the case officer of Lee Harvey Oswald in 1959. It was Nosenko's opinion that Oswald was considered unimportant by the KGB and that the KGB had not been involved in the assassination of President Kennedy. Sometime during this period he discovered that the KGB had kept a surveillance file on his father despite the fact that he was well known for his patriotism and loyalty. This disturbed Nosenko, and his disillusionment with the KGB grew.

When the United States arrested KGB spy Igor Ivanov in 1963, the

KGB decided to arrest an American citizen in hopes of trading him. Nosenko was assigned to pick out an American, Frederick Barghoorn, a Yale political science professor, but when the KGB began to believe that he was a personal friend of President Kennedy, he was released a month later. After this incident he was assigned as a security officer at the Geneva conference. It was here that he made his decision to defect. But for Nosenko his troubles were just beginning.

When the CIA discovered that Nosenko had been Oswald's case officer and that according to Nosenko the KGB had no involvement in the Kennedy assassination, many in the CIA began to believe that Nosenko was an agent sent to throw the CIA off on KGB involvement. Many in the CIA believed that he was a disinformation agent sent to cover up the KGB relationship with Oswald. There was a vigorous debate in the CIA about his credibility. Nosenko did help point toward the spy John Vassall in Great Britain and gave the location of over 40 listening devices in the U.S. embassy in Moscow; a CIA mole in the KGB confirmed that Nosenko had damaged the KGB, rolling up its operations in New York due to the defection. Despite this, a civil war waged within the CIA over Nosenko's credibility.

Nosenko was kept in a house surrounded with barbed wire and searchlights at Camp Peary, the CIA training base near Williamsburg, Virginia, where he was occasionally drugged, interrogated constantly, and confined until 1968. The CIA head of counterintelligence, James Angleton, became obsessed with the theory that Nosenko was a KGB plant. Many in the CIA felt Nosenko's harsh treatment was outrageous. After 1968 Nosenko's treatment improved, and he was given a regular salary as a CIA contract adviser. (Andrew and Gordievsky, *KGB*; Barron, *The KGB*; Brook-Shepherd, *The Storm Birds*; Halpern and Peake, "Did Angleton Jail Nosenko?" *IJIC*; Mangold, *Cold Warrior*)

416 Nunn-May, Alan (b. 1911).   Born in Great Britain, he attended Cambridge in 1930, graduating in 1933. He later earned a doctorate in 1936 in physics. He visited the Soviet Union as a student and became a confirmed Communist. While teaching at Cambridge, he joined the Cambridge team on the Tube Alloys atom bomb project in April 1942. While in Canada, he made contact with Soviet intelligence. The Soviet GRU assigned him the code name "Alek" while he was working on the Manhattan Project where he provided the Soviets with samples of uranium 235 used in the Hiroshima bomb. In January 1943, he went to Montreal for the Atomic Energy Division of the Canadian National Research Council.

When Igor Gouzenko defected, he exposed the Canadian spy ring. Nunn-May returned to London in 1946 where he pled guilty and was sentenced to ten years; he was released in 1952. (Gouzenko, *The Iron Curtain*;

Hyde, *The Atom Bomb Spies*; Lucas, *The Great Spy Ring*; Moorehead, *The Traitors*)

417   Nut, Bernard.   Lieutenant Colonel Nut, French counterintelligence official, was found dead February 1983 near a mountain road in the French Alps. Lying near his car a few feet away was a .375 Magnum with three shots fired. He was shot in the back of the head. At first it was believed to be suicide, but an autopsy revealed that Nut's death was a murder. Several theories were discussed. One stated that Nut was killed by a double agent after Nut had discovered him. (*Facts on File*, 1983; *New York Times*, April 6, 1983)

Obieglo, Hubert see Klopfleisch, Erich

418   Ogorodnikova, Svetlana.   In July 1985, Ogorodnikova was sentenced to eighteen years for espionage. She was the female lure who trapped FBI agent Richard Miller into spying for the KGB. Ogorodnikova and her husband, Nikolai (sentenced to eight years), pled guilty to espionage. Both had emigrated to the United States in 1973 and had been under occasional FBI surveillance since 1980. The FBI began constant surveillance of her when she began frequenting the Soviet consulate in San Francisco. The FBI then discovered that Miller had met her in 1984. The FBI described her as an amateur spy who did small-time operations. She would often brag about being a KGB major. The prosecution argued that Svetlana's role was to trap Miller into an affair and convince him to provide classified documents. Miller claimed that he was attempting to infiltrate the KGB in California. (Allen and Polmar, *Merchants of Treason*; Corson and Crowley, *The New KGB*; Romerstein and Levchenko, *The KGB Against the "Main Enemy"*)

419   Oldfield, Maurice (1915–81).   Head of British MI6 from 1973 till his retirement in 1978. During World War II he served in the Intelligence Corps in the Middle East. At the end of the war, he joined MI6. While in MI6, he served in a variety of posts in Asia and as station chief in Washington. His security clearance was withdrawn in 1980 when he admitted to being a homosexual. Oldfield had worked under Soviet spy Kim Philby for a time. Rumored to be the model of John le Carré's fictional character George Smiley and the character of "M" from Ian Fleming's James Bond novels. (Andrew, *Her Majesty's Secret Service*; Knightley, *The Master Spy*; West, *The Circus*; Wright, *Spy Catcher*)

Olivier, Louis Leon see Lundahl, Frederick Boyce

420   Opatrny, Jiri, and Zdenek Pisk.   In July 1966, the U.S. State Department expelled Opatrny, attaché for the Czech embassy, for planning to place a listening device in a State Department office. The operation had begun in 1961 by Zdenek Pisk, a second secretary, but he turned the operation over to Opatrny when he returned to Czechoslovakia in May 1963. A Czech-speaking employee of the State Department passport office, Frank John Mrkva acted as an undercover agent for the FBI after informing authorities of Pisk's approach. When Opatrny gave Mrkva a listening device to install in the office, authorities arrested him in May 1966. It was intended to be planted in the office of Raymond E. Lisle, director of European Affairs. Opatrny reportedly told Mrkva that a second operation would be launched to place a bug in the office of Undersecretary of State George W. Ball. (*Facts on File,* 1966; *New York Times,* July 14, 16, 1966)

421   Osborne, Richard W.   In March 1983, the Soviet Union ordered Osborne expelled for espionage. Osborne, a U.S. diplomat, had been detained by Soviet authorities after he was caught operating a portable radio device used for the transmission of data via the U.S. Marisat communications satellite. Osborne had been a first secretary in the economics section in Moscow since August 1982. *Izvestia* accused Osborne of being a CIA agent, claiming that he had been caught with a special radio that was used with the Marisat communications satellites. Notes found on Osborne reportedly could dissolve in water in case of emergencies. (Kessler, *Moscow Station;* Richelson, *American Espionage and the Soviet Target*)

422   Ostenrieder, Gerda.   In September 1977, Ostenrieder was sentenced in a West German court to three years for giving over 500 Foreign Ministry classified documents to East Germany from 1964 to 1973. (*Facts on File,* 1977)

423   Ostrovsky, Victor (b. 1949).   Raised as a Zionist in Holon, Israel, but of Canadian origin, he joined the army at the age of 18 and nine months later became a second lieutenant in the military police, then the youngest officer in the Israeli army, serving at the Suez Canal, Golan Heights, and along the Jordan River.

In November 1971, Ostrovsky left the military and moved back to Edmonton, Canada, missing the Yom Kippur war. He returned to Israel in May 1977 and joined the navy, serving as a captain, head of the weapons system testing branch of the Israeli Navy's operations section.

Ostrovsky was recruited by the Mossad, and after several meetings and examinations he rejected the offer when he was told that the job would require considerable time away from his family. Mossad harassed him and his wife by phone for the next eight months. Ostrovsky actually wanted the position but wanted to maintain his close relationship with his family. Finally succumbing to their harassment, he joined the Mossad in the fall of 1982.

After an extensive and exhaustive preemployment process, including two polygraphs, an English examination, numerous questionnaries, psychological and physical examinations, including a six-hour interview of his wife, Ostrovsky was accepted into the Mossad's two-year training program. According to Ostrovsky, they hold a course every three years, and that is made up of only 15 people. Whether any of these people pass the course is not a predetermined result. Of the five thousand interviews they give, they pick only 15 for the course. He arrived at the Mossad training base January 1983.

In a bizarre incident in August 1984 at the Mossad academy, Ostrovsky and two other recruits stumbled upon a sex party at the academy pool. About 25 people, nude, mostly secretaries, female soldiers, and top Mossad brass, including the present head of Mossad, Mark Hessner, were dancing, playing in the pool, engaging in sex, and swapping partners. Ostrovsky would later discover that the parties were quite frequent.

Ostrovsky's days at Mossad became numbered after several odd events took place. The first came when another Mossad trainee approached him with a homosexual advance. After complaining to Mossad brass about the behavior, he was forcefully told to forget it. The second incident came in a Mossad break-in at the special investigative police headquarters in Jerusalem where they removed a file on the police investigation of the veteran religious cabinet minister Yosef Burg. Ostrovsky complained about Mossad's internal interference in Israeli politics, a clear violation of regulation, and was warned not to complain. The third incident came two weeks after he became a *katsas* (case officer) when he was ordered to transfer a parcel that had arrived from the Far East to Panama. But when he arrived at the airport, he discovered a huge container containing smaller packages. After loading it on an Israeli Air Force Hercules transport carrier, he discovered it was illegal drugs. After he complained to officials in Mossad, he discovered that it was Mossad's Mike Harari who was involved in the Panamanian operation.

He was sent to Cyprus to pose as a middleman in an arms shipment to a European who had been supplying arms to the PLO. The idea was to involve European police in the investigation after Mossad provided evidence of their involvement in illegal gunrunning. After the success of this operation, another one came into play, one that resulted in his termination from Mossad, serving as a middleman between Mossad and a Metsada combatant watching the Tripoli airport in Libya. When a Libyan Gulfstream 11 executive jet filled with some of the most wanted PLO terrorists took off, the Metsada agent contacted Ostrovsky, who notified the Israeli

Air Force waiting to intercept the jet. Unexpectedly, Ostrovsky accidently discovered that it was a trick by the PLO, who were on to the Israeli plan. After desperately trying to warn Mossad, he was ignored. When the airplane was intercepted and landed in Israel, it was found not to contain the terrorists but some Arab businessmen. Israel was embarrassed by the scandal that followed, and Mossad conveniently, and intentionally, blamed Ostrovsky for the mess.

When he finally returned to Mossad headquarters, he was told to resign in March 1986. He soon discovered that his military file had been ordered activated and that he was to be sent to serve as a liaison for the southern Lebanese army and Israel, clearly an overt attempt to get him killed, for serving such a position would have been a death sentence for an ex–Mossad agent. Fearing for his life, he escaped Israel and fled back to Canada where he wrote his book detailing his experiences. (Black and Morris, *Israel's Secret Wars;* Ostrovsky and Hoy, *By Way of Deception*)

424   Oswald, Lee Harvey.   There are a variety of conspiracy theories surrounding the assassin of Pres. John F. Kennedy. One of those theories is based on a belief that Oswald was part of a CIA plan to assassinate Kennedy. In 1964, Oswald's mother testified that she believed that Oswald was employed in some fashion for the CIA. The CIA denied any association with Oswald. Another theory is that he had been recruited by the KGB for the assassination. Oswald had lived in the Soviet Union for several years. (Brook-Shepherd, *The Storm Birds;* Epstein, *Legend;* Garrison, *On the Trail of the Assassins;* Groden and Livingstone, *High Treason*)

425   Ott, Bruce D.   In January 1986, Ott, an airman first class, was arrested and convicted to 25 years for attempting to sell confidential data to the Soviets. Ott, a clerk, worked on the SR-71 spy planes. Ott had contacted the Soviet consulate general in San Francisco to sell data. He met two FBI agents posing as KGB officers and attempted to sell confidential data to them for $160,000. (Allen and Polmar, *Merchants of Treason; Facts on File,* 1986)

426   Owda, Faisal Abdel Kader.   In 1965, Owda, a secret service agent from Egypt, was granted political asylum in Iran. The Iranian state security organization described Owda as an important member of Egyptian intelligence organization. Iranian authorities also stated that Owda was preparing to tell about Egyptian espionage activities. Owda had arrived in Iran after fleeing Beirut, Lebanon, where Iranian security officials said he was on an important mission for Egyptian President Nasser. Egyptian authorities denied that Owda was involved in Egyptian intelligence or security operations. (*Facts on File*, 1965; *New York Times*, January 10, 11, 1965)

427   Owen, William James.   In January 1970, British officials arrested Owen, Labour party member of the House of Commons, for violating the Official Secrets Act by providing data to a foreign power between August 26, 1961, and December 1969. In April 1970, Owen resigned from the House of Commons. In May 1970, a jury found Owen not guilty of the charges. Owen had been accused of providing Czech agents with classified information from the defense committee on which he served as a member. Owen was accused of accepting money from the Czech agents. Owen admitted accepting money from Czech agents for information that he claimed was not classified and was often falsified. He had been recruited in 1957 during a visit in Czechoslovakia. Elected to Parliament in November 1954 and in February 1960 appointed to the Defence Estimates Committee, he supplied the Czechs with both political and military data. Though acquitted of the charges, he did agree to reveal the Czech relationship to MI5 after the trial. Code-named "Lee" by Czech intelligence, he had been recruited in 1954 by Czech intelligence officer Jan Paclik (alias Novak). (Andrew and Gordievsky, *KGB*; Frolik, *The Frolik Defection*; West, *The Circus*)

428   Pacepa, Ion.   In August 1978, Pacepa, the director of the Rumanian foreign intelligence service (DIE), defected to the West while in West Germany. Reportedly, General Pacepa was the vice-minister of the Rumanian security police and a close aid to Rumanian President Nicolae Ceauşescu. (Andrew and Gordievsky, *KGB*; *Facts on File*, 1978)

429   Paisley, John S. (d. 1978).   Former deputy chief of the CIA's Office of Strategic Research and a member of the CIA-DIA study group on the Soviet military budget. Even though Paisley had retired from the CIA in 1974, he continued on as a consultant.

On September 24, 1978, Paisley, 55, set sail in Chesapeake Bay on a sailboat. The next day the sloop was found floating empty, and on October 1 Paisley's body was discovered in the Chesapeake Bay, weighted down with driving belts with a bullet wound in the left side of the head.

Maryland State Police concluded suicide, but numerous senators, including Sen. William V. Roth (R, Del), stated the circumstances surrounding the death were suspicious. Despite the conclusion of the state police coroner George Weems. A Marina owner, Harry Lee Langley, who saw the body at the scene, stated there were large markings around the throat indicating a rope burn or knife cut which the state police coroner failed to report. Maryland prosecutors Naji P. Maloof and Lawrence Lampson, investigating the death, complained vigorously about the CIA's refusal to cooperate with the state police investigation.

Even though the Senate Intelligence Committee investigated the circumstances surrounding the death, no conclusive evidence emerged linking Paisley's death to his activities with the CIA. Numerous theories about Paisley's death were discussed. One linked Paisley's death to the theft of KH-11 satellite manuals from CIA headquarters, which Paisley had worked on. A second theory was that Soviet defector Yuri Nosenko, a friend of Paisley's, discovered that Nosenko was a double agent and that he was killed by the KGB to stop him from revealing his identity. A third theory was that Paisley was a Soviet mole killed either by the CIA or by his Soviet handlers for unknown reasons. The last theory was that Paisley committed suicide due to personal problems, but his family and lawyer said he had no financial or personal problems. (*Facts on File*, 1978–79; Prados, *The Soviet Estimate*)

430 Pak Yong. In 1981 South Korean authorities announced the arrest of a family engaged in spying for North Korea. Pak, his wife, two sons, and a brother were charged with providing military and economic information to North Korea with a radio for 24 years. (*Facts on File*, 1981)

431 Pakhtusov, Yuri N. Lieutenant Colonel Pakhtusov, assistant military attaché for the Soviet embassy in Washington, was expelled March 9, 1989, for espionage. The FBI arrested Pakhtusov for obtaining classified documents on a U.S. government computer system. The Soviets retaliated by expelling U.S. assistant military attaché Lt.Col. Francis Van Gundy for espionage on March 15. The State Department retaliated and expelled Sergei Malinin, a Soviet trade official, for unspecified reasons. (*Facts on File*, 1989; *New York Times*, March 10, 11, 1989)

432 Pallais, Maria Lourdes. Double agent for the Sandinista government in Nicaragua against the CIA. Pallais, a niece of the late dictator of Nicaragua Anastasio Somoza, was an Associated Press reporter when she was recruited by the CIA but instead was working for the Sandinista intelligence service. (*Facts on File*, 1988)

433 Paques, Georges. Deputy chief of the NATO headquarters press office in Paris, he was arrested on August 10, 1963, while meeting his KGB contact. In 1962 he was made deputy chief of the French section press and information service of NATO in Paris until his arrest. Under questioning, he admitted that he had spied for the Soviets from 1944.

Recruited in 1944 by Aleksandr Guzovsky at the age of 29 while in Algiers with the Free French as head of political affairs in the broadcasting service, after the war during the Fourth Republic he worked as an adviser for numerous ministers in Paris. In 1958, with the beginning of the Fifth Republic, Paques gained access to defense data when he was assigned to the general staff of the Ministry of National Defense.

His KGB case officers at the time were Nikolai Lysenko and Vasili Vlasov. He provided them with the entire NATO defense plan for Europe. He handed over the military plans of the joint Anglo-French attack on Suez in 1956. During the Berlin crisis, he provided the Soviets with NATO defense plans for West Berlin, which convinced the Soviets to build the wall. Paques claimed his KGB handlers showed him a letter from Khrushchev thanking him for the data that prevented a war in Europe.

It was the defection of the KGB officer Anatoliy Golitsyn to the West that provided the French the first indication that there was a Soviet mole in NATO. The general description pointed toward Paques, who was put under surveillance. This eventually led to a meeting between Paques and his KGB handler Vladimir Khrenov. He was convicted in a French court and sentenced to life. He argued at his trial that he had provided the data to the Soviets in the interest of world peace. Paques suffered from a large ego, which his KGB handlers would exploit by telling him that his information was of great importance. (Andrew and Gordievsky, *KGB*; Brook-Shepherd, *The Storm Birds*; Faligot and Krop, *La Piscine*; Rositzke, *The KGB*)

Parr, Bertram L. see Althoff, William

434   Pash, Boris T.   In the early 1950s U.S. Army Colonel Pash was assigned to the CIA to serve as chief of a special operations group in the Office of Policy Coordination, called Program Branch 7 (PB/7), aimed at East-bloc countries. The unit was responsible for conducting assassinations and kidnapping in Eastern Europe. Reportedly, PB/7 never carried out any operations. (Ambrose, *Ike's Spies*; Corson, *The Armies of Ignorance*; U.S. Govt., *Church Committee Report*)

435   Paskalian, Sarkis O.   In September 1975, Paskalian admitted in a U.S. court that he had photographed classified documents for the KGB. Paskalian was a New York diamond cutter who emigrated to the United States from the Soviet Union in 1971 with the purpose of espionage. When Paskalian arrived in the United States, he contacted a relative, Sahag K. Dedeyan, who was employed with Operations Research, Inc., to get him to provide classified data. Paskalian managed to photograph a 70-page NATO classified document, "Vulnerability Analysis: U.S. Reinforcement of NATO," which was provided by Dedeyan. Dedeyan was also arrested but apparently was unaware of Paskalian's activities. Paskalian pled guilty and was sentenced to 22 years for spying. Dedeyan stated

stated that he had been coerced by the FBI to testify against Paskalian. (*Facts on File*, 1975; *New York Times*, June 28, 1975; Rositzke, *The KGB*)

436   Pathe, Pierre-Charles.   The KGB took notice of Pathe in 1959 after he published an article placing the Soviet Union in a favorable light. The KGB found him to be anti–U.S. and anti–NATO. A KGB officer on the staff of UNESCO in Paris recruited Pathe in 1960 as an agent for disinformation operations. In 1960–79 he published over 100 articles for the KGB. He printed KGB articles about Latin America, China, NATO, and the CIA in his private political newsletter funded by the KGB, called the *Synthesis*. The newsletter was popular among politicians and businessmen. He also collected information on French journalists, politicians, and government officials, and provided analysis on French political events. His main job involved improving French attitudes toward the Soviet Union. He was an active member of the movement for the independence of Europe and encouraged anti–U.S. programs in the movement. He was arrested in 1979 at the age of 70 as an agent of influence for the Soviet Union. He was sentenced in May 1980 to five years for his activities. (Barron, *KGB Today*; Bittman, *The KGB and Soviet Disinformation*; Rositzke, *The KGB*)

437   Pattis, Jon.   Pattis, a U.S. engineer, was arrested in Iran in 1986 for spying for the CIA and Iraq and sentenced to ten years in prison. Reportedly, Pattis had been carrying a false Italian passport. Pattis appeared in October 1986 on Iranian TV confessing to passing data to the CIA through his company, Cosmos Engineers, including data that helped Iraq attack an Iranian telecommunications center. Pattis also stated that he reported to his CIA liaison Kavi Austin. (*Facts on File*, 1986–87; *New York Times*, August 9, 27, October 15, 1986; January 7, April 23, 1987)

438   Pavlichenko, Vladimir Pavlovich.   In October 1971, a *New York Times* article accused Pavlichenko, a UN Public Information Office director of external relations, of being a veteran KGB officer. He denied the charges. A former KGB defector, Peter Deriabin, also accused Pavlichenko of being a KGB agent and having worked in the Moscow headquarters of the KGB 1952–53. Ironically, a few days after the article was published, the UN renewed his contract for two years. (Barron, *KGB*; *Facts on File*, 1971; *New York Times*, October 5, 1971)

439   Pawar, P. B.   In September 1963, Pakistani authorities requested the removal of four members of the Indian High Commission on charges that they were engaged in espionage. A Pakistani Air Force officer had been arrested a few weeks before for spying for India. The officer stated that he had delivered documents to India's mission air adviser, Group Captain Pawar. In retaliation, the Indian government announced the expulsion of the Pakistan High Commission's air adviser and three personal staff members on charges of espionage. (*Facts on File*, 1963; *New York Times*, September 9, 1963)

440   Pawlowski, Jerzy.   In April 1976, Polish authorities announced that Pawlowski, former Polish Olympic fencing champion, had been sentenced to 25 years by a Polish military court for spying for a NATO country. Pawlowski, a former lieutenant colonel in the Polish Army, had reportedly conducted espionage since 1965 for financial reasons. He was arrested in June 1975 for spying for the French government. Pawlowski was a well-known writer and law professor in Poland and had a variety of international contacts. (*Facts on File*, 1975–76; *New York Times*, August 9, 15, 1975; March 31; April 11, 1976)

441   Pelton, Ronald W.   Pelton served in the Soviet Division of the National Security Agency as a low-level staff member from 1965 to 1979. Despite his position, Pelton had access to classified information gathered from 60 Soviet signals and communications links. While still at the NSA, in 1979, Pelton filed bankruptcy and then resigned his $24,500 position. After a few business failures Pelton contacted the Soviet embassy in Washington in 1980 and spoke to Vitaly Yurchenko about selling some information to the Soviets. Pelton met with the KGB in Vienna to be debriefed while staying at the Soviet ambassador's residence. He was paid $35,000 for sensitive NSA information worth millions of dollars. In two meetings at the Soviet Embassy in Vienna, he provided the Soviets with extensive data on U.S. signal and communications intelligence targeted at the Soviet Union.

One of the most sensitive NSA operations to be compromised was the Ivy Bells operation. Ivy Bells was an advanced eavesdropping operation that tapped into a military communications cable at the bottom of the Sea of Okhotsk between the Soviet mainland and the Kamchatka Peninsula. Pelton also compromised the seven-code-word operation run out of the U.S. embassy in Moscow, and another unnamed joint U.S.-British operation. Pelton was arrested after a tip from KGB defector Vitaly Yurchenko in November 1985 and was sentenced in 1986 to three life terms. (Allen and Polmar, *Merchants of Treason*; Kessler, *Escape from the CIA*; Wise, *The Spy Who Got Away*; Woodward, *Veil*)

442   Penkov, Victor.   In July 1978, Colonel Penkov, assistant military attaché at the Soviet embassy, was expelled by the French government after engaging in espionage activities. French counterintelligence agents arrested Penkov after catching him in the act. He was later released and ordered to leave the country. (*Facts on File,* 1978; *New York Times,* August 1, 1978)

443   Penkovskiy, Oleg Vladimirovich (1919–63).   Penkovskiy served as an artillery officer in Ukraine during World War II as commander of the 41st Guards Anti-Tank Regiment. After the war he attended the Frunze Military Academy in Moscow from 1945 to 1948. In 1949 he joined the GRU and served as military attaché to the Soviet embassy in 1955. From 1956 to 1958 he served at the GRU headquarters in Moscow.

In 1961 Penkovskiy took the opportunity to inform Greville Wynne, a British agent, that he wanted to offer his services. Penkovskiy traveled to London as head of a trade delegation, and he met with CIA and MI6 for further discussions. Wynne continued to serve as his case officer in Moscow till his arrest. Penkovskiy handed to the West considerable data on Soviet missile programs, Khrushchev's activities, space satellite data, military and industrial secrets.

In 1963, Penkovskiy and Greville Wynne were tried and convicted in the Soviet Union for espionage for Britain and the United States. Both men pled guilty. Penkovskiy was sentenced to death and executed. Wynne was sentenced to three years in prison and five years in a labor camp.

His motivation for spying appears to be disillusionment with the Communist system, particularly Khrushchev's activities. Penkovskiy had been the deputy head of the Foreign Department of the State Committee for Scientific Research and Coordination. He admitted to spying for Britain and the United States over a period of a year and half, providing data on Soviet missile technology and East European troop movements and a variety of political and economic data, using up to 5,000 miniature film clips.

Wynne served as a courier between Penkovskiy and British embassy diplomats Roderick Chisholm and his wife at the British embassy in Moscow. Wynne had complained that he wanted to stop his activities due to fear of being caught but that British intelligence officials threatened to interfere in his business affairs. He had been traveling in Hungary as managing director of Mobile Exhibitions, Ltd. He was arrested in 1962 in Budapest. (Maclean, *Take Nine Spies;* Penkovskiy, *The Penkovskiy Papers;* Wynne, *The Man from Moscow*)

444   Peri, Michael A.   Peri, a former U.S. Army specialist, pled guilty in 1989 to espionage charges in West Germany and was sentenced to 25 years for spying for East Germany. Peri had been an electronic signal interceptor expert in the intelligence section of the 11th Armored Cavalry Regiment of the U.S. Army's Five Corps. Peri had escaped to East Germany in February with sensitive computer equipment but returned a month later. (*Facts on File*, 1989; *New York Times*, March 17; June 22, 25, 1989)

445   Perkins, Walter T.   Former Air Force Master Sergeant Perkins, the chief noncommissioned officer in the intelligence division of the Air Defense Weapons Center at Tyndall Air Force Base in Florida, had access to all the classified material at the center. He was convicted for attempting to give Soviet agents classified military documents on radar detection systems and missile systems. Perkins's lawyers blamed his alcoholism for his behavior, and he pled not guilty by insanity induced by his acute alcoholism.

He had been arrested on October 1971 attempting to board a plane for Mexico at the Panama City airport in Florida with sensitive documents on a classified radar detection system and Air Force data on countermeasures to Soviet and Eastern European missile systems. His Soviet handler waited in vain in Mexico City for Perkins to arrive. When Oleg Andreevich Shevchenko learned of the arrest, he fled to Cuba. Perkins was sentenced to three years. (Allen and Polmar, *Merchants of Treason*; Barron, *KGB*; Rositzke, *The KGB*)

446   Petersen, Arne Herlov.   A Soviet agent of influence, Petersen, a Danish leftist writer, was recruited in 1973 by Leonid Makarov for the KGB. Petersen was a romantic leftist who admired the leadership of Pol Pot, Muammar Qadaffi, and Kim Il Sung. Petersen helped organize propaganda drives financed by the KGB to support the "Nordic Nuclear Weapons Free Zone" movement, which wanted to eliminate NATO nuclear weapons from northern Europe. In 1981 Petersen also sponsored a nuclear-free march, also financed by the KGB, from Oslo, Norway, to Paris. He wrote numerous articles, political tracts, and advertisements under the direction of the KGB. Petersen also was responsible for two booklets, probably written by the KGB, called *Cold Warriors* (1979) and *True Blues* (1980), which attacked the anti–Soviet position of Margaret Thatcher. Both publications were poorly written and were riddled with common errors.

Danish counterintelligence agents observed 23 meetings between Petersen and his KGB contact, Major Vladimir Dmitrevich Merkulov, who was the active measures officer for the Copenhagen KGB residency. In 1981, Petersen was arrested, and Merkulov was expelled. He was charged with operating for the KGB but was released in 1982 based on arguments that the true culprits, and authors, the KGB agents, had left the country. (Andrew and Gordievsky, *KGB*; Barron, *KGB Today*; Bittman, *The KGB and Soviet Disinformation*)

447 Petersen, Joseph Sydney. On October 9, 1954, FBI agents arrested Petersen for espionage. He was the first National Security Agency employee to be arrested for espionage. He had served in the U.S. Army during World War II, decoding Japanese diplomatic codes. It was at this time that he met and became friends with a Dutch Army colonel, J. A. Verkuyl, a Dutch liaison officer also working on Japanese codes. Petersen joined the NSA in 1941 and continued his friendship with Verkuyl, who was working on the creation of a Dutch COMINT agency. Petersen would send him ideas on the organization of the new agency and new methods of cryptography without the knowledge of the NSA.

In 1948 he began passing this information to Giacomo Stuyt, communications officer at the Dutch embassy in Washington. A search of Petersen's apartment revealed a cache of classified documents that had been returned by Stuyt. After a careful examination of the documents, they noticed that the Dutch agents had taken the staples out of the documents to photocopy them and then restapled them with an odd-shaped staple. This helped security trace the documents that had been passed to the Dutch.

Petersen was fired on October 1, 1954, while a debate raged on whether he should be prosecuted since a "friendly" nation was involved. After a court battle, Petersen pled guilty December 22, 1954, and was sentenced to seven years and released in 1958. Security officials, overwhelmed with the paranoid belief that Petersen would try to get revenge on the NSA by contacting the KGB with information, decided to bug his apartment for several months without authorization. After several months, no indication that he intended on getting revenge was found and the bugs were removed. The Dutch government announced that it had accepted information from Petersen with the understanding that it was officially sanctioned by the U.S. government. (Bamford, *The Puzzle Palace;* West, *The SIGINT Secrets;* Wise and Ross, *The Invisible Government*)

448 Peterson, Martha. Peterson arrived in Moscow in 1975 under cover as a vice consul but worked instead for the CIA. The KGB had roughed her up during an interrogation, and the CIA was upset by the treatment. Apparently the KGB was upset that her cover as vice consul had fooled them. Her cover position was played out in full, with her working in the visa department of the embassy interviewing Soviet citizens seeking visas for immigration and helping with passport problems for visiting Americans. She was arrested in July 1977 while servicing an agent dead drop. According to *Izvestia*, she had placed a hollow stone in a crevice on a bridge over the Moscow River at the Lenin Hills. The hollowed rock contained cameras, two poison pills, gold, and a microphone.

A year after her expulsion, on July 12, 1978, *Izvestia* published a picture of Peterson standing in front of a table containing the hollowed-out rock and its contents. The article accused her of providing poison to be used on an unnamed Soviet citizen. No reason was given for the delay in publishing the picture, but it did come shortly after the United States accused the Soviet Union of bugging the U.S. embassy in Moscow. (Deming, "We Still Need Spies," *Newsweek*; Richelson, *American Espionage and the Soviet Target*; Turner, *Secrecy and Democracy*; Wise, *The Spy Who Got Away*)

449 Petrov, Vladimir (1907–91). Petrov served for three years in the Soviet Navy's Baltic fleet as a cipher clerk before joining the secret police in 1933 as a cipher clerk in Moscow till 1937, when he was briefly assigned on a mission to China. In 1938 he was transferred to the cipher section of the NKVD and later became chief. In 1942 he was sent to the Soviet embassy in Stockholm as a cipher clerk and counterintelligence officer. In 1951 he was made resident of the station in Australia. In April 1954 he defected, along with his wife, Evdokia, a cipher clerk at the embassy. When he defected, he brought numerous classified documents revealing Soviet intelligence operations in Western countries. (Brook-Shepherd, *The Storm Birds*; Petrov, *Empire of Fear*; Romerstein and Levchenko, *The KGB Against the "Main Enemy"*; Toohey and Pinwill, *Oyster*)

450 Pham Xuam An. North Vietnamese spy during the U.S. conflict in Vietnam. Serving as a colonel in the North Vietnamese Intelligence Regiment, he first infiltrated the Presidential Social Research Service, which was actually an intelligence organization for Ngo Dinh Diem's Can Lao party. At the PSRS, he evaluated intelligence reports for Tran Kim Tuyen, who headed PSRS. Later, he served as a news correspondent for *Time* magazine and the British news agency Reuters. His press credentials allowed him into sensitive civilian and military bases and access to top civilian and military personnel. In later years, an unconfirmed report stated that he served for the Vietnamese UN mission under the alias Hoang Mong Bich. Today he is officially retired and breeds German shepherds for a living, but a senior Vietnamese military intelligence official stated that he was in charge of keeping tabs on foreign journalists. (Safer, *Flashbacks*; White, "Saigon Fourteen Years After," *National Geographic*)

451 Philby, Harold Adrian Russell ("Kim") (1912–88). Soviet double agent in MI6, the "third man" of a Soviet spy ring that included Guy Burgess and Donald Maclean. He attended Cambridge in 1929 and graduated in 1933. During these years, he befriended Anthony Blunt, Guy Burgess, and Donald Maclean. At Cambridge he became disillusioned by British society and began studying Marxism-Leninism.

After college he worked as a journalist covering the war in Spain, then in France in 1939 for the *London Times*, but at the same time he was sending intelligence reports back to the Soviets. In 1939 he returned to Great Britain and joined MI6; by 1944, he was the head of the Russian desk. In 1946 he served as MI6 liaison to the CIA in Washington. It was Philby who notified the Soviets of the CIA-MI6 Albanian operation in 1949–51, which resulted in the death of hundreds of Albanians.

In January 1963, Elliott Nicholas, MI6 intelligence officer, flew to Beirut on a mission to confront Philby. Upon his arrival, he told Philby that there was strong evidence against him. Philby admitted to Elliott that he had been a Soviet spy since 1934. He continued by stating that he had been recruited in Vienna and had recruited Burgess. He admitted that it was he who sabotaged the British-U.S. Albanian operation. Elliott encouraged him to return to London with him, but Philby argued that he needed more time. Philby then escaped to Moscow. His presence in Moscow was confirmed when a journalist accidently met Philby in January 1965. In 1980 Philby received the Order of People's Friendship. Philby had already received the Order of the Red Banner and the Order of Lenin. In 1965 Philby became involved in an affair with codefector Donald Maclean's wife. Philby's wife, angered by the affair, returned to Great Britain. (Boyle, *The Fourth Man*; Knightley, *The Master Spy*; Newton, *The Cambridge Spies*; Page, Leitch, and Knightley, *The Philby Conspiracy*; Philby, *My Silent War*; Seale and McConville, *Philby*; Trevor-Roper, *The Philby Affair*)

452   Phillips, David Atlee (1922–88).   Former CIA chief of Latin American and Caribbean operations. He joined the U.S. Army in 1943 and was shot down in a B-24 near the Adriatic coast. After a year in a German POW camp, he escaped. After the war he moved to Chile where he attended the University of Chile 1948–49, and in 1949 he bought the English-language newspaper, *South Pacific Mail.* His business relationships, knowledge of the country, and the newspaper attracted the attention of the CIA station chief, and the CIA recruited him as a contract agent in 1950.

By 1954, he was a full-time employee for the CIA and was sent to Guatemala to work with E. Howard Hunt on propaganda projects designed to overthrow the government. After the success of the coup, he joined the psychological warfare department and he was sent to Cuba. In 1957 he was sent to Lebanon. In 1960 he was assigned as propaganda chief of the Bay of Pigs operations. In 1961 he was sent to Mexico City as senior covert action specialist. In 1965 he became chief of station in the Dominican Republic and helped coordinate the U.S. military invasion of the country. In 1968 he was chief of the Cuban Operations Group of the Western Hemisphere Division. In 1970 he was made chief of station to Brazil. In 1973 he was made chief of the Western Hemisphere Division till his retirement in 1975. He founded the Association of Former Intelligence Officers (AFIO) for the purpose of improving the CIA's image, becoming its first president. His efforts also included the production of an intelligence journal edited by former CIA officers, *The International Journal of Intelligence and Counterintelligence*. (Phillips, *The Night Watch*; Prados, *Presidents' Secret Wars*; Ranelagh, *The Agency*)

453   Pickering, Jeffrey L.   A hospitalman third class while stationed at the Naval Regional Medical Clinic in Seattle, he gave a five-page classified document to the Soviet embassy in Washington in June 1983. He was arrested in 1983, sentenced to five years' hard labor, and dishonorably discharged. (Allen and Polmar, *Merchants of Treason*)

454   Pienaar, Andre.   A major in South African military intelligence, he was arrested in 1986 for spying for the African National Congress and passing data to an unnamed African state bordering South Africa; he was convicted in May 1987 on charges of espionage. (*Facts on File*, 1987)

455   Pieterwas, Wladyslaw.   In April 1970, West German authorities arrested Pieterwas, a Polish government employee in the inland shipping. He was discovered with technical equipment common to espionage. With him was a West German research specialist on opinion polls from Dresden, Gottfried Sommer, who was also arrested and charged with document forgery and espionage. (*Facts on File*, 1970)

Pisk, Zdenek see Opatrny, Jiri

456   Polednak, Alois.   In July 1971, a Czech court sentenced Polednak to two years for espionage from 1968 to 1970. He had been the director of the Czech film industry. Five others were convicted: Jaroslav Sedivy, historian and former member of the Institute of International Politics and Economics, was sentenced to 18 months for espionage; Edita Cerenska, former secretary of the Federal Assembly, sentenced to one year; Vaclav Cerenska, a Czech retired army colonel, and Edita's husband, sentenced to seven years; Milada Kubiasova, an interpreter at the French embassy, sentenced to ten years; Hubert Stein, an interpreter at the Dutch embassy, sentenced to 12 years. (*Facts on File*, 1971)

457   Polgar, Thomas (b. 1922).   Born in Hungary to a Jewish family, he escaped to the United States during the Nazi purges of the 1930s. When World War II began, he joined the U.S. Army and was given a commission due to his command of six languages. He was recruited into the

Office of Strategic Services (OSS), where he parachuted behind German lines to set up an agent network in Berlin. He was successful and survived the war. He joined the CIA and was first stationed in West Germany as an assistant to chief of station in the early 1950s. From 1961 to 1970, he was chief of station in Argentina. It was here that Polgar became a hero within the CIA. An airliner was hijacked by American dissident radicals. Polgar walked onto the plane to negotiate. He was able to talk them into releasing the hostages and gave them drugged bottles of Coke. After they were unconscious, Polgar was able to bring in Argentine security forces. This made him a hero in the CIA, and he was given the post of chief of station of Saigon in January 1975, despite his lack of experience in Asia.

When Polgar arrived in Saigon, he found himself in a disintegrating country. Despite the negative reports from the field from seasoned CIA officers, Polgar continued insisting that the South Vietnamese government would survive. Polgar was accused of stopping reports from the field from reaching CIA headquarters about the growing strength of Communist forces and the demoralization of South Vietnamese military forces. Reportedly, Polgar threatened his case officers by insisting that each case officer must visit each province he claimed to be Vietcong-controlled to verify it. Of course, they would have been killed or captured. Since no case officer would attempt such an act, Polgar could satisfy himself with the statement to headquarters that there was no positive proof that the VC controlled the countryside. Reports to headquarters were full of gross errors and inconsistencies, and continued till a few weeks before the fall of Saigon. The CIA was totally unprepared for an evacuation when it came and was forced to rely on helicopters from the U.S. military and Air America to evacuate. The CIA was forced to leave some of its best agents and assets to be captured by North Vietnamese forces. Many of the secret files containing the identities of Vietnamese contacts were captured intact. (Colby, *Lost Victory*; DeForest and Chanoff, *Slow Burn*; McGehee, *Deadly Deceits*; Snepp, *Decent Interval*; Stockwell, *In Search of Enemies*)

458 Pollard, Jonathan Jay.   While working for the U.S. Navy Investigative Service's Anti-Terrorist Alert Center (ATAC) as a civilian intelligence expert on terrorism, Pollard approached the Israelis in 1984 and offered classified data. He was handled by Israel's Liaison Bureau for Scientific Relations (LAKAM), not Mossad, as is commonly believed. Pollard provided the Israelis with national security estimates, naval intelligence data, and intelligence provided by the Defense Intelligence Agency (DIA).

Information provided to Israel included specifics on the PLO headquarters in Tunisia, which allowed for an Israeli air raid. Data also included capabilities of the Libyan air defense system, which the Israelis were able to avoid during their attack on Tunisia. In 1985 Pollard was arrested and later pled guilty. According to the prosecutors, Pollard received $45,000 for his services, but Pollard maintained that he was justified in his actions by his Jewish origins.

Ironically, Pollard had claimed openly to friends, including a senior deputy in the ATAC, that he was an agent for the Israelis. Israel was embarrassed politically by the Pollard scandal and dismantled LAKAM. Counterintelligence agents believe that there is a second Israeli agent with the Department of Defense, due to statements made by Pollard that Israeli agents handling him asked for specific documents according to control numbers and dates, data which Pollard did not have access to and which indicated that the Israelis had another spy.

Pollard was sentenced to life in 1987. His wife, Anne Henderson Pollard, was sentenced, as an accessory, to five years. Pollard helped authorities in the investigation of Israeli Air Force officer Aviem Sella and Israeli intelligence officer Rafi Eitan; a former scientific attaché from the Israeli consulate in New York, Joseph Yagur; and a secretary of Israel's embassy in Washington, Irit Erb — all of whom had handled him as a spy. (Blitzer, *Territory of Lies*; Henderson, *Pollard*; Ostrovsky and Hoy, *By Way of Deception*; Raviv and Melman, *Every Spy a Prince*)

Poluchkin, Y. N. see Bychkov, H. E.

459   Polyakov, Dmitri Fedorovich.   In January 1990, an article in the Soviet newspaper *Pravda* stated that a Soviet diplomat described as "Donald F" had been executed for spying for the United States. The article stated that he had been recruited by the West in 1961 when he was attached to the Soviet mission to the UN. He later worked in Soviet embassies in Burma and India. Former CIA intelligence officers identified him as Polyakov. (*Facts on File*, 1990; *New York Times*, January 23, 1990)

460   Pontecorvo, Bruno (b. 1913).   Born in Italy to Jewish parents, Pontecorvo escaped Italy in 1936 due to the anti–Jewish and anti–Communist Fascist campaign. Pontecorvo's family members were high officials in Italy's Communist party. He fled to France, where he worked with the well-known Communist scientist Pierre Joliot-Curie, but escaped in 1940 to the United States after the fall of France.

In 1943 he joined the Anglo-Canadian atomic research team at Chalk River in Ontario, Canada. He was well liked and nicknamed "Ramon Navarro" due to his movie-star looks. Sometime between 1943 and 1945 he sent a letter to the Soviet embassy offering his services. Initially, Soviet officials thought it was a trap and ignored his offer. Pontecorvo then delivered a sample of classified documents to the embassy. The Soviets quickly established contact with him. In 1949 he was transferred to the

British atomic research team at Harwell, England, and granted British citizenship. He worked at Harwell till the arrest of Klaus Fuchs in 1950. Neither the Canadians nor the British had conducted a security check on Pontecorvo, both assuming that the other government had investigated him before his employment. The arrest of Klaus Fuchs turned Security on the staff, and background investigations were launched. Pontecorvo went through six different security checks, and outside of finding a few relatives in Italy who were Communists, no specific information was discovered that linked him to espionage. The FBI raided Pontecorvo's home in the United States, which provided some evidence that Pontecorvo was pro–Communist. The data was sent to British MI6 liaison officer in Washington, Kim Philby, who was a Soviet spy and suppressed the information till Pontecorvo could escape in October 1950.

Pontecorvo was one of the few scientists who worked with the production of lithium deuteride, essential to the production of the H-bomb. Pontecorvo, granted Soviet citizenship in 1952, continued to work on the H-bomb for the Soviets and was awarded two Orders of Lenin for his activities. (Andrew and Gordievsky, *KGB*; Costello, *Mask of Treachery*; Moorehead, *The Traitors*; Pincher, *Too Secret Too Long*)

461 Pope, Allen Lawrence (b. 1929). Pope grew up in Florida and attended the University of Florida for two years before dropping out and joining the Air Force. Pope flew 55 missions during the Korean War, earning the Distinguished Flying Cross. In March 1954, he began working for Civil Air Transport, a CIA proprietary first based in Taiwan, and flew missions dropping supplies to the besieged French outpost at Dien Bien Phu. During this period he lived in Saigon with his wife and raised a family.

In April 1958, he began flying B-26 missions for the CIA against the Indonesian Army in support of the provincial rebels in Sumatra, who were opposed to Sukarno. He flew several missions during the campaign from the base in the Philippines. After attacking the airstrip on Ambon Island in the Moluccas on May 18, 1958, he was shot down by government antiaircraft guns. A round hit the right wing, setting it on fire. He bailed out and broke his leg after parachuting into a tree.

President Eisenhower denied that Pope was a government employee, referring to him as a mercenary. But captured documents on the downed plane revealed considerable evidence to the contrary. The CIA was forced to withdraw all its paramilitary personnel in the field. The operation was wrapped up, and the rebels were quickly overwhelmed and surrendered. Sukarno turned the incident into a propaganda tool and threatened to have him executed.

According to several versions, Pope accidentally bombed a church during his last mission, killing most of the congregants. Another story states that Pope accidentally bombed a hospital, killing numerous patients, but the more probable story, the one presented at Pope's trial in Jakarta, was that he accidently bombed the Ambon marketplace while attacking the airfield, killing numerous people headed to church on Ascension Thursday.

On December 28, 1959, Pope went to trial in Jakarta and was accused of deaths of 23 Indonesians. The trial lasted till April 29, 1960, when he was sentenced to death. Robert Kennedy visited Indonesia in February 1962 and asked Sukarno to release Pope, but it was not until July 1962 that he was released. After his release he went to work with another CIA air proprietary, Southern Air Transport, based in Miami. (Powers, *The Man Who Kept the Secrets*; Robbins, *Air America*; Smith, *Portrait of a Cold Warrior*; Wise and Ross, *The Invisible Government*)

462   Popov, Pyotr Semyonovich (d. 1963).   In 1953 Popov, a lieutenant colonel of the Soviet GRU, dropped a note in a U.S. diplomat's car in Vienna offering information. He described himself as a GRU officer with the Soviet Group Forces headquarters in Baden bei Wien. He was given the code name ATTIC and was assigned a CIA case officer, George Kisvalter.

Popov was a graduate of the Military Diplomatic Academy. Popov gave the CIA an extensive history of GRU operations in Vienna. He provided the names and position of every GRU officer in Vienna and the cryptonyms of 370 Soviet "illegal" agents working in the West. He also gave in-depth data on Soviet military strategy and equipment.

In July 1954, he returned to the Soviet Union on leave for three weeks. While on leave, he accessed more data on nuclear weapons, guided missiles, and nuclear submarines. In 1955 he was transferred to the illegal support section of GRU in East Berlin. While in East Germany, he was assigned a MI6 officer who served as a liaison between him and the CIA, George Blake, who turned out to be a double agent for the Soviets. In December 1958, he was ordered to return to Moscow and arrested upon his arrival. The Soviets allowed him to pass disinformation for a while, but he was arrested during a meeting on a Moscow bus with his Moscow CIA case officer, Russell Langelle, serving under cover as chief security officer, on October 16, 1959, by five Soviet agents.

Popov reportedly was severely tortured into revealing his activities, and in 1963 he was put on trial and executed. Yuri Nosenko, a KGB defector, reported that the KGB had used a special powder Langelle's Soviet maid had placed in his shoes that allowed the KGB, using dogs, to trace him to Popov. Popov was executed by being thrown alive into a furnace in the basement of GRU headquarters. Reportedly, his execution was filmed and showed to GRU recruits as a reminder of the fate of traitors.

They released Langelle and expelled him from the country. The Soviet news agency Tass reported that Langelle had been seen giving a Soviet citizen 20,000 rubles in payment for information. The Soviets also explained that a notebook found on Langelle contained specific references to espionage activities. Langelle stated that the Soviets threatened his family in an attempt to recruit him. (Andrew and Gordievsky, *KGB*; Brook-Shepherd, *The Storm Birds*; Hood, *Mole*; Prados, *The Soviet Estimate*; Richelson, *American Espionage and the Soviet Target*; West, *The Circus*)

463 Porst, Hannsheinz. In November 1970, Porst, a West German Marxist millionaire, was released after serving half his sentence for spying for East Germany. Porst, owner of a large West German photo supply company, was convicted in July 1969 for passing classified political information to East German agents for over 14 years. He was sentenced to two years and nine months. Two accomplices were also convicted: Alfred Pilny and Peter Neumann. Porst confessed to being a member of the East German Socialist Unity party but denied that he had been a spy. The West German government argued that Porst had used his position in the West German Free Democratic party to obtain information. (*Facts on File*, 1969–70; *New York Times*, July 9, 1969)

464 Powers, Francis Gary (1929–77). He joined the U.S. Air Force in 1950 and was assigned to Strategic Air Command. In 1956 he was recruited by the CIA to pilot the U-2 reconnaissance spy plane. He was sent to the U-2 base in Nevada, where he was trained. After training he was sent to the Incerlik Air Force Base at Adana, Turkey. Powers flew several missions over the Soviet Union till May 1, 1960, when he was shot down over Sverdlovsk. At 68,000 feet, he was believed to be safe from surface-to-air missiles.

Khrushchev made a public show trial of Powers and embarrassed President Eisenhower, who had publicly stated before the incident that the United States was not flying spy planes over the Soviet Union. Powers was put on trial in August 1960, pleading guilty of espionage, and was sentenced to ten years. Powers testified at the trial that he had been hired by the CIA in 1956 as a pilot and that the NASA was used as a cover for reconnaissance missions. He was released on February 10, 1962, during an exchange for convicted Soviet agent Rudolph Abel. Powers was criticized after his return to the United States for not initiating the self-destruct button and committing suicide. Despite the criticism, he was given the Intelligence Star for his service. In August 1977, Powers died in a helicopter crash as a TV reporter in California. (Beschloss, *Mayday*; Powers, *Operation Overflight*; Wise, *The U-2 Affair*)

465 Prager, Nicholas Anthony (1928–81). In 1948 Prager's father retired in Britain after working for the British consulate in Prague as a clerk. In 1949 Prager falsely claimed to have been British at birth on his Royal Air Force application, and within five years he had become an accomplished radar technician while stationed at Fighter Command Headquarters at Stanmore. Prager was a committed Communist, also missed by a security check. By 1956, he had access to classified data at the RAF Wittering base where he had access to V-bomber radar systems.

In 1959 Prager visited his native Czechoslovakia and was recruited by Czech intelligence officers from the Statni Bezpecnost (StB), who gave him the code name Marconi. He delivered technical data on the Blue Diver and Red Steer nuclear V-bombers. Prager then went to work for English Electric in 1961 as an electrical engineer working on classified defense projects. Reportedly, Prager supplied Czech agents with classified documents on RAF radar jamming equipment. In 1971 two Czech intelligence defectors, Joseph Frolik and Frantisek August, provided details that resulted in Prager's arrest and sentence to 12 years. A search of Prager's home found one-time cipher pads and other evidence. Frolik pointed out that Prager's father had worked for Czech intelligence while working as a clerk in the British consulate in Prague. Frolik and August had worked as Prager's case officer, 1961–63.

In June 1971, British court convicted Prager on two counts of spying for Czechoslovakia. During the trial Prager first claimed to have been blackmailed into being a spy but later blamed his Czech wife, who he argued was a Czech intelligence agent. During the trial it was revealed that Prager's passport had a Czech visa stamp issued by Bohumil Malik, a well-known Czech intelligence officer. According to authorities, Prager's wife was having an affair with another RAF technician who was also working for Czech intelligence and disappeared in June 1971. Both are believed to have escaped to Czechoslovakia. (Andrew and Gordievsky, *KGB*; Pincher, *Too Secret Too Long*; West, *The Circus*)

Prieur, Dominique see Mafart, Alain

466 Prime, Geoffrey Arthur (b. 1938). He joined the Royal Air Force in 1956, attending the Russian-language school. In 1964, after a tour of duty in Kenya, he was stationed in Gatow, Berlin's military base, for four years, working on East-bloc SIGINT intercepts. In his Russian-language studies he became interested in Soviet society. In January 1968, Prime, returning to the RAF SIGINT station in West Berlin, passed a note to a Soviet officer near the checkpoint, expressing an interest in spying. The Soviets trained him in espionage before his return to London to work at the Processing Group, where he worked as a transcriber (Sept.

1968–Mar. 1976). He maintained contact with the KGB with a special short-wave radio. He later joined the Government Communications Head-quarters (GCHQ) in March 1976 (similar to the U.S. National Security Agency). By March 1976, he was working in the Soviet section of J Division, the most sensitive Soviet intercept section, and by November 1976, he was promoted to head J Division. The pressures of spying for the Soviets, his job at GCHQ, and marital problems brought on odd behavior by Prime. In September 1977, he quit his job and became a taxi driver in Cheltenham. He broke contact with the KGB for three years until 1980 when he renewed contact and handed over classified documents that he had kept after leaving GCHQ.

Ironically, Prime did not come to the authorities' attention due to his espionage activities. Instead, Prime was first arrested in 1982 for sexually assaulting women in Cheltenham. After Prime was arrested, it was his wife who told authorities that Prime had been spying for the Soviets. During his interrogation Prime admitted his activities and explained that he spied due to a romantic belief in Soviet socialism and some personal psychological problems. In November 1982, he was sentenced to 35 years for espionage and three years for sexual assault. Prime had suffered a harsh childhood, his parents having a variety of marital problems, and he was sexually molested by a relative. (Andrew and Gordievsky, *KGB*; Bamford, *The Puzzle Palace*; Corson and Crowley, *The New KGB*; West, *The SIGINT Secrets*)

467 Pripolzev, Valentine Alexandrovich.   After serving as an officer in the Soviet Army, Pripolzev was recruited into the KGB. He served in numerous Soviet trade missions in Asia and Europe until his assignment in the Soviet trade mission in Cologne, West Germany, in 1959 under cover as an engineer. His assignment was to gather information on the F-104G Starfighter, NATO missile program, and nuclear reactor plans. His second mission was to activate German "sleeper" agents. These were former German POW soldiers captured by the Soviets during the war who had agreed in writing to spy for the Soviets in some distant future; in this case, 15 years had passed. Many of them had become successful business-men with important contacts in the government and military. However, many were reluctant to participate in espionage, and the local police were notified. West German counterintelligence officials (BfV) had already begun an intensive surveillance operation on Pripolzev due to a tip from Werner Grunhagen, an editor for an engineering technical journal.

Pripolzev had befriended Grunhagen and asked him to provide copies of articles about the F104G Starfighter published by the journal. Pripolzev paid Grunhagen generously for the articles and later pushed for non-published technical reports on numerous types of military aircraft including helicopters. Eventually Grunhagen was receiving large payments for more sensitive information, which Pripolzev instructed him to place in a drop box to avoid being traced. Grunhagen eventually became worried about the direction of the interaction and contacted German officials. The BfV encouraged him to continue the meetings with Pripolzev under surveillance, and on August 25, 1961, Pripolzev was arrested. In July 1962, Pripolzev was exchanged for four Soviet-held Germans accused of espionage. Pripolzev was then sent to the Soviet trade mission in North Vietnam. (*Facts on File*, 1962; Hagen, *The Secret War in Europe*)

468 Profumo, John Dennis (b. 1915).

The Profumo affair can be compared easily to the controversy surrounding Alger Hiss. There was little evidence to support a case of espionage; both individuals lived charmed and successful careers; and both were persecuted with accusations of collusion with Soviet spies.

Profumo grew up in a wealthy upper-class family in England. He attended Brasenose College, Oxford, with a degree in agriculture and political economy. He joined the University Air Squadron and flew biplanes part-time. After college he traveled around the world, spending time in China, Japan, Russia, and the United States.

In 1939 he was adopted as prospective Conservative candidate for Kettering at the age of 24 and became the youngest MP at Westminster. When the war started, he joined the British Army while remaining in his elected post. In the 1945 general election he lost his seat at Kettering, and in 1947 he left the army and went back into politics.

He began working for the Conservative central office as a broadcasting adviser. In 1952 he took office as joint parliamentary secretary at the Ministry of Transport and Civil Aviation in Winston Churchill's government. In 1957 he became parliamentary under secretary for the colonies. In 1960 he was chosen as secretary of state of war. It was at this time that Profumo became involved in an affair with Christine Keeler, a high-class prostitute who was also sleeping with Eugene Ivanov, a Soviet GRU officer.

When MI6 learned from Oleg Penkovsky that Eugene Ivanov was a GRU officer at the London embassy, MI5 placed him under surveillance. MI5 was led to the house of Stephen Ward where Ivanov was visiting Keeler. At the time Profumo was using the same girl. Profumo met Keeler in 1961 at the home of Lord Astor, where she was swimming in the pool naked. Profumo chased her around the pool awhile. They began meeting in London for several sessions at the apartment of Stephen Ward. Ward's connections to the KGB and Profumo's visits sparked rumors that Profumo had been compromised. Profumo was warned by MI5 that Ward was dangerous, and he broke off the relationship with Keeler. But a year later Ward was in trouble with the law over Keeler's prostitution and quickly implicated Profumo. The British press converged on Profumo, who quickly resigned in 1963. The affair also led to the downfall of Prime Minister Harold Macmillan's Conservative government, and Ward committed suicide while facing a prostitution charge shortly after Profumo's resignation. (Irving, *The Anatomy of a Scandal*; Kennedy, *The Trial of Stephen Ward*; Knightley and Kennedy, *An Affair of State*; Summers and Dorrill, *Honeytrap*)

Pronine, Victor see Negrino, Azelio

469   Raborn, William Francis (b. 1905).   Director of the Central Intelligence Agency (DCI) from April 1965 to June 1966 under President Johnson. He graduated from the U.S. Naval Academy in 1928 and the Naval War College in 1952. From 1955 to 1962 he served as the director of the Special Projects Office for the U.S. Navy on the development of the Polaris missile system. In 1962–63, he served as deputy chief of naval operations. He retired from the navy in 1963; earned the Distinguished Service Medal and the National Security Medal for his service. (Cline, *Secrets, Spies and Scholars*; Jeffreys-Jones, *The CIA and American Democracy*; Ranelagh, *The Agency*)

470   Radzhabov, Akper.   In March 1978, Soviet officials announced that Radzhabov, a technician in the food-processing industry, had been sentenced to 13 years of solitary confinement for spying for the United States. Reportedly, Radzhabov had met U.S. officials initially to defect to the United States but was encouraged to supply data. (*Facts on File*, 1978)

471   Raghunath, Krishnan, and Padmanab Vijai.   In June 1967, Chinese authorities expelled two Indian diplomats on charges of espionage. India retaliated by expelling two members of the Chinese embassy in New Delhi. Raghunath, second secretary, and Vijai, third secretary, were accused of photographing a restricted military area outside Beijing in June. Raghunath was also accused of conducting military and political espionage since the beginning of the Cultural Revolution. The Indian government responded that Raghunath had photographed a tourist Buddhist temple and nothing of military value. When the two diplomats arrived at the airport, a crowd of Red Guards attacked the two, beating them and dragging them around the airport. India expelled Chen Lu-chih, first secretary, and Hsieh Cheng-hao, third secretary, at the Chinese embassy in New Delhi for military espionage. (*Facts on File*, 1967; *New York Times*, June 13, 14, 1967)

472   Ratkai, Stephen Joseph.   Convicted in February 9, 1989, of espionage for the Soviets, he was arrested in Newfoundland as the result of a two-year sting operation called Operation Station Zebra, run jointly by the Canadian Security Intelligence Service (CSIS), the Royal Canadian Mounted Police (RCMP), and the U.S. Navy Investigative Service (NIS). In December 1986, a female U.S. Navy lieutenant walked aboard the Soviet scientific research ship in the port at St. John's, Newfoundland, to offer classified data. In February, Ratkai, a Canadian citizen who spent considerable time in Eastern Europe, contacted her and offered money for classified data. Ratkai, alias "Michael," had stolen classified documents from the U.S. Navy base at Argentia, Newfoundland, which monitored surface ship and submarine activity in the North Atlantic. Ratkai pled guilty to the charges. (*Facts on File*, 1989)

473 Redin, Nicolai Gregorovich. He was arrested by the FBI in 1946 on espionage charges for attempting to gather data on the U.S. destroyer tender *Yellowstone*, which was assigned to take part in the atomic tests at Bikini Atoll. Lieutenant Redin was a member of the Soviet Purchasing Commission. Redin was later acquitted of the charges. (*Facts on File*, 1946; *New York Times*, March 27; April 11, 23, 1946)

474 Reichwald, Jurgen. In September 1981, West German authorities arrested Reichwald for providing classified data on the Tornado fighter. Reichwald, an engineer who was working on the project, had provided data to an East German agent, Rolf Hecht, who was also arrested. (*Facts on File*, 1981)

475 Revin, Valentin A. In September 1966, the U.S. State Department announced the expulsion of Revin, Soviet third secretary at the Soviet embassy in Washington, for attempting to purchase space, missile, and aircraft classified data. In an elaborate FBI sting operation, Revin had been discovered when a U.S. citizen who had been approached by Revin went to the FBI. Working with the FBI, the citizen provided declassified data to Revin for money. (*Facts on File*, 1966; *New York Times*, September 3, 1966)

476 Rhodes, Roy Adair (b. 1917). In 1957 Master Sergeant Rhodes testified at the espionage trial of Rudolph Abel that he had sold the Soviets military secrets while stationed at the U.S. embassy in Moscow, 1952–53. Rhodes was in charge of the embassy motor pool. Lonely during his stay in Moscow, one night he went on a drinking spree with some Russians. The next morning he awoke in the bed of a young Russian woman. She later confronted him, claiming to be pregnant, and demanded that he take responsibility. He agreed to supply her and her "brother" with classified data. Clearly, this was a classic sex trap, with the threat of exposure to his wife and colleagues. Receiving payments in rubles equal to $2,500–$3,000, Rhodes had been discovered when Reino Hayhanen mentioned that Abel had sent him to contact Rhodes in the United States. Rhodes was later charged with espionage for the Soviets. (Barron, *KGB Today*; Bernikow, *Abel*; Donovan, *Strangers on a Bridge*; Rositzke, *The KGB*)

477 Richter, Ursula. In August 1985, Richter disappeared and was suspected to have fled to East Germany as a spy. Richter, a secretary in the accounts department at the League of Expellees, was suspected of being the head of an East German spy network in West Germany. Several other disappeared during this time: Lorenz Betzing, friend of Richter and a messenger with an army administrative office in Bonn; Sonja Lueneburg, the personal secretary of the Economics Minister; and Heinz Tiedge, division head of the counterintelligence service of the BfV, who later defected to East Germany. (*Facts on File*, 1985; Richelson, *Foreign Intelligence Organizations*)

478 Rickett, Walter A. Rickett was arrested in China in the 1950s and convicted of espionage. When he was released in 1955, he announced that he had been an agent for the United States collecting military intelligence on China. (*Facts on File*, 1955; *New York Times*, August 2, 1955)

479 Ritchie, Rhona Janet. In November 1982, Ritchie, a British diplomat, pled guilty in a British court to spying for the Egyptian government. Ritchie admitted that while she served a second secretary at the British embassy in Israel, she provided confidential embassy cables to her lover, an Egyptian diplomat, Rifaat al-Ansari, the data including information on multi national peacekeeping forces in the Sinai and negotiations between the British and American governments pertaining to the Middle East. She was given a nine-month suspended sentence after she pled guilty. She joined the British Foreign Office in August 1979. She spoke several languages. In July 1981, she was assigned to the British embassy in Tel Aviv as press attaché. She met Rifaat al-Ansari, second secretary, at a cocktail party at the Egyptian embassy in Tel Aviv. She fell in love, and he used the relationship for information. They did not hide their relationship, and Shin Bet notified British officials that she was delivering sensitive data from the embassy telex machines. It was revealed to her that Rifaat had a wife and family in Egypt and that he was a professional intelligence officer. The judge called her actions more foolish than evil. (*Facts on File*, 1982; Raviv and Melman, *Every Spy a Prince*)

480 Rockstroh, Herbert. Sergeant Rockstroh, of the East German State Security Service, defected to the West in 1963. Rockstroh had worked in the department responsible for East-bloc spy operations in West Berlin. He brought classified documents to the West when he defected. (*Facts on File*, 1963)

481 Rodriguez, Felix I. (alias Max Gomez). He served for the CIA in Cuba, Congo, Bolivia, Vietnam, and Central America. He served as the Contra logistics chief at Ilopango base in El Salvador in the 1980s. He was a well-known anti–Castro veteran who participated in Operation 40 and helped blow up a Spanish freighter in 1964 under Manuel Artime's orders. While working with Green Berets in 1967 tracking down Che Guevara, he interrogated Che Guevara just before his execution and reportedly still wears Guevara's wristwatch as a memento. He later served as a special airmobile counterinsurgency specialist in Vietnam. In 1981 he was involved with training Argentine commandos stationed in Honduras, who pulled out during the Falklands war, bitter over U.S. support for Britain. Then he went to El Salvador to handle the Contra supply shipments at Ilopango air force base. (Byrne, *The Chronology*; Cockburn, *Out of Control*; Marshall, Scott, and Hunter, *The Iran-Contra Connection*; Rodriguez, *Shadow Warrior*; U.S. Govt., *The Tower Commission Report*; Walker, *Reagan versus the Sandinistas*)

482 Rogalsky, Ivan N. In January 1977, Rogalsky was arrested by the FBI for attempting to sell classified data to the Soviet Union. The U.S. government also filed a complaint against Yevgeny P. Karpov, an official of the Soviet UN delegation, as a coconspirator, but no criminal charges were filed. Reportedly, Rogalsky, a Soviet émigré living in the United States since 1971, had been receiving information from Paul Y. Nekrasov, an engineer for the RCA Space Center who had cooperated with the FBI. In a sting operation, the FBI had Nekrasov give Rogalsky classified documents detailing U.S. satellite communications. (*Facts on File*, 1977; Rositzke, *The KGB*)

483 Rohrer, Glen Roy. Rohrer, sergeant first class, claimed that he had joined the U.S. Army Counterintelligence Corps in 1949 in the mistaken belief that he would be hunting down Nazi war criminals but ended up working against Communist governments in Europe. In 1965 Rohrer defected to Czechoslovakia, where he appeared on Prague TV describing U.S. espionage in Czechoslovakia and claiming had become disenchanted by the activities. (*Facts on File*, 1977; *New York Times*, January 7, 1977)

484 Ronget, François. In December 1974, a Lebanese military court in Beirut sentenced Ronget, a French citizen, to death for assisting an Israeli commando team in Beirut an April 1983 that killed three Palestinian terrorists. Reportedly, Ronget was discovered with five forged passports used by the commandos to enter Lebanon before the attack. (*Facts on File*, 1974; *New York Times*, December 22, 1974)

485 Roosevelt, Archibald "Archie" Bulloch (b. 1918).

Grandson of Theodore Roosevelt, he studied a variety of languages while attending Harvard (class of 1939), including ancient Greek, Arabic, French, and Italian. He joined the U.S. Army in 1942, serving in the military intelligence unit G-2. His first assignment landed him in the invasion of North Africa by Allied forces, called Operation Torch. While in Morocco, he wrote several reports on the political situation of the Muslim population. He was later put in charge of censorship of the Arabic broadcasts on Radio Maroc in Rabat. Later he was transferred to Allied headquarters in Algiers in the psychological warfare branch, where he studied Axis propaganda efforts against the local populace. He returned to the United States in 1943 and worked in the Office of War Information headquarters in Washington, working on a propaganda project aimed at the Muslim population of North Africa. He was later made an instructor at Camp Sharpe, teaching various foreign nationals combat tactics. He was assigned to Cairo, to the Joint Intelligence Committee, Middle East (JICME), as an intelligence analyst, then transferred to the Counter Intelligence Center in Iraq (CICI) as an assistant military attaché to the U.S. legation there till the end of the war. In 1946 he was sent to Iran as a military attaché. He resigned from the U.S. Army in 1947 as a captain and joined the CIA as a Middle East specialist. He started out in the Voice of America, aiming propaganda at the Middle East, then served in several Middle Eastern posts, including Lebanon, Turkey, and station chief in London. His specialty was propaganda and political action. He participated in anti–Castro propaganda after the failure of the Bay of Pigs invasion and retired from the CIA in 1974. (Blum, *The CIA*; Roosevelt, *For Lust of Knowing*; Wise and Ross, *The Espionage Establishment*)

486 Roosevelt, Kermit (Kim) (b. 1916).

The grandson of Theodore Roosevelt and a distant cousin of Franklin Roosevelt, he graduated from Harvard in 1938 and continued there as a professor in history. In 1941 he joined the Office of Strategic Services (OSS), serving in the Near East branch. Roosevelt joined the CIA and served as special assistant in political operations in the Near East Division.

It was Roosevelt who engineered the CIA coup (Operation Ajax) against Prime Minister Mossadegh in Iran in 1953. When Mossadegh nationalized the Anglo-Iranian Oil Company, the United States and Britain quickly panicked. The British suggested overthrow, and the CIA quickly brought a plan together. The British froze Iranian assets, and a naval blockade was enforced to stop oil shipments. Roosevelt brought in General H. Norman Schwarzkopf, an old friend of the shah, to help in the operation. The shah fled to Rome and waited for the CIA operation to take hold. On August 19 a CIA-sponsored rally of 100,000 "supporters" of the shah began rioting. They attacked pro–Mossadegh newspapers and offices. A gun battle erupted between pro–Mossadegh and pro-shah forces at Mossadegh's estate. Mossadegh, fearing arrest, fled the country. Three hundred people were killed during the coup. Roosevelt argued that it was not the nationalization of Anglo-Iranian Oil but the Iranian Tudeh Communist party that the United States was afraid would take over.

He left the CIA in 1957 to become vice president for governmental relations of Gulf Oil 1958–64, then a partner in a Washington public relations firm that represents, among other clients, Iran. (Ambrose, *Ike's Spies*; Eveland, *Ropes of Sand*; Roosevelt, *Countercoup* and *War Report of the OSS*; Rubin, *Paved with Good Intentions*; Smith, *OSS*)

487   Rose, Fred.   Canadian Communist MP arrested on charges of espionage in 1946 for attempting to sell RDX secrets to the Soviet Union. Born Jacob Rosenberg in Poland to Russian Jewish parents, he was a Communist party organizer in Quebec and a member of the Canadian Parliament, elected to Parliament in 1943 and re-elected in June 1945. He was handled by GRU agent Colonel Nikolai Zabotin of the Soviet embassy. When Igor Gouzenko defected, he revealed Rose and the Canadian spy network. (Andrew and Gordievsky, *KGB*; Brook-Shepherd, *The Storm Birds*; Gouzenko, *The Iron Curtain*; Rositzke, *The KGB*)

Rosenberg, Ethel see Rosenberg, Julius

488   Rosenberg, Julius (1918–53), and Ethel (1915–53).
Julius Rosenberg first became awakened to the political Left in 1933 when he became absorbed by the plight of the West Coast labor leader Tom Mooney, who was serving a life sentence for killing ten people in a bombing. Julius collected signatures for a petition drive to free Mooney. In 1934 Rosenberg entered City College of New York (CCNY) and became involved in student anti–Fascist organizations. He participated in the founding of CCNY's branch of the American Student Union, which supported the New Deal policies of Roosevelt and endorsed the Loyalist side in the Spanish Civil War. He also became a member of the Steinmetz Club, a branch of the Young Communist League (YCL), while in college. Julius graduated in February 1939 with a major in electrical engineering. Shortly after graduation, he married Ethel Greenglass.

After school, he joined the Federation of Architects, Engineers, Chemists and Technicians (FAECT), a militant union ran by a leftist leadership. Julius soon found work as a civilian engineer with the Army Signal Corps until 1945 when he was fired for being a member of the Communist party. After Rosenberg was fired, he went to work at the Emerson Radio Corporation, where he was an engineer on military projects. After that, he and David Greenglass started the G&R Engineering Company, but the business flopped, and Greenglass blamed Rosenberg for its failure.

When Klaus Fuchs was arrested in England in 1950, Fuchs confessed to being a spy for the Soviets since the early 1940s. During his confession he told about a courier by the name of Raymond. The FBI quickly got on his trail and discovered him to be Harry Gold. During Gold's confession, he gave the identities of two other spies: David and Ruth Greenglass. The Greenglasses implicated the Rosenbergs. Greenglass claims that Rosenberg assured him during the Fuchs arrest that if they were indangered of arrest, they would have to defect to the Soviet Union. It was Greenglass who had worked at Los Alamos during the production of the atom bomb. Greenglass was a devoted Communist nicknamed "Doovey." Both David and Ethel grew up in New York's Lower East Side. Ethel, seven years his senior, had brought home leftist political tracts that influenced her younger brother David.

Ethel graduated from high school at the age of 15, skipping several grades. She found her first job as a clerk in a shipping company but was fired four years later for starting a strike. She was very union-oriented. Ethel was a very strong-willed person who had dominance over Julius's mild manner. Since Julius spent so much time in Ethel's home before they were married, Ethel's younger brother David became close to Julius. Graduating from CCNY in 1939, Rosenberg had joined the Communist Party (CP) on December 12, 1939. David and Ruth were members of the YCL. But Ethel and Julius dropped out of the CP quietly in 1943. The Greenglasses charged that they dropped out to take another, more secretive role in the effort to help the Soviets. When the Rosenbergs left the party, they even canceled their subscription to the *Daily Worker*.

When David Greenglass went to Los Alamos, the Rosenbergs seized the opportunity and recruited him to spy. According to Greenglass, he supplied the Rosenbergs with the layout and operations of Los Alamos installations, some of the names of the scientists working there, notes on a high-explosive lens mold, and an arrangement of shaped charges used to create an implosion shock wave (a plutonium-fired implosion device). Rosenberg introduced David to his courier and made arrangements for another exchange of information. While Greenglass was at Los Alamos, Harry Gold showed up and took some more sketches on the implosion device.

It was felt that since Julius was not talking, putting pressure on Ethel might convince him to cooperate and reveal his network. Many of Rosenberg's friends fled the country when the arrests began. When Greenglass was arrested in June 1950, Joel Barr and Morton Sobell escaped to Mexico; Barr's best friend, Al Sarant, disappeared on July 27.

According to Greenglass, when Rosenberg was inspector for the Signal Corps, he handed over copies of tube manuals to help the struggling Soviet radio and electronics industry. At Emerson he stole a proximity fuse, a fire-control device used in connection with the Norden bombsight. According to David Greenglass during the trial, Rosenberg had been working for the Soviets when he was employed by the Signal Corps and by 1945 had delivered atom bomb secrets to the Soviets. Greenglass also stated that Rosenberg had been a master spy who controlled a large network of spies in New York and Ohio, that Ethel had known about his activities and approved of them. Since Greenglass and his wife had already been caught, it is fair to say that they pointed the finger at Rosenberg out of convenience. The Rosenbergs had past connections to the Left, and there had been some family dispute earlier about the failure of their joint business. The frustration the U.S. government had experienced with the Fuchs sentence of just 14 years may have led to the harsh sentence the Rosenbergs were given. When the judge sentenced the Rosenbergs to death, he called their crime "worse than murder," blaming them for the Korean War and for the millions that would eventually die in a nuclear conflict between the United States and the Soviet Union.

The Rosenbergs never admitted any involvement and always maintained their innocence. They were executed in the electric chair in Sing Sing Prison on June 19, 1953. The Rosenbergs were charged with conspiracy to commit acts of espionage, in violation of the Espionage Act of 1917. (Hyde, *The Atom Bomb Spies*; Meeropol and Meeropol, *We Are Your Sons*; Philipson, *Ethel Rosenberg*; Radosh and Milton, *The Rosenberg File*)

489 Rositzke, Harry August (b. 1911). A Harvard graduate with a Ph.D. in English literature, from 1936 to 1942 he taught English at Harvard. He served in the U.S. Army from 1942 to 1944, then transferred to the Office of Strategic Service (OSS), serving in London, Paris, and Germany during World War II. After the war he joined the CIA, serving for 25 years. In the early 1950s, he conducted intelligence operations in the Soviet Union and Eastern Europe while stationed in Munich, West Germany. In 1957–62 he served as station chief in New Delhi, India, where his principal intelligence targets were Chinese and Soviet personnel and operations. In 1962–70 he worked in Washington on domestic intelligence operations against Soviet and Eastern European officials in the United States and coordinated operations against Communist parties abroad. From 1962 to 1970 he pursued domestic intelligence operations against Soviet and Eastern European agents in the United States. He retired in 1970. (Blum, *The CIA*; Prados, *Presidents' Secret Wars*; Rositzke, *The CIA's Secret Operations*, and *The KGB*; Smith, *OSS*)

490   Roski, Franz Arthur.   In August 1985, a high official of the West German border police was sentenced for spying for East Germany. Roski gave classified data on border tactics, defenses, and intelligence. Roski was arrested in 1984 after his wife, Sylvie, alerted authorities to his activities. Sylvie was motivated by religious reasons to denounce her husband. (*Facts on File*, 1985; *New York Times*, September 12, 1985)

491   Rotsch, Manfred.   Rotsch, a West German engineer, had given the Soviet Union data on the Tornado jet fighter. He was sentenced to eight years for espionage in 1986, exchanged along with Klaus Schmidt and Wolfgang Klautzsch by West Germany for East German–held spies Christa-Karin Schumann and Wilhelm Wilms in 1987. (*Facts on File*, 1987)

492   Roussilhe, Francis.   In January 1971, a French court sentenced Roussilhe to 20 years for espionage. He confessed to passing classified NATO documents to Rumanian agents. Roussilhe, a Frenchman, had worked in NATO's secret documents section in Brussels as a translator and reportedly supplied twelve thousand pages of classified documents for $18,000. (*Facts on File*, 1969, 1971; *New York Times*, August 13, 1987; Rositzke, *The KGB*)

493   Russell, McKinney H.   In May 1971, the Soviet newspaper *Literaturnaya Gazeta* accused Russell, chief cultural affairs officer at the U.S. embassy in Moscow, of attempting to recruit a Soviet scientist, identified only as Viktorov, for spying. Reportedly, Russell sought background data on scientists participating in the U.S.-Soviet scientific exchange program and information on defense production plants. According to the article, Viktorov supplied Russell with false data. The U.S. embassy denied the charges. (*Facts on File*, 1971; *New York Times*, May 6, 1971)

494   Rybachenko, Vladimir.   In February 1977, French authorities expelled Rybachenko, a Soviet envoy, for industrial espionage. Rybachenko worked in the scientific section of the UN Educational, Scientific, and Cultural Organization (UNESCO) and was caught receiving classified data on a new computer system by French agents. (*Facts on File*, 1977; *New York Times*, February 20, 1971)

495 Sakharov, Vladimir Nikolaevich. Graduating from Moscow's Institute of International Relations in 1968 as a member of its first graduating class of Arab specialists, he joined the Ministry of Foreign Affairs and was sent to Alexandria, Egypt, as an assistant attaché. Upon his arrival, he learned the KGB had acquired him, unwillingly, into the service. He was assigned to numerous tasks, including the recruitment of Abdel Madsoud Fahmi Hasan, the chief of an intelligence unit assigned to monitor foreign embassies. Later he translated intelligence reports for Hasan from Arabic to Russian and defected in Kuwait to the United States (Barron, *KGB*; Bittman, *The KGB and Soviet Disinformation*; Prados, *The Soviet Estimate*; Sakharov, *High Treason*)

496 Sarant, Alfred (d. 1979). Sarant was a close associate of Julius Rosenberg. Sarant oversaw the development of control computers and airborne computers for Soviet aircraft and microelectronics. When Rosenberg was arrested, Sarant fled to Mexico, then Czechoslovakia, finally settling in Leningrad. At the time of his escape, he worked on an atom-smasher project for Cornell University in New York. In 1969 Sarant was recognized by the Soviet government for his efforts and was named a Soviet state prize laureate. (Walter and Miriam Schneir, *Invitation to an Inquest*; Radosh and Milton, *The Rosenberg File*)

497 Sattler, James Frederick. Worked for the Atlantic Council of the United States, a nongovernmental organization established in 1961 to promote better relations among NATO nations. When he applied for a job in 1976 as a minority staff consultant for the House International Relations Committee, the FBI informed the committee that Sattler's contacts with East Germany were under investigation. Sattler learned about the FBI investigation and out of desperation filed a foreign agent's registration statement with the Department of Justice in March 1976 but later panicked and escaped to East Germany.

When asked if he was involved with a foreign government he described his recruitment in 1967 by an East German intelligence officer named Rolf. He had given East Germans sensitive documents from NATO and government agencies in West Germany, the United States, Great Britain, Canada, and France. He admitted that he was working for an East Berlin organization called the Combined Intelligence Services of the Warsaw Pact. He stated that he had received training in codes, microphotography, and clandestine drops, photographing documents on a microdisc camera, and mailing them to East Berlin. The East German Ministry of State Security awarded him with an "honor decoration" for his services. After Sattler disappeared, the Justice Department announced that no prosecution would be pursued due to the lack of witnesses. (Allen and Polmar, *Merchants of*

Treason; Bittman, *The KGB and Soviet Disinformation;* Romerstein and Levchenko, *The KGB Against the "Main Enemy"*)

498   Savich, Boris Trofimovich.   In April 1970, Belgian authorities expelled Savich, a Soviet truck salesman, for espionage. They discovered miniature cameras, and other espionage equipment. He had been arrested in March in Brussels for spying for the Soviet Union. Reportedly, he was attempting to get data on Belgian and NATO military bases, and planning on setting up a spy ring within the Supreme Headquarters Allied Powers Europe (SHAPE) while posing as a Soviet truck salesman for Skaldia-Volga. (Barron, *KGB; Facts on File,* 1970)

499   Scarbeck, Irvin Chambers.   Arrested and convicted in 1961 for espionage charges, Scarbeck had been a U.S. State Department foreign service officer working as second secretary in the U.S. embassy in Warsaw since 1958. Scarbeck was accused of giving political classified documents to Polish agents between January and May 1961. Scarbeck had joined the State Department in 1952, receiving the State Department's meritorious service award for the development of the student exchange program in 1959. At the Warsaw embassy he was involved in simple maintenance duties for the compound.

Reportedly, Scarbeck, married with four children, had been seduced by a beautiful young Polish female, Urszula Discher, and in December 1960 was blackmailed when Polish agents stormed into her apartment, photographing them in a compromising position. Discher was granted a visa to West Germany as part of Scarbeck's demands for his cooperation, but Scarbeck refused to hand over codes and sensitive data. This was the first espionage charge ever filed against a foreign service officer in the State Department. Scarbeck was convicted and sentenced to 30 years in 1961, but was released in May 1966. (Cookridge, *Gehlen; Facts on File,* 1961, 1966)

500   Schadock, Horst, and wife, Marie-Luise.   In December 1977, West German authorities arrested this East German couple for spying on Western military installations. They had been living in the Netherlands, using their home as a base for conducting missions into West Germany. Since they were East German citizens, their extravagant lifestyle drew the attention of Dutch authorities, who began surveillance on their movements. (*Facts on File,* 1978; *New York Times,* January 5, 1978; Rositzke, *The KGB*)

Schadock, Marie-Luise see **Schadock, Horst**

501 Schlesinger, James Rodney (b. 1929). Director of Central Intelligence Agency (DCI) from February 1973 to July 1973 under President Nixon. From 1955 to 1963 he served as a professor of economics at the University of Virginia; a senior staff member 1963–67 for the RAND Corporation, director of strategic studies, 1967–69; assistant director and acting director of the Bureau of the Budget, 1969–70; assistant director of the Office of Management and Budget, 1970–71; chairman of the Atomic Energy Commission, 1971–73. After his tenure as DCI, he served as secretary of defense from 1973 to 1975, secretary of energy 1977–79, and a counselor to the President's Commission Strategic Forces, 1983. (Cline, *Secrets, Spies and Scholars;* Jeffreys-Jones, *The CIA and American Democracy;* Ranelagh, *The Agency*)

502 Schpeter, Henrich Natan. In June 1974, Schpeter, a Bulgarian economist and a former diplomat to the UN, 1966–72, was sentenced to death by a Bulgarian court for espionage. The Bulgarian government accused Schpeter of being on the payroll of an unnamed foreign intelligence organization. UN officials appealed on his behalf. Schpeter, who was Jewish, was released in August 1974 and flew to Israel. (*Facts on File,* 1974; *New York Times,* June 6, 7, 14; July 5, 1974)

503 Schulze, Reinhardt, and Sonja. In 1986, the Schulzes were sentenced in London to ten years for attempting to pass classified data to East Germany in 1980–85. There was no concrete evidence that they passed secrets, but evidence was strong enough to convict them of attempting espionage. They were directly connected to the espionage case of Margaret Hoeke and arrested in August 1985 while carrying false passports. Few doubted that they had been active intelligence agents for East Germany. (*Facts on File,* 1985–86)

504 Schumann, Christa-Karin. Schumann and Wilhelm Wilms were swapped by East Germany for several West German–held spies in 1987. West Germany released three spies — Manfred Rotsch, Klaus Schmidt, and Wolfgang Klautzsch. Schumann, an East German physician, had been arrested in 1979 and was serving a 15-year sentence. (*Facts on File,* 1987; *New York Times,* August 13, 1987)

505 Schwarzkopf, H. Norman (1895–1958). Graduating in 1917 from West Point and serving in the U.S. Army, he left the military to serve as the New Jersey State Police chief. During the 1931 kidnapping of the Lindbergh baby, he headed the investigation. In 1935 he reentered the military and during World War II was sent to Iran to organize the national police force, the Imperial Iranian Gendarmerie. He was sent by the U.S. to underdeveloped countries to help teach foreign governments how to maintain law and order. In 1948 he was promoted to brigadier general and left Iran for West Germany.

In August 1953, he participated in Operation AJAX, a CIA operation to support the shah of Iran. During the crisis Schwarzkopf met with the shah to convince him to act against the growing Communist party, Tudeh, and pro–Mossadegh forces. It was Schwarzkopf's trained police that the shah used to stop the Tudeh and pro–Mossadegh forces rioting in the streets. Schwarzkopf delivered a bag of money to CIA officer Kermit Roosevelt (reported to be a million dollars) to buy officials and others to support the shah. They were able to organize hundreds of pro–Shah groups that would march and riot against pro–Mossadegh supporters. It was his son, "Stormin'" Norman H. Schwarzkopf, that lead coalition military forces in Operation Desert Storm against Iraqi forces in the liberation of Kuwait in 1991. (Ambrose, *Ike's Spies*; Corson, *The Armies of Ignorance*; Prados, *Presidents' Secret Wars*; Roosevelt, *Countercoup*)

506   Schwirkmann, Horst.   In September 1964, Schwirkmann, an electronics technician specialist in debugging for the West German embassy in Moscow, was injected in the buttocks with nitrogen mustard gas while on a sight-seeing trip to the Zagorsk monastery. The gas nearly killed him; as it began eating away at his skin, he was rushed to a German hospital for treatment. The gas had been produced at the KGB labs of the Technical Operations Directorate. Reportedly, Schwirkmann had antagonized Soviet intelligence agents by finding and eliminating several key wiretaps and other electronic eavesdropping devices found in the West German embassy. Each time he found a microphone, he would run intense levels of voltage through it, giving the listener a painful hello. (Barron, *KGB*; Rositzke, *The KGB*)

507   Scranage, Sharon M.   Scranage, a clerk for the CIA, was arrested in July 1985 at a Virginia motel where she was planning a lovers' rendezvous. She plead guilty in 1985 for disclosing the identities of Ghanaians working for the CIA to her Ghanaian boyfriend, Michael Agbotui Soussoudis. Due to her disclosures, one CIA asset was reportedly murdered. She also revealed classified data on communication and radio traffic.

Soussoudis, first cousin of Ghana's leader, Flight Lieutenant Jerry Rawlings, was convicted of espionage and sentenced to twenty years before a spy exchange with Ghana. Her sentence was reduced in 1986, citing the fact that Soussoudis was released to return to Ghana.

They met in Accra in 1983, the Ghanaian capital, when she was working under embassy cover as a clerk but was actually a CIA operations support assistant, and he was working for his cousin as an intelligence officer. On her second day there, she met Soussoudis, and they became lovers. For the next two years, she provided secrets and sex to Soussoudis. When the ambassador discovered that she was dating Soussoudis, she ordered the station chief to inform her to cease the relationship. She did not.

She copied data from CIA cables in shorthand, passing them to Soussoudis. She also provided the identities of eleven informants and five CIA employees. Many within the intelligence community believe that much of the data went Kojo Tsikata, the pro–Marxist head of Ghanaian intelligence, who passed the data to intelligence services in Cuba, Libya, East Germany, and the Soviet Union. She left Ghana in May 1985 and was asked to continue spying while at the CIA headquarters in Virginia. Soussoudis pled guilty to espionage charges and was expelled. Scranage was sentenced to two years. (Allen and Polmar, *Merchants of Treason; Facts on File*, 1985–86)

508   Sella, Aviem (b. 1946).   Sella, born in Haifa, Israel, joined the Israel Air Force in 1964 as a pilot, flying in the 1967 Six Day War. In 1969–71 he served as a junior deputy to the F-4 Phantom squadron commander, flying combat missions during the 1970 air attack on Egypt. In 1971 he earned a BA in economics at Jerusalem University. In 1972–74 he served as first deputy to a Phantom squadron commander flying combat missions during the 1973 war. In 1974–76 served as a staff officer at the Air Force headquarters, developing air combat tactics. In 1976 he took command of the 201st Fighter-Bomber (F-4E) Squadron at Hatzor air base. In 1979 he attended Tel Aviv University earning an M.A. in business administration. In 1980–83 he was chief of Air Force operations and led the famous Israeli bombing raid on the Iraqi nuclear reactor in 1981. In 1982 he helped plan the raid on Syrian antiaircraft missile system during the invasion of Lebanon. In 1984, while attending New York University, he began studying for his Ph.D. in computer science.

It was in May 1984 that Jonathan Jay Pollard was introduced to Sella in New York. Sella was able to learn from Pollard that he was interested in providing Israel specific intelligence from his position at the U.S. Navy's Anti-Terrorism Alert Center (ATAC). Sella acted as Pollard's handler for the Israeli Defense Ministry's Liaison Bureau for Scientific Relations. In late 1984 Sella turned Pollard over to another Israeli and returned to Israel with a promotion to brigadier general, given command of the Tel Nol air base. Sella later returned to the U.S. and was planning to meet Pollard for dinner the day FBI agents searched Pollard's apartment. When Sella learned of Pollard's impending arrest, he left the U.S. under a false passport, fearing arrest.

Though indicted by a U.S. court in 1987 for espionage, Sella was in

Israel and unlikely to be extradited to the U.S. United States officials complained about Sella's promotion and claimed that U.S. officers would refuse to work with Sella in the future. Sella resigned his post but remained in the air force as head of the Israel Defense Forces staff college. Israel's recruitment and use of Pollard as a covert spy in the U.S. was a violation of the 1951 intelligence cooperation agreement between the U.S. and Israel. (Black and Morris, *Israel's Secret Wars*; Blitzer, *Territory of Lies*; Raviv and Melman, *Every Spy a Prince*)

509 Sellers, Michael. In March 1986, Sellers, under cover as second secretary in the political section of the U.S. embassy in Moscow, was accused of spying and ordered to leave the USSR. The Soviets reported that Sellers had been caught during a secret meeting with a Soviet spy. Sellers, a CIA officer, may have been the victim of retaliation by the Soviets to the U.S. order to reduce their Soviet, Ukrainian, and Byelorussian missions to the UN. Many believe it was the former CIA officer Edward Lee Howard that exposed him to the KGB. (Allen and Polmar, *Merchants of Treason*; Kessler, *Moscow Station*; Wise, *The Spy Who Got Away*)

510 Semichastny, Vladimir Yefimovich. Participated in the ouster of Khrushchev in October 1964. Replaced by Yuri Andropov in May 1967 as head of the KGB, in October 1961 Semichastny had replaced Alesandr Shelepin as head of the KGB. Interestingly, the same day that *Pravda* announced the replacement of Semichastny, it also announced the death of KGB Maj. Gen. Vasilii Lukshin in the line of duty. No connection has yet been established. (Andrew and Gordievsky, *KGB*; Barron, *KGB*; Corson and Crowley, *The New KGB*; Knight, *The KGB*)

511 Serov, Ivan Alexandrovich (1905–63). When the KGB became suspicious of Oleg Penkovsky, it was Serov who wrote a letter of support for his old drinking buddy Penkovsky. After Penkovsky's arrest, Serov was fired as head of GRU. Despondent, he drank heavily and finally shot himself in the head.

Graduated from the Frunze Military Academy in 1939, he entered the NKVD and was appointed chief of Ukraine. In 1941 was promoted to deputy people's commissar of state security. He served as the deputy chairman of the NKGB during World War II and was responsible for the Katyn Forest massacre. In 1945 Serov became deputy chief of SMERSH (military counterintelligence) in the Soviet zone of Germany, then, 1946–53, was first deputy minister of the MVD. In 1958 he was replaced as KGB chief and put in as chief of GRU. He was chairman of the KGB from April 1954 to December 1958. (Andrew and Gordievsky, *KGB*; Brook-Shepherd, *The Storm Birds*; Corson and Crowley, *The New KGB*; Knight, *KGB*)

512   Sevastyanov, Gennadi G.   In 1963, Sevastyanov, a Soviet attaché at the Soviet embassy, was expelled from the U.S. for attempting to recruit a Soviet defector who was working for the CIA. The employee stated that his brother, Vododya, whom he had not seen in over twenty years, and Sevastyanov, using the alias "Ivan Ivanovich," approached him in April and May to encourage him to spy for the Soviet Union. There were threats against his family back in the Soviet Union if he did not cooperate. Vododya had entered the U.S. under the alias Vladimir I. Gridnev, a Soviet government official. The CIA employee went to the FBI, notified them of the approach, and monitored two meetings between them. (*Facts on File*, 1963; *New York Times*, July 2, 1963; Wise and Ross, *The Invisible Government*)

513   Shackley, Theodore George, Jr. (b. 1927).   He served in the U.S. Army from 1945 to 1947, then attended the University of Maryland in 1951, rejoining the Army from 1951 to 1953. After leaving the U.S. Army, he joined the CIA. Nicknamed the "blond ghost," Shackley worked as a Clandestine Service officer for the CIA. After the Bay of Pigs fiasco, he was made chief of JM/WAVE, the CIA base in Miami, Florida, for the express purpose of organizing covert operations in Cuba.

As CIA station chief in 1966 Vientiane, Laos, in the mid–1960s he encouraged counterinsurgency tactics, which emphasized nonmilitary action. Shackley used methods more familiar to Peace Corps members than CIA agents. The CIA encouraged land reform, cooperative stores, vocational training schools, and fish ponds. Many of the projects were successful, and Meo tribesmen would turn their backs on the Pathet Lao Communist insurgents. In 1969 Shackley became chief of station in Saigon. Ironically, as chief of station, he deemphasized the CORDS program, which was designed on the same theories that Shackley used in Laos, and concentrated on traditional intelligence methods. In 1972 Shackley headed the Western Hemisphere Division. He was in a difficult position when he was forced to close numerous CIA operations in Latin America due to their exposure by former CIA agent Philip Agee. He was later made deputy to the chief of the Clandestine Service and finally a member of the CIA's Policy and Coordination staff. He retired in 1979. (Agee, *Inside the Company*; McCoy, *The Politics of Heroin*; Prados, *Presidents' Secret Wars*; Shackley, *The Third Option*; Smith, *Portrait of a Cold Warrior*; Snepp, *Decent Interval*)

514   Shadrin, Nicholas George.   His name was Nickolai Fedorovich Artamonov before his defection as a Soviet destroyer commander when he sailed across the Baltic Sea to Sweden in his motorboat in 1959. He worked for the U.S. Office of Naval Intelligence and for the Defense Intelligence Agency as a consultant. When he was approached by KGB officers, the CIA asked him to be a double agent. In 1975 he met the KGB in Vienna and was kidnapped. According the Vitaly Yurchenko, Shadrin was killed after KGB agents administered a lethal amount of chloroform when the KGB tried to kidnap him in Austria to be returned to the Soviet Union. (Hurt, *Shadrin*; Kessler, *Escape from the CIA*; Martin, *Wilderness of Mirrors*)

Sharovatov, Viktor S. see Netrebsky, Boris

Shaw, Joseph see Larrimore, Don

515   Shelton, Ralph W. ("Pappy").   Reportedly, Major Shelton commanded a team of Green Berets assigned by the CIA to train a six-hundred-man force of Bolivian Indians to hunt down Che Guevara, who was organizing a Communist guerrilla movement in Bolivia. Guevara was finally captured and executed by the Bolivian Army in 1967. Reportedly, Bolivian military officers were so terrified of the capabilities of the CIA army that they insisted that it be disbanded. (*Facts on File*, 1969)

516   Shevchenko, Arkady Nikolaevich (b. 1930).   In 1974 Shevchenko informed U.S. officials that he wished to defect, but the CIA convinced him to stay. The CIA assigned the code name "Andy," and he delivered information on policy and political matters. In April 1978, he officially defected to the U.S., the most senior Soviet official to defect.

In 1949–54 he attended Moscow's State Institute of International Relations, studying French and international law. After his graduation he joined the Foreign Ministry in 1955 as an attaché in the UN and worked on arms-reduction strategy. In 1958 he was sent to the UN as a disarmament specialist with the Soviet delegation for three months. That same year he was made a member of the Communist party. In 1960 he returned to the UN as a full member of the Soviet delegation, along with Nikita Khrushchev, who banged his shoes on the podium of the UN General Assembly. He returned to the UN in 1963.

While a senior Soviet diplomat at the UN, he spied for the CIA 1975–78, providing the CIA with Soviet plans in Central America and Africa, and Soviet position papers for Strategic Arms Limitation II. Shevchenko defected to the U.S. in April 1978 when Soviet authorities began to suspect him. While at the UN, he was the undersecretary-general for political and Security Council affairs.

In October 1978, Shevchenko was involved in a scandal when he was accused by Judith Taylor Chavez of using CIA funds, $40,000 given to her in the form of gifts and cash. Shevchenko stated that the money was from his severance pay from the UN and that he regretted the relationship with

Chavez, who he claimed was with a Washington escort service. (Brook-Shepherd, *The Storm Birds;* Richelson, *American Espionage and the Soviet Target;* Shevchenko, *Breaking with Moscow*)

517 Sheymov, Victor Ivanovich. A KGB major responsible for cipher communications. The CIA arranged for his escape from the Soviet Union in May 1980.

After he defected, he worked for the CIA as a consultant 1980–90. Granted U.S. citizenship in 1985, he took the name Victor Orlov. In a 1990 press conference Sheymov announced that the Soviets had two sources in the State Department providing information on foreign policy, negotiation positions and strategy, and arms-control positions. He also claimed that KGB chief Yuri Andropov had made a special request to gather information about the security arrangements of Pope John Paul II, claiming that it was basically an order to kill the pope and that there was a KGB plan to break the legs of ballet star Rudolf Nureyev. (*Facts on File,* 1990; *New York Times,* March 3, 13, 1990)

518 Shkolnik, Isaac. In April 1973, Shkolnik, a Soviet Jew from Vinnitsa, Ukraine, was sentenced by a Soviet court to ten years for treason. Reportedly, Shkolnik had been charged with spying for Israel. Due to international pressure, his sentence was reduced to seven years. (*Facts on File,* 1973; *New York Times,* February 12; July 4, 1973)

519 Sigl, Rupert. In April 1969, Sigl, an Austrian national trained in East Germany but working for the KGB, defected to West Germany. He gave them specific data covering a 20-year period of espionage activities. While in the West, he was placed in protective custody by the CIA. He had been assigned by the KGB in East Berlin as head of a spy ring 1957–69.

He was assigned a variety of odd jobs for the KGB and handled a variety of agents recruited by the KGB. No arrest was made of Laurence, who claimed that the KGB had approached him several times since 1963 but that he had refused their propositions. Another was Franz von Wesendonck, a lawyer in the Common Market secretariat in Brussels, and Darley Lambeth Apusumah, a Ghana diplomat who was arrested in Ghana. (Barron, *KGB;* Rositzke, *The KGB;* Sigl, *In the Claws of the KGB*)

520 Sillitoe, Percy. Director-general of MI5 1946–53. He joined the South African police in 1908 and three years later transferred to the Northern Rhodesia police till 1923. He was appointed chief constable of Chesterfield in 1923, then Kent in 1943. In April 1946, he was appointed chief of MI5, replacing Sir David Petrie. Despite the fact that the British government was rampant with Soviet spies (Klaus Fuchs, Guy Burgess, Kim Philby, Anthony Blunt, and Donald Maclean), MI5 was able to uncover only one major spy, William Martin Marshall, while Sillitoe was chief. Upon Sillitoe's retirement, Roger Hollis was appointed. (Costello, *Mask of Treachery;* Pincher, *Too Secret, Too Long;* West, *The Circus, MI5;* Wright, *Spy Catcher*)

521   Silvestri, Franco.   In September 1971, Italian authorities arrested Silvestri on espionage for the Soviet Union. His Soviet contact, a unidentified commercial counselor, a GRU colonel, for the Soviet embassy, left Italy after the arrest of Silvestri. Reportedly, Silvestri, a petty officer in the Italian navy who worked in the NATO headquarters in Naples, provided the Soviets with classified NATO documents. (*Facts on File,* 1971)

522   Simko, Svetozar.   In February 1977, Simko, a Czech agent working in West Germany, defected to Great Britain. Simko served as a military intelligence officer and had worked in West Germany in espionage operations for six years undercover as a foreign correspondent for the Czech news agency (CTK). Simko described the locations of money and communication equipment hidden in rural West Germany to be used in case of war by East-bloc agents for sabotage purposes. Simko also identified seventeen Czech diplomats as intelligence agents. (*Facts on File,* 1977)

Sims, Barbara see Cunningham, Alden

523   Sinclair, John ("Sinbad").   In April 1956, MI6 sent a frogman to examine the hull of the Soviet cruiser *Ordzhonikidze* in Portsmouth harbor. It was hoped that something could be learned from the ship's antisubmarine equipment. The frogman, Lionel "Buster" Crabb, disappeared, and only a headless body was found later. The Soviets lodged a complaint, and the British government apologized for the incident. Sinclair, as head of MI6, received most of the blame. (Costello, *Mask of Treachery;* Pincher, *Too Secret, Too Long;* West, *The Circus, MI5*)

524   Sites, Erik.   Sites, a CIA officer undercover as aide to the military attaché at the U.S. embassy in Moscow, was expelled from the Soviet Union in 1986 for spying. On May 7 the KGB arrested Sites along Malaya Priogovskaya Street. The Soviets discovered he was carrying a blue bag containing an electric razor that concealed a miniature camera. The Soviets announced that a major spy operation had been stopped. Many believe that it was Edward Lee Howard, a former CIA officer who defected to the Soviet Union, who identified Sites to the KGB. (*Facts on File,* 1986; *New York Times,* May 15, 1986; Wise, *The Spy Who Got Away*)

525 Sitte, Kurt (b. 1910). Sitte, born in the Sudetenland of Czechoslovakia to a non–Jewish German family, studied in Prague where he excelled in math and physics. The Nazis arrested him and sent him to Buchenwald concentration camp because his wife was Jewish. While in prison, he befriended Communists who joined the Czech intelligence service after the war and recruited him as a spy. He continued his studies in Great Britain in nuclear physics and taught the subject at Syracuse University in New York. The FBI discovered that he was a Communist spy and recruited him as a double agent, but he left the U.S. for Brazil in 1953 for unexplained reasons.

In 1955 he went to Israel to lecture at the Technion, in Haifa, and took the post of chairman of the physics department. He began reporting to a Czech intelligence officer from the Czech embassy. Finally Shin Bet discovered the mole and on June 16, 1960, arrested him at his home shortly after he returned from an international science conference in Prague. Sitte had penetrated Israel's scientific community. In 1961 Sitte was convicted in Israel, charged with espionage for Czechoslovakia, and sentenced to five years. (*Facts on File*, 1961; *New York Times*, February 8; June 29, 1961; Raviv and Melman, *Every Spy a Prince*)

526 Skardon, William James (Jim) (d. 1987). British counterespionage agent for MI5 as head of the Watcher Service in MI5. Probably the best intelligence interrogator in the history of British intelligence. His most famous case involved the interrogation of Klaus Fuchs, who confessed his participation in espionage for the Soviets to Skardon. Fuchs confessed in January 1950, leading to his arrest in February. He also interrogated Kim Philby in 1951 but came to no conclusion. (West, *The Circus, MI5*; Williams, *Klaus Fuchs, Atom Spy*; Wright, *Spy Catcher*)

527 Skinner, Dennis G. In June 1983, Skinner, Midland Bank representative, died after a fall from his apartment in Moscow. The death was ruled a murder after a British coroner's investigation. Soviet authorities ruled that it was an accident. Skinner's wife, Soviet-born Lyudmilla Skinner, stated that her husband had contact with British intelligence and with the KGB in the fourteen years he lived in Moscow. Two days before his death, Skinner, in a life-or-death tone, gave a note to a neighbor to deliver to the British embassy stating that there was a spy within their security forces.

The two governments began to expel diplomats as a result of the inquiry. The Soviets expelled John Burnett, first secretary and head of security at the British embassy in Moscow. Burnett had testified at the coroner's inquest and had met Skinner the night before his death in his apartment. (*Facts on File*, 1984; *New York Times*, June 16, 17, 1984)

528 Skripov, Ivan Fedorovich. In 1963 the Australian government ordered the expulsion of Skripov for espionage activities. Reportedly, in 1961, Skripov, first secretary at the Soviet embassy in Canberra, elicited the help of a female agent to act as a courier in the formation of a spy network in Australia. The Australian Secret Intelligence Organization (ASIO) placed the couple under surveillance, photographing and documenting the couple's activities. (*Facts on File*, 1963; *New York Times*, February 8, 9, 11, 1963)

529 Slack, Alfred Dean. U.S. chemist arrested in 1950 on espionage charges for supplying Harry Gold defense secrets. Slack had worked for the Holston Ordnance Works in 1943–44 and the Manhattan project in Oak Ridge, both in Tennessee. He was also accused of giving high-explosive RDX secrets to the Soviets through Harry Gold. (Barron, *KGB*; *Facts on File*, 1950)

530 Smirnov, Valery. In July 1977, Lieutenant Commander Smirnov, Soviet naval attaché, was accused by Canadian authorities of engaging in industrial espionage during a 16-month Royal Canadian Mounted Police (RCMP) surveillance period. A researcher working at Bell-Northern Research, near Ottawa, informed RCMP that Smirnov had approached him to provide classified data. RCMP authorized the researcher to provide nonclassified data to Smirnov during a sting operation. He was expelled from Canada. (*Facts on File*, 1977)

531 Smith, Edward Ellis. The CIA was not allowed to station an officer at the Moscow embassy till 1953 when they sent Smith, who was quickly seduced by a KGB agent under cover as a maid. They were photographed, and the KGB showed him the pictures in the hope of blackmailing him into spying for them. He went to his superiors, who withdrew him from the station. (Kessler, *Moscow Station*; Smith, "The First Moscow Station," *IJIC*)

532 Smith, John Discoe (b. 1926). In 1967 the Communist party of India published Smith's book *I Was a CIA Agent in India*, which ignited continued suspicion whether the CIA had attempted to assassinate Chou Enlai, the Chinese premier, in 1955. In his book he claimed that while working as a cipher clerk and communications specialist at the U.S. embassy in New Delhi in 1954–59, he served as a courier between the CIA and Nationalist Chinese agents, delivering a package to them. He later learned it was the two time bombs later placed aboard the Air India plane that was chartered to carry Chou Enlai and his delegation to the Bandung Conference in Indonesia. The plane exploded, crashing into the South China

Sea on April 11, 1955, killing everyone aboard except the crew. Chou Enlai had departed the plane in Burma, with instructions for the plane to continue without him. The only proof of Smith's statements was his listing in the *State Department Bibliographic Register* as stationed in India in 1954–59, then to an unnamed Southeast Asian country where he was possibly recruited by the KGB. He was later reported to be in Moscow and participated in the anti–CIA propaganda broadcasts of Peace and Progress Radio, where he detailed CIA operations in India. (Blum, *The CIA; Facts on File*, 1955–56; *New York Times*, April 12, 30; August 3, 4, September 3, 1955; November 22, 1967; Rositzke, *The KGB*)

533   Smith, Joseph Burkholder (b. 1921).   He attended Harvard till he joined the U.S. Army in February 1943 as a Japanese-language specialist and then as an Army Military Intelligence Language Specialist Fifth Class. He left the Army in February 1946 and finished his degree.

He joined the covert action arm of the CIA's Far East Division in September 1951 as a Southeast Asian psychological warfare expert. In 1953 Smith was transferred to Indonesia to evaluate a difficult covert operation involving several bookstores selling anti–Communist books. The project was dropped because a bookstore was difficult to justify as a cover in an impoverished and largely illiterate country like Indonesia, particularly a store run by the CIA.

Smith was then assigned to Singapore as chief of covert operations in April 1953. During his tenure in Singapore, the events in Vietnam had gained the attention of the CIA. Smith used agents in Singapore in the local news service to write some black propaganda stories about the crisis in Vietnam. One story stated that the Chinese were providing armed support for the Vietminh.

He returned to CIA headquarters in July 1956 and began coordinating covert operations against Sukarno. Sukarno had intended on moving Indonesia into the Sino-Soviet bloc, which infuriated his military officers. The first operation was support for a group of rebel military officers who declared a coup on February 15, 1958. The revolt was supported by CIA air support and bombers.

With the threat of an anti–CIA government coming to power in the Philippines, Smith was sent there on March 10, 1958, undercover as a civilian Air Force employee. CIA concentrated its efforts on the upcoming elections by supporting Genaro Magsaysay, but the election was won by Ferdinand Marcos.

By November 1960, Smith was the chief of the Propaganda Guidance Section, a unit within the Covert Action staff, producing propaganda guidelines about Castro's Cuba for all overseas stations, called *Bi-Weekly Propaganda Guidance.* The idea was to inform the various stations around the world what the CIA felt was important, so that propaganda projects could bolster the CIA's position. A few months prior to the Bay of Pigs invasion, Smith was encouraging propaganda projects that would bolster the case in favor of the liberation of Cuba.

After the Bay of Pigs disaster Smith was transferred to the Western Hemisphere Division as the chief of the Venezuelan desk in August 1961. Fearing an attempt by Castro to start a revolution in oil-rich Venezuela, the CIA was ordered to checkmate his activities in South America. One project Smith helped sponsor was the production of an anti–Communist newspaper *La Republica* in Caracas.

In June 1962, Smith was sent to the Buenos Aires station under the alias Arthur H. Toohill, where he was in charge of the propaganda project jointly run with the Argentine security agency. While in Argentina, Smith focused on anti–Cuban propaganda operations and collecting data on Ernesto "Che" Guevara. Smith left Argentina on August 29, 1966.

In June 1969, he was sent to Mexico City to participate in the station's MHCHAOS operation. MHCHAOS was the CIA domestic spying operation on Vietnam protesters in the U.S. The Mexico City station kept tabs on U.S. citizens organizing antiwar activities in Mexico. The last year of his Mexico tour was spent rolling up CIA operations former CIA officer Philip Agee's *Inside the Company* had exposed in Latin America. Ironically, Agee had failed to mention Smith in his book despite the fact that they had worked together in Argentina in 1965.

Smith retired from the CIA after 22 years of service; in June 1973, he was awarded the CIA Medal of Meritorious Service. (Blum, *The CIA*; Smith, *Portrait of a Cold Warrior*)

534 Smith, Raymond D.   Commander Smith, serving as assistant naval attaché at the U.S. embassy in Moscow, was arrested and deported in 1962 for espionage. Smith had been arrested in Leningrad in October carrying a Minox camera, tape recorder, and high-powered binoculars. The Russians said he was photographing naval installations. The U.S. embassy said he was taking a walk in the park. Reportedly, Soviet security agents roughed up Smith during the arrest. The State Department claimed that Smith's arrest and expulsion was in response to the Cornelius Drummond discovery and expulsion of several Soviet agents. (*Facts on File*, 1962; *New York Times*, October 6, 7, 9, 11, 1962; Wise and Ross, *The Invisible Government*)

535 Smith, Richard Craig.   In April 1984, Smith, a former U.S. Army counterintelligence specialist, was arrested by the FBI for espionage at Washington's Dulles International Airport. However, Smith admitted taking $11,000 from a Soviet agent in Tokyo in return for classified data on U.S. intelligence operations which revealed the names of six double agents.

Smith had worked for the army's Intelligence and Security Command from 1973 to 1980, first as a noncommissioned officer and later as a civilian employee, where he managed U.S. double agents and developed cover stories for them in an operation called Royal Mitre.

He left the Army in 1980, starting a video company in his home state, Utah. In June 1981, he went to Tokyo on a business trip looking for Japanese investors. Smith stated that two men, Ken White and Danny Ishida, approached him, stating that they were from the CIA and asking him to help in a plan to penetrate the KGB in Japan. They told him to portray himself as broke and dying of cancer, with a wife and four children, desperate to sell secrets. This was based on the truth. He did have four children, and his video business was bankrupt. The mysterious CIA operatives never contacted him, and Smith went to the FBI. He stated that he was indeed a spy, but for the U.S., not the Soviet Union, describing it as a CIA operation to infiltrate the KGB. The CIA did not support Smith's story, but a federal jury found him not guilty in 1986.

He claimed that Charles Richardson, a retired CIA officer, had recruited him for the operation, but Richardson denied the story. Smith claimed that he had worked through a Hawaiian investment firm (Bishop, Baldwin, Rewald, Dillingham and Wong, Inc.), which was used as a front for the CIA operations in Asia. The firm went defunct in 1983, and Ronald Rewald was accused of defrauding investors of $20 million. Rewald claimed that the CIA had drained the firm while using it as a front. (Allen and Polmar, *Merchants of Treason*; Corson and Crowley, *The New KGB*)

536   Smith, Walter Bedell (1898–1961).   Director of Central Intelligence Agency (DCI) from October 1950 to February 1953 under President Truman. Promoted to general in the U.S. Army in August 1951, he became under secretary of state in February 1953. He served as chief of staff of the Allied forces in North Africa and the Mediterranean, later chief of staff to General Eisenhower, Supreme Headquarters, Allied Expeditionary Forces. He was promoted to lieutenant general in January 1944 and served as U.S. ambassador to the Soviet Union from 1946 to 1949. He retired from the U.S. Army in February 1953. (Darling, *The Central Intelligence Agency*; Leary, *The Central Intelligence Agency*; Ranelagh, *The Agency*)

537   Snepp, Frank W.   After completing his master's degree from Columbia University's School of International Affairs, he joined the CIA upon the encouragement of a professor and to avoid being drafted during the Vietnam War. Initially Snepp was assigned to the European Division as an analyst on NATO affairs. However, one day some colleagues decided to play a practical joke and signed his name to a job assignment for Vietnam. After being accepted, Snepp pleaded in vain but was warned that he would jeopardize any future opportunities for foreign assignments.

In 1969–71 he completed one tour under Ted Shackley at the Saigon station, where he prepared strategic estimates and briefings, also handling interrogations and informant networks. After his first stint in Vietnam, Snepp returned to CIA headquarters to serve in the CIA's Vietnam Task Force, but for political reasons he was removed from that position. Snepp returned to Vietnam for his second tour in 1972, first as the CIA interrogator of Nguyen Van Tai, Le Van Hoai, and Nam Quyet, then as the senior intelligence analyst in the station's Indications Analysis branch till the evacuation of the U.S. embassy in April 1975.

Snepp was then assigned to Thailand to debrief journalists and refugees escaping Vietnam. In August 1975, he was recalled to CIA headquarters where he received a promotion and earned the Intelligence Medal of Merit for "analytical acuity" during the final month of the war. Three weeks later he resigned after futile attempts to generate interest in an official after-action report.

Determined to set the record straight on the CIA's mismanagement in Vietnam, particularly the disastrous final days, Snepp wrote *Decent Interval* in 1977. The CIA argued that Snepp had violated the secrecy agreement he signed when he joined the CIA and sued for the profits of the book in 1978. The suit went to the Supreme Court in 1980, and the Court voted in favor of the CIA in *Snepp v. U.S.*, 444 U.S. 507 (1980). Snepp had to hand over the profits from his book. Snepp was also forced to submit his novel *Convergence of Interest* to the CIA for approval in 1980. The book was about a CIA officer's involvement in the assassination of President John F. Kennedy. (Bittman, *The KGB and Soviet Disinformation*; Breckinridge, *The CIA and the U.S. Intelligence System*; Johnson, *America's Secret Power*; Snepp, *Decent Interval*)

538   Soble, Jack, and Robert Soblen.   They were born in Lithuania as Ruvelis Leiba Sobolevicius (1990) and Abromas Sobolevicius (1903) to a rich Jewish merchant. Robert changed his name from Sobolevicius to Soblen when he left Lithuania.

In 1929–32 both brothers were close confidants of Leon Trotsky while he was living in Turkey, both actually spying on him for Soviet intelligence. The two brothers appeared to be loyal followers of Leon Trotsky. They quickly rose in the ranks. It is unknown whether Trotsky knew they were brothers. They played a major role for the Soviet intelligence service in spying on Trotsky and disrupting his movements.

They were later to operate a major Soviet spy ring in the U.S. Jack Soble arrived in the U.S. in 1941 and inherited the Rabinowitz spy ring. The most famous member of the ring was courier Boris Morros, a Hollywood producer. A letter given to Morros to deliver to Moscow was intercepted by the FBI. His entire ring was arrested. Both had given the Soviets national security data. Jack Soble pled guilty to spying for the Soviet Union in 1957 in a New York courtroom.

Jack Soble testified against his brother in court, stating that his brother often complained about the amount of money the Soviet were paying him. Since he suffered from cancer and was expected to die soon, he was temporarily released on bail. In June 1962, Soblen escaped to Israel but was extradited to the United States. On the plane back, Soblen attempted suicide by stabbing himself with a dinner knife and was rushed to a London hospital and applied for asylum in England, but he committed suicide when he was being returned to the airport to be returned to the U.S. He died five days later in a London hospital. (Andrew and Gordievsky, *KGB*: Romerstein and Levchenko, *The KGB Against the "Main Enemy"*; Rositzke, *The KGB*)

Soblen, Robert see Soble, Jack

539   Sokolov, Aleksander (b. 1919).   In October 1964, Sokolov and his wife were deported to Czechoslovakia for spying for the Soviet Union. One of the prosecution's main witnesses against the Sokolovs was a Finn, Kaarlo Rudolph Tuomi, who had worked as a double agent in Soviet intelligence. Both had been charged with conspiring to commit espionage in Washington and New York City 1957–63 and attempting to gather data on U.S. missile sites, nuclear weapons shipments, and military data. They pleaded not guilty to the charges. The original espionage charges had to be dropped due to security concerns. Sokolov, a Soviet citizen, had originally requested to be deported to Czechoslovakia rather than the Soviet Union, and both were placed aboard an Air India flight for the journey to Prague. (Cookridge, *Spy Trade*; Wise and Ross, *The Espionage Establishment*)

Solousov, Anatoly see Tsekovisky, Victor

540   Soloviev, Mikhail.   In October 1976, Soloviev, a member of the Soviet embassy's trade department, was expelled from France for espionage activities. French agents arrested Soloviev in a church in Paris after he had received classified documents about a secret jet engine program. Soloviev had contacted the engineer working on the project, who notified French counterintelligence. French agents set up a sting operation with the engineer to entrap Soloviev. (*Facts on File*, 1976; *New York Times*, October 17, 1976)

541   Souers, Sidney William (1892–1973).   First Director of Central Intelligence Group, forerunner of the CIA, from January 1946 to June 1946, under President Truman. A former lieutenant commander in the U.S. Naval Reserve during World War II, he became a rear admiral and deputy chief of naval intelligence in 1945. From 1947 to 1950 he was executive secretary of the National Security Council and special consultant to President Truman during the Korean War. (Cline, *Secrets, Spies and Scholars*; Darling, *The Central Intelligence Agency*; Leary, *The Central Intelligence Agency*)

542   Souther, Glenn Michael (d. 1989).   Former U.S. Navy petty officer, defected to the Soviet Union in 1986. Souther had served as an intelligence specialist in satellite intelligence with the Sixth Fleet 1975–82. When Souther learned in May 1986 of an FBI-NIS investigation, he disappeared from Norfolk, went to Italy, then defected to the Soviet Union. His name surfaced in 1989 in Moscow when the *Red Star* announced that he had died June 22. The article went on to describe him as a major in the KGB by the name of Mikhail Yevgenyevich Orlov. Reportedly, KGB chief Vladimir A. Kryuchkov admitted later that Souther had committed suicide. (Allen and Polmar, *Merchants of Treason*; *Facts on File*, 1989; *New York Times*, June 28, 29, 1989)

543   Spencer, George Victor.   In April 1966, Spencer, a Vancouver postal clerk, was found dead by natural causes in his home. He had been under investigation for spying for the Soviet Union. Reportedly, Spencer had sold information to two Soviet diplomats at the Ottawa embassy. Both were expelled from Canada in 1965 as a result of the charges. (*Facts on File*, 1966; *New York Times*, March 6, 8, 11, 1966)

544   Stashynsky, Bogdan (b. 1931).   A Soviet KGB defector in 1961, he confessed to the murder of two anti–Soviet exiles, Ukrainian nationalists Leo Rebet in 1957 and Stefan Bandera in 1959, in Munich, West Germany. Stashynsky had sprayed prussic acid into their faces that once inhaled, caused instant death by cardiac arrest, making it look like a simple heart attack. He was awarded the Order of the Red Banner for the two assassinations. Stashynsky was trained to serve as an illegal in West Germany, Department 13 (assassination and sabotage).

In 1951 he was sent to infiltrate the Organization of Ukrainian Nationalists, in which he succeeded. After several months he was withdrawn and sent to Kiev to learn German. In January 1956, he traveled to Munich as a courier for a Soviet agent named Bisaha who worked on the staff of the Ukrainian nationalist newspaper, which put him into position for the assassination. He was sentenced to eight years for their murders in a West

German court in 1962. (Barron, *KGB; New York Times,* November 18, 1961; Romerstein and Levchenko, *The KGB Against the "Main Enemy")*

545 Steadman, Alastair Duncan. In March 1975, former Royal Air Force nuclear bomber pilot Flight Lieutenant Steadman was charged with spying for the Soviets. British MI5 agents arrested Steadman after surveillance for a week. A search of his home revealed radio equipment for transmitting messages to the Soviet Union. He was convicted of selling NATO and British classified data to the Soviet Union and sentenced to nine years. Steadman claimed that a Soviet consular official, Mikenberg, had threatened the lives of his family if he did not cooperate. (*Facts on File,* 1975)

546 Stern, Alfred K. (1897–1986), and wife, Martha Dodd (b. 1908). Indicted for spying for the Soviet Union in a New York court, they escaped their home in the U.S. for Mexico in 1953, then fled to Czechoslovakia in 1957. When they arrived, they renounced their U.S. citizenship and called the charges false. They were later spotted in the Soviet Union in 1957. The charges stemmed from accusations from Boris Morros, Russian-born Hollywood movie producer-composer, who reportedly worked as a "counterspy" for the U.S. government, during testimony at the House Un-American Activities Committee.

The Sterns were wealthy and influential leftists. The 1957 indictment stated that the Sterns used their home in Connecticut to meet Soviet agents. Morros stated that the Sterns had given him $100,000 to set up a business that would act as a front for Soviet espionage activities.

Stern lived in Prague as a consultant at the construction ministry until his death in 1986. The U.S. Justice Department dropped charges against them in 1979 when all the witnesses had died. (*Facts on File,* 1957, 1979; Romerstein and Levchenko, *The KGB Aainst the "Main Enemy")*

Stern, Martha Dodd see **Stern, Alfred K.**

547 Stockwell, John R. He grew up in Kasai Province of the Belgian Congo, learning the local dialect, Tshiluba. After ten years in Africa, he returned to the U.S. and attended the University of Texas. After college he joined the Marine Corps and served one tour in a parachute reconnaissance company, then served on a U.S. Navy ship as a Marine Corps intelligence officer, visiting numerous African ports.

He joined the CIA in 1964 as an operations officer in the African Division, served as chief of the Lubumbashi base in Zaire, then chief of station in Bujumbura, the capital of Berundi on Lake Tanganyika. In 1972 he served as chief of the Kenya-Uganda section till 1973 when he was sent to Vietnam as a case officer in Tay Ninh Province of South Vietnam after the previous officer committed suicide. After Tay Ninh fell to the North Vietnamese, he worked briefly with Orrin DeForest in Bien Hoa, where he continued to handle agents. After the fall of Saigon in 1975, he earned the Medal of Merit for his service in Vietnam.

In 1975 the Angola Task Force was created by the CIA to help anti–Cuban forces in Angola, and Stockwell was made chief. Shocked by the disclosures of the Church and Pike committees investigating the CIA activities, Stockwell decided to resign. The point of disclosure that bothered him personally was the CIA plot to kill Patrice Lumumba, with whom he had shared similar experiences in Africa. These disclosures, combined with Stockwell's experiences in Vietnam and Angola, convinced him to resign after 12 years of service, on April 1, 1977. He wrote an open letter to DCI Stansfield Turner in the *Washington Post* (April 10, 1977), calling for reform measures in the CIA.

Stockwell later wrote *In Search of Enemies* (1978), detailing the Angolan program, but the U.S. government sued him in March 1980 to retain the profits of the book, arguing that Stockwell had violated the secrecy agreement he signed when he joined the CIA. Stockwell agreed in June 1980 to forfeit all future profits from his royalties to the government. Today, Stockwell writes and lectures about the CIA. (Bittman, *The KGB and Soviet Disinformation*; DeForest and Chanoff, *Slow Burn*; Snepp, *Decent Interval*; Stockwell, *In Search of Enemies, The Praetorian Guard*)

548   Stolz, Richard F., and Kenneth A. Kerst.   In January 1965, the Soviet Union accused Stolz, first secretary of the U.S. embassy, and Kerst, former first secretary of the U.S. embassy, of espionage. Stolz was ordered to leave the country, but Kerst had already left in November 1964. Soviet authorities stated that a Soviet citizen identified as "B" had been arrested for espionage and was said to have worked with Stolz and Kerst. U.S. authorities stated that the Soviets were retaliating to the U.S. expulsion of Boris V. Karpovich, information counselor at the Soviet embassy in Washington. (*Facts on File*, 1965; *New York Times*, January 29, 1965)

549   Stonehouse, John.   When a Czech intelligence officer defected, he named Stonehouse, a minister, as a Czech asset. He was a former labor minister in the Aviation and Technology ministries, and later postmaster-general and minister of posts and telecommunications. It was claimed that Stonehouse had been recruited by sexual entrapment while visiting Czechoslovakia. Stonehouse denied the allegations, and no evidence was presented. Later, Stonehouse attempted to fake his death by suicide to escape continued investigation, but when it was learned that there was no strong evidence, he reappeared under an alias in Australia and was arrested and returned to Great Britain where he was sentenced to seven years for eighteen charges of fraud and theft in 1976.

After his release, he wrote a novel, *Ralph*, in 1982 describing blackmail operation by East Germans. His novel describes now an official in the European Commission, Ralph Edmonds, is seduced in a sex trap by East German intelligence. He describes a wild sexual encounter with the seductress Lotte, only to notice the large oval ceiling mirror afterward when he is handed pictures of his affair by East German agents. In 1974, with business problems and an MI5 investigation, he faked suicide and escaped with his mistress to Australia. (Andrew and Gordievsky, *KGB*; Frolik, *The Frolik Defection*; Pincher, *Too Secret, Too Long*; West, *The Circus*)

550 Suh Kyung Won.   Possible North Korean spy. Suh, an opposition member of South Korea's National Assembly, had made a secret visit to North Korea in 1988 and met with North Korean leader Kim Il Sung. Reportedly, Suh accepted a payment of $100,000 for information. The South Korean government arrested Suh in June 1989 and charged him with espionage, and on December 20, Suh was sentenced to 15 years. Suh claimed he had been forced to sign a confession. Suh was a member of Kim Dae Jung's Party for Peace and Democracy and may have been a political target rather than an agent for the North Koreans. (*Facts on File*, 1989; *New York Times*, December 21, 1989)

551 Suranov, Oleg.   In February 1980, Spanish authorities arrested Suranov, head of Soviet Aeroflot operations in Spain, for espionage charges and expelled him. Suranov was also accused of having contacts with left-wing extremist groups. Another Soviet, a first secretary for the Soviet embassy, Anatoly Krasilnikov, was also expelled from Spain. Both men were accused of stealing classified military secrets on the Spanish military. (*Facts on File*, 1980; *New York Times*, February 17, 1980)

552 Susdaryanto, Johannes Batista.   In August 1984, a U.S. military court convicted Lieutenant Col. Susdaryanto of spying for the Soviet Union and sentenced him to ten years. Susdaryanto worked in the U.S. Navy's hydrographic department and had provided the Soviets with classified maps and documents from 1976 to 1982. Some of the documents included joint surveys by the U.S. and Indonesia of the strategic Makasar Strait, used by the U.S. Seventh Fleet. (*Facts on File*, 1984)

553 Suslov, Ilya M.   Suslov, a Soviet journalist, was arrested in the Soviet Union in 1986 for espionage for West German intelligence and sentenced to fifteen years in prison. Suslov had been the editor of the

Novosti news service and the host of *Man, Earth, Universe*, a popular Soviet TV program on space exploration during the 1970s. The West German BND was receiving military and scientific secrets from the mid–1970s till his arrest. His West German contact was Pavel Arsene, the Soviet representative of a West German company that was a front for the BND. (*Facts on File*, 1986; *New York Times*, July 31, 1986; Richelson, *Foreign Intelligence Organizations*)

554 Sutch, William Ball. In February 1975, Sutch, former head of the Department of Industries and Commerce, was acquitted by a New Zealand court for espionage. Sutch had been accused of meeting secretly with Soviet diplomats in 1974. Two Soviets were expelled from New Zealand — Dimitri Razogovrov, first secretary, and U. F. Pertsev, administrative staffer. (*Facts on File*, 1974–75)

554A Sutterlein, Heinz, and wife, Leonore. Sutterlein was sent to West Germany to romance one of three secretaries working for the Foreign Ministry. He settled on a secretary by the name of Lenore. After a brief romance, they were married in December 1960. She soon began giving him classified documents that he would photograph during her lunch breaks. They were handled by KGB Lt. Col. Eugen Runge, but he defected in 1968 to the West, revealing Sutterlein's activities.

A West German court in Cologne sentenced Sutterlein to seven years in November 1969 for passing classified documents to the Soviet Union. His wife, Leonore, had passed 3,000 political and NATO documents over a seven-year period. (Andrew and Gordievsky, *KGB*; Barron, *KGB*)

Sutterlein, Leonore see **Sutterlein, Heinz**

555 Suvorov, Victor (b. 1947). Real name Vladimir Bogdanovich Rezun, defected to the British in June 1978. He used the pseudonym Suvorov. He was able to give the West the best glimpse into the Soviet GRU and the infamous Spetsnaz (or Special Purpose Forces). In 1958, at the age of 11, he entered military cadet school (till 1965), then entered the All-Army Higher Military Counterintelligence School. He joined the Communist party in 1967.

In 1968 he participated as a lieutenant in the Soviet invasion of Czechoslovakia, as a company commander of a regiment. The invasion, called Operation Danube, caused his disillusionment. After this he was stationed at a GRU station in Geneva with the rank of captain. After four years he defected to the British embassy in Vienna. (Brook-Shepherd, *The Storm Birds*; Suvorov, *Inside the Aquarium, Inside Soviet Military Intelligence*, and *Spetsnaz*)

556   Svenson, Alfred E.   In 1964 Captain Svenson returned after defecting to East Germany in May 1963. Svenson, a U.S. Army intelligence officer before his defection, was returned against his will by Soviet authorities. No specific reason was given for returning him, and no exchange took place. Since Svenson had been an intelligence officer, many wondered what, if any, information was provided to the East Germans and Soviets. He was found guilty in a West German court of deserting, defecting, and stealing a Jeep. He was sentenced to seven years' hard labor. (*Facts on File*, 1964; *New York Times*, July 1, 3, 9, 10, 1964)

557   Sveshnikov, Gennady Vassilievich.   In July 1977, Spanish Foreign Ministry officials expelled Sveshnikov for espionage activities. Sveshnikov had been arrested while in the possession of classified documents in the city of Aranjuez. Sveshnikov worked for Intramar, a Soviet-Spanish company that built logistical equipment for the Spanish fishing fleet based in the Canary Islands. (*Facts on File*, 1977)

558   Tarasov, Vasily.   In April 1964, Canadian officials expelled Tarasov, a Soviet correspondent for *Izvestia*, for espionage. According to Canadian officials, Tarasov had attempted to obtain classified data on industrial processes from a civilian government employee. The employee informed authorities of Tarasov's approach, and he was arrested after a meeting. (*Facts on File*, 1964; *New York Times*, April 29, 1964)

559   Telli, Diallo.   In August 1976, Telli, a former Guinea justice minister who was charged in the attempt to overthrow the government, stated that he had been working for the CIA and had been recruited in 1974 for the purpose of supplying the CIA with data on Guinea's domestic situation. The U.S. government denied the charges. (*Facts on File*, 1976)

560   Terpil, Frank E. (b. 1939).   He joined the U.S. Army in 1958 and was stationed in the Far East. In 1965 he joined the CIA as a contract employee in the Technical Services Division, basically a low-level communications technician. In the CIA he was well known for stories of his cloak-and-dagger adventures, petty theft, and womanizing. Wherever he was assigned overseas, he would become involved in the black market of currency, liquor, and stolen goods. He would become involved in back-alley deals with a variety of shady characters.

In 1970 Terpil was assigned to the CIA station in New Delhi, India. This would be his last station post, for he became immersed once again in the black market. While he was in Afghanistan in 1971 finalizing an illicit currency transfer, the India-Pakistan War broke out, and the borders were closed, trapping Terpil in Afghanistan. Unable to return to his duty station in New Delhi at a time of crisis, he was shipped home after the war and fired by the CIA.

After the CIA he roamed around the Middle East and Central America, reacquainting himself with old contacts and suggesting he was still with the CIA on special unofficial missions, but he was actually working as a middleman for arms merchants. He was able to build a large network within a few years.

Former CIA officer Ed Wilson, who was looking to make contacts with Libya, met with Frank Terpil to make a business proposition with the Libyan government. Terpil would act as a contact man with the Libyans, and Wilson would organize the equipment and delivery from London. In 1976 the Libyans provided long lists of special weapons, silencers, timing devices, C-4 explosives, and surveillance equipment. Both Wilson and Terpil taught classes on assassination, espionage tradecraft, and escape-evasion techniques.

In 1976 Terpil and Wilson later attempted to recruit three Cuban exiles with ties to the CIA to assassinate a Libyan exile. Wilson and Terpil were charged with attempting to hire assassins to kill Libyan dissident Umar Abdullah Muhayshi for the Libyan government. Terpil and Wilson offered $1 million to three Cuban exiles — Rafael "Chi Chi" Quintero and Raul Villaverde and Raul's brother during two meetings. Quintero, a Bay of Pigs veteran, notified the CIA of Terpil and Wilson's activities. The three Cubans met in Geneva with Terpil and Wilson in the belief that they were being hired to kill Carlos the Jackal, an infamous terrorist. But upon arrival, they were told their real target was an anti–Qaddafi dissident by the name of Umar Abdullah Mahayshi living in Cairo. The Cubans balked and returned to Miami.

In 1977 Terpil and Wilson went their separate ways. Terpil went to Uganda to work for Idi Amin as his security advisor, supplying a variety of poisons, drugs, and torture equipment to Idi Amin. In December 1979, Terpil became involved in an arms deal in New York City and was arrested by undercover agents. He was released on bail and fled to Beirut in September 1978. In May 1981, while still in Beirut, he was tried in absentia in the U.S. and convicted and sentenced to 53 years for trying to sell arms to two undercover agents posing as Latin American revolutionaries.

In November 1981, Terpil was indicted for conspiring to provide guns, ammunition, decoding equipment, and torture equipment in 1979 to Idi Amin of Uganda. Terpil then moved to Damascus, Syria, and opened a restaurant. Syrian intelligence officers arrested him and returned him to Beirut. (Goulden, *The Death Merchant*, Maas, *Manhunt*; Marshall, Scott, and Hunter, *Iran-Contra Connection*)

561   Terrell, DuWayne, and William Thomas.   In early 1980, two Americans were arrested in North Yemen and accused of being spies. Thomas was accused of being a CIA agent, and Terrell was accused of being a spy for Israel. Both were reportedly tortured into making confessions, which both denied when they were released in February 1981. Terrell had been arrested in February 1980, Thomas in April 1980. Terrell had arrived in North Yemen in November 1979 from Israel, where he had worked with the Southern Baptist Church in Jerusalem. While in North Yemen, he was employed by Thomas's Washington-based marketing business in North Yemen. Thomas had been in North Yemen since December 1977. U.S. officials pressed the government to release both men, and they were finally released, after being found not guilty by a court, a day after the Iranian government released the 52 Americans it held in Teheran. (*Facts on File*, 1981; *New York Times*, February 17, 19, 1981)

562   Thomas, Louis C.   In June 1983, Thomas, an electronics specialist assigned to the U.S. embassy security division, was expelled from the Soviet Union for espionage. Reportedly, Thomas had been caught in an act of espionage in Moscow. Thomas had been at his assignment with the U.S. embassy for two years. The State Department did not respond to the allegations. (*Facts on File*, 1983; Kessler, *Moscow Station*; *New York Times*, June 5, 1983)

Thomas, William see **Terrell, DuWayne**

563   Thompson, Robert Glenn.   Thompson, a former U.S. Air Force airman second class, was arrested for spying for the Soviet Union. Reportedly, Thompson had spied for the Soviets between June 1957 and July 1963 within the U.S. and abroad while in the Air Force. Two Soviet diplomats were named as coconspirators: Fedor D. Kudashkin (also called John Kurlinsky), who worked as the chief of the Russian section of verbatim reporters at the UN and also served as third secretary of the Soviet UN delegation, and Boris Vladimorovich Karpovich, who served as an interpreter at the UN and later as an information counselor in the Soviet embassy in Washington.

Thompson, in the Air Force 1952–58, began spying for the Soviet Union in December 1957 while stationed in West Berlin. According to authorities, Thompson provided the Soviets with pictures of U.S. military equipment, military installations, missile sites, codebooks, counterintelligence operations, and a variety of classified documents. Thompson used a shortwave radio to receive instructions from Soviet handlers.

Thompson pled guilty in March 1965 to spying for the Soviet Union between June 1957 and July 1963. He also stated that he had received special training in the Soviet Union for espionage activities. He was sentenced to thirty years.

In May 1978, he was exchanged for an East German–held American who was arrested for helping East Germans flee into West Germany in the trunk of his car — Alan Stuart Van Norman. Thompson claimed that he had been born in Leipzig and was entitled to return there.

In June 1957, while stationed in West Berlin, he walked across the sector border and contacted East German intelligence officials. While attached to the Air Force Office of Special Investigations, he served the East Germans, detailing U.S. counterintelligence and intelligence operations against East Germany. Thompson also supplied the East Germans with a list of air force intelligence safe houses in West Berlin and helped identify CIA and army safe houses. The Soviets stepped in and provided Thompson with espionage training during a secret trip to the Soviet Union. (Allen and Polmar, *Merchants of Treason*; Romerstein and Levchenko, *The KGB Against the "Main Enemy"*; Rositzke, *The KGB*)

564   Thyraud de Vosjoli, Philippe L. (b. 1920).   Head of the Washington station for the French intelligence service (SDECE) for twelve years. He had taken part in resistance operations during World War II in his native region of Romorantin in France. After the war he joined French intelligence. In April 1951, he was sent to Washington as the liaison between the CIA and SDECE, code-named LAMIA, under cover as embassy counsellor. While he was stationed in Washington, the CIA apparently recruited him. Thyraud organized networks of agents in the Caribbean, Haiti, and Cuba. In August 1962, his networks in Cuba picked up signs of the installation of Soviet missiles, which he reported to the CIA. In late 1962 he was sent back to Paris and was commanded to report all his contacts in Cuba by name. He resisted but later gave the name of the Cuban agent who identified Soviet missiles in Cuba. Later the agent was arrested and executed by Cuban security forces. No doubt a KGB plant in French intelligence gained access to the information. In September 1963, Thyraud was fired from the SDECE. He charged later that the SDECE had assassinated Enrico Mattei, an Italian oil magnate, and a *Time* magazine correspondent who supported the Algerian revolution, who died in a mysterious plane crash. (Faligot and Krop, *La Piscine*; Powers, *The Man Who Kept the Secrets*; Thyraud de Vosjoli, *Lamia*)

565   Tiedge, Hans Joachim.   In August 1985, Tiedge, division head of the West German counterintelligence service (BfV) disappeared. He was later discovered to have defected to East Germany. Tiedge's defection caused an espionage scandal in West Germany affecting the office of Chancellor Helmut Kohl. Tiedge was described as the third most important intelligence official in West Germany, with 20 years of experience in counterintelligence.

Tiedge, depressed with his wife's death three years before, suffered from financial problems and alcoholism. Tiedge was a notorious drinker who had his driver's license revoked. His daughters were reportedly heavily involved in the Cologne drug culture. Tiedge betrayed two Western agents in East Berlin Communist party circles. At the same time, several other people disappeared and were believed to be part of an East Germany spy network warned by Tiedge to escape: Sonja Lueneburg, personal secretary to the economics minister; Ursula Richter, secretary for the League of Expellees; and Lorenz Betzing, a friend of Richter, messenger for the army administrative office in Bonn; Astrid Willner, a secretary in the chancellor's office; Herbert Willner, a senior official with a foundation, with ties to the liberal Free Democratic party. (Glees, *The Secrets of the Service*; Richelson, *Foreign Intelligence Organizations*)

566   Tikhomirov, Aleksandr V.   In February 1970, FBI agents arrested Tikhomirov, a Soviet working as a translator for the UN secretariat, on espionage charges in Seattle, Washington. But charges were later dropped on condition that he return to the Soviet Union. Tikhomirov had approached a U.S. Air Force technical sergeant and offered him money for information in December 1969. The sergeant went to authorities, who used him in a sting operation. The FBI arrested the Soviet after the sergeant had given him classified documents. (Allen and Polmar, *Merchants of Treason*; Newman, *Famous Soviet Spies*)

567   Tipanut, Virgil.   In June 1975, Tipanut, third secretary of the Rumanian embassy in Oslo, Norway, defected. He named forty Rumanian intelligence agents working in five European countries: Britain, Denmark, Norway, Sweden, and West Germany. The target of most of the agents was sensitive industrial and technological data. Military and political intelligence was secondary. Many of the agents had already escaped back to Rumania when Tipanut defected. Titus Petrila, an exchange student, was charged with espionage in Norway and confessed under questioning. (*Facts on File*, 1975; *New York Times*, August 31, 1975)

568   Titov, Gennadi Fyodorovich (b. 1932).   Titov, nicknamed "the Crocodile," was an unpopular KGB officer with his colleagues but well liked by superiors. When Titov was a young child, his father was arrested by Stalin's security forces and executed. Despite the fact that his father had been accused of being a traitor, he was accepted in the Leningrad Military Institute in 1955, joining the KGB after graduation. In 1972–77 he served as KGB resident in Norway, handling Arne Treholt, a spy in the

Norwegian government till he was expelled in 1977. In 1979–84 he was head of the Third Department and was responsible for Britain, Ireland, Scandinavia, and Australia. (Andrew and Gordievsky, *KGB*; Romerstein and Levchenko, *The KGB against the "Main Enemy"*)

569   Titov, Igor Viktorovich.   In March 1983, Titov, a correspondent for the Soviet magazine *New Times*, was expelled for attempting to recruit an American student in Great Britain while in charge of political intelligence in London as deputy resident. After returning to KGB headquarters, he became head of the British desk of the KGB. (Andrew and Gordievsky, *KGB*; *Facts on File*, 1983; *New York Times*, April 1, 1983)

570   Tobias, Michael T.   In August 1984, Tobias and his nephew Francis X. Pizzo were arrested for attempting to sell navy cryptographic key cards to the Soviet Union. Tobias was a third class radioman on USS *Peoria*, a U.S. Navy tank landing ship based in California. Tobias had offered the codes to the Soviet consulate in San Francisco for $100,000, apparently unsuccessfully, because they then offered to sell them to federal agents for $1,000 and a promise of immunity. He was sentenced to 12 years for theft of government property and extortion. (Allen and Polmar, *Merchants of Treason*; *Facts on File*, 1984)

571   Tofte, Hans V. (1912–87).   Head of CIA covert operations 1950–51, while stationed in Japan, Tofte established extensive CIA bases throughout Japan to help service Civil Air Transport and helped build networks in North Korea to help downed pilots during the Korean War.

After his retirement from the CIA, he was involved in a scandal. Tofte had placed his Georgetown home on sale, and while a realtor was showing the house to a customer who had connections with the CIA, he noticed stacks of classified documents in Tofte's closet. CIA security removed the documents. Tofte was outraged, claiming that the CIA had entered his home illegally and that some of the security men had stolen some of his wife's jewelry. He sued the CIA director, Richard Helms, and the CIA, who considered countercharges of having unauthorized possession of classified documents. (Hunt, *Undercover*; Leary, *Perilous Missions*; Smith, *OSS*; Powers, *The Man Who Kept the Secrets*)

572   Tolkachev, Adolf G.   Soviet aviation specialist who spied for the CIA, captured by Soviet authorities and executed in 1985. Edward Lee Howard, former CIA agent, had revealed to Soviet authorities the identities of Tolkachev and his CIA handler, Paul M. "Skip" Stombaugh, who was using the cover of second secretary at the U.S. embassy in Moscow.

Tolkachev, a defense researcher at the aviation institute in Moscow, provided data related to Soviet research on aviation technology, electronic guidance, radar and stealth technology. Tolkachev, an asset since the Carter administration, may have been the agent who supplied data on the building of a large phased-array radar at Krasnoyarsk. Edward Lee Howard had been briefed on Tolkachev and was supposed to take over as his case officer in Moscow. Tolkachev was arrested during a meeting with Stombaugh in June 1985, and Stombaugh was expelled. A *Pravda* article on September 22, 1985, announced the arrests of Stombaugh and Tolkachev. (Kessler, *Moscow Station*; Richelson, *American Espionage and the Soviet Target*; Wise, *The Spy Who Got Away*; Woodward, *Veil*)

573 Torriente, Jose Elias de. In April 1974, a sniper shot Torriente, former Cuban minister of agriculture, in his Miami home. Torriente had been accused by Fidel Castro of working for the CIA. A Cuban political group calling itself Zero took responsibility for the assassination. Torriente had been a leader of the Cuban exiles living in Miami. (*Facts on File*, 1974; *New York Times*, May 14, 1974)

Tran Ngoc Duc see Nguyen Song Hai

574 Travkov, Gennady. In February 1980, French authorities arrested Travkov, a Soviet consular official, as he was receiving classified documents concerning the Mirage 2000 fighter from a drop site. Reportedly, Travkov had made attempts to obtain classified data from the company that built the Mirage 2000, which was scheduled to take the place of the Mirage 3 in 1984. Travkov was expelled from France. (*Facts on File*, 1980)

575 Treholt, Arne. Former Norwegian diplomat and labor deputy minister convicted of spying for the Soviet Union and Iraq in a Norwegian court. Treholt, deputy press secretary at the Norwegian Foreign Ministry, provided military and political secrets to the Soviet Union and Iraq from 1974 to 1984. Treholt was arrested in January 1984 at the Oslo airport attempting to leave the country to meet KGB agents. Authorities discovered classified documents from the Foreign Ministry in his luggage. Treholt was described as one of the Soviets' best agents in the West.

Treholt had gained that information while a student at a Norwegian military academy in 1983–84. Treholt provided details of the meetings of Norwegian political leaders and visiting foreign dignitaries, including British Foreign Minister Lord Carrington, West Germany's Chancellor Helmut Schmidt, and Henry A. Kissinger, U.S. secretary of state. Treholt served as deputy minister 1976–78, and had access to cabinet documents.

Treholt had played a significant role in the negotiations with the Soviets concerning territorial and fishing rights, and the division of the Barents Sea continental shelf. Reportedly, authorities are now concerned that Treholt may have provided the Soviets with an advantage in those negotiations. Treholt also delivered information about NATO defense plans. Treholt, paid $81,000 for his services, was sentenced to 20 years.

Several Soviet diplomats were expelled in connection with Treholt's arrest: embassy counselor Leonid Makarov, described as the head of KGB operations in Norway, First Secretary Stanislov Cherbotok, and First Secretary Yuri Anisimov.

In the late 1960s Treholt became a strong opponent of American foreign policy. The KGB noticed his anti–American activities and recruited him in 1968. He was handled from 1968 to 1971 by KGB officer Yevgeni Belyayev, from 1972 to 1977 by Gennadi Titov. In late 1978 Treholt was appointed to the Norwegian mission to the UN in New York City. From 1982 to 1983 he was at the Norwegian Defense College and had access to NATO Cosmic material. A KGB officer turned double agent, Oleg Gordievsky, identified Treholt to his handlers, and surveillance began. (Andrew and Gordievsky, *KGB; Facts on File*, 1984–85; *New York Times*, January 22, 24, 25, 28, February 2, March 20, 1984; February 25–27, March 3, June 21, 1985).

576 Treu, Alexander Peter. The McDonald Commission of the Canadian government, investigating the counterintelligence activities of the Royal Canadian Mounted Police (RCMP), reported in 1980 that Treu, a communications engineer, had sold NATO classified data to China. The commission reported that RCMP had discovered in 1973 that Treu had given classified data on technical, scientific, and military information regarding NATO's air defense communication and surveillance systems to the Chinese. In 1974, Treu admitted to passing the information to China. Nonetheless, Treu was not prosecuted for espionage but on two counts of leaking classified data, which he was later acquitted for in 1979. (*Facts on File*, 1980)

577 Treumann, Andrezej. In July 1982, Treumann, the highest-ranking Polish banker in the United States, defected. Treumann was the North American representative for Bank Handlowy, a Polish foreign trade bank, but was also a high-ranking Polish intelligence agent. U.S. intelligence agents debriefed Treumann and discovered a spy network in the U.S. (*Facts on File*, 1982; *New York Times*, October 22, 1982)

Trevisin, Gabriela see **Farcetti, Paolo**

Truong Dinh Hung see **Humphrey, Ronald L.**

578   Tsekovisky, Victor, and Anatoly Solousov.   In 1983 these two Soviet diplomats were expelled from Canada for espionage. Tsekovisky worked in the Soviet trade mission, and Solousov worked in the international secretariat of the International Civil Aviation Organization, a UN agency. Both were accused of attempting to steal classified high technology. (*Facts on File*, 1983)

579   Turner, Stansfield (b. 1923).   Director of Central Intelligence Agency (DCI) from March 1977 to January 1981, under President Carter. Graduated from the U.S. Naval Academy in 1946; Rhodes Scholar, Oxford University, B.A., 1950, M.A., 1954; director of Systems Analysis Division in the office of the chief of naval operations 1971–72; vice admiral, 1972; president of U.S. Naval War College 1972–74; commander, U.S. Second Fleet 1974–75; admiral 1975, commander-in-chief of Allied Forces in South Europe (NATO) 1975–77.

Turner, facing the CIA horrors disclosed in congressional hearings in the mid–1970s, detailing assassination attempts, bungled coups, and the Vietnam debacle, felt compelled to exorcise the demons from the CIA. In October 1977, on Halloween weekend, Turner dispatched 850 pink slips to employees in the clandestine services — known in the CIA as the "Halloween Massacre." The CIA lost some of the most experienced career officers in the history of its clandestine services. A few years later, during the Iran hostage crisis, many blamed Turner's firings for allowing the CIA to be unprepared for the crisis. Though Turner had toned down the human intelligence factor, he increased funds and support to technical intelligence such as satellites and signal intelligence (SIGINT). (Breckinridge, *The CIA and the U.S. Intelligence System*; Johnson, *America's Secret Power*; Ranelagh, *The Agency*; Turner, *Secrecy and Democracy*)

580   Vacek, Evgen.   In January 1967, Vacek, a Czech employed at the UN's Political and Security Council Affairs Department, resigned after U.S. officials showed evidence to UN Secretary-General U Thant that Vacek had attempted to obtain classified scientific and military data. (*Facts on File*, 1967; *New York Times*, January 10, 1967)

581   Vandenberg, Hoyt Sanford (1899–1954).   Second director of the Central Intelligence Group (CIG), forerunner of the CIA, from June 1946 to May 1947, under President Truman. Graduate of U.S. Army War College, 1936; former deputy commander of U.S. Army War College, 1936; former deputy commander of U.S. Army Air Forces; commanded Ninth Air Force in Europe during World War II; assistant chief of staff, G-2,

War Department General Staff till 1946; October 1947, vice chief of staff of U.S. Air Force as general; from 1948 to 1953, U.S. Air Force chief of staff. (Darling, *The Central Intelligence Agency*; Leary, *The Central Intelligence Agency*; Ranelagh, *The Agency*)

582   Vandiver, Richard S.   In April 1984, the Afghanistan government in Kabul ordered Vandiver expelled for espionage. The State Department announced that the charges were groundless. Vandiver was the second diplomat to be expelled in a year. The Soviet newspaper *Izvestia* stated that the Soviet Union believed that Vandiver was a CIA agent who had been caught by an Afghan double agent. Reportedly, the double agent had provided Vandiver with false information about the war. A secondary report from the U.S. government stated that the Afghan government might be responding in vain to the damage of a successful CIA penetration of the Afghan government. (*Facts on File*, 1984; *New York Times*, April 12, 29, 1984)

583   Vanunu, Mordechai (b. 1954).   A former Israeli nuclear technician, he worked in the secret plutonium-extraction and bomb-making factory in the Negev Desert, at Dimona, 1976–1985. Vanunu had taken sixty pictures of the underground factory located under the nuclear reactor at Dimona and given them to the *Sunday Times* of London, who discovered that the Israelis had manufactured 100–200 nuclear bombs, with the capability of producing neutron and hydrogen bombs.

Vanunu, whose family emigrated to Israel in the early 1960s from Morocco, joined the Israeli Army as a corporal in the engineering corps. He failed his physics course at Tel Aviv University but managed to get accepted in a trainee technician program at the Nuclear Research Center in Dimona in November 1976.

After becoming a shift manager, Vanunu began to experience some radical personality shifts. First he rejected his orthodox Jewish upbringing and began a secular lifestyle. When Israel invaded Lebanon in 1982, he became disillusioned and joined several radical leftist groups at Beersheba University, where he was taking classes in philosophy. He joined the Israeli Communist party and began to do a variety of odd things: posed as a nude model for art students and participated in pro–Palestinian demonstrations and causes. In 1985 security officials discovered his odd behavior and warned him to cease. but Vanunu continued and was fired in November 1985.

He drifted through Asia, ending up in May 1986 in Australia where he had a religious experience and converted to Christianity. It was here that he revealed to a journalist friend that he had two rolls of film of the ultrasecret nuclear bomb plant. After encouragement from his friend, he contacted the *London Times*. A week before the article was to be published,

Vanunu met a young American tourist by the name of Cindy, actually an Israeli agent. She showed some interest in Vanunu and was able to lure him out of Great Britain on a holiday in Rome where she promised to have sex with him.

He left for Rome September 30, 1987, and Israeli officials announced November 30 that he was in Israel under arrest. Apparently, when he arrived in Rome, Cindy took him to an apartment where he was jumped by two Israeli agents and drugged. He was then put aboard the Israeli merchant ship *Tappuz*, bound for Israel. Cindy was believed to be Cheryl Chanin Ben-Tov, an American married to a captain in Israeli military intelligence. Interestingly, she had a sister named Cindy.

On March 24, 1988 he was convicted for espionage and treason in an Israeli court and sentenced to eighteen years. No reporters were allowed at the seven-month trial, held in secret. (Black and Morris, *Israel's Secret Wars;* Ostrovsky and Hoy, *By Way of Deception;* Raviv and Melman, *Every Spy a Prince*)

584 Vargas Garayar, Julio (d. 1979). Vargas, a former noncommissioned Peruvian Air Force officer, was executed by firing squad in January 1979 for spying for Chile. Vargas was convicted of selling Peruvian military secrets to Chile. He was arrested in October 1978 for selling photographs of Peruvian air bases to four Chilean embassy diplomats. The Peruvian government expelled the diplomats, along with two Chilean naval officers who were caught taking photographs of an air base. The Chilean government admitted that they had recruited Vargas as a spy. Vargas was the first to be executed in Peru during peacetime in the twentieth century for spying. Reportedly, Vargas was bitter about being discharged from the military and needed money but only earned $380 for his services. (*Facts on File*, 1979; *New York Times*, January 21; February 15, 1979)

585 Vartanyan, Igor P. In 1978, Canadian authorities expelled Vartanyan for espionage activities. Vartanyan, who was listed as the first secretary in charge of sports and cultural affairs at the Soviet embassy in Ottawa, had been meeting an agent of the Royal Canadian Mounted Police (RCMP). The unnamed RCMP counterintelligence agent had been approached in 1977 by Soviet agents. The RCMP agent told his superiors, who then arranged for him to pass nonclassified data to Soviet agents as bait. The RCMP agent met with Vartanyan on several occasions and was paid several thousand dollars for the unclassified and fabricated documents. The Canadian authorities were able to identify 13 Soviet officials as KGB. In February 1978, they expelled members of the embassy believed involved. (*Facts on File*, 1978)

586   Vassall, William John Christopher (b. 1924).   Vassall worked as a clerk in the office of the naval attaché for the Admiralty and was assigned to the British embassy in Moscow from March 1954 to June 1956. Vassall started spying for the Soviets within six months of arriving in Moscow when he was blackmailed. Vassall claimed he was blackmailed when he had gotten drunk with several Russians in Moscow and was photographed engaging in homosexual acts.

When he returned to London, he moved into an expensive apartment on Dolphin Square despite the fact that he was a mid-level clerk. When Yuri Nosenko and Anatoliy Golitsyn defected to the West, they mentioned a spy in the British Admiralty but did not know his name. Nosenko mentioned that he was a homosexual, which helped to focus the investigation. Despite intensive surveillance of his apartment and a search of his office in the Admiralty, no evidence could be found until a search of his apartment was conducted in September 1962. They discovered two special document cameras, espionage-related equipment, and film hidden in a bookcase containing 170 classified documents. He was arrested and sentenced to 18 years for espionage for the Soviet Union in 1962, released in October 1972. (Vassall, *Vassall*; West, *The Circus*; West, *The Vassall Affair*; Wright, *Spy Catcher*)

Vijai, Padmanab see Raghunath, Krishnan

587   Vinogradov, Arkady A.   In June 1983, Vinogradov, a Soviet diplomat in Japan, was expelled for espionage. He was accused of attempting to steal computer secrets from Hitachi. Vinogradov and a confederate, Boris N. Kakorin, an engineer of the Soviet embassy, had approached an executive at the company and suggested that the Soviet Union would help him finance his own computer company to be used as a front for Soviet espionage efforts against industrial targets. The Public Security Investigation Agency (PSIA) had had both Kakorin, who left Japan in 1982, and Vinogradov under surveillance since 1978. Vinogradov was the first foreign diplomat ordered to leave the country since World War II. (*Facts on File*, 1983; *New York Times*, June 22, 1983; Richelson, *Foreign Intelligence Organizations*)

588   Voelkner, Hans.   In February 1970, a Paris court sentenced Voelkner, East German intelligence agent, to 12 years for espionage. Two women also arrested were Marthe Danilo and Simone Leman, who received suspended sentences. Voelkner reportedly ran a spy ring that gathered information on NATO. (*Facts on File*, 1970)

589   Vrajik, Arnost.   In October 1971, Czech authorities sentenced Vrajik, a Czech journalist writing under the name of Arnost Prazak, to ten years for espionage for the U.S. Reportedly, Vrajik had given the U.S. embassy information about Soviet military troop locations and strength in Czechoslovakia, information about Czech foreign affairs negotiations, and military maneuvers from the summer of 1968 to 1970. The Czech government ordered Samuel Wise, first secretary at the U.S. embassy, to leave the country for being Vrajik's contact. (*Facts on File*, 1971)

590   Walker, John Anthony, Jr. (b. 1937).   (The Walker spy ring: John Walker, retired navy warrant officer; son **Michael Lance Walker,** sailor assigned to the aircraft carrier *Nimitz;* John's brother **Arthur James Walker (b. 1934),** retired submarine officer; close friend **Jerry Alfred Whitworth (1939);** all recruited to spy for the Soviet Union.)

John Walker, the head of the ring, delivered submarine, missile, and communications plans, allowing the Soviets to decipher U.S. codes and duplicate U.S. cryptographic equipment. Walker helped the Soviets improve their defenses by selling the U.S. Navy strategic plans for a war with the Soviet Union.

Walker's estranged wife, Barbara, had notified the FBI on several occasions from November 1984 to January 1985 but was unable to convince them of her former husband's activities. The FBI finally began to pay attention to her when details about drops and espionage techniques were discussed. The FBI launched Operation Windflyer to capture Walker in the act of selling data to the Soviets.

Walker had a flawless navy career, retiring as a chief warrant officer after 20 years of service. He had been a radioman, starting out with service on an old post–World War II diesel submarine and moving up to nuclear-powered submarines and then shore duty where he had access to the most sensitive secrets in the Atlantic and Pacific fleets.

In June 1955, John Walker was arrested after a burglary of a clothing store. The judge offered to suspend the probation if John joined the navy. John, wanting to follow his older brother Arthur's footsteps, entered the submarine service. He entered submarine school in 1960, the U.S. Navy submarine base in Connecticut. It was here that he began to get access to sensitive data. In 1961 he was sent as a radioman to the diesel submarine USS *Razorback,* his first submarine. In 1962 he was selected to serve as a radioman aboard the new SSBN *Andrew Jackson,* a nuclear ballistic missile submarine in California. It was aboard this submarine that John gained excess to the war plans against the Soviets called the Single Integrated Operational Plan (SIOP). In 1963 he was sent to Crypto Repair School, Naval Schools Command, in Vallejo, California, where he had unlimited access to cryptographic equipment. He returned to the *Andrew Jackson* in 1963 as chief radioman. In 1965 he was transferred to the SSBN *Simon Bolivar* where he became sénior chief radioman and obtained top secret clearance for the first time. He stole his first secret in December 1967, the keylist for a KL-47 cryptographic machine. He then strolled into the Soviet embassy in Washington, offering to sell military secrets.

His wife became suspicious when in 1968, living in Norfolk, they began living beyond his financial means. His wife made a search of his desk and found a tin box with details of his espionage for the Soviets. At that time Walker was providing data on secret codes. John also supplied the Soviets with data and locations of the SOSUS hydrophones in the Atlantic. It was the KW-7 cryptographic machine data that probably cost valuable lives in Vietnam. He later gave the keylists and manuals for several other machines: KWR-37, KW-8, KY8, KG-14, KL-47, and KW-7.

The Soviets supplied him with a Minox camera and high-speed black-and-white film. While at the Naval Submarine Force, Atlantic Fleet, Norfolk, Virginia, in 1967, he served as a communications watch officer and message center officer. Here he knew the location and mission of every U.S. attack submarine as well as U.S. intelligence and techniques for locating Soviet submarines and surface vessels.

Ironically, Walker was known as a staunch anti–Communist, had joined the John Birch Society in 1965, and was a member and recruiter for the Ku Klux Klan.

Walker was transferred from Norfolk to San Diego to teach cryptography in 1969, and it was there that he met Jerry Whitworth, recruiting him as a spy on the Pacific Fleet. After leaving San Diego, Walker was sent to the USS *Niagara Falls,* a combat store ship that serviced navy vessels off the coast of Vietnam. He served as a courier, carrying data sensitive for radio communications, and would meet Soviet agents in Hong Kong. Radio traffic dealt with the time and place of naval air strikes and their coordination with Air Force land strikes based in Thailand and in Vietnam. When American pilots continually found themselves flying into an enemy prepared with SAMs and AA missiles, it had to be more than coincidence. During the Vietnam War, the Soviets were able to decode U.S. messages on ship movements, troop movements, and where U.S. bombers were going to strike next. The intercepted message also told the Soviets at what ranges the U.S. could detect Soviet subs.

The Soviets made Walker an admiral in the Soviet Navy. In 1974 he was sent back to Norfolk and retired in 1976. In May 1985, Walker went to make a drop of material to Soviet Vice-Consul Aleksey Tkachenko, who was assigned to make the pickup. The FBI managed to pick up the drop and scared the Soviets away. Walker wandered the area, looking for his money, but was frustrated. He was arrested the next day at the Ramada Inn in Rockville, Maryland.

The FBI discovered that his son Michael Walker, serving on the aircraft carrier *Nimitz*, had also worked for him. They found a box containing fifteen pounds of classified documents. He joined the navy in December 1982 and was first assigned to Fighter Squadron VF 102 at the Oceana Naval Air Station, Virginia Beach, but did not have access to classified data till his assignment on the USS *America* aircraft carrier. John Walker offered to pay his son for secret data, but it was not until he was back at Oceana that he first stole secret documents. When he was stationed on the *Nimitz* in 1984, he had access to U.S. Navy exercises, ship coordinates, operations, and Defense Intelligence Agency (DIA) messages. He was put in charge of burn bags, from which he was able to steal the documents.

Arthur Walker, arrested on May 20, 1985, also provided John Walker with data. He had been in the navy for 21 years, retiring as a lieutenant commander in 1973, and worked for a defense contractor in Norfolk, the VSE Corporation, with access to classified data. On November 12, 1985, Arthur was sentenced to three life terms and forty years.

Jerry Whitworth met John Walker in 1970. In 1967 he was sent to radioman's school in Bainbridge, Maryland. Jerry also attended the navy's ultrasecret satellite communications school at Fort Monmouth, New Jersey. Jerry had access to numerous machines: KWR-37, KW-7, and KW-36. Whitworth served on the USS *Constellation* aircraft carrier as the classified material system custodian.

He would meet John in Hong Kong to make drops. Whitworth was a communications instructor, and Walker was the assistant director of the Radioman School at the navy's Service Schools Command in San Diego. But Walker did not recruit Whitworth till 1974. Whitworth joined the Naval Reserve out of high school.

John Walker would meet Whitworth's ship, the USS *Enterprise*, in Hong Kong and San Francisco to make pickups. In 1976 he was the chief radioman aboard the aircraft carrier USS *Constellation*, and he had access to a variety of secret data. In 1979 he was sent to the Alameda Naval Air Station in California where he became senior chief radioman until 1982. He retired in 1983 as a chief petty officer. He turned over top secret cryptographic keylists, technical manuals, and intelligence messages.

John Walker was sentenced to life but was given a plea bargain after promising to cooperate with the government investigation. Michael Walker received 25 years. Jerry Whitworth, who also provided data on the KWR-37 broadcast system, was sentenced to 365 years. Whitworth had received $332,000 for data he provided to John Walker. Vitaly Yurchenko described the Walker spy ring as the most important Soviet spy operation in the United States. (Barron, *Breaking the Ring*; Blum, *I Pledge Allegiance*; Earley, *Family of Spies*; Kneece, *Family Treason*)

Walker, Michael Lance see Walker, John Anthony

591   Wang Chia-sheng.   In July 1980, a Chinese court sentenced Wang to death for spying for the Soviet Union. Wang had defected to the Soviet Union in 1975 but had returned to China twice on espionage assignments. Chinese authorities accused Wang of being a KGB agent. (*Facts on File*, 1980)

592   Webster, William Hedgcock (b. 1924).   Director of Central Intelligence Agency (DCI) from 1987 to 1991, under Presidents Reagan and Bush. Webster had been the director of the FBI since 1978. In May 1991, Webster resigned as director of the CIA, reportedly due to the numerous complaints from the White House and Congress that Webster's tenure as DCI failed to predict the collapse of the Soviet empire and the Iraqi invasion of Kuwait. (*Facts on File*, 1987, 1991; Johnson, *America's Secret Power*)

Weischenberg, Carl Lutz see Heiser, Carl John

593   Welch, Richard Skeffington (1929–75).   On December 23, 1975, Welch, CIA station chief in Athens, Greece, was assassinated by three gunmen outside his home by a group calling itself the Revolutionary Organization of November 17th. Welch had a love for things Greek, and had studied ancient Greek in college. It was his goal to rise to the rank of station chief of the Athens CIA station. Welch was working under cover as a State Department special assistant to the ambassador. Welch's identity had been revealed in the *Athen News* in the November issue, which identified Welch and gave his home address as a CIA agent, the name taken from a list published in Philip Agee's *CounterSpy* magazine, which was dedicated to the disruption of CIA operations. In the same issue, Agee stated in an article that CIA agents should be identified and then "neutralized" by "the people." Agee later stated that what he meant by "neutralize" was to expose, thus blowing the agents' cover and forcing them out of the country. Agee also argued that an East German book, *Who's Who in the CIA*, had listed Welch's name in 1968 and that it was well known that Welch was the station chief in Athens. Welch had previously served as station chief in Peru in 1972–73 and had served at the CIA stations in Guyana, Guatemala, and Cyprus. The furor over Welch's name being printed and Agee's activities resulted in Public Law 97-200, the Intelligence Identities Protection Act of 1982, which provided for stiff punishment for those who publish the names of active CIA agents. (Agee, *On the Run*; Johnson, *A Season of Inquiry*; Mader, *Who's Who in the CIA*; Phillips, *The Night Watch*)

594   Wennerstrom, Stig Eric (b. 1906).   In 1963, Wennerstrom, a Swedish disarmament specialist, was arrested in Sweden for spying for the Soviet Union. Wennerstrom, a retired air force colonel, was accused of giving the Soviets military data on Sweden's military, NATO, and the U.S. Strategic Air Command (SAC). Wennerstrom confessed to spying since 1948. Wennerstrom served as Swedish air attaché in Washington 1952–57. During an interrogation, Wennerstrom stated that he had visited several U.S. military installations and weapons factories, supplying the Soviets with information from those visits.

In a secondary development, Wennerstrom had reportedly been recruited in 1946 by a U.S. air attaché in Stockholm to work as a spy for the U.S. United States intelligence officials denied ever making contact with Wennerstrom.

In June 1964, a Swedish court convicted him of espionage for the Soviet Union and sentenced to life. In October 1964, Wennerstrom attempted suicide by taking sleeping pills but survived the attempt. His prison sentence was reduced in 1972 from life to 20 years, and he was released in September 1974.

When Wennerstrom was arrested, he admitted that he was a spy for the Soviets and had been made a major general in the KGB. He was recruited while serving as the air attaché in Moscow 1948–51, then served as air attaché in Washington from April 1952 to March 1957. The CIA became suspicious of Wennerstrom when an undisclosed East German double agent identified a spy working in the air force section of the Swedish command's headquarters at the Ministry of Defense. Swedish intelligence was alerted, and surveillance began on Wennerstrom in November 1959 and continued till his arrest in 1963. He identified his Soviet contacts and handlers. Two Soviet diplomats were expelled from Sweden due to their involvement: Major General Vitali A. Nikolsky, military attaché; Georgi P. Baranovsky, first secretary. (Barron, *KGB*; Costello, *Mask of Treachery*; West, *The Circus*; Whiteside, *An Agent in Place*)

595 Wesolowska, Alicja.

In 1980, Wesolowska was sentenced to seven years for spying for an unnamed NATO country in Poland during a secret military trial. Wesolowska, a Polish citizen, was employed by the UN Development Program. According to Polish authorities, Wesolowska pled guilty to the charges. From the time of her arrest, she was held in solitary confinement for six months. She was released in 1984 after negotiations between UN officials and Polish authorities. At her release she declared her innocence of the charges. (*Facts on File*, 1980, 1984; *New York Times*, February 14; March 2, 5, 6, 8; April 10, 15, 1980)

596 Whalen, William Henry.

In 1966, Whalen, a retired U.S. Army lieutenant colonel, was arrested selling classified data on U.S.

atomic and missile projects between December 1959 and March 1961 to the Soviets.

Whalen had been a member of the support staff of the Joint Chiefs of Staff. He provided the Soviets with a variety of information on nuclear weapons, missiles, military intelligence reports, SAC operations and targets, and troop movements, for $5,000. He pled guilty and was sentenced to 15 years in March 1967. The FBI began surveillance in 1959 when he was seen meeting two GRU officers — First Secretary Mikhail M. Shumaev and Colonel Sergei A. Edenski. (Corson and Crowley, *The New KGB*; Marchetti and Marks, *The CIA and the Cult of Intelligence*; Prados, *The Soviet Estimate*; Romerstein and Levchenko, *The KGB Against the "Main Enemy"*; Rositzke, *The KGB*)

597   White, Roscoe.   In August 1990, Ricky White, the son of Roscoe White, held a press conference announcing that his father had been one of the assassins, including Lee Harvey Oswald, hired by the CIA to kill President John F. Kennedy. According to Ricky White, his father had joined the Dallas Police two months before the shooting to be in position for the assassination. His father had kept a detailed diary describing the operation, which Ricky White claimed he had given to the FBI, who later mysteriously lost it. (*Facts on File*, 1990)

Whitworth, Jerry Alfred see Walker, John Anthony

598   Wiedemann, Henrich.   A former West German judge, retired in 1949, he was accused (but not arrested) in March 1970 of being the head of an East German spy ring since his retirement. Along with Wiedemann, Irene Schultz, who worked as a clerical aide to Science Minister Hans Leussink, and Liane Lindner, employed as a psychologist in Cologne under the name of Ingeborg Weber, were arrested. Reportedly, Schultz and Wiedemann had passed classified documents to Lindner, who was caught with the documents in her possession at the time of her arrest. (*Facts on File*, 1970; *New York Times*, March 5, 7, 1970)

Wiegel, Jürgen see Lutz, Lothar Erwin

599   Williamson, Earl J. ("Ted").   In February 1971, Williamson, the CIA chief of station in Costa Rica, was recalled due to accusations that he had been involved in a CIA plot to overthrow President Jose Figueres Ferrer. Reportedly, Williamson had been upset by the fact that Costa Rica was opening relations with the Soviet Union. Listed as first secretary of the embassy, he was actually the CIA station chief. He had boasted at a party that the Figueres government would soon be toppled.

Costa Rican officials heard of the comments and demanded his removal. Williamson maintained his post, and a scare ran through the Costa Rican government when a rumor spread that the merchant vessel *Waltham* was unloading weapons on an isolated beach.

Fearing a coup, Figueres went into hiding and demanded that Williamson be removed. Williamson's previous post included the CIA station in Cuba before the revolution. (Blum, *The CIA; Facts on File*, 1971; *New York Times*, February 11, 1971)

600 Willner, Herbert Adolf, and Herta-Astrid. The Willners defected to East Germany in September 1985. Herta-Astrid was a secretary in the office of Chancellor Helmut Kohl from 1973 and was chief secretary to the head of the department for internal affairs, which included domestic security policy. She denied giving East Germany classified data on West German–U.S. communications and space weapons research.

Herbert Willner worked for a research organization, the Friedrich Naumann Foundation, closely related to the Free Democratic party, as a consultant from 1969. He fled East Germany in 1960, worked briefly with *Der Spiegel* for four years, and joined the FDP in 1965, working in several departments.

During World War II he had fought as a soldier in the Nazi Waffen SS and after the war joined the West German Communist party. He was later expelled due to his history with the Nazis, but was eventually readmitted. The Willners made their defection public in two individual letters stating their reasons for leaving. They disappeared while traveling in Spain on a vacation. Hans Tiedge, who also defected, was a counterintelligence official who had the Willners under investigation. (*Facts on File*, 1985; *New York Times*, September 18, 19, 1985)

Willner, Herta-Astrid see **Willner, Herbert Adolf**

601 Wilmoth, James. Wilmoth served on the USS *Midway* but had no security clearance. Despite this, he was charged with attempted espionage, contacting a Soviet agent, and the use and sale of hashish. He was court-martialed in Yukosuka, Japan. He was sentenced in 1989 to 35 years for spying for the Soviet Union. (*Facts on File*, 1989; *New York Times*, October 5, 27, 1989)

602 Wilms, Wilhelm. A former West German counterintelligence officer, he was serving a life sentence when he was exchanged by East Germany for West German–held East German spies. Wilms was exchanged along with Christa-Karin Schumann for Manfred Rotsch, Klaus Schmidt, and Wolfgang Klautzsch. (*Facts on File*, 1987)

603   Wilson, Edwin Paul (b. 1928).   Former CIA contract employee and arms dealer. In 1947 Wilson signed on as a merchant seaman, joining the Seafarers International Union. From here he traveled the Pacific visiting Asian ports for a year, visiting Shanghai during the frantic last days of the Nationalist government of Chiang Kai-shek.

When he returned to the U.S., he enrolled at the University of Portland, graduating in 1953 with a B.A. in psychology. He joined the U.S. Marine Corps (USMC) after college and attended the Marine Corps Officer Candidate School at Quantico, Virginia, finishing OCS in June 1953, a few days before the Korean War ended. Wilson was sent to Korea and later to Japan. His duties included escort officer to prisoners, running a base laundry, and other boring desk jobs. Wilson, bored and frustrated, began to drink and womanize. In later years Wilson would tell stories about being a company commander, losing some friends in the war, even being wounded in battle.

Wilson left the USMC on October 31, 1955, as a first lieutenant. On November 1, 1955, he joined the CIA as a contract support agent. Since he was a contract employee, he lacked the training and security clearances of other employees. His entry position was that of a junior security officer; he supervised uniformed guards at bases for the supersecret U-2 spy plane. Later, Wilson told outrageous stories about his leadership during the U-2 program.

It was Wilson's next assignment that placed him in the clandestine world of espionage. His next contractual assignment was to pose as a union staff member and infiltrate left-wing labor unions in European ports. Since he had been a merchant seaman and a member of SIU, he was perfect for the job. Wilson was given credentials as an SIU staff member and put on the payroll of SIU, first as a lobbyist in SIU's Washington office, then as an international representative, Later he was sent to Brussels as an assistant port representative for the SIU. Here he posed as a leftist American seaman and made contacts with socialists in other labor groups. He remained in Europe for two years and returned to the U.S. in 1961.

Wilson claimed to have trained anti–Castro forces at the CIA base in Nicaragua and to have helped run agents in and out of Cuba. Though Wilson claims intimate involvement in the CIA's Bay of Pigs fiasco, CIA personnel involved in Cuba do not recall him. Actually, Wilson played a minor role as a paymaster on one isolated phase of the operation, and there was some controversy about where the money actually went.

In the 1960s Wilson became known in the CIA as a specialist at creating and operating proprietary companies. These were businesses that were set up as cover for CIA operations. Wilson set up one company called the Maritime Consulting Associates (MCA), which handled maritime traffic around the world. One problem the CIA had was in handling maritime traffic in southeast Asia. Cargo that commercial shippers would not carry to war-torn Vietnam Wilson's company would take. MCA was the sea version of Air America, shipping arms to Africa, the Middle East, Latin America, and Asia for client armies of the CIA.

Wilson began to make money in real estate in Virginia. When he put down a CIA proprietary as an asset, the bank called the company. Officials in the CIA were upset with Wilson's disclosure, and his contract with the CIA was not renewed in 1971. Wilson then became a contract employee for Task Force 157, a special top secret unit of the Office of Naval Intelligence. He created a company that would be a cover for TF 157 agents. He went on their payroll and started a firm called Consultants International, which helped the TF 157 monitor Soviet maritime activities.

In 1976 Wilson was fired when he tried to bribe Bobby Inman into helping to get the Congress to buy the F-16. Wilson also wanted Inman to disband TF 157 and create a new and bigger intelligence organization under Wilson's leadership.

Wilson started a new career and was allowed to keep Consultants International, which by then had been established as a worldwide trading company. He went into business with a former CIA technician, Frank Terpil, who had been fired by the CIA for misconduct. Wilson believed that Libya would be a lucrative market for weapons, and both Terpil and Wilson made contact with the Libyan government and began acting as arms merchants. The relationship began to develop further when the Libyans requested that they arrange the assassination of a Libyan dissident. Fortunately, the plot failed, and both were charged with offering $1 million to three Cuban refugees with ties with the CIA to assassinate Umar Abdullah Muhayshi in 1976. Prosecutors argued that the plot had been planned to gain favor with the Libyan government.

He was also convicted in 1983 for planning the murders of two federal prosecutors and six witnesses against him. He was sentenced to 25 years. Wilson had offered $1 million for the assassination of nine people to an undercover FBI agent. The list included federal prosecutors E. Lawrence Barcella, Jr., and Carol E. Bruce. In 1983, Wilson offered $1 million to fellow inmates to have his wife and Wayne Trimmer, who was testifying against him, killed. Interestingly, one of the targeted witnesses, Ernest Keiser, was shot and wounded in December 1984 outside a restaurant near Washington by an unknown assailant escaping with Keiser's briefcase. According to Keiser, the briefcase contained sensitive documents on the fugitive Robert L. Vesco. Keiser had helped the federal government lure Wilson out of Libya in 1982 and was a prosecution witness against Wilson. Keiser was not sure if it was Vesco or Wilson who was responsible for the shooting.

Wilson was convicted in 1982 for arms smuggling to Libya. Wilson was found guilty in 1983 of illegally shipping forty thousand pounds of plastic explosives to Libya in 1977. Wilson argued that he was working as a "de facto" agent for the CIA at the time of his actions.

Wilson had been living in Libya since his indictment in the U.S. in 1980. He was enticed into leaving Libya for the Dominican Republic by associates who were working in cooperation with the U.S. government. Wilson was carrying an Irish passport under the name Philip McCormick. He was arrested when he arrived in the Dominican Republic on June 12.

Kevin P. Mucahy, a former CIA technician who worked for Wilson, informed federal authorities of Wilson's activities in 1976. Mucahy was to be a key witness against Wilson and Terpil but was found dead at his cabin of unknown cause. The FBI launched an investigation when the coroner autopsy could not find the cause of death. It was reported that Mucahy had suffered from bronchial pneumonia and advanced emphysema.

An associate of Wilson's, Douglas M. Schlachter, reportedly made contact with two CIA officials, Theodore G. Shackley and Thomas Clines, who approved of his activities and gave him assignments to carry out while in Libya. Schlachter reportedly told them that he was shipping explosives to Libya and training them in the construction of bombs, and that Wilson had brought in former Green Berets to help in the training. Clines had asked him to carry out intelligence-gathering operations while in Libya. Schlachter was indicted in August 1982 for illegally shipping explosives to Libya but agreed in a plea bargain to testify against Wilson. (Goulden, *The Death Merchant*, and "The Rogue of Rogues," *IJIC*; Maas, *Manhunt*; McCoy, *The Politics of Heroin*; Turner, *Secrecy and Democracy*)

604   Winkler, Martin. In August 1985, Winkler, an East German diplomat in Buenos Aires, defected to West Germany. Winkler, a specialist in Latin American affairs, was a senior East German diplomat. Rumors claimed that Winkler's defection was caused by the defection of the BfV counterintelligence chief Hans Tiedge to East Germany. (*Facts on File*, 1985; *New York Times*, August 30, 1985)

605   Woikin, Emma. A cipher clerk for the External Affairs Department of Canada, she pled guilty to espionage for the Soviet Union in 1946. She admitted giving the Soviets secret data and was sentenced to two years. Though not a Communist party member, she was firmly dedicated to the cause. (Brook-Shepherd, *The Storm Birds*; *Facts on File*, 1946; *New York Times*, March 1; April 5, 1946)

606   Wolf, Hans Guenther. In June 1975, a Swiss court convicted an East German couple, Wolf and his wife, Gisela, for military, political, and economic espionage. The couple confessed to spying and using

Switzerland as a base for gathering data on NATO and West Germany. They were sentenced to seven years. (*Facts on File,* 1975)

607   Wood, James D.   In August 1973, U.S. Air Force Sergeant Wood was charged with spying for the Soviet Union. Reportedly, Wood had passed classified data to a Soviet agent, Victor Tchernyshev, first secretary of the Soviet embassy in Washington. On July 21, 1973, the FBI arrested Viktor Tcherynshev for espionage during a meeting with Sergeant Wood in New York City. The sergeant had counterintelligence data. He had been with the Air Force Office of Special Investigations since March 1973 and had transferred from Travis Air Force Base in California. (Allen and Polmar, *Merchants of Treason;* Barron, *KGB;* Rositzke, *The KGB*)

608   Wright, Peter (b. 1916).   Former assistant director of MI5. At the outbreak of World War II, he joined the navy and served in the Admiralty Research Laboratory (ARL), working on anti-midget-submarine detection systems. Developed the technical know-how to use X-Craft midget submarines to cripple the German battleship *Tirpitz.* After the war he continued in the navy and began work as a principal scientific officer at the Services Electronic Research Laboratory in 1946.

In 1949 British intelligence asked Wright to study technical and scientific initiatives that would help run agents in Eastern Europe. Given the title "external scientific adviser," an unpaid position, he used the resources of the Services Electronics Research Laboratory to develop new microphones and develop ways of getting sound reflections from office furniture.

When a concealed microphone was discovered in the great seal of the U.S. on the wall of the U.S. ambassador's office in 1951, Wright was given the device to study. He discovered that it was a new type of eavesdropping device and helped to develop a British prototype code-named SATYR. The SATYR project established Wright's credentials as a scientist with MI5, even though officially he was still in the Admiralty. In 1955 Wright joined MI5, becoming MI5's first scientist. He started out in MI5's technical department, called A2, as the scientific officer and dealt primarily with counterintelligence branch problems with the Soviets. One of Wright's first assignments was to provide a microphone for the interrogation by MI6 of one of their own men suspected of being a Soviet spy — Kim Philby, the infamous "third man." Philby was cleared and defected to the Soviet Union years later.

In 1956 Wright was the first to crack the codes of cipher machines by using highly sensitive microphones to record the distinctive sounds made during the setting. The technique became known as ENGULF. This advance helped during the Suez crisis when Wright placed a bug in the phone in the cipher room of the Egyptian embassy in London where they were able to decipher the cable traffic.

The first A2 operation Wright became involved in was Operation CHOIR, the bugging of the Russian consulate. But the Russians discovered the bugs and erected a soundproof partition across the wall. His next operation came in 1956 when he was sent to Canada to help the Royal Canadian Mounted Police (RCMP) with the installation of microphones in the Russian embassy in Ottawa, called Operation DEW WORM. The microphones would be located near the KGB security sanctum, but the Russians suddenly moved it to another point in the embassy.

In a third operation in Canada in 1957, Wright assisted in the installation of SATYR microphones in the new Polish consulate in Montreal. But after the installation the Poles discovered the devices. Wright began to get suspicious of the sudden defensive actions the Soviets were taking with each new installation.

In 1959 Wright discovered signs that the Soviets had a mole within MI5. When he brought the evidence to Roger Hollis, the director-general, he shut the investigation down. In 1961 the hypothesis was borne out when more evidence came out due to the Krogers-Lonsdale spy ring investigation, but Hollis terminated any further investigation.

In 1963 Wright was named to head the Fluency Committee, investigating the possibility of Soviet infiltration into MI5. By 1964, Wright became convinced that Hollis was the mole. From 1963 the evidence from the Golitsyn interrogations began to point toward Hollis, and Wright actually faced Hollis in an informal meeting to discuss his accusations just before Hollis retired. Hollis countered each argument with a different conclusion about the material Wright proposed. An investigation on Hollis as a possible Soviet spy was launched in 1969 but in vain. Another investigation was started in 1974 but also failed to prove anything.

Wright retired in January 1976 and in 1987 published a book about his experiences, *Spy Catcher,* which infuriated the British government. Numerous legal attempts were made to stop the publication of the work, but they were unable to stop it. (Pincher, *Too Secret, Too Long;* Turnbull, *The Spy Catcher Trial;* Wright, *Spy Catcher*)

609 Wynne, Greville Maynard (1919–90). He served in British Army Intelligence during World War II. After the war he became a successful businessman who traveled throughout Eastern Europe and the Soviet Union in international trade, but at the same time he was working for MI6. In 1960 he attended a trade delegation in Moscow and met GRU officer Oleg Penkovskiy, who asked him to contact British intelligence. Wynne returned to London and notified MI6 of Penkovskiy's offer. MI6 continued using Wynne as a contact source. When Penkovskiy was arrested in 1962, Wynne was quickly arrested in Budapest and flown back to Moscow for his trial. He was put on trial in 1963 and sentenced to eight years. After 18 months in a Soviet prison, he was released in April 1964 in exchange for a Soviet spy, Gordon Lonsdale. (Andrew and Gordievsky, *KGB*; Maclean, *Take Nine Spies*; Penkovskiy, *The Penkovskiy Papers*; West, *The Circus*; Wynne, *The Man from Moscow*)

610 Yager, Joel. Marine Corporal Yager, stationed in Iwakuni, Japan, at the Marine Corps air station, was arrested in September 1977 for attempting to pass classified documents to an undercover Naval Investigative Service (NIS) agent posing as a foreign national. Yager was not court-martialed. (Allen and Polmar, *Merchants of Treason*)

611 Yakushkin, Dmitri Ivanovich. KGB station chief in Washington from March 1975 to January 1982, he served 1963–69 in the Soviet delegation to the UN as head of KGB operations in New York. Upon his return to Moscow in 1982, he was named chief of the First Chief Directorate's First Department. He had a degree in economic science. Fluent in English, he became the symbol of the new KGB — sleek, sophisticated, and a snake. (Andrew and Gordievsky, *KGB*; Bittman, *The KGB and Soviet Disinformation*; Corson and Crowley, *The New KGB*; Shevchenko, *Breaking with Moscow*)

612 Yariv, Aharon (b. 1921). He was born in Moscow under the name Aharon Rabinowitz. His family moved to Lithuania in 1925, then to Palestine in 1935. He joined the British Army during World War II, serving in the Jewish Brigade as a captain. After the war he joined the Jewish underground army, the Haganah. After the war of independence he became an instructor at the Israeli Army war college. He attended the French Military College in 1950 and helped create Israel's first staff college. Then he became the Israeli military attaché in Washington in 1957. In March 1960 he was given command of his own brigade, the Golani Brigade, but in 1961 he became deputy to the chief of Israeli military intelligence, the Aman, under Meir Amit. In 1963 he became chief of Aman when Amit became chief of Mossad. Yariv became instrumental in gathering intelligence before and during the Six Day War in 1967. He left Aman in November 1972 to become P.M. Golda Meir's adviser on terrorism. (Black and Morris, *Israel's Secret Wars*; Eisenberg, Dan, and Landau, *The Mossad*; Raviv and Melman, *Every Spy a Prince*; Steven, *The Spymasters of Israel*)

613 Yermishkin, Oleg N. In 1984, Yermishkin, a Soviet Olympic attaché, was denied entry into the United States due to his ties to the KGB. The State Department announced that Yermishkin had definite ties to the KGB and that his intention to travel to California, high on the Soviet list of high-technology producers, would be unwise. Yermishkin, according to the Soviets, was preparing arrangements for the Soviets' participation in the 1984 Summer Olympic Games in Los Angeles. (*Facts on File*, 1984; *New York Times*, March 2, 3, 1984)

614 Yildirim, Huseyin.   Sentenced to life for spying for the Soviet Union, Yildirim, a Turkish-born naturalized U.S. citizen, a former civilian mechanic for the U.S. Army in West Germany, admitted to participating with James Hall, also convicted of spying for the Soviets, in selling secrets to an FBI agent posing as a Soviet agent. The confession was videotaped. Yildirim had sold data to the Soviets since 1982. He later claimed to be a double agent working for the U.S. government, but no one believed him. (*Facts on File*, 1989; *New York Times*, July 17–21, 1989)

615 Yurchenko, Vitaly Sergeyevich (b. 1936).   He served in the Soviet Navy till he was recruited into the KGB. He attended the Third Chief Directorate counterintelligence school, then served in the Third Chief Directorate. Served as chief KGB security officer at the Soviet embassy in Washington between 1975 and 1980. From September 1980 to March 1985 he was chief of the Fifth Department (internal security) of Directorate K (counterintelligence) for the First Chief Directorate. From April to July 1985 he was assigned as deputy chief of the First Department.

In June 1985, Yurchenko defected to the U.S. embassy in Rome and then in a bizarre turn of events returned to the Soviet Union in November in Washington. A 25-year KGB veteran, Yurchenko identified two traitors in the U.S. government: Ronald Pelton, in the National Security Agency, and Edward Lee Howard, in the Central Intelligence Agency. Just before his defection to the U.S., he had been promoted to deputy in the First Department of the KGB. Yurchenko was the highest-level KGB defector to the United States.

Yurchenko escaped from his CIA handlers in November in a French restaurant in Georgetown and returned to the Soviet embassy. At the embassy he gave a press conference, claiming that the CIA had kidnapped him, drugging him while in captivity. In 1985 rumors that Yurchenko was executed by firing squad were discovered to be untrue. Reportedly, Yurchenko today holds a high-level post in the Soviet Navy. Many intelligence officials believe that Yurchenko was a KGB plant to embarrass the U.S. But rumors that Yurchenko's defection was due to a love affair with a wife of a Soviet diplomat in Ottawa were widespread.

Yurchenko later boasted that when he had a private dinner with CIA Director William Casey, the director's fly was open. There was heavy criticism of the CIA's handling of Yurchenko. The CIA failed to provide Russian-speaking debriefers despite his repeated requests. His motivations for defecting were criticized and repeatedly questioned by his CIA handlers.

His requests for secrecy and revelations to debriefers were ignored and widely published in newspapers. (Kessler, *Escape from the CIA*; Romerstein and Levchenko, *The KGB Against the "Main Enemy"*; Wise, *The Spy Who Got Away*; Woodward, *Veil*)

616   Zabotin, Nikolai.   Colonel Zabotin, the GRU resident in Ottawa, was awarded the Order of the Red Banner and the Order of the Red Star in 1945 for acquiring data on the details of the bomb dropped on Hiroshima, provided by Alan Nunn-May. Arriving in Ottawa in June 1943, Zabotin recruited heavily from the Canadian Communist party. When Gouzenko defected, he exposed the spy ring. (Andrew and Gordievsky, *KGB*; Bittman, *The KGB and Soviet Disinformation*; Brook-Shepherd, *The Storm Birds*; Rositzke, *The KGB*)

617   Zacharski, Marian W.   Zacharski, a Polish intelligence officer, recruited William Holden Bell, an aerospace engineer, to sell sensitive information. Reportedly, the FBI had Zacharski under surveillance when he first entered the U.S. He arrived in the U.S. on a commercial visa in 1977 as a representative of the Polish American Machinery Company. He moved into the same condominium where Bell lived, and they became close friends. In 1978 Bell complained about serious financial problems, and Zacharski offered him $5,000 for classified documents from Hughes Aircraft where Bell worked. Bell testified against Zacharski during the trial. He was sentenced to life in 1981 for spying but was exchanged for East German–held spies in 1985. (Allen and Polmar, *The Merchants of Treason*; Bittman, *The KGB and Soviet Disinformation*)

618   Zakharov, Gennadi Fyodorovich.   Zakharov worked as a scientific officer at the Center for Science and Technology for Development at the UN. Zakharov had recruited a Guyana foreign student who worked for a defense contractor. However, the student notified the FBI of Zakharov's recruitment attempts, and the FBI arranged to have the student hand over unclassified documents to Zakharov. In 1986 Zakharov was making an exchange of money for documents in a New York City subway when he was arrested. Zakharov was later exchanged for American reporter Nicholas Daniloff, who was arrested on espionage charges. (*Facts on File*, 1986–87; *New York Times*, August 24–26, 28; September 1–30; October 1, 3, 9, 20, 1986)

619   Zamir, Zvi ("Zvicka") (b. 1924).   Succeeded Meir Amit as head of Israel's Mossad in 1968. He was a former major general in the Israeli Army with no intelligence experience. He was born in Poland, arriving in Palestine in 1925 as an infant. His family changed their name from

Zarzevsky to Zamir. He joined the Palmach (Jewish self-defense army) in 1942, became divisional commander in 1944, and saw combat in the 1948 war for independence. He was arrested and jailed by the British for illegal immigration activities. He fought as a battalion commander during the battle for Jerusalem. In 1950 he was assigned as a special instructor for senior army officers and in 1953 attended British Army officer's school in England. After he returned, he became the head of the infantry school and in 1956 took a position in training command in the Ministry of Defense. In 1957 he attended Hebrew University, earning a B.A. in humanities. He was promoted to brigadier in charge of the Training Command, and in 1962 he took control of the Southern Command.

He was appointed as military attaché to London in July 1966, missing the Six Day War. Upon his return, he was appointed chief of Mossad. While Mossad chief, he implemented a tough antiterrorist program that resulted in numerous assassination operations against Black September, a branch of the PLO responsible for the death of Israeli Olympic athletes at the Munich airport in September 1972. Zamir had watched the massacre in the control tower at the Munich airport and became obsessed with revenge.

Mossad agents, sent to avenge the death of the athletes, were to kill Salameh, Black September's operations officer who planned the Munich attack, but mistakenly killed a Moroccan by the name of Bouchiki in Lillehammer, Norway. It caused a major scandal for Mossad and Israel. Norwegian authorities were irate with the Israelis.

The disaster of the Yom Kippur war and the Lillehammer scandal put a black mark on his record as chief. Many accused Mossad of spending too much time and resources hunting down Palestinian terrorists and failing to detect the growing Arab military buildup resulting in the Yom Kippur war, which Israeli intelligence passed off as military exercises. He was accused of not acting fast enough to the growing evidence. He retired in 1974. (Black and Morris, *Israel's Secret Wars*; Eisenberg, Dan, and Landau, *The Mossad*; Raviv and Melman, *Every Spy a Prince*; Steven, *The Spymasters of Israel*)

620   Zangira, Juma Thomas.   In October 1977, a Tanzanian court sentenced Zangira, a former Tanzanian intelligence officer, to twenty years for espionage. Zangira had been arrested in July for engaging in a six-year correspondence with John Wilson, a British citizen who asked for and received specific information on espionage and sabotage operations in Tanzania regarding guerrilla rebel groups in southern Africa. (*Facts on File*, 1977)

621   Zborowski, Mark (b. 1907) (alias Etienne).   In 1958 Zborowski was discovered to have worked with Jack Soble for the Soviet Union. Zborowski had arrived in the U.S. in 1941, becoming a U.S. citizen in 1947. In 1956 he admitted that he had been a Soviet spy in France in the 1930s but claimed he no longer worked for them. But Soble insisted that Zborowski was a Soviet agent.

Zborowski had been identified by a description given by Soviet defector General Alexander Orlov, former head of the KGB in Spain, who defected in 1954 as a Soviet agent in the U.S. In 1957 he did admit to having given two Soviet agents some classified data.

During the 1930s he was recruited in France by Soviet intelligence and was ordered to infiltrate Trotsky's inner circle. He befriended Trotsky's son Lev Sedov and stole Trotsky's archives in Paris. (Andrew and Gordievsky, *KGB*; Corson and Crowley, *The New KGB*; Rositzke, *The KGB*; Romerstein and Levchenko, *The KGB Against the "Main Enemy"*)

622 Zehe, Alfred. Zehe, an East German physicist, was arrested in November 1983 for espionage for East Germany at a meeting of the American Vacuum Society. Zehe had worked for the East German Ministry of State Security as an intelligence agent. He pled guilty to espionage for East Germany. Zehe provided U.S. national security data to East Germany in 1983. Zehe had recruited a U.S. Navy civilian employee from the U.S. Navy's Electronic Systems Engineering Command in South Carolina, who went to the FBI, to provide the documents. The employee provided documents for Zehe in Mexico and to East German embassy officials in Washington in 1982 and 1983. The employee was paid a total of $21,300 for his services. The FBI and the Naval Investigative Service (NIS) began Operation Showdown, which trapped Zehe in the act. Zehe was sentenced to eight years but exchanged in July 1985 for several East German–held spies. (*Facts on File*, 1983, 1985; *New York Times*, November 4, 5, 1983)

623 Zhang, Nikolai Petrovich. In July 1980, Zhang, a Soviet citizen, was sentenced to seven years by a Chinese court for spying. Zhang was accused of attempting to photograph a military defense installation on China's border with the Soviet Union and attempting to steal military information. (*Facts on File*, 1980; *New York Times*, July 21, 1980)

Zinyakin, Vladimir Petrovich see **Chernyayev, Rudolph**

624 Zlatovski, George (b. 1913), and wife, Jane Foster (b. 1912). Indicted in a New York court for espionage charges in 1957 for the Soviet Union, the Zlatovskis had been living in Paris for the last eight years, and the French government refused to extradite them to the U.S. They were tied to the Jack and Myra Soble spy scandal.

Zlatovski was a naturalized U.S. citizen, originally from Kiev, and later served in the U.S. Army in 1943–48 as an intelligence officer. Jane Zlatovski had worked at the Board of Economic Warfare, Office of Strategic Services, and the army's Information Service branch in Vienna and Salzburg.

The indictment stated that since 1940 the Zlatovskis had collected U.S. classified defense data for the Soviet Union. The indictment also stated that he used the aliases George Michael and Rector, his wife the name Slang.

Following the Japanese surrender, one of the first Americans to reach Indonesia was an OSS Indonesian specialist, Jane Foster, educated at Mills College, who had spent several years in Java before the war. After meeting with Sukarno, she reported that the Indonesian nationalist was not a Communist or pro–Soviet. Jane Foster was accused of passing her OSS Indonesian reports to the Soviets in 1945. Jane Foster, born in California, went to work for the Board of Economic Warfare as an analyst in 1942. In December 1943, she transferred to the OSS until January 1946. From September 1947 to August 1948 she worked for the U.S. military in Austria at the European Command Headquarters in Salzburg. She spoke French, Malay, Dutch, and German. Jane joined the Communist party in the 1930s while living in the Dutch East Indies from 1936 to 1940. Jane met with Jack Soble and provided classified OSS documents on Indonesia. While in Austria, she gained access to sensitive counterintelligence documents in 1947–48. While in the OSS, she was stationed throughout Asia, including Ceylon, India, Burma, Siam, and Thailand.

Her husband, George, was born in Russia and came to the U.S. with his parents in 1922 as a child. He joined the U.S. Army in November 1942 and left as a lieutenant in February 1948. He spoke Russian, German, French, and Spanish. In an interview in 1938, he mentioned joining the Abraham Lincoln Brigade fighting in Spain. George joined the Communist party while living in Minnesota in the early 1930s. George attended the U.S. Intelligence School in 1946 and served as an interrogations officer in the Military Intelligence Section of the U.S. forces in Austria. (Corson and Crowley, *The New KGB*; Romerstein and Levchenko, *The KGB Against the "Main Enemy"*; Smith *OSS*)

Zlatovski, Jane Foster see Zlatovski, George

625 Zolotarenko, Vladimir. In November 1980, Zolotarenko was arrested by French authorities for providing NATO classified documents to Soviet agents. Zolotarenko, French-born to Russian parents, was employed by the Aerospace Research and Development Agency in France. He confessed to providing classified documents to two Soviet agents he had met at a party. The French government expelled two Soviet diplomats. (*Facts on File*, 1980)

626 Zorn, Heinz Bernhart. In August 1980, French authorities arrested General Zorn, former chief of staff of the East German Air Force for espionage. He had retired from the military three years before. Zorn entered France in August under a tourist visa and was placed under surveillance by French counterintelligence agents. When Zorn was arrested, authorities discovered classified documents detailing French tanks and antitank weapons. After six days of interrogation, he was charged with espionage. (*Facts on File*, 1980; *New York Times*, September 7, 1980)

627 Zotov, Anatoly Pavlovich. In December 1982, Zotov, naval attaché for the Soviet embassy in London, was expelled for spying. The British government accused Zotov of being a member of the Soviet GRU. Zotov denied any improper activities. The Soviets retaliated by expelling Captain Bruce Richardson of the British embassy in the Soviet Union. (*Facts on File*, 1982; *New York Times*, December 3, 4, 18, 24, 1982; Suvorov, *Inside the Aquarium*)

Glossary

Agent in place: An agent who has legal access to secret data.

Agent of influence: An agent in high places who can help shape events favorably for the opposition.

Agent provocateur: An agent who uses covert action to stimulate an opposing faction to foolish action.

Ajax, Operation: CIA-sponsored coup in Iran in 1953.

ASIO: Australian Security and Intelligence Organization.

ASIS: Australian Secret Intelligence Service.

Asset: An intelligence resource.

Bag Job: Illegal Entry.

BfV: Federal Office for the Protection of the Constitution (West Germany).

Black operator: An agent working covertly or undercover.

Black propaganda: The dissemination of false information.

BOSS: Bureau of State Security (South Africa).

BND: Federal Intelligence Service (West Germany).

Camp Peary: CIA training facility located near Williamsburg, Virginia. Also referred to as the Farm.

Case officer: Individual in charge of handling and recruiting agents.

CAT: Civil Air Transport (CIA).

Chief of station: CIA head of operations at an embassy.

CIA: Central Intelligence Agency (U.S.).

CIG: Central Intelligence Group (preceded CIA).

COMINT: Communications Intelligence.

Company, the: Euphemistic term for the CIA.

COMSEC: Communications Security.

Confutation: Euphemistic term for defection.

CORDS: Civil Operations and Rural Development Support (U.S.).

CREEP: Committee to Re-Elect the President (Nixon).

Cryptanalysis: Breaking coded messages.

Cryptography: Enciphering a message so that it must be deciphered to be read.

Cut-out: A mediator between a handler and spy.

DCI: Director of Central Intelligence (CIA).

Dead drop: Hiding place for depositing and collecting messages and material.

Defector: An individual who flees his country for political reasons.

DGI: Cuban Intelligence Service.

DIA: Defense Intelligence Agency (U.S.).

DOD: Department of Defense (U.S.).

Double agent: Spy working for the opposition while pretending to be loyal to his handlers.

DST: French Internal Intelligence Service.

ECM: Electronic Countermeasures.

ELINT: Electronic Intelligence.

FBI: Federal Bureau of Investigation (U.S.).

FBIS: Foreign Broadcast Information Service (U.S.).

GCHQ: Government Communications Headquarters (British).

Gold, Operation: Joint British-U.S. intelligence operation which involved the digging of a tunnel from West Berlin into East Berlin to tap into Soviet communication lines.

Gray propaganda: The use of half-truths to confuse or influence the opposition.

GRU: Military Intelligence (USSR).

Honey trap: Sexual entrapment operation intended for blackmail.

HUMINT: Human Intelligence.

INR: Bureau of Intelligence and Research, U.S. State Department.

JCS: Joint Chiefs of Staff (U.S.).

KCIA: Korean Central Intelligence Agency.

KGB: Committee for State Security (USSR).

MfS: East German Ministry of State Security.

MI5: British Counterintelligence Service.

MI6: British Secret Intelligence Service.

Mole: Infiltrator within a spy organization.

Mongoose, Operation: CIA operation designed to overthrow Castro.

Mossad: Israeli Intelligence Service.

MVD: Soviet Ministry of Internal Affairs.

NFIB: National Foreign Intelligence Board (U.S.).

NIE: National Intelligence Estimate (U.S.).

NIS: Naval Investigative Service (U.S.).

NKGB: Soviet People's Commissariat for State Security.

NKVD: Soviet People's Commissariat for Internal Affairs.

NSA: National Security Agency. (U.S.).

NSC: National Security Council (U.S.).

NTS: National Alliance of Russian Solidarity.

OGPU: State Political Administration (USSR).

OSS: Office of Strategic Services (U.S.).

PDB: President's Daily Brief (U.S.).

PFIAB: President's Foreign Intelligence Advisory Board.

PHOTINT: Photographic Intelligence.

Pickle factory: Euphemistic term for the CIA.

PNG: Persona non grata. The official designation that an individual has been expelled from a country for improper activities.

Proprietary company: CIA-owned companies that serve as fronts for covert operations. Example: Air America.

RCMP: Royal Canadian Mounted Police.

SAC: Strategic Air Command.

Safe house: A house, apartment, or facility that serves as hiding or meeting place for espionage purposes.

SB: Polish Intelligence Service.

SDECE: French Counterintelligence Agency.

SIGINT: Signal Intelligence.

SIS: Secret Intelligence Service (MI6).

SMERSH: Secret police units within the Soviet Army during World War II.

Spook: Nickname for a spy.

SSD: East German Intelligence Service.

STB: Czech Intelligence Service.

Tradecraft: Espionage technique.

UN: United Nations.

USMACV: United States Military Assistance Command Vietnam.

Watchers: Counterintelligence agents.

Zapata Plan: CIA-sponsored invasion of Cuba. Often referred to as the Bay of Pigs invasion.

Chronology

1946

January 22: President Truman creates Central Intelligence Group (CIG) under direction of National Intelligence Authority (NIA). Rear Adm. Sidney W. Souers serves as director of Central Intelligence (DCI) till June, when Air Force Lt. Gen. Hoyt Vandenberg replaces him as DCI.

March 4: Canada breaks up a Soviet spy ring working out of the Soviet embassy at Ottawa; spy ring was involved in atomic espionage.

March 19: Alan Nunn-May pleads not guilty to espionage for the Soviets at his arraignment in London.

March 26: FBI arrests Soviet Lt. Nicolai Redin on espionage charges for attempting to obtain data on the destroyer tender *Yellowstone* due to take part in the atomic tests at Bikini Atoll.

March 28: Canadian Communist MP Fred Rose is arrested for attempting to give RDX secrets to the Soviets. Sentenced to ten years for espionage.

April 12: Emma Woikin, a cipher clerk in the External Affairs Department, pleads guilty in a Canadian court to giving secret data to the Soviets.

June 10: Truman appoints Lt. Gen. Hoyt S. Vandenberg as director of the Central Intelligence Group; he holds the post till May 1947.

1947

May 1: Roscoe H. Hillenkoetter is appointed director of the Central Intelligence Group (till October 1950).

May 20: U.S. Army's foreign intelligence network and the FBI's Latin American organization are revealed to have stopped all operations after a political battle with the National Intelligence Authority over jurisdiction.

August 1: The Royal Canadian Mounted Police (RCMP) announces that Samm Carr, former Labor-Progressive party organizer sought during the 1946 Soviet spy probe, has escaped to Mexico.

September 18: Central Intelligence Agency and the National Security Council are created by the National Security Act of 1947, replacing the Central Intelligence Group (CIG) and National Intelligence Authority (NIA).

October 9: Ontario Supreme Court convicts Harold Samuel Gerson for conspiracy to aid Soviet espionage.

December 6: Raymond Boyer is convicted in Montreal, Canada, for conspiring to sell RDX (high explosive) secrets to the Soviets.

1948

June 18: The Office of Policy Coordination (OPC) is created within the CIA by NSC Directive 10/2.

1949

The year: The CIA and MI6 jointly run Operation Valuable, aimed at overthrowing the Communist government in Albania. Operation is a failure.

March 4: The FBI arrests a Soviet, Valentin A. Gubitchev, and a Justice Department employee, Judith Coplon, for spying for the Soviets.

August 29: The Soviet Union detonates its first nuclear device, reportedly, taking Western intelligence services by surprise.

October: China creates the Ministry of Public Security (MPS) as a counterintelligence service.

October: A joint CIA-MI6 trained Albanian rebel group is captured by the Albanian secret police shortly after parachuting into the country.

October 10: Ervin Munk, Czech consulate, is expelled by the U.S. for espionage.

October 24: Jan Horvath, Czech embassy, is expelled by the U.S. for espionage.

1950

February 3: Klaus Fuchs is arrested in London as a Soviet spy. Fuchs is later sentenced to fourteen years after pleading guilty to giving atomic secrets to the Soviets.

March 9: Valentin A. Gubitchev, UN secretariat, is expelled by U.S. for Soviet espionage.

April: East Germany's Ministry for State Security created.

April 15: U.S. Army court-martial in West Germany convicts Air Force Cpl. Gustav Mueller of attempting to give military secrets to the Soviets.

May 23: Harry Gold is arrested by the FBI on espionage charges.

July 6: U.S. court convicts David Greenglass of atomic espionage.

July 17: FBI arrests Julius Rosenberg in New York City on a charge of atomic espionage.

July 29: Abraham Brothman and Miriam Moskowitz are arrested by the FBI as conspirators in the Fuchs-Gold spy ring.

August 11: FBI arrests Ethel Rosenberg in New York on a charge of atomic espionage.

September: West Germany creates the Office for the Protection of the Constitution (BfV).

September 18: Alfred Dean Slack is found guilty of espionage charges in a U.S. court, accused of passing RDX secrets to the Soviets.

October 7: Gen. Walter Bedell Smith is appointed director of the Central Intelligence Agency (till February 9, 1953).

1951

January 31: New York federal grand jury indicts Julius and Ethel Rosenberg, Morton Sobell, David Greenglass, and Anatoli A. Yakovlev for espionage for the Soviets between June 1944 and June 1950.

February 7: U.S. federal grand jury finds William W. Remington guilty of espionage for the Soviets.

March–April: Julius Rosenberg and wife, Ethel, are convicted of espionage; executed in 1953.

April: China arrests Hugh F. Redmond as a U.S. spy. Sentenced to life in 1954.

April 5: Julius and Ethel Rosenberg are sentenced to death for espionage for the Soviets.

May: China creates the United Front Work Department and the International Liaison Department. Both institutions are involved in espionage activities.

May: Guy Burgess and Donald Maclean, members of the British Foreign Ministry, defect to the Soviet Union.

June: CIA-MI5 parachute sixteen Albanian rebels into Albania, captured immediately by the Albanian secret police.

July 15: Peter Varkonyi, Hungarian legation, is expelled by the U.S. for espionage.

July 15: Sandor Louis Nagy, Hungarian legation, is expelled by the U.S. for espionage.

September: Israel reorganizes the Secret Service into the Central Institute for Intelligence and Special Assignments (Mossad).

1952

February 25: U.S. federal court of appeals upholds the death sentences of Julius and Ethel Rosenberg.

April: CIA memorandum suggests using individuals with high ESP skills to work as agents. The document also expressed an interest in Soviet and Nazi ESP experiments, and possibility of using dogs as ESP team members.

May 23: Joseph W. Weinberg, "Scientist X," is indicted by a U.S. federal grand jury in Washington, D.C., on charges of perjury before the House Un-American Activities Committee, is accused of giving atomic secrets to the Soviets.

June 13: William M. Marshall, British Foreign Office radio operator, arrested for espionage for the Soviets.

July: CIA parachutes four Chinese members of Team Wen into the Manchurian province of Kirin to establish an agent network.

July 12: Great Britain orders the expulsion of Second Secretary Pavel S. Kuznetzov of the Soviet Embassy for espionage.

September 4: CIA officers Wayne H. Richardson and Miller Holland are held in contempt by a U.S. federal district court in Seattle for refusing to testify in the trial of Harry A. Jarvinen, who was charged with giving the CIA false information.

September 15: South Korea announces the arrest of seventeen men and seventeen women in Pusan as spies for the Communists, Lee Hae Chong as the leader of the men, and Hong Chung Cha as the leader of the women.

September 21: USAF S. Sgt. Giuseppe Cascio arrested in Korea for attempting to sell secret data on the Sabre jet to the Communists.

September 29: Director of the Central Intelligence Agency Walter Bedell Smith announces that Communists have infiltrated nearly every security and intelligence organization in the U.S. government, including CIA.

October: National Security Agency created by presidential directive.

November 19: CIA officers Richard G. Fecteau and John T. Downey captured in China after their Civil Air Transport cargo plane is shot down; both charged with espionage. Fecteau is released in 1971, Downey in March 1973.

December: President Eisenhower approves the U-2 spy plane program.

December 2: Tony Ernest Dewick is court-martialed by a British court for espionage for the Soviets.

December 13: The United Nations announces the dismissal of Nikolai Skvortsov as a Soviet spy.

1953

The year: CIA begins recruiting Tibetan refugees for a secret army to fight the invading Chinese.

January 14: Yuri V. Novikov, Soviet embassy, is expelled by the U.S. for espionage.

January 19: Otto Verber and Kurt L. Ponger indicted in a Washington court for espionage for the Soviets.

January 27: A Polish military court sentences to death Rev. Joseph Lelito, a Roman Catholic priest, and Michal Kowalik and Edward Chanclica, laymen, as spies for the U.S. and Vatican.

February 26: Allen Dulles appointed director of the Central Intelligence Agency (till November 1961).

April 26: CIA parachutes four Ukrainian exiles from a U.S. bomber into the Soviet Union; all caught and executed by firing squad.

May 20: Christache Zambeti, Rumanian legation, is expelled for espionage by the U.S.

June 19: Julius and Ethel Rosenberg are executed in the electric chair in Sing Sing Prison for espionage.

August: CIA stages coup d'état in Iran deposing Prime Minister Mohammed Mossadegh and placing the Shah, Mohammed Reza Pahlevi, into power; called Operation Ajax.

October 31: During a U.S. Army court-martial in Berlin, Pvt. Robert W. Dorey receives a fifteen-year sentence for fleeing to East Germany and twice returning to the U.S. zone with Soviet agents, whom he guided around U.S. military installations.

November 4: Polish authorities charge that the U.S. parachuted two spies into Poland.

November 15: Vietnamese secret police in Hanoi report breaking up a Chinese spy ring in northern Vietnam.

November 28: CIA experiments with LSD result in tragedy when an unwitting Frank Olsen is given the drug and dives through the tenth-story window of the Washington Statler Hotel, plunging to his death.

December 5: A Korean military court in South Korea sentences to death Chung Kook Eun, former editor of the *Seoul Yun-Hap Shinmoon*, for spying; executed in February 1954.

1954

February 3: Igor A. Amosov, Office of Naval Attaché, is expelled for espionage by the U.S.

February 3: Aleksandr P. Kovalev, United Nations mission, is expelled for espionage by the U.S.

February 25: A Viet Minh spy ring discovered in the French channel port of Le Havre; French also seize antiwar propaganda aimed at discouraging support for the war.

May 7: French garrison at Dien Bien Phu surrenders to Viet Minh forces.

May 29: Leonid I. Pivnev, Office of Air Attaché, expelled for espionage by the U.S.

June: CIA stages coup d'état in Guatemala, overthrowing President Jacobo Arbenz Guzman and placing a military junta headed by Col. Carlos Castillo Armas; called Operation Success.

July 24: East Germany reports that Roman Catholic Bishop Stephan Trochta of Litomerice, Rev. Frantisek Rabas, Rev. Frantisek Vicek, and Rev. Bohumil Landsmann are tried and convicted of spying for the Vatican before the Czech Supreme Court.

August: Construction begins on Berlin tunnel by CIA and SIS; called Operation Gold, designed to reach sensitive Soviet communication lines for tapping.

September 2: South Korean national Hong Ki Khung, alias Kyung Ki Chang, is arrested by the Philippine Army, along with an unidentified Filipino who received secret SEATO documents.

October 9: Joseph Sydney Petersen, former NSA analyst, arrested by FBI agents on charges of espionage on behalf of the Dutch government.

November: CIA creates the Freedom Company in the Philippines to develop anti–Communist programs.

November 2: China's Public Security Ministry announces that of the 230 Nationalist and CIA-trained agents sent into China since 1951, 106 have been killed and 124 captured.

November 22: China sentences eleven U.S. Army airmen and two CIA officers (John Thomas Downey, 24, and Richard George Fecteau, 27) as spies. In addition, nine Chinese Nationalists working for the CIA are sentenced to death or life. The eleven U.S. airmen included Col. John Knox Arnold, commander of the 581st Air Resupply and Communications Wing of the Far East; Maj. Wm. H. Baumer, operations officer of the 91st Strategic Reconnaissance Squadron of the FEAF: Capt. Eugene John Vaadi; Capt. Elmer Fred Llewellyn: Lt. Wallace L. Brown; Lt. John Woodrow Buck; Sgt. Howard Wm. Brown; and Airmen Harry Martin Benjamin Jr., John Walker Thompson, Steve Edward Kiba Jr., and Daniel C. Schmidt; all captured after their planes were shot down over China.

December 21: Egypt announces that Max Bennett, an Israeli agent, had committed suicide in his prison cell.

December 22: Joseph Sydney Petersen Jr., former analyst, pleads guilty to one of three charges in an espionage indictment.

1955

January 31: Egypt hangs two Israeli spies, Moussa Lieto and Samuel Azar.

February 21: Maksim Martynov, UN mission, is expelled for espionage by the U.S.

February 25: Berlin tunnel reaches communications lines.

April 12: An Air India passenger plane carrying Chinese delegates to the Bandung Conference is blown up by a time bomb over the South China Sea; later evidence points to CIA involvement.

August 1: The first U-2 spy plane is test-flown.

1956

February: President's Foreign Intelligence and Advisory Board (PFIAB) is created by President Eisenhower.

February 11: Guy Burgess and Donald Maclean hold a news conference in a Moscow hotel room, ending the mystery of their 1951 disappearance.

April: West Germany creates the Federal Intelligence Service (BND) as an intelligence-gathering service.

April 21: Soviets discover Berlin tunnel.

April 25: Aleksandr K. Guryanov, UN mission, expelled for espionage by the U.S.

June 14: Ivan A. Bubchikov, Office of Military Attaché, expelled for espionage by the U.S.

June 22: Boris F. Gladkov, UN mission, expelled for espionage by the U.S.

July 1: The first U-2 mission flies over Moscow, Leningrad, and Baltic coast.

August 20: Rostislav E. Shapovalov, UN mission, expelled for espionage by the U.S.

August 23: Viktor I. Petrov, UN secretariat, dismissed for Soviet espionage.

October 28: Cuban Military Intelligence chief, Col. Antonio Blanco Rio, is assassinated and two members of his party are wounded after leaving a Havana nightclub.

October 29: Konstantin P. Ekimov, UN mission, expelled for espionage by the U.S.

November: Fidel Castro and eighty followers arrive in Cuba to overthrow the government of Batista.

1957

The year: U.S. State Department Bureau of Intelligence and Research is created.

January 14: Yuri P. Krylov, Office of Military Attaché, expelled for espionage by the U.S.

January 25: Vasily M. Molev, Soviet embassy, expelled for espionage by the U.S.

February 5: Jack Soble, Myra Soble, and Jacob Albam indicted by a U.S. federal grand jury in New York on charges of espionage.

February 6: Soviet TV displays four imprisoned spies, Nikolai I. Yakuta, Mikhail P. Kydryavtsev, Alexander Novikov, and Konstantin Khmelnitsky, claiming they parachuted into the USSR to carry out espionage and subversion activities; all claim they were trained by U.S. intelligence specialists in West Germany.

February 7: USSR expels USMC Capt. Paul Uffelman, USN Lt. William S. Lewis, assistant U.S. embassy attachés, in Moscow for espionage activities.

March 12: A Swedish court sentences Bedros Zartaryan, Turkish engineer, to ten years at hard labor for espionage for the Soviets.

March 25: Vladimir A. Grusha, UN mission, expelled for espionage by the U.S.

April 17: Gennadi F. Mashkantsev, Soviet embassy, expelled for espionage by the U.S.

May: Karoly Meszaros, Hungarian legation air attaché, expelled for espionage by the U.S.

May: Pal Racz, UN Hungarian mission, expelled for espionage by the U.S.

July 8: New York federal grand jury indicts Russian-born George Zlatovski, and U.S.-born wife, Jane Foster Zlatovski, on espionage.

August 7: Soviet spy Rudolf Ivanovich Abel, KGB colonel, is indicted by a New York federal grand jury for espionage.

September 24: The KGB announces the arrest in Latvia in July of C. P. Bromberg and his assistant, L. N. Zarinsh, as U.S. spies.

October: USSR launches the Sputnik 1 satellite.

1958

February 15: CIA begins support for Indonesian rebel soldiers in a coup attempt against Sukarno; ends in June 1959 in failure.

April 17: Czechoslovakia expels Second Secretary Joseph R. Jacyno of the U.S. embassy in Prague for spying.

April 23: Italian Foreign Ministry announces that Aleksandr Solovyev, Soviet embassy assistant military attaché in Rome, was detained on espionage charges.

May 7: Einar Blechingberg, Danish embassy trade counselor in Bonn, West Germany, is returned to Denmark and charged with spying for an unnamed East European government.

May 9: Max Ulrich, former federal police inspector and Swiss counterintelligence agent, is convicted in Switzerland for spying for France. Ulrich supplied French Colonel Marcel Mercier with data on Arab diplomats during the 1956 Suez crisis.

May 18: CIA Civil Air Transport B-26 bomber, flown by Allen Pope, is shot down during an attack on Ambon Harbor by the Indonesian Army.

June 6: Nikolai I. Kurochkin, Soviet embassy, is expelled for espionage by the U.S.

July 18: British court sentences Brian F. Linney to four years for spying for Czechoslovakia.

August 16: Israeli Mossad announces the arrest of fourteen Arabs as part of a Syrian spy ring.

October 16: Chinese radio announces that Stanley Ernest Jones along with Harold George King, British citizens, are charged with running a U.S. spy ring in Shanghai.

November 13: Israel announces the arrest of ten Arabs as members in a United Arab Republic spy ring.

1959

May 13: In an informal request, the U.S. asks Evgeni A. Zaostrovtsev, Soviet embassy, to leave the country, for espionage.

1960

January 7: Vadim A. Kirilyuk, UN secretariat, is dismissed for Soviet espionage.

March 17: President Eisenhower orders CIA to begin the training of a Cuban exile army in Guatemala; army would later be renamed Brigade 2506 and take part in the Bay of Pigs invasion.

April: TIROS (Television and Infra-Red Observation Satellite) is launched into orbit by the U.S.

May: A Soviet gift of a wooden carving of the great seal of the United States to the U.S. ambassador to the UN, Henry Cabot Lodge, is discovered to contain an electronic listening device.

May 1: U-2 pilot Gary Powers shot down over international waters in the Barents Sea by a Soviet fighter jet.

July 22: Petr Y. Ezhov, Soviet embassy, expelled for espionage by the U.S.

August 13: Valentin M. Ivanov, Soviet embassy, expelled for espionage by the U.S.

1961

January 17: Patrice Lumumba assassinated by Congolese soldiers loyal to Joseph Mobutu; CIA blamed after CIA plan to assassinate Lumumba is revealed.

January 31: SAMOS-2 (Satellite and Missile Observation System) reconnaissance satellite is placed into orbit by the U.S.

March 24: Igor Y. Melekh, UN secretariat, expelled for espionage by the U.S.

April 16–19: Bay of Pigs invasion by CIA-trained Cuban army.

June 13: Miroslav Nacvalac, UN Czech mission, expelled for espionage by the U.S.

August: U.S. Defense Intelligence Agency created.

October (to October 1962): Operation Mongoose – CIA covert plan involving sabotage and assassination aimed against Cuba.

November 29: John McCone is appointed director of the Central Intelligence Agency (till April 1965).

1962

February 10: U-2 pilot Frances Gary Powers traded by the USSR for U.S.-held Soviet spy Rudolf Abel.

April: The CIA approaches Mafia contact John Rosselli about planning of a Mafia assassination of Castro.

April 26: The SR-71 reconnaissance aircraft ("the Blackbird") first flown by the U.S.

August 7: Yuri V. Zaitsev, UN secretariat, receives informal request to leave the U.S. for Soviet espionage.

September 9: Chinese shoot down a U-2 spy plane piloted by a Nationalist Chinese.

September 29: Evgeni M. Prokhorov, UN mission, expelled for espionage by the U.S.

September 29: Ivan Y. Vyrodov, UN mission, expelled for espionage by the U.S.

October 15: U.S. discovers nuclear missiles in Cuba.

October 22–28: Cuban missile crisis.

October 27: Cuba shoots down U-2 spy plane.

1963

July 1: Gennadiy G. Sevastyanov, Soviet embassy, expelled for espionage by the U.S.

October 11: Ivan Egorov, UN secretariat, expelled for Soviet espionage.

October 11: Aleksandra Egorova expelled for Soviet espionage by the U.S.

October 16: The VELA reconnaissance satellite first launched by the U.S.; VELA detected nuclear explosions.

October 30: Gleb Pavlov, UN mission, expelled for espionage by the U.S.

October 30: Yuri Romashin, UN mission, expelled for espionage by the U.S.

October 30: Vladimir Olenov, UN mission, expelled for espionage by the U.S.

November 22: CIA provides Rolando Cubela with a poisoned pen to kill Castro.

November 22: President John F. Kennedy assassinated.

1964

April 7: President Johnson stops all CIA activities against Cuba and Castro.

December 14: Vasiliy V. Zadvinskiy, Soviet Office of Military Attaché, expelled for espionage by the U.S.

December 14: Aleksandr V. Udalov, Soviet Office of Air Attaché, expelled for espionage by the U.S.

December 14: Vladimir P. Grechanin, Soviet Office of Military Attaché, expelled for espionage by the U.S.

1965

January 7: Boris V. Karpovich, Soviet embassy counselor, expelled for espionage by the U.S.

January 15: Kazimierz Mizior, Polish embassy, expelled for espionage by the U.S.

April 28: William Raborn appointed director of the Central Intelligence Agency (till June 1966).

June 2: Stefan M. Kirsanov, Soviet embassy, expelled for espionage by the U.S.

July 7: Valentin P. Novikov's contract as UN secretariat not renewed due to Soviet espionage activities.

1966

February 2: Vadim A. Isakov, Soviet assigned to UNICEF and UNSEC, expelled for espionage by the U.S.

May 4: Stefan Starzewski, Polish embassy, expelled for espionage by the U.S.

May 20: Tadeusz Wisniewski, Office of Polish Military Attaché, expelled for espionage by the U.S.

June 30: Richard Helms appointed director of the Central Intelligence Agency (till February 1973).

July 13: Jiri Opatrny, Czech embassy, expelled for espionage by the U.S.

September 2: Valentin Revin, Soviet embassy, expelled for espionage by the U.S.

October 31: Aleksay R. Malinin, Soviet embassy employee, expelled for espionage by the U.S.

1967

March 29: President Johnson orders stop of all covert CIA financing of private and voluntary organizations. These organizations included the National Student Association, AFL-CIO United Automobile Workers, the magazine *Encounter*, International Cooperative Development, and the Asia Foundation.

May: The Civil Operations and Revolutionary Development Support (CORDS) program is initiated in Vietnam as a joint undertaking by the State Department Agency for International Development and USMACV. One of the programs under CORDS was the infamous Phoenix program operated by the CIA.

June 8: USS *Liberty*, SIGINT platform, cruising off the coast of the Sinai, is attacked by Israeli planes and ships.

October 9: Che Guevara is executed by CIA-trained Bolivian troops.

1968

January 23: USS *Pueblo*, U.S. Navy SIGINT platform, is captured by the North Koreans.

July: CIA begins Operation Chaos, a domestic program designed to spy on student groups opposed to the Vietnam War.

September 29: CIA recruiting office in Ann Arbor, Michigan, destroyed by a bomb.

November 20: CIA recruiter physically removed by angry students from South Bend, Indiana, while recruiting Notre Dame University students for employment with the CIA.

1969

April 14: A U.S. Navy EC-121 reconnaissance airplane shot down by two North Korean fighters.

May 23: Viktor V. Kopytin, Soviet embassy, *Tass* employee, expelled for espionage by the U.S.

Christmas Day: Israel initiates Operation Noah's Ark with the smuggling of five gunboats out of the French Cherbourg harbor.

1970

February 17: Aleksandr V. Tikhomirov, Soviet UNSEC employee, expelled for espionage by the U.S.

February 17: Boris Mikhaylovich Orekhov, *Pravda* correspondent in New York, expelled for espionage by the U.S.

April 24: China begins satellite reconnaissance program with the launching of *China One.*

November 8: Leonid Nikolaevich Zhegalov, a *Tass* correspondent in Washington, D.C., expelled for espionage.

1971

March–May: An anti–Castro group releases the African swine virus into Cuba. The Cuban government was forced to kill 500,000 pigs to prevent the spread of the virus. CIA intelligence officers delivered a sealed container that contained the virus to the Cuban group in Ft. Gurlick, Panama Canal Zone, a few months before it was released. The CIA paramilitary training center helped train members of the group in paramilitary operations.

June 15: U.S. launches first KH-9 reconnaissance satellite.

August: White House orders CIA's Technical Services Division to supply E. Howard Hunt with the equipment used in the burglary of the office of Daniel Ellsberg's psychiatrist.

September 3: Former CIA employee E. Howard Hunt and some assistants break into the office of Daniel Ellsberg's psychiatrist.

September 24: British government orders the expulsion of ninety Soviet citizens on charges of espionage.

October 27: Karel Simunek, Czech embassy, expelled for espionage by the U.S.

1972

June 17: (2:00 A.M.): Five men arrested for breaking and entering at the Democratic National Committee headquarters at the Watergate Hotel in Washington, D.C. Two of the burglars are former CIA employees.

November 20: President Nixon fires CIA director Richard Helms for failing to participate in the Watergate cover-up.

May 19: Valery I. Markelov, UN secretariat, expelled for Soviet espionage by the U.S.

1973

February 2: James Schlesinger appointed director of the Central Intelligence Agency (till July).
March 6: The first U.S. Rhyolite reconnaissance satellite launched, positioned over the horn of Africa to monitor Soviet microwave communications.
September 4: William E. Colby appointed director of the Central Intelligence Agency (till January 1976).

1974

August: President Nixon resigns the presidency.

1975

January 4: President Ford creates the Commission on CIA Activities chaired by Vice President Nelson Rockefeller. The commission submits its report June 6, 1975.
January 27: The Senate Select Committee to Study Government Operations with Respect to Intelligence Activities created, chaired by Senator Frank Church (D, Idaho).
February 19: The House Select Committee on Intelligence established to investigate the activities of the CIA. Chaired by Representative Otis G. Pike (D, New York). On January 29 House votes to withhold public access of the final report.
April 30: South Vietnam falls to North Vietnam.
December 23: Richard S. Welch, CIA chief of station in Athens, Greece, assassinated by left-wing terrorists.

1976

January 30: George Bush appointed director of the Central Intelligence Agency (till January 1977).
February 19: Executive Order 11905 signed by President Gerald Ford; sets new intelligence policies as well as the establishment of an intelligence oversight mechanism.
April 26: The Church committee, U.S. Senate Select Committee to Study Intelligence Activities, releases its report noting defects in the CIA Office of Inspector General, recommending administrative and statutory actions.
May 19: Senate Select Committee on Intelligence established as an oversight committee on U.S. intelligence organizations.
June: Edwin Wilson, former CIA agent, signs first mercenary contract with Libya.
July 4: Israeli raid on Entebbe.
July 14: House Permanent Select Committee on Intelligence created as an oversight committee with jurisdiction over the CIA, chaired by Representative Edward Boland (D, Mass.).
July 14–December 15: Reportedly, CIA agents attempt to assassinate Jamaican Prime Minister Michael Manley three times, each attempt a failure.
August: Australian Secret Intelligence Service (ASIS) and Japan's Cabinet Research Office (Naicho) begin a liaison relationship.
December 19: U.S. launches KH-11 reconnaissance satellite.

1977

January 16: FBI agents arrest Christopher Boyce for spying for the Soviets.

February: Congress forces the CIA to stop payments to King Hussein for a free hand in Jordon, called Operation No-Beef.

March 9: Stansfield Turner appointed director of the Central Intelligence Agency (till January 1981).

May 23: A second U.S. Rhyolite reconnaissance satellite launched, positioned over Borneo to monitor signals from China and USSR.

October: DCI Turner abolishes 850 positions within the CIA, concentrating on the Clandestine Service; referred to as the "Halloween Massacre."

1978

January 24: Executive Order 12036 is signed by President Carter, restructures U.S. intelligence organizations, placing guidelines on intelligence activities.

August: Vladimir Kostov, Bulgarian exile living in Paris, assassinated by the KGB.

1979

November 4: Iranian students seize U.S. Embassy in Tehran, accusing the staff of spying.

December 22: State Department revokes former CIA agent Philip Agee's right to hold a U.S. passport.

December 24: Soviet Union invades Afghanistan.

1980

January 18: Japanese authorities arrest retired General Yukihisa Miyanaga, who served in the intelligence branch of Japan's Self Defense Force, for spying for the Soviets.

February 9: French counterintelligence agents arrest Soviet consular official Gennady Travkov for espionage.

February 14: Spanish authorities arrest Oleg Suranov, chief of Spanish Office of Aeroflot, for espionage.

February 21: DCI Turner announces he allowed the CIA to recruit clergymen, academics, and journalists as CIA operatives.

April 25: A hostage rescue mission by U.S. forces aborted at Desert One in the Iranian desert; eight Americans die when a helicopter collides with a C-130 transport plane.

June 30: Iranian government orders expulsion of Vladimir Goloanov, first secretary of the Soviet embassy, for espionage.

July 4: Three men armed with machine guns attack the home of a CIA officer, Richard Kinsman, attached to the U.S. embassy in Jamaica.

December: CIA begins providing Afghan rebels with arms and equipment.

1981

January 20: Iran releases U.S. hostages after 444 days of captivity.

January 28: William Casey appointed director of the Central Intelligence Agency.

February 11: U.S. expells Ricardo Escartin, Cuban diplomat, for espionage.

March 4: Mozambique accuses four U.S. embassy officials of espionage and orders their expulsion.

March 9: President Reagan authorizes the CIA to undertake covert activities against Nicaragua.

May 2: A former CIA official, Carl Duckett, confirms reports that Israel had developed nuclear weapons.

June 22: Zambia expells two U.S. diplomats for espionage.

July 18: The Soviets shoot down an Argentine CL-44 turboprop cargo plane carrying military equipment from Israel to Iran.

July 23: Senator Barry Goldwater states that William Casey, director of CIA, should resign.

September: TR-1 reconnaissance aircraft is first flown by the U.S.

September 15: Egypt orders expulsion of Soviet ambassador Vladimir Polyakov and six embassy employees for fomenting unrest among conservative Muslims.

October: Fifty U.S. citizens living in Peru sign a petition protesting the appointment of Frank Ortiz as U.S. ambassador; reportedly, Ortiz had CIA ties.

October 19: West Germany exchanges Gunther Guillaume for nine West Germans held by East Germany.

October 20: President's Foreign Intelligence Advisory Board is reestablished by President Reagan.

November 23: Reagan issues National Security Decision Directive 17, which authorizes a CIA plan to create a Contra army to oppose Nicaragua.

1982

January 20: U.S. Ensign Stephen Baba sentenced to eighteen years for espionage for the Soviets.

February 2: Andrew Pyke, British executive of a helicopter company, released by Iran after being arrested in 1980 for espionage.

February 3: U.S. expells GRU officer, Maj. Gen. Vaily Chitov, for espionage.

March 14: CIA-trained demolition team blow up the Rio Negro and Ocotal bridges in Nicaragua.

April 2: France creates the General Directorate of External Security (DGSE).

April 2: Argentina invades the Falkland Islands.

April 5: U.S. Justice Department dismisses William Kennedy for publicly identifying Mexican police chief, Miguel Nassar Haro, as CIA operative.

April 21: Bobby Ray Inman resigns as deputy director of the CIA; during a speech to the American Newspaper Publishers Association, he described the quality of U.S. intelligence capabilities as "marginal."

June 15: Former CIA agent Edwin P. Wilson arrested in New York City for selling arms to Libya.

June 23: Public Law 97-200, Intelligence Identities Protection Act, signed by President Reagan. The new law imposes criminal penalties for those who reveal the names of covert intelligence personnel; probably signed as a result of the activities of Philip Agee.

June 24: Polish military court sentences Ryszard Herczynski, scientist, to two years for espionage for the U.S.

July 19: A twin-engine aircraft purchased by the CIA attempts to bomb petroleum storage facilities in Nicaragua.

October 22: Polish banker and spy, Andrzej Treumann, defects to the U.S.

December 3: Britain expells Soviet GRU officer, Anatoly Pavlovich Zotov, for espionage.

December 7: British court sentences Hugh Hambleton to ten years for spying for the Soviets.

December 10: In a stunning vote, 411–0, U.S. House of Representatives prohibits the CIA from continuing support for paramilitary operations against the government of Nicaragua.

December 22: France creates Directorate for Surveillance of the Territory (DST) as a counterintelligence service.

1983

January 26: South African officials announce the arrest of Dieter Gerhardt for espionage for the Soviets.

March 10: Soviet officials announce the expulsion of Richard Osborne, a U.S. diplomat, for being a CIA agent.

March 31: British officials announce expulsion of three Soviets for espionage.

April: Australian Security and Intelligence Organization exposes and expells Valery Ivanov as a spy working out of the Soviet embassy under the cover of third secretary.

April 18: The U.S. embassy in Beirut, Lebanon, badly damaged in a suicide bomb attack by an Islamic extremist. Among the sixty-three people killed are seven CIA officers, including the station chief, Robert Ames.

April 24: FBI Director William Webster announces that there are over one thousand Soviet and Eastern European spies operating within the U.S.

June 17: U.S. officials announce that a Soviet diplomat, Arkady Vinogradov, attempted to steal computer secrets.

August 20: The *Washington Post* reveals that a top secret U.S. Army intelligence unit that was formed in 1980 to deal with the Iran hostage rescue is still in operation; called the Intelligence Support Activity.

September 1: Soviets shoot down a 747 Korean Airlines Flight 007, killing 269 people after it strayed over Soviet territory.

September 8: CIA plane crashes after dropping a bomb on Managua's airport. The pilot, Agustin Roman, and bombardier, Sebastian Mueller, are killed when the blast forces the plane down.

September 9: A plane provided by the CIA to the Contras attacks the port of Corinto, Nicaragua.

September 12: Canada expells two Soviet diplomats for espionage.

September 23: FBI agents arrest Penyu Kostadinov, Bulgarian trade representative, for espionage.

October: CIA produces the manual *Psychological Operations in Guerrilla Warfare* (TAYACAN) for the Contras. It suggests neutralizing government officials to achieve political ends.

October 10: CIA-trained Contras attack fuel storage tanks in Corinto, Nicaragua.

October 20: President Reagan awards the National Security Medal to former DCI Richard Helms.

October 23: Marine compound in Beirut destroyed by a suicide car-bomb attack; 241 killed.

October 25: U.S. troops invade Grenada.

November 10: U.S. federal grand jury indicts East German physicist Alfred Zehe on eight counts of espionage.

December 3: India announces arrest of three retired military officers for espionage for the U.S.

1984

January 1: CIA contract agents mine Nicaraguan ports and harbors.

January 11: Nicaragua shoots down a U.S. helicopter, killing a U.S. Army pilot, Warrant Officer Jeffrey Schwab; helicopter manages to land one hundred yards within the Honduras border.

January 20: Arne Treholt, deputy press secretary at the Norwegian foreign ministry, arrested for espionage for the Soviets.

February 2: CIA "Latino" contract agents bomb a communications center in Nicaragua.

March 1: U.S. State Department denies a visa to Oleg Yermishkin, Soviet Olympic attaché, due to his ties to the KGB.

March 16: William Buckley, CIA chief of station in Beirut, is kidnapped by Iranian-backed extremist group calling itself Islamic Jihad; Buckley reportedly died as the result of torture in the basement of the Iranian embassy in June 1985.

March 21: The *New York Times* reports that Col. Nicolas Carranza, head of El Salvador's Treasury police, was a paid informant for the CIA.

March 23: A CIA DC-3 crashes in Costa Rica.

April 11: Afghan officials expell U.S. diplomat Richard Vandiver for espionage.

April 16: A British court sentences MI5 agent Michael Bettany to twenty-three years for espionage for the Soviets.

May 14: James Harper sentenced to life for selling U.S. missile secrets to Polish agents.

May 31: Bomb explodes at a press conference of Contra leader Eden Pastora in a Nicaraguan village, wounding Pastora and killing four journalists; Pastora blames the CIA for the attack.

September 20: Car bomb destroys U.S. embassy annex in Aukar, Christian East Beirut, Lebanon.

October 3: FBI agents arrest FBI counterintelligence agent Richard Miller for Soviet espionage.

October 15: The Central Intelligence Agency Information Act is signed by President Reagan.

November 27: FBI agents arrest former CIA agent Karl Koecher for espionage for the Soviets.

December 18: FBI agents arrest Thomas Cavanagh for selling stealth technology to the KGB.

1985

February 25: Poland orders expulsion of U.S. Army Col. Frederick Myer for espionage activities.

March 8: In a vain attempt to kill a militant Shiite leader, CIA-trained Lebanese intelligence agents set off a car bomb in Beirut, killing eighty people, and miss their target.

March 24: Soviet soldiers shoot and kill U.S. Maj. Arthur Nicholson in East Germany.

April 15: India announces arrest of nineteen Indian officials for espionage for Poland, France, and East Germany.

May 20: John Walker arrested by FBI agents for Soviet espionage.

June 13: Soviet authorities arrest Paul Stombaugh, CIA officer, for espionage.

June 14: TWA 747 hijacked by two Lebanese Shiite Hezbollah terrorists; one hostage, a U.S. sailor, killed; the hostages are released June 30.

July 10: French DGSE agents blow up and sink *Rainbow Warrior* in Auckland, New Zealand; one crew member dies.

July 11: FBI announces arrest of CIA employee Sharon Scrange for espionage for Ghana.

July 14: The White House contacts Iran with a proposal to sell one hundred TOW missiles to secure the release of U.S. hostages in Lebanon.

September 15: Iran receives four hundred TOW missiles from the Israelis, who act as a mediator for the U.S., which replaces the TOW missiles the Israelis have delivered. In exchange for the missiles, the Iranians order the release of U.S. hostage Rev. Benjamin Weir. Later, U.S. delivers another one thousand TOWs in direct shipment from the U.S. to Iran.

September 25: Former CIA agent Edward Lee Howard disappears while under FBI surveillance.

October 1: Israel attacks PLO headquarters in Tunis; attack not possible without help of the American spy Jonathan Pollard.

October 4: Islamic Jihad announces that CIA station chief William Buckley has been killed; CIA sources believe Buckley was killed over the summer.

November 18: Jonathan Jay Pollard arrested on espionage for Israel.

November 23: FBI agents arrest former CIA analyst Larry Chin for espionage for the Chinese.

November 25: FBI agents arrest former NSA analyst Ronald Pelton for espionage for the Soviets.

1986

January: Iranian arms merchant Manucher Ghorbanifar suggests using profits from arms sales to Iran to aid the Contras.

February 4: France expells four Soviet diplomats for espionage.

March 14: Soviet Union orders expulsion of CIA officer Michael Sellers.

April: Oliver North begins using the profits from Iranian arms sales to fund Contras.

April 14: U.S. fighters and bombers attack Libya.

May 25: Secret trip to Iran by Oliver North and Robert McFarlane to negotiate the sale of arms for the release of hostages in Lebanon.

August 7: Soviet officials announce the defection of former CIA agent Edward Lee Howard.

August 8: Iranian authorities arrest Jon Pattis, American communications engineer, for espionage activities.

September 5: U.S. Congress agrees to provide $100 million in lethal and nonlethal aid to Contras.

October 5: CIA Southern Air Transport shot down in Nicaragua, Eugene Hasenfus captured by Sandinista troops after parachuting to safety.

October 22: Soviet authorities announce the execution of Adolf Tolkachev for spying for the CIA.

October 29: India announces sentencing of six for espionage for the U.S.

November 2: Lebanese magazine *Al-Shiraa* reveals arms-for-hostage deal between the U.S. and Iran.

November 13: President Reagan denies in a TV speech being involved in an arms-for-hostage deal with Iran.

December 12: Nicaraguan authorities arrest Sam Hall, U.S. citizen, for espionage activities.

1987

February 2: White House announces resignation of William Casey as director of the CIA.

February 5: Roger Cooper appears on Iranian TV, confessing to having worked for the British intelligence in an attempt to build an agent network within Iran.

March 2: Robert Gates withdraws nomination as Director of the CIA due to attacks on his possible role in Iran-Contra affair.

March 3: William Webster, former FBI director, appointed director of the CIA.

April 1: East and West Germany swap eight spies.

May 5: Cuba announced the arrest of two people for spying for the CIA.

May 6: Former director of the CIA William Casey dies of brain tumor.

May 19: Japanese police break up a Soviet spy ring in Tokyo.

July 7–14: North testifies before the Iran-Contra committee under immunity from prosecution.

August 12: East and West Germany swap five spies.

December 18: U.S. State Department announces arrest of Soviet diplomat Mikhail Katkov for espionage.

1988

January 14: U.S. Army Sgt. Daniel Richardson arrested by authorities at the Aberdeen Proving Grounds for espionage for the Soviets.

February 2: French intelligence agent Jacques Merrin assassinated in Christian East Beirut.

March 24: Mordechai Vanunu convicted of treason in an Israeli court for revealing details of Israel's atomic bomb program.

March 28: West German officials announce the arrest of six Soviet spies.

June 11: Canadian authorities announce the arrest of Stephen Ratkai for espionage for the Soviets.

August 25: West German officials announce the arrest of Clyde Conrad for espionage.

December 21: U.S. Army Warrant Officer James Hall arrested for espionage for the Soviets and East Germany.

1989

January 10: Former U.S. Navy CPO Craig Kunkle arrested for espionage for the Soviets.

March 9: U.S. State Department expells Lt. Col. Yuri Pakhtusov for espionage.

April 17: An Afghan tribunal sentences Jordanian to sixteen years for spying.

April 24: U.S. federal grand jury indicts Joseph Fernandez, former CIA station chief in Costa Rica, on four criminal counts relating to his role in Iran-Contra affair.

June 21: U.S. Army Specialist Michael Peri pleads guilty to espionage.

July 20: Huseyin Yildirim convicted of spying for the Soviets by a U.S. federal court.

October 4: U.S. Navy announces that Airman James Wilmoth convicted and sentenced to thirty-five years for espionage for the Soviets.

October 19: Sue Dobson, agent for the South African Bureau of Information, appears in London to announce her participation in espionage operation against the African National Congress.

December 20: South Korean legislator Suh Kyung Won sentenced to fifteen years for spying for North Korea.

1990

February 26: Costa Rican judge signs order of extradition for U.S.-born John Hull for participation in the 1984 bombing at La Penca, Nicaragua, in attempt to assassinate Eden Pastora.

March 10: Iraqi court sentences Farzad Bazoft, freelance journalist, to death for espionage.

June 8: U.S. Titan-4 rocket launched into orbit carrying electronic eavesdropping satellite.

June 10: U.S. newspapers confirm the role CIA played in arrest of Nelson Mandela by South African police in August 1962; retired CIA officer confirmed that a paid informant within the ANC had given the location of Mandela's hideout to the CIA.

August 2: Iraq invades Kuwait.

August 6: Ricky White, son of Roscoe White, announces at a news conference that his father had been one of three men who shot President John F. Kennedy.

August 29: NBC News reports that CIA and U.S. Special Forces had provided covert aid to the Kuwaiti guerrillas.

September 18: Former CIA agent Thomas Clines convicted of four counts of income tax evasion stemming from his involvement in the Contra arms sales.

November: U.S. State Department dismisses career diplomat Felix Bloch under suspicion of espionage.

November 15–20: Space shuttle *Atlantis* carries out secret military spy satellite mission.

1991

February 3: Jordan executes Jordanian Air Force pilot and a truck driver by hanging for spying for Israel. The pilot had been recruited while on a training course in Germany in 1990. The Israelis used a female agent to seduce the pilot.

February 23: U.S. and Allied ground forces attack Iraqi positions: Operation Desert Storm.

May 8: William Webster resigns as director of the CIA.

May 14: Robert Gates named as the next director of the CIA.

May 17: Iraq sentences British engineer Douglas Brand to life for spying for Great Britain.

June 12: Gen. H. Norman Schwarzkopf scolds U.S. intelligence services (CIA) for poor performance during war with Iraq.

July 13: News agencies report that CIA had a variety of relationships with the Bank of Credit and Commerce, Inc. (BCCI), the bank accused of a variety of illegal banking transactions with terrorists and criminal organizations.

August 12: U.S. begins using U-2 spy planes over Iraq to locate weapons-research sites that satellites could not locate.

August 15: President Bush signs covert-activities limitation bill designed to prevent Iran-Contra–style activities.

August 19: Communist conservatives attempt coup d'état.

August 21: Coup attempt in Soviet Union falls apart.

August 27: Gorbachev announces that a full-scale purge of the KGB is under way.

September 6: Clair George, former CIA director of operations, indicted on ten felony counts of lying about Iran-Contra affair to Congress.

Bibliography

Reference Works

Becket, Henry S. A. *The Dictionary of Espionage: Spookspeak into English.* New York: Stein and Day, 1986.

Blackstock, Paul W., and Frank L. Schaf, Jr. *Intelligence, Espionage, Counterespionage, and Covert Operations: A Guide to Information Sources.* Detroit, MI: Gale Research Company, 1978.

Buranelli, Vincent, and Nan. *Spy/Counterspy: An Encyclopedia of Espionage.* New York: McGraw-Hill, 1982.

Constantinides, George C. *Intelligence and Espionage: An Analytical Bibliography.* Boulder, CO: Westview Press, 1983.

Deacon, Richard. *Spyclopedia: The Comprehensive Handbook of Espionage.* New York: William Morrow, 1987.

Dobson, Christopher, and Ronald Payne. *The Dictionary of Espionage.* London: Harrap, 1984.

Facts on File. New York: Facts on File, 1946–1991.

Goehlert, Robert, and Elizabeth R. Hoffmeister. *The CIA: A Bibliography.* Public Administration Series: Bibliography P-498. Monticello, IL: Vance Bibliographies, June 1980.

Lazitch, Branko, and Milorad M. Drachkovitch. *Biographical Dictionary of the Comintern.* Palo Alto, CA: Hoover Institution Press, 1973.

Mader, Julius. *Who's Who in the CIA.* East Berlin, 1968.

New York Times, 1946–1991.

O'Toole, G. J. A. *The Encyclopedia of American Intelligence and Espionage: From the Revolutionary War to the Present.* New York: Facts on File, 1988.

Pforzheimer, Walter, ed. *Bibliography of Intelligence Literature.* Washington, DC: Defense Intelligence College, 1985.

Research Reports on Intelligence for Teaching Faculty. Consortium for the Study of Intelligence under the direction of the National Strategy Information Center, Washington, DC, 1985.

Rocca, Raymond G., and John J. Dziak. *Bibliography on Soviet Intelligence and Security Services.* Boulder, CO: Westview Press, 1985.

Seth, Ronald. *The Encyclopedia of Espionage.* London: New English Library, 1972.

Smith, Myron J. *The Secret Wars.* 3 vols. Santa Barbara, CA: ABC-Clio, 1980.

Watson, Bruce W., Susan M. Watson, and Gerald W. Hopple. *United States Intelligence: An Encyclopedia.* New York: Garland Publishing, 1990.

Monographs and Periodicals

Agee, Philip. *Inside the Company: CIA Diary.* New York: Bantam, 1975.
_____. *On the Run.* Secaucus, NJ: Lyle Stuart, 1987.
_____, and Louis Wolf, eds. *Dirty Work: The CIA in Western Europe.* Secaucus, NJ: Lyle Stuart, 1978.
Aguilar, Luis. *Operation Zapata: The Ultrasensitive Report and Testimony of the Board of Inquiry on the Bay of Pigs.* Frederick, MD.: University Publications of America, 1981.
Aldouby, Zwy, and Jerrold Ballinger. *The Shattered Silence: The Eli Cohen Affair.* New York: Coward-McCann, 1971.
Allen, Thomas B. and Norman Polmar. *Merchants of Treason: America's Secrets For Sale from the Pueblo to the Present.* New York: Delacorte Press, 1988.
Ambrose, Stephen E., and Richard H. Immerman. *Ike's Spies: Eisenhower and the Espionage Establishment.* Garden City, NY: Doubleday, 1981.
Andrade, Dale. *Ashes to Ashes: The Phoenix Program and the Vietnam War.* Lexington, MA: Lexington Books, 1990.
Andrew, Christopher. *Her Majesty's Secret Service: The Making of The British Intelligence Community.* New York: Viking Penguin, 1986.
_____, and Oleg Gordievsky. *KGB: The Inside Story of Its Foreign Operations from Lenin to Gorbachev.* New York: Harper Collins, 1990.
Andrews, Bert, and Peter Andrews. *A Tragedy of History: A Journalist's Confidential Role in the Hiss-Chambers Case.* Washington, DC: Robert B. Luce, 1962.
Bamford, James. *The Puzzle Palace: Inside the National Security Agency, America's Most Secret Intelligence Organization.* New York: Penguin Books, 1982.
Barron, John. *Breaking the Ring.* Boston: Houghton Mifflin, 1987.
_____. *KGB: The Secret Work of Soviet Secret Agents.* New York: Bantam, 1974.
_____. *KGB Today: The Hidden Hand.* New York: Reader's Digest Press, 1983.
Beck, Melvin. *Secret Contenders: The Myth of Cold War Counterintelligence.* New York: Sheridan Square, 1984.
Bernikow, Louise. *Abel.* New York: Trident Press, 1970.
Beschloss, Michael R. *Mayday: Eisenhower, Khrushchev and the U-2 Affair.* New York: Harper and Row, 1986.
Bethell, Nicholas. *Betrayed.* New York: Times Books, 1984.
Bittman, Ladislav. *The Deception Game: Czechoslovak Intelligence in Soviet Political Warfare.* Syracuse, NY: Syracuse Research Corporation, 1972.
_____. *The KGB and Soviet Disinformation: An Insider's View.* Washington, DC: Pergamon-Brassey's, 1985.
Black, Ian, and Benny Morris. *Israel's Secret Wars: A History of Israel's Intelligence Services.* New York: Grove Weidenfeld, 1991.
Blake, George. *No Other Choice: An Autobiography.* New York: Simon and Schuster, 1990.
Blitzer, Wolf. *Territory of Lies.* New York: Harper and Row, 1989.
Blum, Howard. *I Pledge Allegiance: The True Story of the Walkers; An American Spy Family.* New York: Simon and Schuster, 1987.
Blum, William. *The CIA: A Forgotten History; U.S. Global Interventions Since World War II.* New Jersey: Zed Books, 1986.
Bobb, Dilap. "Indecent Exposures: Pamella Singh Bordes." *India Today,* 15 April 1989, 38–46.

_____. "The Hersh Heresy: Morarji Desai." *India Today*, 30 June 1983, 46–49.

_____. "The Spy Sensation." *India Today*, 15 February 1985, 12–21.

Boettcher, Robert. *Gifts of Deceit: Sun Myung Moon, Tongsun Park and the Korean Scandal*. New York: Holt, Rinehart and Winston, 1980.

Bourke, Sean. *The Springing of George Blake*. New York: Viking, 1970.

Boyle, Andrew. *The Climate of Treason: Five Who Spied for Russia*. London: Hutchinson, 1979.

_____. *The Fourth Man: The Definitive Account of Kim Philby, Guy Burgess, and Donald Maclean and Who Recruited Them to Spy for Russia*. New York: Dial, 1979.

Breckinridge, Scott D. *The CIA and the U.S. Intelligence System*. Boulder, CO: Westview Press, 1986.

Brook-Shepherd, Gordon. *The Storm Birds: The Dramatic Stories of the Top Soviet Spies Who Have Defected Since World War II*. New York: Weidenfeld and Nicolson, 1989.

Burchett, Wilfred. *The Second Indochina War*. New York: International, 1970.

Byrne, Malcolm, ed. *The Chronology: The Documented Day-by-Day Account of the Secret Military Assistance to Iran and the Contras*. New York: Warner Books, 1987.

Carr, Barbara. *Spy in the Sun*. Cape Town, South Africa: Timmins, 1969.

Cave-Brown, Anthony. *The Last Hero: Wild Bill Donovan*. New York: Times Books, 1982.

Cecil, Robert. *A Divided Life: A Personal Portrait of the Spy Donald Maclean*. New York: William Morrow, 1989.

Chambers, Wittaker. *Witness*. New York: Random House, 1952.

Cline, Ray S. *Secrets, Spies, and Scholars: Blueprint of the Essential CIA*. Washington, DC: Acropolis Books, 1976.

Cockburn, Leslie. *Out of Control: The Story of the Reagan Administration's Secret War in Nicaragua, the Illegal Arms Pipeline, and the Contra Drug Connection*. New York: Atlantic Monthly Press, 1987.

Colby, William. *Lost Victory: A First Hand Account of America's Sixteen-Year Involvement in Vietnam*. Chicago: Contemporary Books, 1989.

_____, and Peter Forbath. *Honorable Men: My Life in the CIA*. New York: Simon and Schuster, 1978.

Cook, Alistair. *A Generation on Trial: USA vs. Alger Hiss*. New York: Knopf, 1952.

Cookridge, Edward H. *Gehlen: Spy of the Century*. New York: Random House, 1971.

_____. *The Many Sides of George Blake, Esq.: The Complete Dossier*. New York: Vertex, 1970.

_____. *The Spy Trade*. London: Hodder and Stoughton, 1971.

_____. *The Third Man*. New York: G. P. Putnam, 1968.

Corson, William R. *The Armies of Ignorance: The Rise of the American Intelligence Empire*. New York: Dial Press/James Wade Books, 1977.

_____, and Robert T. Crowley. *The New KGB: Engine of Soviet Power*. New York: William Morrow, 1986.

Costello, John. *Mask of Treachery: Spies, Lies, Buggery and Betrayal*. New York: Warner Books, 1988.

Daniloff, Nicholas. *Two Lives, One Russia*. New York: Avon, 1990.

Darling, Arthur B. *The Central Intelligence Agency: An Instrument of Government, to 1950*. University Park, PA: Pennsylvania State University Press, 1990.

Deacon, Richard. *The Chinese Secret Service.* New York: Taplinger, 1974.

DeForest, Orrin, and David Chanoff. *Slow Burn: The Rise and "Bitter" Fall of American Intelligence in Vietnam.* New York: Simon and Schuster, 1990.

Deming, Angus. "We Still Need Spies: The Arrest of Martha Peterson in Moscow." *Newsweek,* 26 June 1978, 38.

Deriabin, Peter. *Watchdogs of Terror: Russian Bodyguards from the Tsars to the Commissars.* New Rochelle, NY: Arlington House, 1972.

_____, and T. H. Bagley. *The KGB: Masters of the Soviet Union.* New York: Hippocrene Books, 1990.

_____, and Frank Gibney. *The Secret World.* New York: Doubleday, 1959.

De Silva, Peer. *Sub Rosa: The CIA and the Uses of Intelligence.* New York: Times Books, 1978.

de Toledano, Ralph and Victor Lasky. *Seeds of Treason: The True Story of the Hiss-Chambers Tragedy.* New York: Funk and Wagnalls, 1950.

Donovan, James B. *Strangers on a Bridge: The Case of Colonel Abel.* New York: Atheneum, 1964.

Dooley, Thomas A. *Dr. Tom Dooley's Three Great Books: Deliver Us from Evil, The Edge of Tomorrow, and The Night They Burned the Mountain.* New York: Farrar, Straus and Cudahy, 1962.

Driberg, Tom. *Guy Burgess: A Portrait with Background.* London: Weidenfeld and Nicolson, 1956.

Duffy, Brian. "Tinker, Tailor, Soldier, Deputy Chief of Mission." *U.S. News and World Report,* 7 August 1989, 21.

Dulles, Allen. *The Craft of Intelligence.* New York: Harper and Row, 1963.

_____. *The Secret Surrender.* New York: Harper and Row, 1966.

Dzhirkvelov, Ilya. *Secret Servant: My Life with the KGB and the Soviet Elite.* New York: Harper and Row, 1987.

Earley, Pete. *Family of Spies: Inside the John Walker Spy Ring.* New York: Bantam Books, 1988.

Eisenberg, Dennis, Uri Dan, and Eli Landau. *The Mossad, Israel's Secret Intelligence Service: Inside Stories.* New York: New American Library, 1978.

Ennes, James M., Jr. *Assault on the "Liberty": The True Story of the Israeli Attack on an American Intelligence Ship.* New York: Random House, 1979.

Epstein, Edward Jay. *Deception: The Invisible War between the KGB and the CIA.* New York: Simon and Schuster, 1989.

_____. *Legend: The Secret World of Lee Harvey Oswald.* New York: McGraw-Hill, 1978.

Eveland, Wilbur Crane. *Ropes of Sand: America's Failure in the Middle East.* New York: W. W. Norton, 1980.

Faligot, Roger, and Pascal Krop. *La Piscine: The French Secret Service since 1944.* New York: Basil Blackwell, 1989.

Fisher, John. *Burgess and Maclean: A New Look at the Foreign Office Spies.* London: Robert Hale, 1977.

Freemantle, Brian. *CIA.* New York: Stein and Day, 1983.

Frischauer, Willi. *The Man Who Came Back: The Story of Otto John.* London: Muller, 1958.

Frolik, Joseph. *The Frolik Defection.* London: Leo Cooper, 1975.

Garrison, Jim. *On The Trail of the Assassins: My Investigation and Prosecution of the Murder of President Kennedy.* New York: Sheridan Square Press, 1988.

Gehlen, Reinhard. *The Service: The Memoirs of Reinhard Gehlen.* New York: Popular Library, 1972.

Glees, Anthony. *The Secrets of the Service: A Story of Soviet Subversion of Western Intelligence.* New York: Carroll and Graf, 1987.

Golitsyn, Anatoliy. *New Lies for Old: The Communist Strategy of Deception and Disinformation.* New York: Dodd, 1984.

_____. "The Rogue of Rogues." *International Journal of Intelligence and Counterintelligence,* 1 (Spring 1986): 76–82.

Goulden, Joseph C. *The Death Merchant: The Rise and Fall of Edwin P. Wilson.* New York: Simon and Schuster, 1984.

Gouzenko, Igor. *The Iron Curtain.* New York: E. P. Dutton, 1948.

Grey, Anthony. *The Prime Minister Was a Spy.* London: Weidenfeld and Nicolson, 1984.

Groden, Robert J., and Harrison Edward Livingston. *High Treason: The Assassination of John F. Kennedy: What Really Happened.* New York: Conservatory Press, 1989.

Hagen, Louis. *The Secret War in Europe: A Dossier of Espionage.* New York: Stein and Day, 1969.

Halpern, Samuel and Hayden Peake. "Did Angleton Jail Nosenko." *International Journal of Intelligence and Counterintelligence,* 3 (Winter 1989): 451–64.

Harel, Isser. *The House of Garibaldi Street: The First Full Account of the Capture of Adolf Eichmann Told by the Former Head of Israel's Secret Service.* New York: Viking Press, 1975.

Headley, Lake, and William Hoffmann. *The Courtmartial of Clayton Lonetree.* New York: Henry Holt, 1989.

Healy, Melissa. "The Life and Death of an Intelligence Man." *U.S. News and World Report,* 11 May 1987, 22–23.

Heinz, G., and H. Donnay. *Lumumba: The Last Fifty Days.* New York: Grove Press, 1969.

Henderson, Bernard R. *Pollard: The Spy's Story.* New York: Alpha Books, 1988.

Hersh, Seymour M. "The Creation of a Thug: Our Man in Panama." *Life,* March 1990, 81–93.

_____. *The Price of Power: Kissinger in the Nixon White House.* New York: Summit Books, 1983.

Hiss, Alger. *In the Court of Public Opinion.* New York: Alfred A. Knopf, 1957.

Hoare, Geoffrey. *The Missing Macleans.* London: Cassell, 1955.

Hood, William. *Mole.* New York: W. W. Norton, 1982.

Hougan, Jim. *Secret Agenda: Watergate, Deep Throat and the CIA.* New York: Random House, 1984.

Houghton, Harry. *Operation Portland: The Autobiography of a Spy.* London: Rupert Hart-Davis, 1972.

Hunt, E. Howard. *Give Us This Day.* New Rochelle, New York: Arlington House, 1973.

_____. *Undercover: Memoirs of an American Secret Agent.* New York: Berkley/Putnam, 1974.

Hurt, Henry. *Shadrin, The Spy Who Never Came Back.* New York: McGraw-Hill, 1981.

Hyams, Joe. *Flight of the Avenger.* San Diego, CA: Harcourt Brace Jovanovich, 1991.

Hyde, H. Montgomery. *The Atom Bomb Spies.* New York: Atheneum, 1980.

Immerman, Richard H. *The CIA in Guatemala: The Foreign Policy of Intervention.* Austin: University of Texas Press, 1982.

Irving, Clive, Ron Hall, and Jeremy Wallington. *The Anatomy of a Scandal: A Study of the Profumo Affair.* New York: M.S. Mill/William Morrow, 1963.

Jeffrey-Jones, Rhodri. *American Espionage: From Secret Service to the CIA.* New York: Free Press, 1977.

————. *The CIA and American Democracy.* New Haven, CT: Yale University Press, 1989.

John, Otto. *Twice through the Lines: An Autobiography of Otto John.* New York: Harper and Row, 1972.

Johnson, Haynes, Manuel Artime, Jose Perez San Roman, Erneido Oliva, and Enrique Ruiz-Williams. *The Bay of Pigs: The Leader's Story of Brigade 2506.* New York: Dell, 1964.

Johnson, Loch K. *America's Secret Power: The CIA in a Democratic Society.* New York: Oxford University Press, 1989.

————. *A Season of Inquiry: The Senate Intelligence Investigation.* Lexington: University of Kentucky Press, 1985.

Judis, John B. *William F. Buckley, Jr.: Patron Saint of the Conservatives.* New York: Simon and Schuster, 1988.

Kalb, Madeleine G. *The Congo Cables: The Cold War in Africa — From Eisenhower to Kennedy.* New York: Macmillan, 1982.

Kempe, Frederick. *Divorcing the Dictator: America's Bungled Affair with Noriega.* New York: G. P. Putnam's Sons, 1990.

Kennedy, Ludovic. *The Trial of Stephen Ward.* New York: Simon and Schuster, 1965.

Kessler, Ronald. *Escape from the CIA: How the CIA Won and Lost the Most Important KGB Spy Ever to Defect to the U.S.* New York: Pocket Books, 1991.

————. *Moscow Station: How the KGB Penetrated the American Embassy.* New York: Charles Scribner's Sons, 1989.

Khokhlov, Nicolai. *In the Name of Conscience.* New York: McKay, 1959.

Kirkpatrick, Lyman B. *The Real CIA.* New York: Macmillan, 1975.

————. *The U.S. Intelligence Community: Foreign Policy and Domestic Activities.* New York: Hill and Wang, 1975.

Kneece, Jack. *Family Treason: The Walker Spy Case.* New York: Stein and Day, 1986.

Knight, Amy W. *The KGB: Police and Politics in the Soviet Union.* Boston: Unwin and Hyman, 1988.

Knightley, Phillip. *The Master Spy: The Story of Kim Philby.* New York: Alfred A. Knopf, 1989.

————. *The Second Oldest Profession: Spies and Spying in the Twentieth Century.* New York: W. W. Norton, 1987.

————, and Caroline Kennedy. *An Affair of State: The Profumo Case and the Framing of Stephen Ward.* New York: Atheneum, 1987.

Lamar, Jacob V. "North's Other Secret." *Time,* 5 January 1987, 45.

Lamphere, Robert J., and Tom Shachtman. *The FBI-KGB War: A Special Agent's Story.* New York: Random House, 1986.

Lansdale, Edward Geary. *In the Midst of Wars: An American's Mission to Southeast Asia.* New York: Harper and Row, 1972.

Leary, William M., ed. *The Central Intelligence Agency: History and Documents.* Tuscaloosa: University of Alabama Press, 1984.

————. *Perilous Missions: Civil Air Transport and CIA Covert Operations in Asia.* Tuscaloosa: University of Alabama Press, 1984.

Levchenko, Stanislav. *On the Wrong Side: My Life in the KGB.* Washington, DC: Pergamon-Brassey's, 1988.

Lewis, Flora. *Red Pawn: The Story of Noel Field.* New York: Doubleday, 1965.

Lindsey, Robert. *The Falcon and the Snowman.* New York: Simon and Schuster, 1980.

Lonsdale, Gordon. *Spy: Twenty Years in the Soviet Secret Service*. London: Neville Spearman, 1965.

Lotz, Wolfgang. *The Champagne Spy: Israel's Master Spy Tells His Story*. New York: St. Martin's Press, 1972.

————. *A Handbook for Spies*. New York: Harper and Row, 1980.

Lucas, Norman. *The Great Spy Ring*. London: Barker, 1966.

Maas, Peter. *Manhunt: The Incredible Pursuit of a CIA Agent Turned Terrorist*. New York: Random House, 1986.

McCoy, Alfred W. *The Politics of Heroin in Southeast Asia: CIA Complicity in the Global Drug Trade* (revised and expanded). New York: Lawrence Hill Books, 1991.

McFadden, Robert D., Joseph B. Treaster, and Maurice Carroll. *No Hiding Place: Inside Report on the Hostage Crisis*. New York: Times Books, 1981.

McGehee, Ralph W. *Deadly Deceits: My 25 Years in the CIA*. New York: Sheridan Square, 1983.

Maclean, Fitzroy. *Take Nine Spies*. New York: Atheneum, 1978.

Macy, Christy, and Susan Kaplan. *Documents: A Shocking Collection of Memoranda, Letters, and Telexes from the Secret Files of the American Intelligence Community*. New York: Penguin, 1980.

Mangold, Tom. *Cold Warrior; James Jesus Angleton: The CIA's Master Spy Hunter*. New York: Simon and Schuster, 1991.

Marchetti, Victor, and John D. Marks. *The CIA and the Cult of Intelligence*. New York: Dell, 1980.

Marks, John. *The Search for the "Manchurian Candidate": The CIA and Mind Control*. New York: Times Books, 1979.

Marshall, Jonathan, Peter Dale Scott, and Jane Hunter. *Iran-Contra Connection: Secret Operations and Covert Operations in the Reagan Era*. Boston: South End Press, 1987.

Martin, David C. *Wilderness of Mirrors*. New York: Harper and Row, 1980.

Meeropol, Robert, and Michael. *We Are Your Sons: The Legacy of Julius and Ethel Rosenberg*. Boston: Houghton Mifflin, 1975.

Monahan, James, ed. *Before I Sleep: The Last Days of Dr. Tom Dooley*. New York: Farrar, Straus and Cudahy, 1961.

Moody, Sid. *444 Days: The American Hostage Story*. New York: Rutledge Press, 1981.

Moorehead, Alan. *The Traitors*. New York: Harper and Row, 1963.

Morros, Boris. *My Ten Years as a Counterspy*. New York: Viking, 1959.

Moss, Norman. *Klaus Fuchs: The Man Who Stole the Atom Bomb*. New York: St. Martin's Press, 1987.

Myagkov, Aleksei. *Inside the KGB*. New York: Ballantine Books, 1976.

Newman, Joseph, *Famous Soviet Spies: The Kremlin's Secret Weapon*. Washington, DC: U.S. News and World Report, 1973.

Newton, Verne W. *The Cambridge Spies: The Untold Story of Maclean, Philby, and Burgess in America*. Lanham, MD: Madison Books, 1991.

Ostrovsky, Victor, and Claire Hoy. *By Way of Deception: The Making of a Mossad Officer*. New York: St. Martin's Press, 1990.

Page, Bruce, David Leitch, and Phillip Knightley. *The Philby Conspiracy*. New York: Ballantine Books, 1981.

Penkovskiy, Oleg. *The Penkovskiy Papers*. New York: Avon Books, 1965.

Penrose, Barrie and Simon Freeman. *Conspiracy of Silence: The Secret Life of Anthony Blunt*. New York: Vintage Books, 1988.

Persico, Joseph E. *Casey: The Lives and Secrets of William J. Casey from the OSS to the CIA*. New York: Viking Press, 1990.

Petrov, Vladimir, and Evdokia. *Empire of Fear*. London: Andre Deutsch, 1956.

Philby, Kim. *My Silent War*. New York: Grove-Dell, 1968.

Philipson, Ilene. *Ethel Rosenberg: Beyond the Myths*. New York: Franklin Watts, 1988.

Phillips, David Atlee. *The Night Watch: 25 Years of Peculiar Service*. New York: Atheneum, 1977.

Pincher, Chapman. *Their Trade Is Treachery*. London: Sidgwick and Jackson, 1981.

∙∙∙∙∙∙∙∙. *Too Secret, Too Long*. New York: St. Martin's Press, 1984.

Poelchau, Warner, ed. *White Paper Whitewash: Interviews with Philip Agee on the CIA and El Salvador*. New York: Deep Cover Books, 1981.

Powers, Francis Gary, with Curt Gentry. *Operation Overflight: The U-2 Spy Pilot Tells His Story for the First Time*. New York: Holt, Rinehart and Winston, 1970.

Powers, Thomas. *The Man Who Kept the Secrets: Richard Helms and the CIA*. New York: Simon and Schuster, 1979.

Prados, John. *Presidents' Secret Wars: CIA and Pentagon Covert Operations Since World War II*. New York: William Morrow, 1986.

∙∙∙∙∙∙∙∙. *The Soviet Estimate: U.S. Intelligence Analysis and Russian Military Strength*. New York: Dial Press, 1982.

Radosh, Ronald, and Joyce Milton. *The Rosenberg File: A Search for the Truth*. London: Weidenfeld and Nicolson, 1983.

Ranelagh, John. *The Agency: The Rise and Decline of the CIA; from Wild Bill Donovan to William Casey*. New York: Simon and Schuster, 1986.

Raviv, Dan, and Yossi Melman. *Every Spy a Prince: The Complete History of Israel's Intelligence Community*. Boston: Houghton Mifflin, 1990.

Ray, Ellen, William Schaap, Karl van Meter, and Louis Wolf, eds. *Dirty Work 2: The CIA in Africa*. Secaucus, NJ: Lyle Stuart, 1979.

Reese, Mary Ellen. *General Reinhard Gehlen: The CIA Connection*. Fairfax, VA: George Mason University Press, 1990.

Rice, Edward R. *Mao's Way*. Berkeley: University of California Press, 1972.

Richelson, Jeffrey T. *American Espionage and the Soviet Target*. New York: William Morrow, 1987.

∙∙∙∙∙∙∙∙. *Foreign Intelligence Organizations*. Cambridge, MA: Ballinger, 1988.

Robbins, Christopher. *Air America: The Story of the CIA's Secret Airlines*. New York: Putnam's, 1979.

Rodriguez, Felix I., and John Weisman. *Shadow Warrior: The CIA Hero of a Hundred Unknown Battles*. New York: Simon and Schuster, 1989.

Romerstein, Herbert, and Stanislav Levchenko. *The KGB against the "Main Enemy": How the Soviet Intelligence Service Operates against the United States*. Lexington, MA: Lexington Books, 1989.

Roosevelt, Archie. *For Lust of Knowing: Memoirs of an Intelligence Officer*. Boston: Little, Brown, 1988.

Roosevelt, Kermit. *Countercoup: The Struggle for the Control of Iran*. New York: McGraw-Hill, 1979.

∙∙∙∙∙∙∙∙. *War Report of the OSS*. 2 vols. New York: Walker, 1976.

Rositzke, Harry. *CIA's Secret Operations: Espionage, Counterespionage and Covert Action*. New York: Reader's Digest Press, 1977.

∙∙∙∙∙∙∙∙. *The KGB: The Eyes of Russia*. New York: Doubleday, 1981.

Rubin, Barry. *Paved with Good Intentions: The American Experience and Iran.* New York: Oxford University Press, 1980.

Safer, Morley. *Flashbacks: On Returning to Vietnam.* New York: Random House, 1990.

Sakharov, Vladimir, with Umberto Tosi. *High Treason.* New York: Ballantine Books, 1980.

Schlesinger, Stephen, and Stephen Kinzer. *Bitter Fruit: The Untold Story of the American Coup in Guatemala.* Garden City, NY: Doubleday, 1982.

Schneir, Walter, and Miriam. *Invitation to an Inquest.* Baltimore, MD: Penguin Books, 1973.

Seale, P., and M. McConville. *Philby: The Long Road to Moscow.* London: Hamish Hamilton, 1973.

Shackley, Theodore. *The Third Option: An American View of Counterinsurgency Operations.* New York: Reader's Digest Press, 1981.

Shevchenko, Arkady N. *Breaking with Moscow.* New York: Ballantine Books, 1985.

Sigl, Rudolf. *In the Claws of the KGB.* Philadelphia, 1978.

Sklar, Holly. *Washington's War on Nicaragua.* Boston: South End Press, 1988.

Smith, Bradley F. *The Shadow Warriors: OSS and the Origins of the CIA.* New York: Basic Books, 1983.

Smith, John Chabot. *Alger Hiss: The True Story.* New York: Holt, Rinehart and Winston, 1976.

Smith, Joseph B. *Portrait of a Cold Warrior.* New York: Ballantine, 1976.

Smith, Richard Harris. "The First Moscow Station: An Espionage Footnote to Cold War History." *International Journal of Intelligence and Counterintelligence,* 3 (Fall 1989): 333–46.

_____. *OSS: The Secret History of America's First Central Intelligence Agency.* Berkeley: University of California Press, 1972.

Snepp, Frank W. *Decent Interval: An Insider's Account of Saigon's Indecent End Told by CIA's Chief Strategy Analyst in Vietnam.* New York: Vintage Books, 1977.

Stanton, Shelby L. *Green Berets at War: U.S. Army Special Forces in Southeast Asia, 1956–1975.* Novato, CA: Presidio Press, 1985.

Steven, Stewart. *The Spymasters of Israel.* New York: Ballantine Books, 1980.

Stockwell, John. *In Search of Enemies: A CIA Story.* New York: Norton, 1978.

_____. *The Praetorian Guard: The U.S. Role in the New World Order.* Boston: South End Press, 1991.

Summers, Anthony, and Stephen Dorrill. *Honeytrap: The Secret Worlds of Stephen Ward.* London: Weidenfeld and Nicolson, 1982.

Suvorov, Viktor. *Inside Soviet Military Intelligence.* New York: Macmillan, 1984.

_____. *Inside the Aquarium: The Making of a Top Soviet Spy.* New York: Macmillan, 1986.

_____. *Spetsnaz: The Inside Story of the Soviet Special Forces.* New York: W. W. Norton, 1987.

Szulc, Tad. *Compulsive Spy: The Strange Case of E. Howard Hunt.* New York: Viking, 1974.

Thyraud de Vosjoli, Philippe L. *Lamia.* Boston: Little, Brown, 1970.

Toohey, Brian, and William Pinwill. *Oyster: The Story of the Australian Secret Intelligence Service.* Port Melbourne, Victoria: Mandarin Australia, 1989.

Trevor-Roper, Hugh. *The Philby Affair: Espionage, Treason and Secret Services.* London: William Kimber, 1968.

Tully, Andrew. *The FBI's Most Famous Cases.* New York: William Morrow, 1965.

Turnbull, Malcolm. *The Spy Catcher Trial: The Scandal behind the #1 Best Seller.* Topsfield, MA: Salem House, 1989.

Turner, Stansfield. *Secrecy and Democracy: The CIA in Transition.* Boston: Houghton Mifflin, 1985.

U.S. Government. *The Tower Commission Report.* New York: Bantam Books/ Times Books, 1987.

U.S. Government. *The Nelson Rockefeller Report to the President by the Commission on CIA Activities within the United States.* New York: Manor Books, 1975.

Valentine, Douglas. *The Phoenix Program.* New York: William Morrow, 1990.

Vassall, John. *Vassall: The Autobiography of a Spy.* London: Sidgwick and Jackson, 1975.

Walker, Thomas W., ed. *Reagan versus the Sandinistas: The Undeclared War on Nicaragua.* Boulder, CO: Westview Press, 1987.

Weinstein, Allen. *Perjury: The Hiss-Chambers Case.* New York: Knopf, 1978.

West, Nigel. *The Circus: MI-5 Operations 1945–1972.* New York: Stein and Day, 1983.

_____. *MI-5: British Security Service Operations 1909–1945.* New York: Stein and Day, 1981.

_____. *MI-6: British Secret Intelligence Service Operations 1909–1945.* New York: Random House, 1983.

_____. *The SIGINT Secrets: The Signals Intelligence War, 1990 to Today.* New York: William Morrow, 1988.

West, Rebecca. *The Vassall Affair.* London: Sunday Telegraph, 1963.

West, W. J. *The Truth about Hollis.* London: Duckworth, 1989.

White, Peter T. "Saigon Fourteen Years After." *National Geographic,* 176 (November 1989): 604–21.

Whiteside, Thomas. *An Agent in Place: The Wennerstrum Affair.* London: Heinemann, 1967.

Williams, Robert Chadwell. *Klaus Fuchs, Atom Spy.* Cambridge, MA: Harvard University Press, 1987.

Winks, Robin W. *Cloak and Gown: Scholars in the Secret War, 1938–1961.* New York: William Morrow, 1987.

Wise, David. *The Invisible Government.* New York: Random House, 1964.

_____. *The Spy Who Got Away: The Inside Story of Edward Lee Howard, the CIA Agent Who Betrayed His Country's Secrets and Escaped to Moscow.* New York: Random House, 1988.

_____. *The U-2 Affair.* New York: Random House, 1962.

_____, and Thomas B. Ross. *The Espionage Establishment.* New York: Random House, 1967.

Woodward, Bob. *Veil: The Secret Wars of the CIA, 1981–1987.* New York: Simon and Schuster, 1987.

Wright, Peter, and Paul Greengrass. *Spycatcher: The Candid Autobiography of a Senior Intelligence Officer.* New York: Dell, 1987.

Wyden, Peter. *Bay of Pigs: The Untold Story.* New York: Simon and Schuster, 1979.

Wynne, Greville. *The Man from Moscow: The Story of Wynne and Penkovsky.* London: Hutchinson, 1967.

Index